OXFORD HISTORICAL MONOGRAPHS

Oxford Jackson

Architecture, Education, Status, and Style
1835–1924

WILLIAM WHYTE

This book has been printed digitally and produced in a standard specification in order to ensure its continuing availability

OXFORD
UNIVERSITY PRESS

Great Clarendon Street, Oxford OX2 6DP

Oxford University Press is a department of the University of Oxford.
It furthers the University's objective of excellence in research, scholarship,
and education by publishing worldwide in

Oxford New York

Auckland Cape Town Dar es Salaam Hong Kong Karachi
Kuala Lumpur Madrid Melbourne Mexico City Nairobi
New Delhi Shanghai Taipei Toronto
With offices in
Argentina Austria Brazil Chile Czech Republic France Greece
Guatemala Hungary Italy Japan South Korea Poland Portugal
Singapore Switzerland Thailand Turkey Ukraine Vietnam

Oxford is a registered trade mark of Oxford University Press
in the UK and in certain other countries

Published in the United States
by Oxford University Press Inc., New York

ISBN 978-0-19-929658-3

Printed and bound in Great Britain by CPI Antony Rowe, Chippenham and Eastbourne

For
M.G.W., W.S.W., and A.R.W.,
With all my love

Acknowledgements

T. G. Jackson once observed that his work was made possible by friends and by the friends of friends to whom he was recommended. As this book endeavours to explain, his was an important insight. What was true for Jackson is also true for me. In particular, I must thank my supervisors, Jane Garnett and Joe Mordaunt Crook. Jane can scarcely have suspected quite how long and quite how much she would have to teach me. Joe must have tired of my repeated trips to the Athenaeum for tea. But, with immense generosity, each made this project possible. I am also grateful to the examiners of the thesis on which this book is based. Dr Gavin Stamp and Professor José Harris undoubtedly improved my work. Moreover, in a work of real supererogation, José Harris then acted as my editor. Together, she, Anne Gelling, Samantha Lyle Skyrme and Katie Ryde have miraculously turned a thesis into a book.

Other friends also read and re-read the manuscript. Lawrence Goldman, Peter Howell, Matt Kelly, Tom Pickles, Robert Tobin, and—especially—Zoë Waxman, offered helpful criticism and consoling degrees of enthusiasm. My housemates and their partners have not read the text, but at times it must have felt as though they had. I thank Philip Bullock, Dan Butt, Stefano Evangelista, Francesca Galligan, Alan Hamilton, Teresa Shawcross, and Owen Thomas for so patiently putting up with me and my dead architect. Sir Nicholas Jackson and Dr James Bettley, whose edition of Jackson's *Recollections* has been so useful to me, were unfailingly supportive. I am especially grateful to Sir Nicholas, who generously allowed me access to his grandfather's papers. His hospitality was matched by the many people who allowed me to stay with them as I travelled the country in search of Jackson. I owe much to Fiona Ferguson and Tim Pullen, Dave Manington, Jo and Geoff Page, Paul Readman, Helen Southwood, Roey Sweet, and Chris Thomas. Even on holiday, there was no escape from Jackson. I must apologize to Emma Ursich, Sandro Bologna, and Susan Brown, who allowed me to ruin a trip to Croatia by dragging them to Zadar. I do hope that they will find what follows amusing.

Like Jackson, too, I have been more than usually fortunate in the institutions that have helped me. The research for this book would not have been possible without the financial support of the Arts and Humanities Research Board, the Vaughan Cornish Bequest, and the Pollard Fund at Wadham College. Its publication was facilitated by the generosity of the Oxford Modern History Faculty, the Paul Mellon Foundation, and St John's College. The Fellows of Wadham were also kind enough to award me a Senior Scholarship, whilst lectureships at St Anne's and St Peter's, Balliol and Oxford Brookes, brought with them fun and profit. St John's has been a predictably delightful place to finish the book, and I am grateful to my colleagues and my students for their support. So many archivists and librarians responded to my requests for help that it is simply impossible to name them all. I must, though, particularly mention the staff of the Upper Reading Room in the Bodleian Library, whose friendliness is famous and whose helpfulness is legendary.

For permission to consult archives and visit buildings I gratefully acknowledge the Headmaster of Aldenham School, the Headmaster of Brighton College, the Headmistress of Cranbrook School, the Worshipful Company of Drapers, the Provost and Fellows of Eton College, the Senior Master of Giggleswick School, the Headmaster of Harrow School, the Honourable Society of the Inner Temple, the Headmistress of Otford County Primary School, the Headmistress of Oxford High School GDST, the Warden of Radley College, the Headmaster and Governors of Rugby School, the Headmaster of Sir Roger Manwood's School, Sandwich, the Headmaster of Uppingham School, the Headmaster of Westminster School, the Master and Fellows of Balliol College, Oxford, the Principal and Fellows of Brasenose College, Oxford, the President and Fellows of Corpus Christi College, Oxford, the Principal and Fellows of Hertford College, Oxford, the Provost and Fellows of King's College, Cambridge, the Rector and Fellows of Lincoln College, Oxford, the Principal and Fellows of Mansfield College, Oxford, the Warden and Fellows of Merton College, Oxford, the Principal and Fellows of Newnham College, Cambridge, the Provost and Fellows of Oriel College, Oxford, the Master and Fellows of Pembroke College, Cambridge, the Provost and Fellows of The Queen's College, Oxford, the Principal and Fellows of Somerville College, Oxford, the President and Fellows of Trinity College, Oxford, and the Warden and Fellows of Wadham College, Oxford.

Finally, but most importantly, I must thank my family. It has become almost obligatory to dedicate a first book to one's parents and I often suspect this reflects little more than the fact that after several years of sustained research, these are the only people the writer knows well enough to serve the purpose. I should stress that this is certainly not the case for me. My mother and father have been endlessly encouraging, loving, and kind. Far fewer books are dedicated to brothers. Clearly, this is because few brothers are as good as mine. I shan't compel Alasdair to read it, but I dedicate this book to him, and to mum and dad, with all my love and every thanks.

W.H.W.
August 2005

Contents

Illustrations

For permission to reproduce the following images, I am grateful to the Headmaster of Brighton College (3), the Trustees of the Museum of London (98), the Bodleian Library, University of Oxford (2, 4, 18, 23, 49, 50, 54, 61, 66, 68, 69, 70, 84, 85, 86, 87, 93), to the Royal Institute of British Architects (26), to Professor Andor Gomme (42, 43, 44, 100), and—especially—to Professor J. Mordaunt Crook (1, 10, 11, 12, 19, 20, 21, 22, 24, 25, 27, 28, 31, 33, 35, 26, 37, 38, 39, 45, 46, 47, 48, 53, 57, 59, 62, 64, 65, 67, 75, 76, 81, 82, 89, 92).

Abbreviations

ACES	Arts and Crafts Exhibition Society
BAL	British Architectural Library, London
BalCA	Balliol College Archive, Oxford
BCA	Brighton College Archive
BNCA	Brasenose College Archive, Oxford
Bod.	Bodleian Library, Oxford
CamUR	*Cambridge University Reporter*
CCCA	Corpus Christi College Archive, Oxford
CSA	Cranbrook School Archive
CUA	Cambridge University Archive
CUMAA	Cambridge University Museum of Archaeology and Anthropology
DHA	Drapers' Hall Archive, London
ECA	Eton College Archive
EHR	*English Historical Review*
GSA	Giggleswick School Archive
HCA	Hertford College Archive, Oxford
HCRO	Hampshire County Record Office, Winchester
ICBS	Incorporated Church Building Society
ITA	Inner Temple Archive, London
LCA	Lincoln College Archive, Oxford
LPL	Lambeth Palace Library, London
ManCA	Mansfield College Archive, Oxford
MCA	Merton College Archive, Oxford
MOL	Museum of London
NA	National Archive, Kew
NAAA	National Association for the Advancement of Art
NAL	National Art Library, London
NCA	Newnham College Archive, Cambridge
NMR	National Monuments Record, Swindon
OCA	Oriel College Archive, Oxford
OHSA	Oxford High School Archive
ORO	Oxfordshire Record Office, Oxford
OUA	Oxford University Archive
PCA	Pembroke College Archive, Cambridge
RA	Royal Academy, London
RadCA	Radley College Archive
RCA	Royal College of Art, London
RIBA	Royal Institute of British Architects, London
RMSA	Sir Roger Manwood's School Archive, Sandwich
SCA	Somerville College Archive, Oxford

SHC	Surrey History Centre, Woking
SPAB	Society for the Protection of Ancient Buildings, London
TCA	Trinity College Archive, Oxford
USA	Uppingham School Archive
WCA	Wadham College Archive, Oxford

Introduction

Sir Thomas Graham Jackson died on 7 November 1924, aged eighty-eight.[1] As befitted a man of his standing, his obituaries were fulsome in their praise.[2] They paid tribute to his moral qualities, describing a 'dignified figure and a cultivated mind'.[3] They acknowledged his role as one of the 'recognized leaders of all who regarded architecture as an Art'.[4] They complimented him on his value as a thinker, as 'a great scholar and an excellent writer'.[5] And well they might. Jackson was indeed just such a man: a baronet; a RIBA Gold Medallist; a Royal Academician; a Fellow of Wadham College, Oxford, and of the Society of Antiquaries; Associé de l'Académie Royale de Belgique; and an honorary doctor of both the ancient English universities. Above all, it was as an artist and author that he was best known and most respected. He was, after all, 'Oxford's most distinguished architect since Wren'.[6] In particular, Graham Jackson was acknowledged as the dominant architectural influence on elite education: 'the great English architect . . . [whose] work is to be seen at Oxford and Cambridge';[7] the author of buildings at 'nearly half the greater public schools in England'.[8] This was an impressive achievement. There was no doubt in his contemporaries' minds that Jackson had been an important architect, nor that he deserved a biography. 'It is,' wrote one, 'impossible to believe that [his] works . . . will not be a matter of interest and study hereafter.'[9] Hereafter, however, turned out to be somewhat delayed. More than eighty years later, this study represents the very first sustained examination of Jackson's career.

For despite his importance to contemporaries, Jackson has been ignored by most subsequent writers. In part this simply reflects the difficulty of locating material which may be of use to his biographer. There is no Jackson archive, no corpus of documents which could serve as the basis for research. Many of Jackson's office papers were destroyed by his son. The rest were distributed between the institutions for which he had worked. There are designs for Bath Abbey at the Royal Academy; plans for Hertford College, Oxford, in a school at Brighton. Throughout the country, there are small clusters of Jackson's letters and designs, forming a collection of thousands of documents. Only by visiting each of the buildings, and exploring their archives, can an accurate picture of

---

[1] *The Times*, 8 Nov. 1924, 7. His son gives the date as 9 Nov., which would make his *Times* obituary extraordinarily prescient. T. G. Jackson, *Recollections* (ed. Basil H. Jackson; Oxford, 1950), 275.

[2] For a charming sketch of his life see *Country Life* 56 (1924), 740.

[3] *Builder* 127 (1924), 753.   [4] *RIBA Journal* 32 (1924–5), 49.

[5] *Architects' Journal* 60 (1924), 756.   [6] *Oxford Magazine* 43 (1924–5), 126.

[7] *Times*, 10 Nov. 1924, 16.   [8] *Oxford Magazine* 43 (1924–5), 126.

[9] *Architects' Journal* 60 (1924), 758.

1. T. G. Jackson in his early sixties.

Jackson's career be conceived. Nor, until recently, would this effort have seemed worthwhile. For in fact it was not lassitude but lack of interest that prevented historians from pursuing Graham Jackson's trail. More than anything else Jackson was disregarded because he came to be seen as unimportant. By the charitable, he was seen as an example of those 'one or two freaks at the end of the last century whose work is fascinating, but outside the mainstream'.[10] For the less sympathetic, he was a 'never very enterprising figure'; a 'competent decorator' who 'never seemed able to pack more than two rooms together without crushing something and leaving something else sticking out'.[11] Seen in this light, any disregard of Jackson's work is eminently understandable. Dismissed as neither representative nor original, Graham Jackson was easily ignored. Yet the contrast between this attitude and the judgement of his own generation begs

---

[10] John Betjeman, *First and Last Loves* (London, 1969), 141.
[11] H. S. Goodhart-Rendel, *English Architecture since the Regency* (London, 1953), 154–77.

some questions. Why is the disjunction so great? Why was Jackson's reputation so quickly eroded?

Certainly, at the time of Jackson's death his reputation seemed secure. Even two years afterwards his importance appeared to be assured. The 1926 *RIBA Journal*, for example, contained a celebration of Jackson's career by H. S. Goodhart-Rendel, who praised Jackson's 'power and versatility' and claimed that his life typified the tendencies of nineteenth-century architecture.[12] Jackson's work, although increasingly dated, remained popular—far more popular, indeed, than that of his predecessors. 'For Scott, Burges, and Hayward no reprobation could be too severe', recalled John Summerson of the years around 1920. Jackson and his generation, by contrast, were said to have worked 'after "the worst period"', and were thus more acceptable.[13] Nonetheless, an almost universal revulsion against nineteenth-century architecture soon had its effect. Buildings of the Gothic Revival came to be 'accepted as a national misfortune like the weather'.[14] Works like William Butterfield's Keble College, Oxford, were seen as an enormous joke: 'Undergraduates and young dons used to break off their afternoon walks in order to have a good laugh at the quadrangle.' Nor was this abuse born of knowledge; as Kenneth Clark recalled: 'it was universally believed that Ruskin had built Keble'.[15] This combination of ignorance and contempt soon determined responses to later buildings too.[16] Jackson's reputation was inevitably diminished by this reaction. Worse still, even when the work of the Gothic Revival was reassessed, the late-Victorians continued to be condemned. Goodhart-Rendel is a typical figure in this respect. His sensitive appreciation of 1926 was soon replaced by mockery and contempt. Jackson, far from being 'sophisticated and urbane',[17] was now shown as a part of the 'late-Victorian orgy of Bric-à-brac'; a man who had failed to understand his own job.[18]

T. G. Jackson, indeed, was particularly unfortunate. When he was not disparaged he was disregarded. Successive reinterpretations of the period passed him by. Partly this was because of his work in educational architecture. Architectural history has traditionally focused on churches and cathedrals, palaces and country houses. Schools and colleges, as Deborah Weiner observes, have simply not been regarded as major works of art.[19] More importantly still, the preoccupations

[12] H. S. Goodhart-Rendel, 'The Works of Sir T. G. Jackson', *RIBA Journal* 33 (1926), 467–77.

[13] John Summerson, *Victorian Architecture: four studies in evaluation* (New York and London, 1970), 3. [14] Kenneth Clark, *Another Part of the Wood* (London, 1974), 109.

[15] Kenneth Clark, *The Gothic Revival* (London, 1995), 2. See also Basil F. L. Clarke, *Church Builders of the Nineteenth Century* (2nd ed.; London, 1969), p. v. Clarke recalls that he was told 'all the houses in North Oxford were designed by Ruskin'.

[16] For a good example, see H. S. Goodhart-Rendel, *Vitruvian Nights: papers upon architectural subjects* (London, 1932), 6. John Summerson in *The Turn of the Century: architecture in Britain around 1900* (Glasgow, 1976) offers a more sensitive approach.

[17] *RIBA Journal* 33 (1926), 470.

[18] Goodhart-Rendel, *English Architecture Since the Regency*, 177, 225.

[19] Deborah E. B. Weiner, *Architecture and Social Reform in Late Victorian London* (Manchester and New York, 1994), 2.

of previous writers combined to undermine Jackson's importance. When nineteenth-century architecture began to be studied again, it was as part of a much wider programme, with Nikolaus Pevsner setting the trend.[20] In his *Pioneers of Modern Design* (1936) he tried to show that there was a tradition of functionalism in European architecture which led inexorably towards the International Modern style.[21] The subtitle of this work, *From William Morris to Walter Gropius*, made the point. This was Pevsner's apostolic succession.[22] These were the artists who had 'courageously broken with the past and accepted the machine-age'. Modernism was the result.[23] When studying the Victorians, then, he looked for 'possibilities for a twentieth century future'.[24] Those who did not conform to this model were dismissed as 'smugly satisfied with the imitation of the past'.[25] It was a persuasive argument and one that was widely accepted.[26] But it distorted the historical record. As Pevsner himself admitted in 1972, 'no one can as yet write of the nineteenth century without fors and againsts'.[27] Jackson, with his commitment to historicism and unwillingness to 'substitute rolled iron joists for brains', fell into the latter group.[28] Offering no direct line towards Modernism, he could safely be dismissed—and so he was.

Until the 1970s, then, Jackson was perceived as irrelevant at best and obstructive at worst. By 1977, indeed, he was even being attacked for buildings he had not designed. Writing of the late-Victorian period, Peter Levi gave full flow to his prejudice: 'The one really preposterous architect was T. G. Jackson, with whose productions I am sadly familiar. His style used to be called in Oxford Anglo-Jaxon [*sic*] and the Oxford town hall, which replaced a fine Doric building, is his sufficient monument.'[29] Levi was less familiar than he believed. In reality, H. T. Hare was the architect of the Oxford town hall. Jackson was an influence, but no more; it was rather like blaming Ruskin for Keble. And in fact the comparison is telling. Jackson and his closest colleagues had replaced the High Victorian Goths in the popular imagination. They were now dismissed, ignored, or treated with bemusement and disdain. Every successive attempt to rehabilitate them seemed doomed. In 1950, for example, Jackson's *Recollections* were published by his son. They were to prove immensely useful as a source for historians of the period. But initially, at least, they did little for Jackson's

[20] See Peter Draper, ed., *Reassessing Nikolaus Pevsner* (Aldershot, 2004).

[21] William Whyte, 'The Englishness of English Architecture: modernism and the making of a national International Style, 1927–1957', in William Whyte, ed., *Britain and Europe: ideas, identities, institutions, 1750–2000* (forthcoming).

[22] See also J. A. Schmiechen, 'The Victorians, the Historians and the Idea of History', *American Historical Review* 93/2 (1988), 287–316, at 287–90.

[23] Nikolaus Pevsner, *Outline of European Architecture* (London, 1948), 211.

[24] Pevsner, *Studies in Art, Architecture and Design*, (2 vols.; London, 1968), vol. ii, 114.

[25] Pevsner, *Outline of European Architecture*, 197.

[26] Reyner Banham, *Theory and Design in the First Machine Age* (1960; Oxford, 1992); John Summerson, *Heavenly Mansions* (London, 1963), 196.   [27] Pevsner, *Architectural Writers*, v.

[28] *Architects' Journal* 60 (1924), 761.   [29] *Sunday Times*, 4 Dec. 1977.

reputation. At the time, indeed, John Summerson welcomed the book precisely because of its insights into 'the "late", "debased" and "impure" Victorianism on which the sunshine of rediscovery has yet to break'.[30] Whilst this was the case, even his *Recollections* could not help Graham Jackson. He seemed fated to remain misunderstood or ignored.

Slowly but surely, however, the tide began to turn. The work of Mark Girouard, Joe Mordaunt Crook, and dozens of others, started the steady process of rehabilitating and re-evaluating turn-of-the-century architecture, studying it in its own right and rescuing it from the condescension of posterity. Inevitably, this renewed interest in late-Victorian architecture and design refocused attention on T. G. Jackson. His work in Oxford was first seriously reassessed in 1978.[31] In 1982, J. Mordaunt Crook offered a short survey of his career and an analysis of his style.[32] A year later there was an exhibition of his Oxford buildings[33] and a brief history of his Examination Schools was produced.[34] It was little enough—but it was a start.[35] Jackson remained a shadowy figure: 'an architect whose works . . . [have] faded into relative obscurity with the purgative effect of Pevsnerian history';[36] a 'little known Victorian architect', whose reputation had suffered 'a long and undeserved neglect'.[37] Nonetheless, these early intimations were followed by other signs that Jackson was becoming better known and better liked. In subsequent years and in a variety of publications, he was mentioned as an arts and crafts architect; as a post-Ruskinian theorist; as a pioneer of eclectic architecture; as an influence on Croatian design; as a leading figure in collegiate building; and as an important arbiter of taste in late-Victorian Oxford.[38] His glassware and his funerary monuments were also the subject of brief studies.[39] Not all the comment was positive; not all of it was very well

[30] John Summerson, 'A Victorian Architect', *New Statesman and Nation* 40 (1950), 329.

[31] Alistair Martin, 'Oxford Jackson', *Oxoniensia* 43 (1978), 216–21.

[32] J. Mordaunt Crook, 'T. G. Jackson and the Cult of Eclecticism' in H. Searing, ed., *In Search of Modern Architecture* (New York, 1982), 102–20.

[33] James Bettley, ed., *T. G. Jackson: an exhibition of his Oxford buildings* (Oxford, 1983) and 'T. G. Jackson and the Examination Schools', *Oxford Art Journal* 6/1 (1983), 57–66.

[34] Roland Wilcock, *The Building of Oxford University Examination Schools* (Oxford, 1983).

[35] His work in Croatia was also first assessed in Marija Stagličić, 'Zvonik katedrale u Zadru', *Peristil* 25 (1982), 149–58.

[36] Ian Latham, 'Thomas Jackson—Baronet Architect', *Building Design* 665 (11 Nov. 1983), 10.

[37] Paul Oliver in *Building* 245 (1983), 30.

[38] Peter Stansky, *Redesigning the World: William Morris, the 1880s and the arts and crafts* (Princeton, 1985), 121–2; Michael W. Brooks, *John Ruskin and Victorian Architecture* (London, 1989), 261–5; J. Mordaunt Crook, *The Dilemma of Style: architectural ideas from the picturesque to the post-modern* (London, 1987; 1989), 183–4, 18–90; R. A. Lowe and Rex Knight, 'Building the Ivory Tower: the social function of late nineteenth-century collegiate architecture', *Studies in Higher Education* 7/2 (1982), 81–91, at 84; Sonia Bićanić, 'T. G. Jackson's *Recollections* and his campanile at Zadar', *Slavonica* 22/1 (1994–5), 29–38; Howard Colvin, *Unbuilt Oxford* (New Haven and London, 1983), ch. 9.

[39] Judy Rudoe and Howard Coutts, 'The Table-glass Designs of Philip Webb and T. G. Jackson', *Journal of the Decorative Arts Society* 16 (1992), 24–41; Martin D. W. Jones, 'Gothic Enriched: Thomas Jackson's mural tablets in Brighton College Chapel', *Church Monuments* 6 (1991), 54–66.

informed. But taken together, these few dozen pages of analysis, written over the last twenty-five years, offered the beginnings of an understanding of T. G. Jackson.

Moreover, in the last three or four years, interest has continued to grow. The year 2003, in particular, saw a profusion of Jacksonalia, as his *Recollections* were republished and the first truly comprehensive catalogue of his works was compiled.[40] At the same time, too, exhibitions of his watercolours were held at the Royal Academy and at the Croatian Embassy in London.[41] Yet even this renewed enthusiasm for Jackson's architecture has not really recast our ideas about him. His life has been used to prove other points. His career has illustrated innumerable other arguments. No one has focused exclusively on Jackson himself, or on the totality of his work. The importance of Jackson's life demands a full-scale study; a critical account that explores his career in the round. This is not easy, but if we are to understand the man, his work, and the period in which he worked, it is essential. At the most fundamental level, indeed, a substantial account is necessary. The length of Jackson's life and the longevity of his career make this inevitable. He established his practice as an architect in 1862 and was still working at his death in 1924. This sixty-two year career included time as a writer; work as a designer of buildings, glasses, silverware, and furniture; an involvement in educational reform, historical research, and conservation work. Each of these aspects needs to be examined in relation to the others. Both a portrait and a landscape need to be painted: to show Jackson himself and to reveal Jackson in context.

This means starting at the beginning with his birth. Jackson was the son of reasonably prosperous and staunchly Protestant parents. The Jacksons were an 'undistinguished', if respectably ancient family.[42] Originally, they were from the fens, with property in Stamford, Helpstone, and Castor. The family seat, though, was Duddington, in Northamptonshire, and it was here that William Jackson received a Grant of Arms and the right to be called gentleman in 1689. The eighteenth century saw a slow but significant rise in the family's fortune. They intermarried with Hippisleys, Thursbys, and Cartwrights—'the latter,' as Jackson was comically quick to note, 'descended from a sister of Archbishop Cranmer'.[43] His great-uncle, Jeremiah Jackson, a Fellow of St John's College, Cambridge, was Headmaster of Uppingham School between 1777 and 1794. Tobias Hippisley, the architect's grandfather, was High Sheriff of Rutland in 1782. But Jackson's father, Hugh, was the younger son of a younger son, and could not hope to profit directly from his family's success. He trained as a solicitor, and practised in London, rising to become a partner in the firm of Fladgate,

[40] T. G. Jackson, *Recollections: the life and travels of a Victorian architect*, ed. Sir Nicholas Jackson (London, 2003), esp. James Bettley, 'Gazetteer', 266–300.
[41] See also William Whyte, 'Anglo-Jackson Attitudes: reform and the rebuilding of Oxford', *The Victorian* 12 (2003), 4–9. [42] Jackson, *Life and Travels*, 15.
[43] Jackson, *Recollections*, 2.

Young, and Jackson, of 12 Essex Street, the Strand. Back home in Stamford he met and married his wife, Elizabeth Arnold. She came from a medical family: both her grandfather, Thomas, and father, Thomas Graham, were physicians. Consumately professional, the Arnolds were as improving as the Jacksons. Elizabeth's great-aunt was the radical historian Catherine Macaulay. Her uncle wrote books on Italian. Her brothers were both Cambridge educated, and one became Fellow of Trinity College. It was the perfect match, and Hugh Jackson and Elizabeth Arnold were married on 31 March 1834. They moved directly to Hampstead and it was there, on 21 December 1835, that their son, the future architect, was born.

Jackson was the eldest child of a small family. He had two sisters: Emily, who would devote her life to disabled children, and Annie, who would marry her cousin Charles Arnold. Small though it was, Jackson's family was of enormous importance to his life. Family offered him security and support. It also offered him work. Jackson relied on his father for legal advice, whilst his brother-in-law promoted his career.[44] The commission for St John's Church, Wimbledon (1873–6), for example, was due directly to Charles Arnold's influence.[45] More importantly still, his family gave him a set of values to which he remained constant. He finally left home at the age of forty-four, and never seems to have challenged the ideas or opinions of his parents: social, political, or—importantly—religious. Unsurprisingly, for their time and their status, the Jacksons were evangelicals. Elizabeth Arnold had been trained 'to form regular habits of study and self-improvement', and her children were similarly bred amidst a peculiarly Protestant ethic. 'Dancing was thought worldly and was not allowed'; the family shunned the 'mildly high' parish church in favour of more proper worship. This was not Puritanism—after all, there were still parties to attend and games to play.[46] It was not dissent—the Jacksons were staunch Anglicans. Nor was it rigidly enforced. Jackson's aunt enjoyed a dance, and his uncle was an advocate of the suspiciously Catholic idea of church ornamentation.[47] Nonetheless, Graham Jackson never escaped his early evangelicalism.[48] He was to remain 'a deeply religious man' until his death, while hard work, self-improvement, and education dominated his life.[49]

T. G. Jackson's background was also important to him in his work as an architect. He confessed, for example, that the Chapel of Ease which his family attended,

[44] SHC 2508/2 Malden Church, Jackson (16 July 1866).
[45] SHC 2853/3/1 Wimbledon, St John, Minutes of Building Committee (18 March 1873).
[46] Jackson, *Recollections*, 6, 11.
[47] He was also a member of the Cambridge Camden Society: Thomas Kerchever Arnold, *Remarks on the Rev. F. Close's 'Church Architecture Scripturally Considered, from the Earliest Ages to the Present Time'* (London, 1844) and *An Examination of the Rev. F. Close's Reply to 'Remarks' upon his 'Church Architecture Scripturally Considered'* (London, 1844).
[48] In 1898 he resigned from the board of the Incorporated Church Building Society, appalled at its fondness for ritualism. Jackson, MSS, 'Recollections', vol. ii., 520.
[49] *Times*, 7 Nov. 1924, 7.

2. St John's Church, Wimbledon, Jackson's unbuilt tower and spire.

'influenced irresistibly my early conceptions of church architecture'; and he recalled still more significant memories too. For evangelicalism should not be confused with philistinism, or a distrust of the visual arts. Jackson's mother was an accomplished amateur artist. His aunt was the daughter-in-law of Sir William Beechey, RA, the prominent and prolific painter. The family was acquainted with Hampstead's small group of resident artists, including the architects G. G. Scott and C. R. Cockerell. As a child, then, Jackson was introduced to a variety of artistic forms and their creators. In particular, he was 'mad about architecture', and his early life gave him a good opportunity to pursue his interests. Jackson's childhood was divided between houses in Hampstead, Clapham, and Stamford, and each of them brought him into contact with buildings which were to influence his later work. One of his clearest childhood memories was of a trip to Hampton Court, which made an 'enormous impression' on him.[50] His Lincolnshire sojourns introduced him to architectural themes which he was to adopt in many of his most successful works: whether it be the domestic details of Stamford or the grandeur of Burghley House and Kirby, Haddon, and Hardwick Halls. It was the ideal environment for an embryo architect.

Nonetheless, Jackson's youth was by no means extraordinary. He received the usual training of the higher professional classes: prep schools (in Brighton and Clapham) and then, in 1850, boarding school. His father having 'feared the expense' of Harrow, Jackson was sent to Brighton College.[51] This had been founded just five years earlier, 'on Church of England principles for the education of the sons of noblemen and gentlemen'.[52] So new was it, in fact, that Jackson claimed to have been the first college boy to suffer a flogging.[53] This doubtful honour aside, Jackson spent a quiet three years in Brighton: improving his Latin and Greek, illuminating his books with elaborate sketches, and preparing for a place at Oxford. Despite his school prize for Latin, however, he did not win the scholarship to Corpus Christi College for which he was intended, and as a result spent a year with a private tutor.[54] His tutor, the Revd Charles Richmond Tate, was to become a good friend and an early client, but at the time it was more important that he could teach well. Fortunately for Jackson, this was clearly the case. For in 1854 he won a scholarship to Wadham College, Oxford. By now, art and architecture had become a presiding interest for Jackson: in his holidays he haunted Westminster Abbey, sketching every part of the ancient structure.[55] His scholarship to Wadham was won with an essay on an architectural theme.[56] These were important indicators of his future career, but first he had Oxford to enjoy.

---

[50] Jackson, *Life and Travels*, 18–25.   [51] Ibid., 27.
[52] Quoted in S. C. Roberts, ed., *A History of Brighton College* (Brighton, 1957), vii.
[53] Martin D. W. Jones, *A Short History of Brighton College* (Brighton, 1986), 3.
[54] He was, however, matriculated as a Commoner, which explains why some writers have wrongly presumed that he was educated at Corpus Christi.
[55] Jackson, *Recollections*, 17–21.   [56] *Oxford Magazine* 43 (1924–5), 126.

3. Jackson's school book.

Enjoy it he did. Although far from fashionable, Wadham was friendly, hard working, and—above all—evangelical.[57] This was due to its Warden, the 'autocratic and conservative', Benjamin Parsons Symons.[58] He led the evangelical party in Oxford, refused to countenance rowing, and had originally timed his compulsory lectures on the Thirty-nine Articles to coincide with Newman's sermons at the university church. Jackson's native evangelicalism was undoubtedly reinforced by this environment. But other sides of his character were also developed. He abandoned the conservatism of his youth, in favour of an enthusiastic liberalism. He embraced sport in all its forms. Despite the Warden's prescriptions against it, he rowed in the college boat. He acted, danced, and read. He studied painting under 'Turner of Oxford', a gifted artist who had 'left a great future behind him' and resigned himself to teaching.[59] All this activity left Jackson little room for work, though.[60] Despite beginning his revision at an unseasonably early time, he gained only a third in Greats. This was no disaster— it was at least an honours degree at a time when most men left with a pass—but it was a disappointment. Worse still, it would prevent him from obtaining the fellowship that he desired. Nonetheless, he was not without hope. Jackson resolved to sit for a second honours school in Natural Science. As his tutor had advised him, 'They are sure to be very obliging in this School. There are only fourteen men in it, so they can ill afford to lose one-fourteenth of their candidates, for they wish to become popular.'[61] Jackson had a week to get his subject up from scratch and prepare for examination. He got a first.

Here was triumph indeed. But what was to follow? Like many of his contemporaries, Jackson's education had given him little preparation for employment. Worse still, there were no vacant fellowships for him to take up, and with such a poor result, it was unlikely that he could make an academic career out of classics. There was teaching, of course, and Jackson considered a position at Uppingham School. There was also the law, and Jackson expressed an interest in becoming a barrister. His father advised against it, though; he had also declined positions in India on his son's behalf. Rather, he insisted that Graham Jackson should consider becoming an architect.[62] This showed an extraordinary faith in his son's abilities. As a later advice manual put it:

Architecture, as a means of affording elegant amusement, is second only to painting and music; as a means of living it is almost as precarious a thing as either of these professions. A young man, to embrace it, has need of a great and exceptional genius, means of his own, or many friends who will spend money on buildings in his interest.[63]

---

[57] C. S. L. Davies, 'Decline and Revival: 1660–1900', in C. S. L. Davies and Jane Garnett, eds., *Wadham College* (Oxford, 1994), 41–51.   [58] Jackson, *Recollections*, 22–6, 30–3.
[59] Luke Herrmann, 'William Turner of Oxford', *Oxoniensia* 26/27 (1961/2), 312–18, at 313.
[60] An undergraduate notebook of *c.*1856 is preserved at Bod. MS Eng. misc. f. 796.
[61] Jackson, *Life and Travels*, 47–8.   [62] Ibid., 49.
[63] See Francis Davenant, *What Shall My Son Be?* (London, 1870), 145.

The suggestion also relied on Hugh Jackson's useful connections. He sent his son to see Sir Gilbert Scott. For Jackson this was perhaps the most important meeting of his life. He told the distinguished architect of his artistic inclinations, and was shocked to hear an attack on the Pre-Raphaelite Brotherhood in response. 'This roused me to defend them', Jackson recalled, 'for I was steeped in Ruskin and mad about Hunt and Millais.' Strangely, Scott seemed to approve. 'Bring your Pre-Raffaelitism into architecture', he said, 'for it is exactly what architecture is most in need of at the present time.'[64] Burne-Jones himself having advised Jackson to abandon ideas of becoming a painter, the decision was made. On 20 October 1858, Jackson paid the three hundred guinea premium and entered Scott's office as a pupil.

20 Spring Gardens, Gilbert Scott's place of work, was the largest and most important architectural practice in nineteenth-century England, responsible for over a thousand new buildings and restoration projects throughout the country.[65] The office and its founder were, quite simply, a phenomenon. As Goodhart-Rendel put it, 'That the architect who, during a working career of forty years, built or interfered with nearly five hundred churches, thirty-nine cathedrals and minsters, twenty-five universities and colleges, and many other buildings beside, was a remarkable man would be foolish to deny.'[66] Scott's contemporaries were more effusive in their praise. For many—although not all—he was simply the 'foremost architect of his day'.[67] None of this would have been possible without the team of clerks, assistants, and pupils which filled Scott's office. 'In the zenith of his fame', recalled Harry Hems, 'he had a staff of no less than thirty-six.' Such a large practice required ruthless efficiency: 'Contractors were never kept waiting by the hour . . . details and everything were always ready to the minute.' In short, Gilbert Scott 'had at his command splendid specialists who did what he wanted, and who, always in complete touch with their work, had everything ready as it was required'.[68] It was, to all intents and purposes, the first modern architectural office, with its strict organization, common approach, and shared style. Spring Gardens, indeed, became a brand, and an irregular *Sketch Book* was published to advertise its virtues.[69] Jackson could not have joined a more exciting or more promising practice.

The output of Scott's office was not confined merely to buildings. He produced new architects too. During his forty-year career Gilbert Scott trained

[64] Jackson, *Life and Travels*, 50–1.
[65] Surprisingly, Scott has not yet been the subject of a full-scale biography. See: David Cole, *The Work of Sir Gilbert Scott* (London, 1980); Roger Dixon, ed., *Sir George Gilbert Scott and the Scott Dynasty* (South Bank Architectural Papers I, 1980); Joanna Heseltine, ed., *The Scott Family: a catalogue of the drawings collection of the RIBA* (London, 1981).
[66] Goodhart-Rendel, *Architecture since the Regency*, 95–6.
[67] Quoted in Gavin Stamp, 'Introduction' to G. G. Scott, *Personal and Professional Recollections* (1879; Stamford, 1995), p. c.   [68] *Builders' Journal* 11 (1900), 309.
[69] [Spring Gardens Sketch Club], *Spring Gardens Sketch Book* (8 vols; London, 1870–90).

many of the most influential architects of the Victorian period.[70] Notable graduates of Spring Gardens included G. E. Street, G. F. Bodley, and W. H. Crossland. When Jackson joined the twenty-seven strong team, these men were long gone, but his contemporaries were to be no less distinguished. There were both of Scott's sons: George Gilbert junior, and John Oldrid. They joined J. J. Stevenson, E. R. Robson, C. Hodgson Fowler, and Thomas Garner, who was to become Bodley's partner. Able though they were, these were all very different men, with widely varying ideas. What united them—and what bound them to Scott—was a shared love of medieval building. 'The fervour of the Gothic revival was still at its full blast,' recalled Jackson, and 'nothing would pass muster with the young enthusiasts among whom I found myself in Scott's office but severe Geometrical Decorated, or, better still, the severer Transitional.'[71] This was, in fact, a far stricter approach and an earlier style than Scott himself favoured. A Gothic Eclecticism was the hallmark of his secular buildings, as he incorporated details from Flanders and France, Germany and England, Italy and beyond. In his designs for the Government Offices in Whitehall (1862–73), indeed, Scott offered first Gothic, then 'Byzantine', all before building an Italianate edifice.[72] This was exceptional of course. The enthusiasm of his staff and pupils, Scott's own emotional commitment to medieval architecture, and commercial good sense, meant that Spring Gardens remained a predominantly Gothic practice; the home of 'the best Gothic men in the country'.[73]

Jackson never escaped the training which he received in Scott's office. His early works were entirely typical products of the Spring Gardens school. For his old tutor Tate, Jackson built a good Gothic rectory in 1863. Inspired by a Ruskinian 'passion for truth', he exposed the brick corbel course as a cornice around the rooms. This was exactly the same sort of honesty that led Thomas Garner to fall into raptures over a hansom cab: 'It was so "truthful", he said, "so-so-so-medieval"'.[74] Jackson's first great success, a winning design for the Ellesmere Memorial (1867) was similarly 'truthful', and equally 'medieval'.[75] And even as late as 1872, he built a conventional vernacular Gothic primary school in Otford, Kent. This exclusive commitment to medieval revivalism may have waned, but Jackson never transcended its basic principles. Scott's teaching was all-important. Throughout his life, Jackson remained a committed ecclesiastical Goth, believing that only a medieval style was suitable for church building.[76] Nor did his secular work essentially reject Scott's influence. Both men, for example, had a close professional relationship with the marble-carvers Farmer & Brindley.[77]

---

[70] See Cole, *Scott*, 87, 232–5.   [71] Jackson, *Life and Travels*, 55.
[72] David Brownlee, ' "A Regular Mongrel Affair": G. G. Scott's Design for the Government Offices', *Architectural History* 28 (1985), 159–78.   [73] *Builders' Journal* 11 (1900), 309.
[74] Jackson, *Life and Travels*, 56.   [75] *Builder* 26 (1868), 509–10.
[76] T. G. Jackson, *Modern Gothic Architecture* (London, 1873), 107.
[77] Emma Hardy, 'Farmer and Brindley: craftsmen sculptors 1850–1930', *Victorian Society Annual* 1993, 4–17.

4. Ellesmere Memorial (1867–9).

Scott's method of training was far from ideal, though whether it was worse than his contemporaries' remains questionable. Nineteenth-century architectural education was notoriously poor. But Scott's approach evidently omitted much—as he himself recognized—and in particular it left Jackson ill-equipped to cope with complex questions about planning.[78] This problem can be overstated, of course: to some extent, later criticisms reflect changes in fashion as much as anything else.[79] The shift to the formality of neo-classical planning involved a rejection of the informal and additive approach of the Gothic Revival. Certainly, Goodhart-Rendel's sharp criticisms of Jackson reflected his own commitment to *Beaux-Arts* composition, and dislike of the picturesque planning so characteristic of the neo-Goths.[80] In this respect, Jackson was merely typical of his time. Nonetheless, it cannot be denied that he showed little imagination in his plans. He was responsible for no innovations; no breaks from the past comparable to the efforts he made with his façades. Whilst Jackson's schools and colleges pioneered the strikingly modern style with which he was to make his name, their plans reflected no new thinking. Nor were his less well-known commissions any more enterprising. His few houses showed little imagination in their lay-out; they were—as his critics observed—essentially variations on a theme.[81] His churches remained faithful to the ecclesiological training which he received in Spring Gardens.[82] With their distinct chancels, south porches, raised sanctuaries, and exposed roofs, they deviated in no respect from the Cambridge Camden Society's teachings of the 1840s.[83] Worse still, even his contemporaries recognized that his attempts at public building 'did not add to his reputation'. 'Their plans', wrote Arthur Bolton, 'led nowhere, and had the involved character natural, perhaps, to a house planner.'[84]

The explanation for this undoubtedly lay in his pupilage. Gilbert Scott was, himself, an able planner. His rooms were sometimes too large, and his corridors occasionally dark, but overall his work was well thought-out and his buildings were convenient. As a teacher, however, he was clearly deficient. He offered

[78] See Scott's letter to Jackson in *Life and Travels*, pp. xv–xvi.
[79] On Victorian planning, see Jill Franklin, *The Gentleman's Country House and Its Plan* (London, 1981) and Gavin Stamp and André Goulancourt, *The English House 1860–1914: the flowering of English domestic architecture* (London, 1986).
[80] Goodhart-Rendel, *Architecture since the Regency*, 176–7. See also Geoffrey Tyack, *Oxford: an architectural guide* (Oxford, 1998), 261–2, where Goodhart-Rendel's attack is re-articulated.
[81] C. E. Mallows, 'The Complete Work of T. G. Jackson', *Architectural Review* 1 (1896–7), 136–62, at 146.
[82] Scott, *Recollections*, 87–8. See also Gavin Stamp, 'George Gilbert Scott and the Cambridge Camden Society', in Christopher Webster and John Elliott, eds., *'A Church as it should be': the Cambridge Camden Society and its influence* (Stamford, 2000), 173–89.
[83] Cambridge Camden Society, *A Few Words to Church Builders* (3rd ed.; Cambridge, 1844) and *Church Enlargement and Church Arrangement* (Cambridge, 1843). See also, James F. White, *The Cambridge Movement: the ecclesiologists and the Gothic Revival* (Cambridge, 1962).
[84] A. T. Bolton, 'Sir Thomas Graham Jackson RA: an appreciation', *Architects' Journal* 60 (1924), 758–63, at 761.

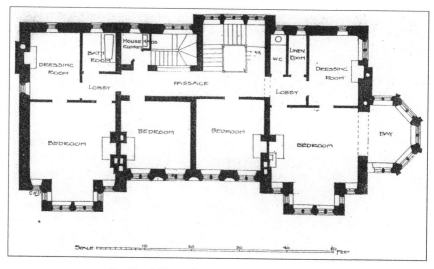

5. President's House, Trinity College, Oxford (1883–8).

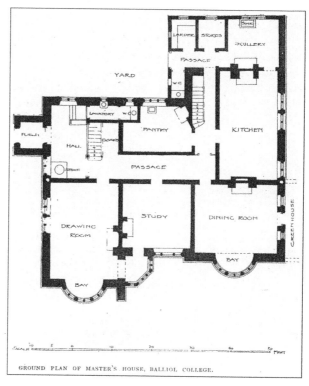

GROUND PLAN OF MASTER'S HOUSE, BALLIOL COLLEGE.

6. King's Mound, Oxford (1892–3).

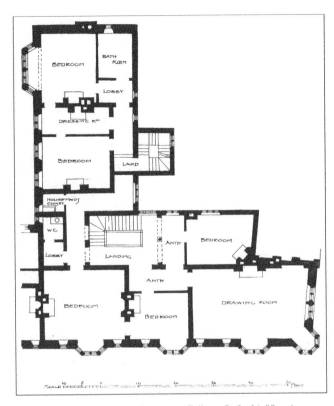

7. Principal's House, Brasenose College, Oxford (1880–9).

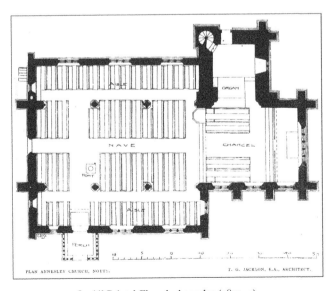

8. All Saints' Church, Annesley (1872–4).

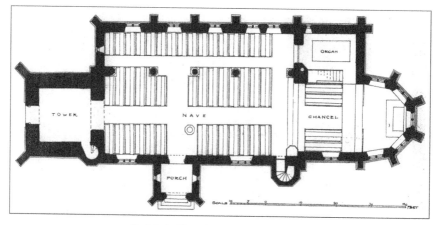

9. St. John's Church, Northington (1887–90).

nothing like the systematic training that would have overcome Jackson's neglect with respect to planning. Indeed, the very basis of his method tended to underrate the importance of a rational plan. For all his Puginian protestations, Scott shared Ruskin's belief that 'architecture is the decoration of construction', and his method consequently focused on the accurate copying of medieval ornamentation; ornamentation that would later be applied to the façade of a building.[85] This training had a profound effect on Jackson. Indeed, as an old man he could still recall the sleepless nights of his first week 'dozing and waking again, and all the time drawing in imagination the west door of Tintern Abbey'.[86] It was an approach that left the young architect with an unrivalled knowledge of medieval details, and an enviable aptitude for architectural illustration. But it inevitably drew his attention away from the plan and towards the elevation. This was a focus that he was never to lose. As even his admirers acknowledged, 'it is in the decoration rather than in the planning . . . that one finds him most at ease. . . . His vocation is, indeed, not planning.'[87] The overwhelming emphasis on the elevation, and on ornamenting the façade, was to affect the young architect's whole career. In that respect, at least, the subsequent criticism of Jackson's work as 'painter's architecture rather than architect's architecture' rings true.[88]

Scott's influence, then, was pervasive and important for good or for ill. It also outlasted Jackson's rebellion against him. For rebel he did. In part, this was a

---

[85] G. G. Scott, *Lectures on the Rise and Development of Medieval Architecture* (2 vols.; London, 1878–9), vol. ii, p. 292. Compare with Ruskin, *Works*, vol. 8, pp. 27–9.

[86] Jackson, *Recollections*, 54.   [87] *Architecture* 2 (1897), 84.

[88] Crook, 'Cult of Eclecticism', 106.

simple reaction against the way in which Spring Gardens worked. 'It need hardly be said that it is an impossibility really to direct so large a staff as Scott's', observed Jackson.

There are many amusing tales which show the slight acquaintance he had with what came out of his office: how he admired a new church from a railway-carriage window and was told it was one of his own; how he went into a church in process of building, sent for the clerk of works, and began finding fault with this and with that till the man said, 'You know, Mr Scott, this is not your church; this is Mr. Street's, your church is down the road'.

Jackson soon came to dislike and distrust this way of working, and he resolved never to imitate it in his own practice.[89] Nor was he alone. Apocryphal stories, like the one in which Scott telegraphed 'Why am I here?' on arrival at a Midland railway station, disconcerted many.[90] Still more importantly, Jackson came to doubt the stylistic preferences of his master too. As he later recalled, Jackson's generation soon 'diverged from the paths of strict Gothic rectitude into tracks where, in the days of our pupilage, we should have thought it sinful to walk'.[91] The fragile unity of Spring Gardens was thus undercut, and the distant—if pervasive—authority of Gilbert Scott was fatally undermined.

Ironically, it was the very success of his office that so damaged Scott. It was in Spring Gardens that the Gothic Revival was killed—and by his own pupils. His absence made this inevitable, for whilst Scott was too busy to teach, his students and staff taught each other. As Jackson recalled:

Perhaps what did us as much good as anything in Scott's office was the sharp fire of criticism that went on and from which none escaped. Even our master's work fared badly . . . and often when sketches came up for some new 'job' we fell upon them and metaphorically tore them to pieces.[92]

This atmosphere of mutual criticism, this unwillingness to listen even to his master's voice, created an environment in which stylistic heresy could be proposed. It eventually led to a re-assessment not just of individual 'jobs', but of the Gothic Revival itself. In the absence of other evidence it is difficult to reconstruct this process of disenchantment. Nor is it true to say that Scott's pupils were alone in their reaction against the Revival. But the record of the Spring Gardens' graduates speaks for itself. Within ten years of their pupilage even Scott's sons had abandoned High Victorian Gothic. Robson for his schools,[93] Stevenson for his houses,[94] G. G. Scott, junior, for his churches:[95] all renounced

[89] Jackson, *Life and Travels*, 57.   [90] Cole, *Scott*, 86.
[91] Jackson, *Life and Travels*, 58.   [92] Ibid., 58.
[93] Malcolm Seaborne, 'Introduction' to E. R. Robson, *School Architecture* (1874; Leicester, 1972), 18–20.
[94] Mark Girouard, 'The Architecture of John James Stevenson', *The Connoisseur* 184 (1973), 166–74; 185 (1974), 106–12.
[95] Gavin Stamp, *An Architect of Promise: George Gilbert Scott (1839–1897) and the Late Gothic Revival* (Donington, 2002).

their High Gothic inheritance. 'I fear that if our revered preceptor and master could return from the grave and see what some of us have been doing', wrote Jackson in 1904, 'he would turn his back on us as renegades and apostates.'[96]

In this sense, Jackson is just one of a group. Whilst others worked on board schools and country houses, he applied the Spring Gardens touch to universities and public schools. Yet although his pupilage was significant, there were at least two other important factors which shaped his career and distinguished his approach. The first was foreign travel. Jackson was an inveterate tourist, and often spent a month or more abroad a year. Even at the height of his success, he would abandon his office for weeks at a time. There was a practical purpose to this, of course. All architects were advised to travel—and those who could afford it did so. Gilbert Scott in particular acknowledged the value of visits to Italy. Not even Benjamin Ferrey endlessly muttering 'Batty Langley' could spoil Venice for him.[97] And so, in 1864, Jackson began a grand tour of Europe. He took as his companion John Oldrid Scott, the younger son of his master. Their itinerary was impressive: Honfleur, Seez, Le Mans, and Chartres; Lucca, Genoa, Pisa, and Siena; not a single ancient town was missed. On this trip, Oldrid Scott played the part of a cross-channel Ferrey. He disliked Italian building, dismissing the campanile at Florence as 'only painter's architecture'. Unsurprisingly, Graham Jackson disagreed. Primed for Italy by Ruskin, he loved what he saw. And at Modena, Scott left for home, leaving Jackson free to explore Parma, Ravenna, and Venice on his own. This tour was to prove formative. Italy taught Jackson the importance of sculpture, painting, and structural polychromy. It revealed the beauty of Italian building. More significantly still, he came back from his travels 'cured of medievalism'. 'I loved the ancient Gothic work, and especially English Gothic no less than heretofore', he wrote, 'but I regarded it henceforth as my tutor rather than my model.'[98] This was certainly an exaggeration. Italy simply confirmed existing doubts. But it was an important experience nonetheless.

Jackson returned to England in changed circumstances too. For in 1864 he was elected a Fellow of Wadham. This was the second of the two key influences on Jackson's career. He was quite well aware of its importance. 'To me', he wrote, 'such a Fellowship has been everything.'[99] In the first place, it was a particularly useful source of income. Jackson was one of the last non-resident, or prize, fellows. These posts were awarded on the basis of an examination and were tenable until marriage. They were only open to graduates from the electing college, and a successful candidate received a stipend but was not required to teach, research, or even live in Oxford. Too good to last, such fellowships were abolished as an abuse shortly afterwards. Whilst they existed, though, they were extremely useful for men like Jackson. In effect, the fellowship gave him the private income every young architect was presumed to require. It also bought him time: fourteen years, in fact. During that period Jackson was not forced to

---

[96] Jackson, *Life and Travels*, 58.   [97] Scott, *Recollections*, 159.
[98] Jackson, *Life and Travels*, 77–88.   [99] Ibid., 75.

support himself with surveying, petty competition work, or the other minor jobs which an impecunious architect might take on to earn ready cash. In an age in which a man could describe himself as a 'Hairdresser and Architect', anything was possible.[100] Rather, Jackson was able to think, to read, and to learn. He was also able to develop new skills, producing 'work of an improving but pecuniarily unprofitable kind'.[101] He designed stained-, painted- and table-glass, embroidery, plate, and a variety of other handiwork. He also wrote, and in 1873 published his first book, *Modern Gothic Architecture*. It was the distillation of a decade's thought and experience. Jackson argued for the abandonment of the Gothic Revival; the use of Renaissance design; the acceptance of a 'judicious eclecticism'.[102] To all intents and purposes, it was the manifesto of the Spring Gardens' Graduates. His fellowship had allowed him to produce it.

Writing books and designing embroidery was all very well. It was not, however, a career. By 1873 Graham Jackson was thirty-seven, unmarried, and 'making a modest income'.[103] He was still living with his parents, first in Sydenham (between 1857 and 1860), then Ewell (1860 to 1867), and finally Sevenoaks. Had the story stopped here, he would have been a tremendous advertisement for the absurdity of prize places at Oxford; further proof that Salisbury was correct to condemn them as 'idle fellowships'.[104] In 1876, though, everything changed. Jackson won the competition to build Oxford's New Examination Schools. The story of his triumph is complex, and long, and is described in Chapter 3. The important point is that the £100,000 project was the start of Jackson's success. It was his first important commission and marked the beginning of his career as a top-flight architect. The Examination Schools was an embodiment of the ideals he had set out in his book—built with precisely the 'judicious eclecticism' he had recommended in *Modern Gothic Architecture*. There were details here from all over Italy: marble from Florence, roofs from Verona, mosaics from Ravenna, and much more besides. Here and there can be found more than a hint of Spring Gardens, too. Jackson had helped his master with the final Foreign Office design, and believed it to be 'the finest thing [Scott] ever did'.[105] The Schools shares a similar evolution—from Gothic to Italianate—and a similar set of assumptions. But it was not a building that looked backwards. It was the foundation of a future style, and a promising career. It made Jackson's a name worth knowing.

The New Examination Schools, then, was critical for Jackson. As Humphry Ward put it: 'The success of the new building, which occupies one of the finest sites in Oxford, was generally admitted, and henceforth Jackson became the Oxford architect *par excellence* ... The public schools followed suit ... He achieved in this way a great position.'[106] All this, and work in Cambridge too. Bit

---

[100] Frank Jenkins, *Architect and Patron* (London, 1962), 225.
[101] Jackson, *Recollections*, 92.   [102] Jackson, *Modern Gothic Architecture*, 110.
[103] Jackson, *Life and Travels*, 109.
[104] Andrew Roberts, *Salisbury: Victorian titan* (London, 1999), 120.
[105] Jackson, *Life and Travels*, 65.
[106] Humphry Ward, *History of the Athenaeum, 1824–1925* (London, 1926), 330.

10. Eagle House, Wimbledon, from the garden.

by bit, Jackson became the chief architect of elite education. Nor did the New Schools just establish the type of building that he would go on to dominate. Its style was similarly significant. 'The carrying out of this great building was quite an education', recalled Jackson, 'and settled me in a style which I think has been rather my own.'[107] This combination of Jacobean work with Italianate details soon became popular, and won still more work. At last (and not before time) Jackson was considered a success. Financially secure, he was now finally able to marry— and did so on 31 March 1880. His wife, Alice Lambarde, came from an old-established Sevenoaks family; Jackson was marrying into the gentry. Soon there were sons: Hugh in 1881 and Basil in 1887, and a new home. Between 1886 and 1887 he bought and restored Eagle House in Wimbledon. It was a striking Jacobean mansion, the 'most important house in Wimbledon', and it was a suit-able symbol of Jackson's success.[108] He took a school—the school, curiously,

---

[107] Jackson, *Life and Travels*, 119.
[108] Ian Nairn and Nikolaus Pevsner, *Surrey* (2nd ed.; 1971), 524. See also *Architect* 46 (1891), 271.

11. The garden front of Eagle House.

12. The Library, Eagle House.

where Schopenhauer had lost his faith—and transformed it into a large family home.[109] The pattern of his life was set. Jackson had become a grandee, a husband, and a father. His marriage was to be intensely happy: his wife was a constant companion, even on his potentially hazardous journeys to the Croatian coast. His sons were a source of profound pride. His family life was deeply fulfilling. In the end, Jackson fully justified his own father's confidence, and his choice of career.

Jackson's success, though, possessed more than purely personal significance. After all, it was hardly unknown for a young architect to be saved by a competition, whilst the roll call of Victorian evangelicals made good is a long and distinguished one.[110] Indeed, Jackson's life in itself is scarcely remarkable. 'Architects', as Gavin Stamp has noted, 'usually lead lives of mundane respectability.'[111] Jackson was no exception to this: happily married, comfortably well off, and professionally fulfilled, he was respectability made manifest. So respectable was he, in fact, that his dark-suited office clerk was popularly supposed to be his private chaplain.[112] What makes Jackson interesting is his work—and, perhaps more particularly, the light that his work casts on his surroundings. In many ways more than most, T. G. Jackson was a product of his environment. Both his success, and the subsequent sudden collapse in his reputation, reflect that and the fact that he thrived in some specific circumstances and declined in others. Only a study of the context in which he worked can explain this. Thus, if we are to understand his career we must learn about his clients, his colleagues, his readers, and his friends.

This, of course, does not mean that the well-worn tools of architectural history should be discarded. Just as knowledge of the architect will help to interpret a building, so knowledge of a building will shed light upon its architect. All buildings carry meaning, and all may convey a message.[113] 'Efforts to construct a meaning-proof architecture have always been *de facto* unsuccessful', as J. P. Bonta puts it. Even 'An architecture designed to be meaningless . . . would *mean* the desire to be meaningless and thus could not actually be meaningless.'[114] In particular, the choice of style must be a critical part of any analysis. Pevsner is not alone in noting that 'If the historian of architecture does not take style dead-seriously, he stops being a historian.'[115] In assessing Graham Jackson's success, this is especially important. From the building of the Examination Schools onwards, Jackson was best known as an idiosyncratic stylist. The 'Anglo-Jackson' style was described by contemporaries as 'Advanced Jacobean'—and it was

---

[109] Patrick Bridgwater, *Schopenhauer's English Schooling* (London, 1988).
[110] Roger H. Harper, *Victorian Architectural Competitions* (London, 1983), xiii–xviii; Ford K. Brown, *Fathers of the Victorians* (Cambridge, 1966), 6.   [111] Stamp, *Architect of Promise*, 2.
[112] Jackson, *Life and Travels*, 72.
[113] William Whyte, 'Reading Buildings Like a Book: the case of T. G. Jackson', in Peter Draper, ed., *Current Work in Architectural History: papers read at the Annual Symposium of the Society of Architectural Historians of Great Britain 2004* (2005), 27–34. More generally see William Whyte, 'How do Buildings Mean? Some issues of interpretation in the history of architecture', *History & Theory* 45 (2006) 153–177.   [114] Juan Pablo Bonta, *Architecture and Its Interpretation* (London, 1979), 22.
[115] *Listener* 65 (1961), 300.

evidently advanced in several important senses.[116] This was a style regarded with distaste by old-fashioned admirers of the Gothic Revival: it was late; it was debased; it was unmedieval.[117] Jackson's choice of a more modern style was seen as progressive: his buildings hummed with modernity. This was important for the architect and for his clients. Both were keen to seem innovative, avant-garde even. They were, as one enthusiast put it, 'very anxious to be up-to-date, and in the fashion'.[118] Jackson's architecture, his books, and even his tableware, all allowed his clients to see and to show themselves as patrons of modern art, as connoisseurs of the latest style. It was Advanced Jacobean for Advanced Victorians.

To be more specific: this was a modern style for a self-consciously modern group of people, England's evolving intelligentsia. They formed a close corps of often inter-related academics, writers, and teachers. Together they were taking over the old universities and the great public schools. They were also reforming them. They re-made Oxford, Cambridge, Eton, and other ancient institutions, and rebuilt them in their own image. Jackson was employed to express their success, to advertise their values, and to emphasize the triumph of reform. His buildings, his style, and his approach were used to articulate the identity of this new group and to proclaim their triumph over other, competing visions of society. He became, in fact, the architect of an intellectual aristocracy. Jackson was particularly successful because he was a part of this group. As a Fellow of an Oxford College, as an author, as an educational reformer, as a member of an educated family, Jackson shared his clients' social status. He was an aristocrat of the intellect in his own right: obviously a safe pair of hands and definitely one of the gang. By examining his place in this new group we can shed light on it, on him, and on his role in expressing their common identity. There is certainly no lack of material to be used. Precisely because they were writers, members of this group have left letters, books, articles, and memoirs. Many of Jackson's clients are themselves the subject of biographies—whether great Victorian *Life and Letters* or more recent monographs. His detractors were similarly voluble, and their attacks are often extremely well expressed. Using this abundance of material, we can begin to understand the reception of Jackson's designs and we can hope to explain their importance to his clients—and to their opponents. We can view Jackson in his true context: assessing his success; providing precisely the broad view that a biography requires and his life demands.

In Chapter 1, Jackson's role as an intellectual in his own right will be examined. He was one of the most prolific architect-authors of the period. His writings offer a unique insight into his thoughts and illustrate his importance as an intellectual. The second chapter deals with Jackson's involvement in the arts and crafts movement, in the restoration of ancient buildings, and in the

[116] H. E. D. Blakiston, *Trinity College, Oxford* (Oxford, 1898), 238.
[117] Mark Girouard, 'Attitudes to Elizabethan Architecture', in John Summerson, ed., *Concerning Architecture* (London, 1968), 13–27, at 25–7.
[118] Mrs Humphry Ward, *A Writer's Recollections* (London, 1918), 119.

reform of art education. In each of these fields, Jackson was a leading figure. His participation in the debates of the day was important for him and for others—and it has been almost universally ignored. Chapter 3 is focused on Jackson in Oxford. For more than a generation he was the chief university architect; a figure so significant that it was even suggested the town should change its name to Jacksonville.[119] Success in Oxford soon led to work elsewhere, and in Chapters 4 and 5, Jackson's buildings for the public schools and at Cambridge will be assessed. Finally, in Chapter 6, the group of people who commissioned him will be identified and explored. The intellectual aristocracy was central to Jackson's achievement and to his identity. In many ways, it is the central theme of his career and his life.

The rationale for this approach is clear. In the absence of any major study of Jackson's work, we must begin with the most basic questions: what did he build, when, where, and why? These questions cannot be divorced from others: who commissioned him and which factors framed this choice? The answers to this series of enquiries will contextualize Jackson's life and explain his success. There is no attempt here to suggest that Jackson founded a school—he did not. Nor to show that he influenced later artists—that is irrelevant to our purposes. It is not even argued that Jackson should enter the supposed pantheon of great architects, whether as 'the Norman Foster of his day', or not.[120] Arguably, the search for a canon of immortals has done more than anything else to distort historical writing. Rather, this book is an attempt to understand Jackson in his own times and on his own terms. Lytton Strachey—a writer with a somewhat different aim—offers a strangely pertinent model. He claimed that 'the history of the Victorian Age will never be written: we know too much about it', but he offered guidance to those foolish enough to attempt such a sisyphian task. 'It is not by the direct method of a scrupulous narration that the explorer of the past can hope to depict that singular epoch', he wrote.

If he is wise, he will adopt a subtler strategy. He will attack his subject in unexpected places; he will fall upon the flank, or the rear; he will shoot a sudden, revealing searchlight into obscure recesses, hitherto undivined. He will row out over that great ocean of material, and lower down into it, here and there, a little bucket, which will bring up to the light of day some characteristic specimen, from those far depths, to be examined with a careful curiosity.[121]

Jackson is perhaps just such a specimen. Uncharacteristic though his prominence made him, he nonetheless illuminates a period and a class. Whether as T. G., as Graham, as Sir Thomas, as 'Anglo', or indeed as 'Oxford' Jackson, his work was critical for his clients and typical of his time.

[119] *Oxford Magazine* 15 (1896–7), 57.
[120] Richard Whiteley, quoted in *Architects' Journal* 211 (2000), No. 17, p. 22.
[121] Lytton Strachey, *Five Victorians* (London, 1942), 221.

I

'Recording our eclectic age'[1]
Jackson and the Dilemma of Style

'It seems to me', wrote T. G. Jackson in 1893, 'that the modern architect's time is half occupied in controversial writing, composing and answering pamphlets, and writing magazine articles. That at least has been my fate this winter.'[2] Trapped, as he was, in the midst of battle over a controversial church restoration, this attitude is unsurprising. But it is also unrepresentative of his usual approach to such work. Jackson, as he himself observed, was 'never quite content unless I have some writing on hand'.[3] He wrote on a wide range of topics, and in a multiplicity of media: letters, articles, and books on architectural history, on artistic theory, and even on politics. Taken together, these thousands of words and hundreds of pages offer a uniquely valuable corpus of material. They show Jackson establishing himself as an author and a public figure; a recognized authority on architecture and architectural history. They reveal a man searching desperately for a way out of the Victorian and Edwardian dilemma of style. They express, sometimes starkly, Jackson's search for a truly modern architecture. He was not unique in this, of course. But sheer effort, originality, and insight made him one of the leading architectural writers of his time. He was an author whose work was often 'worthy of Ruskin or Reynolds', and who left a distinctive and so far under-researched mark on contemporary debate.[4]

In part, this impact was the result of sheer hard work. Jackson's 'vitality was extraordinary'.[5] That he managed to produce quite so much material whilst practising as a professional architect astonished even his contemporaries.[6] In many ways, though, it was a family tradition. Jackson's uncle, Thomas Kerchever Arnold, had an equally exceptional record. This much-published priest had, indeed, to defend himself from charges of over-production and even dishonesty. Arnold's explanation might also be Jackson's: 'The list of my

[1] *The Times*, 20 Jan. 1885, 10.

[2] OUA, NW20/8 St Mary the Virgin, Jackson to Gamlen (27 March 1893).

[3] T. G. Jackson, *Recollections: the life and travels of a Victorian architect* (ed., Sir Nicholas Jackson; London, 2003), 219.   [4] *Architect* 9 (1873), 294.

[5] *Times*, 7 Nov. 1924, 7.   [6] *Architects' Journal* 60 (1924), 761.

works . . . *is* undoubtedly a very long one; but regular industry, and with careful division of times and employments, carried on with hardly any exception for six days in every week, *will* accomplish a great deal.'[7] For most of his career, Graham Jackson operated a similar system: working five days at the office and on Saturdays at home.[8] The result was time enough to think, to draw, and to write: to take part in the great debate which followed the end of the Gothic Revival.

But why? What drove this enterprise? In part, the answer is simply Jackson's environment. He came from a family which wrote, and so he too wrote. His friends were also writers, whether architects or academics. Only a man used to writing—and to being read—would dream of writing to *The Times* to report that a burglar had broken into his house.[9] His letters, in fact, were repeatedly prefaced by the presumption that they would be 'interesting to your readers'.[10] This was more than a stock phrase; it clearly represented Jackson's genuine feelings. He expected people to be interested in his thoughts, and evidently believed that it was his duty to share them. Jackson was, in short, an inveterate correspondent, taking his role as an expert on art and architecture very seriously.[11] After his baronetcy he began to write on still more controversial matters: on the suffragettes (he was antipathetic); on home rule (he was resigned); on war reparations (he was aggressive); on capital levies (he was aggrieved).[12] Jackson became a public figure, whose views on art and politics and other national problems were clearly in demand. Confined to his room for the last six months of his life, he used the time to write another book.[13]

If Jackson's background made him a writer, then his writing made him an influential individual. Through his letters, books, and articles Graham Jackson was able to reach many who would not otherwise have known him. His histories were read on both sides of the Atlantic. They were noted in the *Gazette des Beaux-Arts*,[14] reaching an audience of French artists and academics, who had previously known little—and thought less—of his work.[15] A number of his books were published in America, and others were reviewed in the American press. His occasional papers were periodically abstracted in transatlantic publications.[16] In Ireland, and in Scotland too, it was his books rather than his buildings which gained him some measure of fame.[17] In England, his position as a writer gave him status and a certain authority. As Reginald Blomfield implied,

[7] T. K. Arnold, *A Few Words in Answer to the Attack on My 'Classical School Books' Published in Fraser's Magazine* (London, 1853), 15.

[8] CUA Geol 9/39, Jackson Corresp. (1) 10 Dec. 1896.   [9] *Times*, 14 Jan. 1889, 7.

[10] *Times*, 14 Jan. 1900; 7 Sep. 1917, 5.

[11] e.g., *Times*, 20 Aug. 1887, 4; 28 Dec. 1894, 5; 20 March 1899, 3; 12 Dec. 1905, 4; 20 Dec. 1909, 10; 11 Aug. 1911, 3; 21 Feb. 1914, 9; 25 May 1917, 9; 17 Feb. 1919, 3; 19 May 1920, 12.

[12] *Times*, 16 April 1913, 8; 30 March 1914, 10; 4 July 1914, 12; 22 Nov. 1918, 6; 24 Nov. 1922, 13.

[13] *Oxford Magazine* 43 (1924–5), 126.

[14] *Gazette des Beaux-Arts* 55/1 (1913), 511; 59 (1917), 515; 64/1 (1922), 379; 65/2 (1923), 383.

[15] At least according to C. F. Bell: BalCA D.10.16 (7 Nov. 1911).

[16] *American Architect* 22 (1887), 83–4; 24 (1888), 10–11, 25–6; 87 (1905), 30–2, 51–2.

[17] *Dublin Review* 37 (1888), 234–9; *Scottish Geographical Magazine* 3 (1887), 606–7.

it was through his writing as much as anything else that Jackson became one of the 'recognised leaders' of the architectural profession.[18] Nor was his writing confined to the purely architectural. It included travel journals and even ghost stories.[19] The breadth of his range was exceptional.

Jackson's output was not simply prodigious or merely well known. Indeed, it marked him out as a significant intellectual figure: an arbiter of taste and a public moralist in his own right. In Oxford, as the *Architect* put it, he was '*persona grata . . .* by reason of his scholarship'.[20] In London, his election to the Athenaeum placed him at the heart of the educated class. That he was elected under rule two—which provided for the admission of the truly distinguished—only emphasized his importance to England's intellectual community. Indeed, he was determined to transcend the purely professional, and to address a wider, well-educated public.[21] He wrote for a variety of periodicals—architectural, antiquarian, and much more besides. He was published by the Clarendon and Cambridge University Presses, by John Murray, and Macmillan—all of which were reputable and scholarly. Moreover, unlike most other architects, he could write well.[22] Or, to put it more critically, he had a command of the vocabulary and rhetoric of the educated elite. His books were packed with classical references and Latin tags—the witty wordplay so beloved by his intellectual peers.[23] He was, as one critic put it, 'that rarity, the technical expert who can write like a man of letters'.[24]

Again and again, though, T. G. Jackson returned to the same themes and to similar problems. Much of his most important writing grew out of his building: out of the commissions he received and the controversy that surrounded them. This was a calculated tactic. In the event of a crisis—the rejection of a plan, or assaults on an elevation—Jackson always advised the printing of a controversial letter.[25] His newspaper correspondence and a number of articles and books served a similar function.[26] At all times, however, his aim was to explain as well as to defend. For this the full weight of his rhetorical skills was brought to bear, and with some success.[27] Certainly, he was admired for his persuasive powers, and this literary dexterity was vital to his career.[28] Jackson defended his practice, explained his ideals, and sought to articulate his vision of architecture. More

---

[18] The other was Shaw: Reginald Blomfield, *RIBA Journal* 32 (1924–5), 49–50.

[19] T. G. Jackson, *A Holiday in Umbria* (London, 1917); *Memories of Travel* (Cambridge, 1923); *Six Ghost Stories* (London, 1919).   [20] *Architect* 112 (1924), 301.

[21] *Architectural Review* 54 (1923), 111; *Bookman* 44 (1913), 50.   [22] *Architect* 9 (1873), 294.

[23] *Oxford Magazine* xliii (1924–5), 126; Pierre Bourdieu, *Homo Academicus* (trans. Peter Collier; Cambridge, 1990), 29–30; N. G. Annan, 'The Intellectual Aristocracy', in J. H. Plumb, ed., *Studies in Social History* (London, 1955); reprinted in Annan, *The Dons* (London, 1999), 249.

[24] *Bookman* 44 (1913), 50.

[25] CUA Geol. 9/13/3–5, Jackson to Vice-Chancellor (6 June 1900).

[26] T. G. Jackson, *The Church of St. Mary the Virgin, Oxford* (Oxford, 1897); *Times*, 5 Jan. 1893, 7; 10 Jan. 1893, 11.   [27] As reviewers recognized: *Spectator* 79 (1897), 798.

[28] *Builder* 63 (1892), 516.

than anything else, this attempt unified the whole of his work. In his books and articles—and in the history as much as in the theory—he sought to solve some of the great questions puzzling his contemporaries. He hoped to escape the 'tyranny of style' and to redefine the position of the artist.[29] He intended to find a modern architecture for modern circumstances. He explored the place of the past in the present, and offered a guide to the future direction of his art.

In particular, Jackson was concerned to find a solution to the dilemma of style which had dominated architectural discourse for more than a century.[30] The problem was not a new one. Architects had always struggled to find an appropriate form for each building. Thus, whilst Christopher Wren disliked the Gothic style, he was nonetheless willing to adopt it if the context seemed right. At Westminster Abbey, he proposed a medieval enlargement, seeking to avoid 'a disagreeable Mixture' of Roman and Gothic themes.[31] Similarly, in some of his City churches, he found himself 'oblig'd to deviate from a better style' and take up medieval motifs.[32] Nonetheless, nineteenth-century artists were more than usually self-conscious about style. A new seriousness in antiquarian studies, the rediscovery of Greek and Gothic architecture, the development of new building-types, and the increased availability of iron, plate glass, and other modern materials, all added to their difficulties. At the same time, the debate about style was politicized. The choice of approach—whether Greek or Gothic, Roman or Romanesque—was taken to be a moral question. The Gothic Revival, founded on the assumption that only medieval art was Christian art, proved to be particularly moralistic. A product of the Revival, Gilbert Scott came to feel 'a sort of religious horror at all styles of pagan origin'.[33] Yet even the adoption of medieval architecture had not solved the dilemma. By the end of his life, Scott himself was doubtful about the Revival's success and admitted that no clear solution, no new single style, had emerged.[34] Jackson, trained by Scott in the traditions of the Gothic Revival, wrote in the aftermath of this realization.

He was not, of course, alone in his writing. Most of the front-rank architects of the day were also authors.[35] His master, Gilbert Scott, was phenomenally prolific,[36] writing many of his manuscripts on the train between appointments.[37] Scott's pupil, Street, was the author of two highly influential histories of

[29] T. G. Jackson, *Renaissance of Roman Architecture* (3 vols.; Cambridge, 1921–3), vol. i, p. 188.

[30] J. Mordaunt Crook, *The Dilemma of Style: architectural ideas from the picturesque to the post-modern* (London, 1987).   [31] *Wren Society* (19 vols.; London, 1928–42), vol. xi, 20.

[32] Christopher Wren, *Parentalia* (London, 1750), 302.

[33] G. G. Scott, *Personal and Professional Recollections* (1879; Stamford, 1995), 226.

[34] Ibid., 375–6, 226–7, 373.

[35] David Watkin, *The Rise of Architectural History* (London, 1980), 76–107.

[36] See especially: *Remarks on Secular and Domestic Architecture* (London, 1857); *Gleanings from Westminster Abbey* (Oxford and London, 1861); *Lectures on the Rise and Development of Medieval Architecture* (2 vols.; London, 1878–9).

[37] Gavin Stamp, 'Introduction', to Scott, *Recollections*, pp. f, k.

architecture in Spain and northern Italy.[38] Jackson's generation was still more voluble. G. G. Scott, junior,[39] Basil Champneys,[40] J. J. Stevenson,[41] W. R. Lethaby,[42] and several others, all wrote books, whilst a rather younger group of authors included Reginald Blomfield,[43] Mervyn Macartney,[44] Alfred Gotch,[45] and Edward Prior.[46] Not all were natural writers: William Burges and Norman Shaw preferred pictures to prose, and their books were little more than collected sketches and measured drawings.[47] For all these men, though, publishing formed a significant part of their professional practice. This period, indeed, can be seen as the quintessential age of the literary architect.

These late Victorian writers were following in a grand tradition. After all, both the Greek and the Gothic Revivals were built on books. The work of Winckelman and Riou, Stuart and Revett, and many others, brought a revived Hellenic style to Britain. Similarly, it was the writings of such figures as Horace Walpole, Batty Langley, and the contributors to the *Gentleman's Magazine*, notably John Carter, that popularized Gothic forms in the eighteenth century.[48] Even failed architectural movements had their literary champions—as the abortive Norman Revival showed.[49] And the Gothic Revival of the nineteenth century was especially dependent on, and productive of, articles and monographs. Many of the most important participants in the early years of the movement shared Gilbert Scott's sense of 'awakening' on reading the works of Pugin and the tracts of the Cambridge Camden Society.[50] Later players, like Jackson, were 'steeped in Ruskin' and widely read in Viollet-le-Duc.[51] Books were important, and they were important because they influenced architects.

---

[38] *Gothic Architecture in Spain* (London, 1865); *Brick and Marble in the Middle Ages* (London, 1855).   [39] *An Essay on the History of English Church Architecture* (London, 1881).
[40] *A Quiet Corner of England* (London, 1875); *Memories and Correspondence of Coventry Patmore* (2 vols.; London, 1900).   [41] *House Architecture* (2 vols.; London, 1880).
[42] *Architecture, Mysticism and Myth* (London, 1892); *Medieval Art* (London and New York, 1904); *Architecture* (London, 1911); *Form in Civilisation* (London, 1922); *Philip Webb and his Work* (London, 1935).
[43] *A History of Renaissance Architecture in England* (London, 1897); *Studies in Architecture* (London, 1905); *The Mistress Art* (London, 1908); *A History of French Architecture* (2 vols.; London, 1911–21).
[44] With John Belcher, *Later Renaissance Architecture in England* (2 vols.; London, 1901).
[45] *Architecture of the Renaissance in England* (2 vols.; London, 1891); *Historic Notes on Kirby Hall* (Northampton, 1899); *Early Renaissance Architecture in England* (2nd ed.; London, 1914).
[46] *A History of Gothic Art in England* (London, 1900).
[47] William Burges, *Architectural Drawings* (London, 1870); R. Norman Shaw, *Architectural Sketches from the Continent* (London, 1858): although Burges was responsible for a number of learned articles.
[48] Bruce Allsopp, *The Study of Architectural History* (London, 1970), 58–68; J. Mordaunt Crook, *The Greek Revival* (London, 1972), ch. 1 and *John Carter and the Mind of the Gothic Revival* (London, 1995); Paul Frankl, *The Gothic* (Princeton, 1960), 497–577; Chris Brooks, *The Gothic Revival* (London, 1999), ch. 1.
[49] Timothy Mowl, 'The Norman Revival in British Architecture' (Oxford D.Phil., 1981).
[50] Scott, *Recollections*, 87.   [51] Jackson, *Life and Travels*, 51.

After all, perhaps the most influential figure in the Gothic Revival was John Ruskin. He exercised a vital role not as an architect, but as an author.[52]

This influence was exercised at two levels. In the first place, controversial, polemical, and emotive publications created an environment in which medieval architecture was appreciated and ultimately advocated. From *The Castle of Otranto* to *Dracula*, from *Contrasts* to *The Stones of Venice*, an atmosphere of reverence for medieval art was disseminated and grew in strength, challenging the strong antipathy that had previously been felt towards it. In this sense, it was only a very short step from Walter Scott to Gilbert Scott.[53] Secondly, but no less importantly, the Gothic Revival depended on antiquarian research: a serious attempt to define and understand lost ways of building.[54] The work of men like Thomas Wharton and Thomas Rickman in defining a Gothic style was, in this respect, quite central to the Revival's success.[55] Both aspects were embodied in the work of Augustus Pugin. His books might best be described as polemical archaeology, consisting as they did of highly charged assertions of moral superiority and finely detailed depictions of perpendicular buildings.[56] The combination was captured in W. H. Leeds' new verb 'to Puginise' or to confuse 'political and theological speculations with architectural ones'.[57] This combination of exacting scholarship and claims to a moral and aesthetic monopoly underpinned the whole Gothic Revival. Any challenge to the movement would need new writers, new texts, and new ideas.

There was no attempt, however, to create a new canon. Whilst the Gothic Revival had been built on great weighty tomes, post-Revival architects specialized in quieter volumes. Partly, this reflected doubt; partly it reflected a different approach. As Mark Girouard observes, they 'produced no equivalent to Pugin or Gilbert Scott as an apologist', because they did not want one.[58] Rejecting the perceived dogmatism of the past, the late-Victorians sought to suggest solutions and not prescribe them. Nevertheless, if rigid neo-medievalism was to be overthrown, it had to be confronted on paper. Jackson was simply one of a group of writers who attempted to do just that. The movement included close colleagues: men like J. J. Stevenson, with whom he had trained at Spring

[52] Although, cf. J. Mordaunt Crook, 'Ruskinian Gothic', in John Dixon Hunt and Faith M. Holland, eds., *The Ruskin Polygon* (Manchester, 1982), 68–71, for a useful corrective to an uncritical acceptance of Ruskin's own self-importance.

[53] Amongst the many books on this process, see Kenneth Clark, *The Gothic Revival* (3rd ed., 1962; London, 1995); James Macaulay, *The Gothic Revival, 1745–1845* (Glasgow and London, 1975); Brooks, *Gothic Revival*; and—for a European perspective—Georg Germann, *Gothic Revival in Europe and Britain* (London, 1972).

[54] Rosemary Sweet, *Antiquaries: the discovery of the past in eighteenth-century Britain* (London, 2004).

[55] Frankl, *The Gothic*, 497; Thomas Rickman, *An Attempt to Discriminate the Styles of English Architecture* (London, 1817).

[56] *The True Principals of 'Pointed' or 'Christian' Architecture* (London, 1841) and *Contrasts* (2nd ed., 1841; Leicester, 1975).   [57] Quoted in Crook, *Dilemma of Style*, 42.

[58] Mark Girouard, *Sweetness and Light: the 'Queen Anne' movement, 1860–1900* (Oxford, 1977), 59–63.

Gardens, and Basil Champneys, who was to become a friendly rival in Oxford and elsewhere.[59] They maintained, as Stevenson put it, that 'The attempt to introduce the Gothic style into domestic and civil architecture [had] failed'.[60] And they argued for the abandonment of the Revival and the adoption of a less programmatic approach. Both Stevenson and Champneys were clear about the past, then, but they were less than sure about the future. J. J. Stevenson believed that a new style would evolve unconsciously—as it always had before.[61] Basil Champneys was still less assertive. Arguing for architecture with 'limited ambition', he hoped simply for the spontaneous growth of a 'generally accepted modern standard'.[62] What that standard was to be, he could not say.

Others were less muted in their attacks. J. T. Emmett, in particular, offered a critique of contemporary architecture which was as devastating as it was rude. As a disillusioned former architect he was well informed and well placed to infuriate his former colleagues.[63] His 1872 essay, 'The State of English Architecture' took the attack to a new height. Indeed, it caused a sensation. He argued, and in the most offensive terms, that throughout the nineteenth century the population had been forced to accustom itself to 'the most hideous extent of building that the world ever saw . . . supercilious, conceited, and debased'. With 'neither artists to build, nor critics to discuss, nor a public worthy to approve of any work', Emmett saw little cause for optimism that things would improve.[64] Two years later, in fact, in 'The Hope of English Architecture' (1874), he returned to battle in similar vein, and the architectural world responded with fury. The *Architect* and *British Architect*, the *Builder* and *Building News*, William White and William H. White, Beckett, Kerr, and Phené Spiers all defended their profession. But they were rattled, and a worried Gilbert Scott 'confessed he did not know what the hope of architecture was'.[65] Nonetheless, even Emmett had no programme. His faith in fourteenth-century art and society was touching, but as a way forward it had little to recommend it.[66] Moreover, his alienation from the architectural profession meant that his views had little practical effect.[67] Emmett, Champneys, and Stevenson were an important focus for discontent, but they offered little more than criticism. There seemed to be no clear way forward.

---

[59] Basil Champneys, 'On the Present Relations between Art and Architecture', *Portfolio* 1874, 170–2; 'The Architecture of Queen Victoria's Reign', *Art Journal* 7 (1887), 203–9; 'Style', *British Architect* 31 (1889), 41–3, 61–2, 81. J. J. Stevenson, 'On the Recent Reaction of Taste in English Architecture', *Architect* 11 (1874), suppl. 9–10; 'Queen Anne and Other Forms of Free Classicism', *Architect* 13 (1875), 125–6; *Builder* 33 (1875), 179–81; see also Girouard, *Sweetness and Light*, 59–63.   [60] Stevenson, *House Architecture*, vol. i, p. 381.
[61] *Architect* 13 (1875), 125.   [62] *Portfolio* 1874, 171.
[63] J. Mordaunt Crook, 'Introduction', J. T. Emmett, *Six Essays* (1891; New York and London, 1972), v–xvi; Lethaby, *Philip Webb*, 84.
[64] Emmett, 'The State of English Architecture', in *Six Essays*, 5, 50.
[65] *Architect* 12 (1874), 223–4; *British Architect* 2 (1874), 271–2; *Builder* 32 (1874), 879–80; 33 (1875), 360–1; *Building News* 27 (1874), 501–2, 716, 735–7; Crook in Emmett, *Six Essays*, xii–xv.
[66] *Quarterly Review* 123 (1867), 93–118.
[67] For Champneys' reaction to Emmett, see *Portfolio* 1873, 8–10.

In contrast to these three writers, Jackson's work has been almost totally ignored by historians.[68] Emmett's polemical power, Champneys' and Stevenson's involvement in the 'Queen Anne' Revival, have all made them more attractive subjects for study.[69] Jackson's writings have remained unresearched. Yet his contemporaries would have been amazed at this neglect. Certainly, from the first, Graham Jackson's books were respected, widely read, and well reviewed. His first, *Modern Gothic Architecture* (1873), caused a sensation. It was to be his most important work of theory and it also established the style of writing that Jackson was to make his own. His philosophical training, historical interests, and academic ambitions led him to produce a far more sophisticated treatment of the question than his rival writers. Even E. B. Ferrey, who produced a review designed to defend neo-medievalism, admired Jackson's 'scholarly production'. It was, he wrote, 'almost the only book that has appeared since the Gothic revival, which candidly and impartially discusses the present state of modern architecture'.[70] No one could deny that this was an important contribution to current debate, nor that T. G. Jackson had produced 'a tolerably dispassionate and very temperate, intellectual, and thoughtful treatise'.[71] Not that the book was bland. A quarter of a century later, C. E. Mallows was still shocked by its 'strong language' and impressed by Jackson's 'courage'.[72] The comparisons with Emmett's articles in the *Quarterly Review* were obvious, and led to a tragic mistake. Gilbert Scott came to believe that these anonymous essays were written by Jackson.[73] He must have felt his suspicions confirmed by a reference to Jackson's beloved Wadham in Emmett's essay on 'The Hope of English Architecture'.[74] Scott dropped Jackson, and expelled him from the Spring Gardens circle. They never spoke again.

This unpleasant incident did not halt Jackson's attempts to define a way forward, however. The confusion with Emmett, indeed, was as flattering as it was unfortunate. It reflected the power of his message and the passion of his argument.[75] Contemporary architecture, Jackson maintained, 'was an anachronism, an affectation, a sham'. The Gothic Revival had failed and had always been destined to fail: each age was different, 'and no adopted style can exactly suit those who adopt it'.[76] So it had proved. In a generation, architects had 'twice run through all those varieties of Gothic architecture which represent the steady

---

[68] Although cf. J. Mordaunt Crook, 'T. G. Jackson and the Cult of Eclecticism', in H. Searing, ed., *In Search of Modern Architecture* (New York, 1982), 102; Andrew Saint, *Richard Norman Shaw* (New Haven and London, 1976), 217; Reyner Banham, *Theory and Design in the First Machine Age* (1962; Oxford, 1992), 24, 29–30.

[69] Alan Jerôme Coignard, 'Basil Champneys, architecte (1842–1935)' (Paris IV, Mémoire de Maitrisse, 1984); Mark Girouard, 'The Architecture of John James Stevenson', *Connoisseur* 184 (1973), 166–74; 185 (1974), 106–12; Michael W. Brooks, *John Ruskin and Victorian Architecture* (London, 1989), 257, 266.   [70] *Architect* 10 (1873), 156–70.

[71] *Architect* 9 (1873), 294.   [72] *Architectural Review* 1 (1896–7), 140.

[73] Jackson, *Life and Travels*, 129–30.   [74] Emmett, 'Hope of English Architecture', 27.

[75] Ironically, one reviewer saw *Modern Gothic Architecture* as an attack on Emmett, *Architect* 9 (1873), 294.   [76] T. G. Jackson, *Modern Gothic Architecture* (London, 1873) 182, 11.

growth of four centuries'. Yet the result had been not beauty, but ugliness; not progress, but chaos. Educated men, he declared, 'rue the day when Gothic architecture was revived'. The solution, though, was not to abandon Gothic in favour of Classicism, nor simply to move on chronologically towards the Renaissance. Rather, Jackson sought to create a new style, freed from arbitrary preference and suitable for nineteenth-century England. The answer was what he called 'Judicious eclecticism'; a Gothic freed from antiquarianism and drawing on the insights of Renaissance art. With the architecture of Elizabethan and Jacobean England as a matrix, they would add until they had produced a Gothic moulded and changed 'till it suits the altered circumstances of modern life'; even to the extent that it 'may lose all those features by which we know it'.[77]

It was a radical critique and an inventive solution. But like those of his contemporaries, Jackson's attack on the Gothic Revival did not mean a rejection of all that previous writers had said. This was reform, not revolution, and Jackson himself claimed that much of what he was saying would already have occurred to 'thoughtful students of Architecture'.[78] In particular, his youthful reading of Ruskin was to be of continuing importance to his work.[79] Ruskin argued that the nineteenth century was peculiarly unfortunate in having no style of its own. All was chaos and confusion. 'The architecture of a nation', he wrote, 'is great only when it is as universal and as established as its language; and when provincial differences of style are nothing more than so many dialects.'[80] This would only be achieved by the adoption of a single, commonly-understood approach; one that involved greater craftsmanship, more concern with materials, and a better understanding of the purposes of architecture. Jackson echoed many of these concerns, and the language in which they were articulated. Like Ruskin, he argued that architecture without painting and sculpture was merely building.[81] Like Ruskin, he emphasized the requirement for greater craftsmanship and the urgent need to make the architect an artist again.[82] Like Ruskin, he stressed the importance of agreeing on a modern and representative architecture, a truly nineteenth-century style.[83]

In two key respects, however, Jackson rejected Ruskin and the previous generation. His adoption of a Renaissance style and an eclectic approach were shockingly new. Both were anathema to many. John Ruskin, indeed, had reserved his greatest hatred for precisely this sort of argument. The 'revival of a healthy school of architecture in England', he wrote, would begin with the casting out of everything 'connected with the Greek, Roman or Renaissance architecture, in principle or in form'. The argument was a moral one. These

---

[77] Ibid., 112–13, 4, 24, 26–7, 1–5, 53–67, 88–9, 193–5, 110.   [78] Ibid., iii.
[79] *Builder* 31 (1873), 598.
[80] John Ruskin, *Complete Works*, ed., E. J. Cook and A. Wedderburn (39 vols.; London, 1903–9), vol. 8, p. 252.   [81] Jackson, *Modern Gothic Architecture*, 130; Ruskin, *Works*, vol. 8, pp. 27–40.
[82] Jackson, *Modern Gothic Architecture*, 189; Ruskin, *Works*, vol. 10, p. 201.
[83] Jackson, *Modern Gothic Architecture*, 11–12; Ruskin, *Works*, vol. 8, p. 252.

styles were 'base, unnatural, unfruitful, unenjoyable, and impious'. Their adoption made 'plagiarists of [their] architects, slaves of [their] workmen, and sybarites of [their] inhabitants'.[84] In this, he spoke for a generation. Nor was eclecticism more widely welcomed. J.-B. Lassus called it the plague of art.[85] In 1872, just a year before *Modern Gothic Architecture* was published, J. P. Seddon had cried out against it too. 'Eclecticism! Eclecticism!' he wailed. 'What horrors have been perpetuated in thy euphonious name!'[86] Superficially, Ruskin was more amenable to the idea of mixing styles.[87] But just as Beresford Hope had argued, any 'progressive eclecticism' was expected by Ruskin to be exclusively Gothic. The call to 'eclect from everything that has been collected' did not include classical styles.[88] Jackson's attempt to combine Renaissance style and eclectic approach was thus strikingly novel. His reviewers could barely accept that these prescriptions were honestly meant.[89]

This was not, though, merely inter-generational conflict. There were very real differences between Jackson and his contemporaries too. Although their conclusions often appeared similar, Jackson differed greatly in his approach. Above all else, his critique was both more comprehensive and more strongly sustained than his rivals'. Stevenson's argument for the adoption of 'free classicism', for example, was ultimately dependent on a naïve determinism. Just as the Gothic was superseded by the Renaissance, so the Gothic Revival would now give way to a 'Re-renaissance'.[90] This was precisely the sort of argument by analogy that Jackson sought to avoid. Nor was Basil Champneys any more convincing. Indeed, he failed to convince even himself. By 1898 he was abandoning any defence of 'free classicism' and writing a 'Vindication of the Gothic', frightened that the resurgent Renaissance would sweep the older style away.[91] Champneys, after all, was never entirely lucid in his arguments, and he made 'no claim to any theory or system, nor any leading idea', but this retraction reflected a serious limitation in this thought.[92] As Jackson put it, 'the selection of a style for our modern use can hardly be a fair subject for mere arbitrary preference'. He wanted more. 'There surely must be some principle or rule to guide us in the matter', he wrote.[93] In *Modern Gothic Architecture* Jackson went well beyond his contemporaries in seeking to find it.

Paradoxically, in attempting to create this new style, Jackson argued for the abandonment of stylistic dogmatism. 'It is important at the present day, when the battle of the styles is raging . . . to remember [the] catholicity of art', he

[84] Ruskin, *Works* vol. 11, p. 227.
[85] Stefan Muthesius, *The High Victorian Movement in British Architecture* (London and Brighton, 1972), 161.   [86] Crook, *Dilemma of Style*, 161.
[87] Ruskin, *Works*, vol. 8, pp. 258–9.
[88] A. J. B. Beresford Hope, *The Common Sense of Art* (London, 1858), 13; *Ecclesiologist* 23 (1863), 234; J. Mordaunt Crook, *The Architect's Secret: Victorian critics and the image of gravity* (London, 2003), ch. 3.   [89] *Architect* 10 (1873), 156.
[90] *Architect* 11 (1874), 9–10; *Builder* 33 (1875), 180; *Architect* 13 (1875), 125.
[91] *Builder* 74 (1898), 158.   [92] Champneys, *Quiet Corner*, 7.
[93] Jackson, *Modern Gothic Architecture*, 5.

wrote. All styles had their qualities; all styles could be used.[94] In this respect, judicious eclecticism was simply a means to an end. And that end was 'a living and growing style'; the result of 'the recovery of that artistic temper by which men will be led to express themselves in their work with truth, force, and feeling, just as their forefathers once did'.[95] It was a complicated argument, but Jackson remained true to it throughout his life. Yet, as his career developed his vision broadened. This evolution of ideas, indeed, proved to be another great difference between himself and his contemporaries. For Champneys never produced a great work of synthesis, and as early as 1880 Stevenson concluded that 'the advocacy of my views has become useless, for the world has come round to them'.[96] Although Jackson was only to publish two further works of architectural theory, he nonetheless continued to refine his initial ideas. Whilst the philosophy developed, however, its founding assumptions never changed. It is for this reason that Crook suggests that Jackson's later works were 'a disappointment', merely repeating 'his earlier ideas at greater length and with much less force'.[97] In fact, whilst none of his subsequent writings had the sensational impact of his first, they continued to be acknowledged as important contributions to architectural debate.[98] Indeed, as Jackson continued to write, his ideas became more strongly focused and more strikingly original. He came to offer a real alternative to contemporary architecture.

What was needed, Jackson evidently recognized, was a far clearer definition of fitness for use: what was to be eclected? How was it to be selected? Who would make the choice? All good styles, Jackson had argued, 'obey the same broad catholic principles of truth, honesty and simplicity'.[99] He had not, however, made these principles plain. 'He starts from premises which many readers will not be ready to grant', wrote one critic, 'and which he takes but little pains to establish by proof.' The result was, for some, inspiring. Others found it 'diffuse and inconclusive'.[100] Some were still more blunt. Edmund Ferrey, for one, candidly admitted that 'I cannot follow him in the depths of philosophic argument which he at times indulges in.'[101] In his later books, *Reason in Architecture* (1906) and *Architecture* (1925), and in his letters and his articles, Jackson aimed to identify the ruling principle of fitness for use. The term 'judicious eclecticism' was gradually dropped, although its implications were retained. Rather, Jackson aimed to redefine the concept of 'Gothic architecture', making the values he perceived in Gothic art the criteria for judging fitness.

Ostensibly at least, this approach appeared to drive Jackson even further away from his high Victorian heritage. Rhetorically, he reinforced this idea, condemning Ruskin for his pernicious effect on architecture, and arguing for a

---

[94] Ibid., 7.   [95] Ibid., 21, 20.   [96] Stevenson, *House Architecture*, vol. i., p. 382.
[97] Crook, 'Cult of Eclecticism', 102.
[98] *Builder* 90 (1906), 141–2, 164–5, 193–4, 249–51, 271–3; *British Architect* 65 (1906), 431, 454–63.   [99] Jackson, *Modern Gothic Architecture*, 6.
[100] *Architect* 9 (1873), 294.   [101] *Architect* 10 (1873), 156–70.

wholly new approach.[102] Yet, the project to some extent at least remained very much the same. Ruskin, after all, had made a similar attempt to define the nature of Gothic.[103] Jackson, nonetheless, did develop. In particular he came to use the term Gothic much more freely than his predecessors. In *Modern Gothic Architecture*, he had acknowledged that a building might be 'Gothic in form, but not in spirit'.[104] Now, he expanded on that suggestion, and in true Aristotelian style he sought to separate the essence from the accident in Gothic architecture. Gothic was redefined as 'freedom of design, independence of precedence, conformity to conditions of climate, material, habit, convenience and the general requirements of England and Englishmen'.[105] Style, in that sense, was unimportant; spirit was everything.[106] So it was that Jackson would come to regard 'all buildings which conform to the conditions of English climate, material, and habit as Gothic'.[107]

This was, as Rayner Banham later recognized, a fundamentally functionalist credo.[108] 'Fitness' became the 'prime condition of excellence in Architecture'.[109] The architect's job was to select the most fitting feature: to 'bring his art into conformity with modern life and modern requirements' and to ensure 'the outward expression of good construction'.[110] Jackson was advocating a kind of architectural rationalism. And he went further still. The distinction, Graham Jackson argued, was not between Greek and Gothic, but between authority and reason.[111] Gothic freedom and response to circumstance were contrasted with the supposed slavery of both Vitruvian classicism and Puginian medievalism.[112] The future, Jackson believed, would be a battle between 'the BOND and the FREE'.[113] Gothic—at least in the sense that Jackson had redefined it—was freedom. Gothic was therefore the future. He claimed to have solved the dilemma of style. Jackson was going far beyond the majority of his contemporaries in this. He even concluded that true beauty grew out of functionalism. 'For this reason,' he claimed, 'there are few more satisfactory buildings in modern architecture than the bridges and viaducts and other utilitarian structures of railway engineers.'[114] Clearly, there was still much here from Ruskin, and still more from Viollet-le-Duc.[115] But with his catholic approach and eclectic ambitions, Jackson the Rational Goth went well beyond both. He had developed his own voice and his own unique approach. It was a highly successful synthesis.

[102] T. G. Jackson, *Architecture* (London, 1925), 330.   [103] Ruskin, *Works*, vol. 10, ch. 6.
[104] Jackson, *Modern Gothic Architecture*, 38.   [105] *Times*, 22 Oct. 1901, 10.
[106] *Times*, 21 Feb. 1914, 9; T. G. Jackson, *Gothic Architecture* (2 vols.; Cambridge, 1915), vol. ii, p. 157; *Guardian* 1902, 155.   [107] *Architectural Review* 1 (1896–7), 140.
[108] Banham, *Theory and Design in the First Machine Age*, 29–30, 91.
[109] Jackson, *Reason in Architecture* (London, 1906), 73.   [110] Ibid., 109, 185.
[111] T. G. Jackson, *The Renaissance of Roman Architecture* (3 vols.; Cambridge, 1921–3), vol. i, pp. 188–9; vol. ii., p. 219.   [112] Jackson, *Reason in Architecture*, 3, 14; 247–69.
[113] Jackson, *Architecture*, 330.   [114] Jackson, *Reason in Architecture*, 73.
[115] M. F. Hearn, *The Architectural Theory of Viollet-le-Duc* (Cambridge, Mass., 1990), 7–16.

Contemporaries recognized the importance of this work without necessarily accepting its implications, however.[116] Reginald Blomfield praised Jackson's writing, whilst bemoaning the fact that he had never escaped 'the disastrous legacy of Ruskin'.[117] This was certainly true: after all, Jackson's redefinition of Gothic still depended on an archetypally Ruskinian set of moral categories. But Blomfield's comment would soon sound generous. Things could only get worse. Geoffrey Scott's *Architecture of Humanism* (1914) reflected a growing engagement with precisely the classical canon that Jackson had hoped to escape. More importantly still, Scott's scorn was directed at exactly those arguments used by the post-Gothic generation. Ruskin was certainly guilty of the 'Ethical Fallacy', in which aesthetic and moral concerns were conflated. But Champneys, with his 'prejudice against Order and Proportion' was similarly committing the 'Romantic Fallacy', whilst Stevenson's determinism could be equated with the 'Biological Fallacy', in which an evolutionary metaphor was inappropriately adopted as an explanation of architectural development.[118] Like his colleagues, Jackson was convicted of all these sins, the besetting sins of his generation. When, in 1921, *The Architect* described him as a 'latter-day Ruskin', it was not meant as a compliment.[119] By the end of his life, indeed, Jackson himself acknowledged that there were problems with his approach. He remained optimistic, but he was uncertain about the future. A new style, it was clear, would arise. But its form and its inspiration still seemed harder to define. 'Who can foresee what, if anything, will come of it?' he asked.[120] Despite all his work, despite all his writing, the new style seemed a world away.

Nonetheless, Jackson remained committed to his project, and optimistic about its eventual success. In this respect he differed greatly from those, like Stevenson and Champneys, who stopped writing, and those who wrote only to share their profound sense of gloom: figures like George Aitchison, the Professor of Architecture at the Royal Academy, for example. Jackson and Aitchison shared a similar approach. They often sounded similar.[121] But the contrast between their conclusions was stark.[122] Whilst Jackson continued to experiment, explore, and enthuse well into the 1920s, Aitchison had, by the 1890s, abandoned all hope. Writing in 1902, he posed the rhetorical question of whether the British possessed those capacities which would allow the development of a new and better architecture; answering himself in the bleakest of

---

[116] Some, indeed, were still more critical: *Builder* 91 (1906), 250.

[117] Reginald Blomfield, *Memoirs of an Architect* (London, 1932), 115.

[118] Geoffrey Scott, *The Architecture of Humanism* (London, 1914).

[119] *Architect* 106 (1921), 231.

[120] T. G. Jackson, *Renaissance of Roman Architecture*, (3 vols.; Cambridge, 1921–3), vol. iii, p. 210.

[121] 'Architects are the poets of construction' (Aitchison, *Builder* 78 [1900], 129); 'Architecture is the poetry of construction' (Jackson, *Architecture*, xvi).

[122] Crook, *Architect's Secret*, ch. 1; *Builder* 64 (1893), 65; *Builder* 74 (1898), 252; *Builder* 78 (1900), 130.

terms: 'I am not a prophet', wrote Aitchison, 'but there are no signs of such capacity now existing.'[123] By contrast, although Jackson was no clearer about the future, he was at least happier with it. Change would come, he claimed. It always had done so before; given time it would do so again. This, indeed, was the important point. Unlike most of his fellow writers, Jackson drew comfort from history.

This approach can be found throughout his work. Indeed, *Reason in Architecture* was praised at the time as an 'admirable example of the interpretation of architecture on the historical method'.[124] In part, this reflected a simple personal preference. Jackson loved history. He was the president of his local historical society, a fellow of the Society of Antiquaries, and a man who clearly understood the world in historical terms.[125] More importantly for his career as a writer, this engagement with history placed him clearly within a tradition of architectural writing, the tradition, of course, which had established the Gothic Revival. Both scholarly and polemical publications had, after all, created the movement. Jackson was to use the same tools to challenge the neo-medieval consensus. Moreover, given the problems raised by Jackson's theoretical writing, it was unsurprising that he should increasingly rely on a historical approach. Thus, as the problems grew greater, and his position became more exposed, he turned with ever-greater enthusiasm towards the study of the past.

Jackson's first major work of historical writing was produced in much brighter circumstances, however. This book established him as a gifted and popular historian, and he remained committed to the approach which he had adopted in it. Little wonder: *Dalmatia, the Quarnero and Istria* was perhaps Jackson's most successful book. Published in 1887, it was very widely reviewed and very well received.[126] It remains a standard work on the subject.[127] For although there were a number of guidebooks and general descriptions of the area,[128] as late as 1881 E. A. Freeman complained that 'the best guide to those

---

[123] *RIBA Journal*, 3rd Series 9 (1902), 199.   [124] Blomfield, *The Mistress Art*, 23.

[125] See, for example, his attack on post-war tax increases, and the analogy with the French forced loans of 1795: *Times*, 24 Nov. 1922, 13.

[126] *Academy* 32 (1887), 290–2; *American Architect* 22 (1887), 83–4; *Architect* 37 (1887), 370–1; *British Architect* 27 (1887), 169–70; *Building News* 53 (1887), 123–6; *Dublin Review* 37 (1888), 234–9; *Edinburgh Review* 167 (1888), 81–108; *English Historical Review* 3 (1888), 367–73; *Scottish Geographical Magazine* 3 (1887), 606–7; *Spectator* 60 (1887), 1390–1.

[127] Frank Walker, 'Jackson's Journey', *Building Design* 828 (1987), 28–9. For its influence see Larry Woolf, *Venice and the Slavs: the discovery of Dalmatia in the age of the Enlightenment* (Stanford, Calif., 2001), 346–7.

[128] The RIBA holds Jackson's annotated copy of Emilio Schatzmayer, *La Dalmazia* (Trieste, 1877) [BAL JaT/1/1/1]. See also: A. A. Paton, *Highlands and Islands of the Adriatic* (2 vols.; London, 1844); 'R.H.R', *Rambles in Istria, Dalmatia, and Montenegro* (London, 1875); Viscountess Strangford, *The Eastern Shores of the Adriatic* (London, 1864) and, most importantly, J. Gardner Wilkinson, *Dalmatia and Montenegro* (2 vols.; London, 1848). By 1904 Edith Durham remarked that the road from Kotor to Cetigne 'has been so often written of that it is idle to describe it again' (*London Review of Books*, 17 Feb. 2000, 41).

parts is still the account written by the Emperor Constantine Porphyrogenitus more than nine hundred years ago'.[129] Jackson's work transformed the scholarly treatment of the region, yet, as in his more polemical work, he was writing within a recognizable tradition.[130] In particular, he approached the subject as a follower of both Ruskin and Viollet-le-Duc. From the former, Jackson took a love of Venice and its architecture.[131] The contrast between Gardner Wilkinson's pre-Ruskinian horror at the 'Venetian subjugation' of Dalmatia[132] and Jackson's

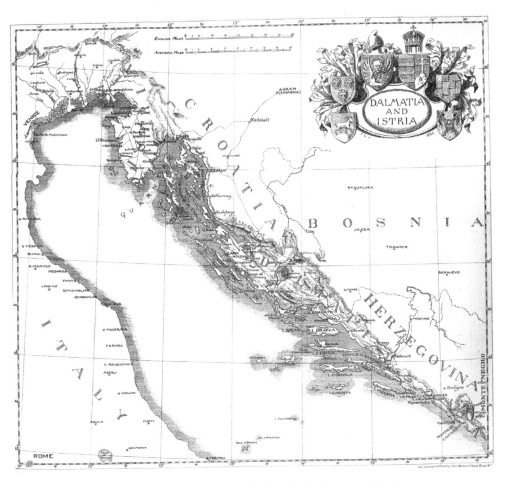

13. Dalmatia. Drawn by Jackson for *Dalmatia, the Quarnero and Istria*.

[129] Edward A. Freeman, *Sketches from the Subject and Neighbour Lands of Venice* (London, 1881), ix.
[130] *Portfolio* 1888, 24.
[131] Jeanne Clegg, *Ruskin and Venice* (London, 1981); Crook, 'Ruskinian Gothic'.
[132] Gardner Wilkinson, *Dalmatia*, vol. i, p. 273.

celebration of Venice's 'greatness' could not be more stark.[133] Viollet-le-Duc offered something rather different. For him, the motive force of any modern architecture was lay and city-based.[134] Graham Jackson found proof of this in Dalmatian art, which was, he argued, 'entirely urban'. Condemning the 'semi-barbarism' of the rural Slavs, he ignored their culture almost entirely.[135] The book's perspective was personal—and the result both original and influential.

It is in his approach to the city of Zadar, which Jackson knew as Zara, that his intellectual preoccupations are most clearly shown. Zadar was the capital of Dalmatia, but it was far from typical of the province as a whole. It was the last Italian-speaking city in the region, a 'small Venice' which was 'never really Dalmatian, or rather Sclavic'.[136] Jackson, unsurprisingly, loved it and devoted two chapters to describing its treasures.[137] More than this, he was commissioned to build within the city. Threatened by the approaching tide of panslavism, the civic authorities experienced a belated burst of *campanilismo*, resolving to complete their half-finished cathedral tower. Admittedly, Jackson's hands were not free to design quite what he wanted. Initially he began with an exuberant essay in Italianate architecture. Then, under the influence of the Austrian government, he was gradually persuaded to adopt a more archaeological approach. But throughout, Jackson's plans for the building revealed his sympathy for the Venetian variants of Dalmatian design. And the tower itself became a powerful symbol of the loyalty to Italy which would keep Zadar within the Italian orbit until 1945.[138]

This obvious bias in favour of Venetian architecture and belief in the superiority of urban life was less damaging to Jackson's scholarship than might be expected. For he combined these strongly stated views with a sophisticated methodology—arguably more sophisticated than that of his rivals. G. E. Street in his books was forced to admit that he had 'not had time or opportunity for examining the documentary history of the buildings' he described.[139] W. R. Lethaby apologized that his 'knowledge of books is only that of a general reader', and explained that he had to rely upon 'inferior editions, translations, and chance extracts' in his works.[140] Jackson, by contrast, used a wide variety of historical evidence.[141] In addition to his acknowledged archaeological skills, he was an intelligent textual critic who used his knowledge of Latin, Greek, Italian, French, and some German to good effect. He searched out new texts and

---

[133] Jackson, *Dalmatia* (3 vols.; Oxford, 1887), vol. iii, p. 439.
[134] E. Viollet-le-Duc, *Entretiens sur l'Architecture* (2 vols.; Paris, 1863–72), vol. i, pp. 239–86.
[135] Jackson, *Dalmatia*, vol. i, pp. 204, 231.
[136] Paton, *Adriatic*, vol. ii, p. 48; Strangford, *Adriatic*, 268.
[137] Jackson, *Dalmatia*, vol. i, chs. 3–4.
[138] Marija Stagličić, 'Zvonik katedrale u Zadru', *Peristil* 25 (1982), 149–58 and "Još o zvoniku zadarske katedrale', *Peristil* 30 (1987), 143–6. See also Sonia Bićanić, 'T. G. Jackson's *Recollections* and his campanile at Zadar', *Slavonica* 22/1 (1994–5), 29–38.
[139] Street, *Brick and Marble in the Middle Ages*, viii.
[140] Lethaby, *Architecture, Mysticism and Myth*, vi.
[141] *English Historical Review* 3 (1888), 368–73.

14. The Hall of Wadham College, Oxford, drawn by Jackson for his *Wadham College, Oxford*.

15. The Chapel of Wadham College, from Jackson's *Wadham College, Oxford*.

retranslated old ones.[142] This 'original research' marked Jackson out as a uniquely diligent worker and capable writer.[143] More than this, it showed that he was a scholar: an original historian and a genuine intellectual. 'Few have possessed the literary ability, artistic faculty, and professional knowledge of such sort that they could do so well', observed one critic.[144] 'The [Oxford] University Press has never produced a work of equal interest to architects', claimed another.[145]

Graham Jackson's use of both antiquarian and archaeological evidence continued in his next two books. Both *Wadham College, Oxford* (1893) and *The Church of St Mary the Virgin, Oxford* (1897) remain the standard works on their subjects.[146] They were, as the titles suggest, the product of filial loyalty: *St Mary*

---

[142] *Academy* 32 (1887), 291; Jackson, *Dalmatia*, vol. ii, pp. 115, 154; vol. iii, p. 40. See also the marginal notes in BAL JaT / 1 / 1 / 1.   [143] *American Architect* 2 (1887), 83.

[144] *British Architect* 28 (1887), 170.   [145] *Architect* 37 (1887), 371.

[146] John Summerson, *Architecture in Britain, 1530–1830* (8th ed.; New Haven and London, 1991), 544; C. S. L. Davies and Jane Garnett, *Wadham College* (Oxford, 1994), 144; Stefanie Knöll, 'St Mary the Virgin Church, Oxford' (Oxford Brookes, MA 1997), 13.

the Virgin was even dedicated *Almae Matri Oxoniae*. They were also convincing proof of the fact that Jackson was committed to a more than usually exacting standard of scholarship. For the history of Wadham, he transcribed the building account books in their entirety, allowing him to offer the first definite identification of the college's architect.[147] Using only the evidence of the masonry itself, he was able to date the construction of St Mary's more accurately than any previous writer.[148] As the proof copy of the book shows, up to the last moment Jackson was improving his text in the light of new archival discoveries.[149] The result was typically authoritative. As an architectural historian, declared the *Spectator*, 'he has no rival'.[150] But, of course, as other reviewers acknowledged, in one respect at least Jackson was hardly alone. The comparisons with Robert Willis's and John Willis Clark's monumental *Architectural History of the University of Cambridge* (1886) were all too obvious.[151] Willis and Clark had used precisely the same approach to their studies as Jackson, marshalling documentary and artifactual evidence to explain both the buildings and the social history of a great academic institution.[152] Theirs was a far greater task, however. In studying the architecture of the whole university they produced 'one of the most remarkable scholarly publications of the nineteenth century,' as David Watkin puts it.[153] Impressive though *Wadham* and *St. Mary the Virgin* were, they could hardly compare to this.

Ignoring the appeals that he should 'do for his university what Messrs. Willis and Clark have done for Cambridge', Jackson moved to a much wider canvas.[154] 'With a zeal which the years are powerless to quell, and a judgment they have ripened', as one admirer put it, between 1913 and 1923 he attempted to account for the development of European architecture from the fall of Rome to the beginning of the nineteenth century.[155] Here was ambition indeed. Ultimately, Jackson published seven volumes: two on *Byzantine and Romanesque Architecture* (1913); two on *Gothic Architecture in France, England and Italy* (1915); and three on *The Renaissance of Roman Architecture* (1921–3) in the same three countries. They were an extremely significant series, suitable for both architect and amateur, and from the first they were 'assured of a permanent place in . . . libraries'.[156] They were not superseded, indeed, until the 1950s;[157] and as late as

[147] T. G. Jackson, *Wadham College, Oxford* (Oxford, 1893), 2.

[148] T. G. Jackson, *The Church of St. Mary the Virgin, Oxford* (Oxford, 1897), 78–82.

[149] Bod., Dep. D. 49, 'St Mary the Virgin', 1, 5–6, 12, 107.

[150] *Spectator* 79 (1897), 798; *Times*, 7 April 1897, 3.

[151] *English Historical Review* 8 (1893), 778; 13 (1898), 607.

[152] A. C. Buchanon, 'Robert Willis and the Rise of Architectural History' (London, Ph.D., 1994), 297–344.

[153] David Watkin, 'Willis and Clark, 1886–1986', *Cambridge Review* 107 (1986), 68–9, 68.

[154] *Athenaeum* 781 (1893), 770.   [155] *Architectural Review* 54 (1923), 110.

[156] *Bookman* 44 (1913), 51. This included libraries overseas, as the catalogue of the *Bibliothèque Nationale* shows. See also *Architect* 95 (1916), 47.

[157] Marcus Whiffen, *Journal of the Society of Architectural Historians* 13/4 (1954), 31. Paul Frankl, *Gothic Architecture* (London, 1962) included the Gothic volumes in his bibliography.

16. Chancel of St Mary the Virgin Church, Oxford, drawn by Jackson for his *Church of St Mary the Virgin, Oxford*.

17. Old Congregation House at St Mary's, playing home to the statues from the Church's tower.

1990, Sir John Summerson was compelled to acknowledge an 'unconscious debt' to Jackson's work.[158] As a whole, the series illustrates the way in which Graham Jackson's architectural vision broadened whilst remaining true to the scholarly methods and theoretical approach that influenced his early work.

In this project, Jackson had few English rivals—or indeed influences. Ruskin remained an important figure for him, as contemporaries acknowledged.[159] The serious-minded and scholarly methods of Robert Willis were similarly seminal.[160] But neither had attempted a great conspectus of European architecture. Many of Ruskin's writings were purely impressionistic, whilst Willis had concentrated his efforts on Cambridge and Italy alone.[161] Of those that did write general surveys, only two bear any real comparison. Banister Fletcher's great work, *The History of Architecture* (1896) encapsulated nineteenth-century architectural thought. He linked the development of art directly to material conditions, and categorized styles on a comparative scale. Every section approached each period systematically, starting with influences on architecture—geographical, geological, social, and so on. It then proceeded to a comparative study of plans, walls, openings, and other features. *The History* was hugely successful, but it offered little challenge to Jackson. More than anything, its title gave it away. Here was a textbook designed for 'the Student, Craftsman and Amateur', rather than the gentleman or the scholar. Jackson was writing for a very different audience. His intended readers were—on the whole—highly educated and intellectually assured; exactly the sort of people already reading James Fergusson's work, in fact. First published in 1855, but frequently re-edited, Fergusson's *Handbook* (later *History*) *of Architecture* was a key text for half a century. But, as Jackson acknowledged, 'Even Fergusson's books, excellent as they are,—capital as far as they go,—are more useful to the amateur than to the student'.[162] Modern scholarship dated them quickly.[163] In addition, their approach was taken almost completely from their French equivalents. It was to the wellspring, then, that Jackson went. He turned, like Fergusson and many others, to France.

Jackson's two chief influences, indeed, came from across the channel. The first was Viollet-le-Duc.[164] However 'fantastic' and 'prejudiced' he might be, Jackson thought him always worth reading—and the effect is quite clear.[165] Just as he had been in Dalmatia, Jackson was clearly attracted by Viollet's historical model, and he also adopted the Frenchman's functionalist analysis as well.[166]

[158] Summerson, *Architecture in Britain*, 541. Interestingly, he also pays tribute to Fergusson and Blomfield.   [159] *Architectural Review* 54 (1923), 110.

[160] As they were for Ruskin: see *Works*, vol. 8, pp. 87, 95.

[161] Robert Willis, *Remarks on the Architecture of the Middle Ages, Especially of Italy* (Cambridge, 1835).   [162] *Builder* 61 (1891), 462.

[163] Reginald Blomfield, *A History of Renaissance Architecture in England, 1500–1800* (2 vols.; London, 1897), vol. 2, p. 270.   [164] *Architectural Record* 40 (1916), 284.

[165] *Builder* 61 (1891), 460–3.

[166] *Architectural Record* 40 (1916), 283–4; T. G. Jackson, *Byzantine and Romanesque Architecture* (2 vols.; Cambridge, 1913), vol. i, p. 205.

Naturally, he did not share Viollet-le-Duc's commitment to the thirteenth century, but his explanation for the development of Gothic architecture came straight out of the *Entretiens*. Gothic, he argued, was the product of free communes and lay architects; it expressed the 'restless temper of the modern world'.[167] Likewise, in its relentless emphasis on the constructional logic of their design, Jackson's article on the development of French cathedral portals could have been an entry in the *Dictionnaire Raisonné*.[168] But Viollet-le-Duc went too far for Jackson. Under the influence of de Gobineau's ethnography, he came to espouse a crudely racist explanation for architectural development,[169] arguing that only peoples of Aryan blood could hope to produce an original architecture.[170] Although Jackson was committed to the idea that each style was the product of national difference, he was clearly unconvinced by the abstraction of Viollet's theory.[171] In this respect, too, he parted company with James Fergusson, who adopted these claims in their entirety and indeed used them as a framework for his own architectural histories.[172]

The link with France did not end there, though. Jackson's second and arguably most important influence was also French. Despite his relative anonymity now, Auguste Choisy was a highly influential figure for Jackson's generation.[173] Although untranslated, his volumes were seriously suggested as a set text for training architects, and were regarded 'as an admirable model for the scientific treatment of architectural history'.[174] Choisy shared a debt to Viollet-le-Duc, but offered a more satisfying explanation for historical change. As a model for architectural development he offered a physiological analogy: architecture as an organism, a microcosm of the evolutionary process. The realities of climate, resources, way of life, and technological skill drove the forms and styles of building throughout history. True architecture, he asserted, grew organically out of its circumstances. This had been the case until the nineteenth century, but now a new age needed a new art. Only by following the example of the past and acknowledging the physiological analogy could this hope to happen.[175] Choisy had broadened the remit of architectural history well beyond its previous limits. His *Histoire* was also more sympathetic to the late Gothic and early Renaissance than either Ruskin or Viollet, or the relevant volumes by Fergusson. It was

---

[167] Jackson, *Gothic Architecture*, vol. i, pp. 53–9.   [168] *Country Life* 39 (1916), 736–8.

[169] Viollet-le-Duc, *Entretiens*, vol. i, p. 343. Compare M. A. de Gobineau, *Essai sur l'inégalité des races humaines* (4 vols.; Paris, 1853–5), vol. i, pp. 350–3 with Viollet-le-Duc, *The Habitations of Man in All Ages* (Trans. Benjamin Bucknall; London, 1876).

[170] Mark Crinson, *Empire Building* (London and New York, 1996), 87–9 and Jacques Gambler, 'In Search of the Primitive', *Architectural Design Profile* 27 (1980), 80–3.

[171] Jackson, *Modern Gothic Architecture*, 58.

[172] Compare James Fergusson, *A History of Architecture* (2nd ed.; 4 vols: London, 1873–5), vol. i, pp. 56–69 with Viollet-le-Duc, *Habitations*, 27, 136–7, 384–9.

[173] Crook, *Architect's Secret*, 90; Blomfield, *The Mistress Art*, 162, 171–4. See also Watkin, *The Rise of Architectural History*, 28.

[174] RIBA Archive, Special Committee Minutes 4 (1899–1908), 107 (1904).

[175] Auguste Choisy, *Histoire de l'Architecture* (2 vols.; Paris, 1899), vol. i, p. 1, vol. ii, p. 762.

Choisy's theory of evolution from style to style, with each reflecting its time and
place, that Jackson echoed in his own later works of history. Both men explained
architecture as an attempt to reconcile constructional necessity with social circumstances. They were not the first to do this, but were perhaps the most successful. As his contemporaries acknowledged, Jackson offered 'not only a new
book, but . . . a new view' of architecture.[176]

Originality was not enough, of course. Jackson's general histories were based
on precisely the same all-consuming effort that had made *Dalmatia*, *Wadham*,
and *St. Mary the Virgin* such a success. They were, as one reviewer noted, 'the
work of a lifetime'.[177] Jackson was unwilling to write about any building that he
had not visited, examined, and sketched;[178] 'information derived at second-
hand', he wrote, 'is only of second-rate importance'.[179] The measured drawings
which resulted from his travels were so accurate that they were borrowed by
other writers for use in their own books.[180] In search of material he travelled all
over Europe, the First World War alone preventing him from exploiting
German examples.[181] Seeking Byzantine building, he even made a trip to Turkey
in 1910,[182] and soon found himself commissioned by the government to report
on the stability of Hagia Sophia.[183] Nor did he abandon his commitment to
archival research and documentary evidence. In the first fifty pages of a typical
volume he quotes from Pliny and Trajan, Horace and Cicero, Theophanes,
Procopius, Tertullian, Justinian, and Paul the Silentiary.[184] Where he lacked
expertise, he relied upon others, with Charles Oman, for one, being thanked for
providing an index of prices for Renaissance France.[185] He produced, as one
writer ornately observed, 'a harvest so goodly that only a churl could spoil his
own enjoyment thereof by withholding his thanks for the feast'.[186] Jackson had
made a monumental contribution to architectural history.[187] Just as Choisy
succeeded Viollet-le-Duc, so Jackson had superseded Fergusson.

What, though, was his message? What was his distinctive contribution to scholarship? In his books Jackson sought to illustrate two main themes: 'the continuity
of architectural history',[188] and the way in which 'the history of the art reflected
that of civilization'.[189] Architecture, he argued, could be explained 'by the social

[176] *Architectural Review* 39 (1916), 36.   [177] *Architectural Record* 40 (1916), 284.
[178] With the exception of T. G. Jackson, 'The Churches of Serbia', *Proceedings of the Society of
Antiquaries of London* 30 (1917–18), 10–17 and Jackson, 'Serbian Church Architecture', in Michael
J. Pupin, ed., *South Slav Monuments I* (London, 1918).
[179] Jackson, *Byzantine and Romanesque*, vol. i, p. v.
[180] Francis Bond, *Gothic Architecture in England* (London, 1906), v.
[181] Jackson, *Gothic Architecture*, vol. i, p. vi.   [182] Jackson, *Life and Travels*, 245–6.
[183] BAL, Ja/1/2/1, Report on Sancta Sophia (1910).
[184] Jackson, *Byzantine and Romanesque*, vol. i, pp. 4–5, 10, 46.
[185] Jackson, *Renaissance of Roman Architecture*, vol. iii, p. viii.
[186] *Building News* 104 (1913), 149.
[187] *English Historical Review* 28 (1913), 552; ibid., 31 (1916), 478.
[188] Jackson, *Byzantine and Romanesque*, vol. i, pp. ix–xx.
[189] Jackson, *Gothic Architecture*, vol. ii, p. 305.

history of the age'.[190] From the fall of the Roman Empire to the rise of the Renaissance, 'one style gave birth to another',[191] under the influence of real national difference.[192] Thus the Romanesque represented 'the vigorous life of the provinces of the old western Empire', whilst Byzantine architecture 'sank into stagnation' under a 'semi-oriental despotism'. Later, control 'passed from the cloister to the lay guilds of workmen' and, 'working now under free conditions', the Gothic was created.[193] This developed on national lines: the English, with their 'love of compromise . . . [and] natural suspicion of theory' rejecting the 'triumphant display of constructive science' that characterized the French approach.[194] This vernacular architecture was retained until the Renaissance, indeed until the rediscovery of Vitruvius. That was 'a Revolution in Art with precedent'.[195] Architecture was never to recover. Certainly it was never to be the same again.

The influences of Ruskin, Viollet-le-Duc, and Auguste. Choisy on this are all too obvious. As David Watkin has observed, this approach was also similar to Reginald Blomfield's.[196] Like Jackson, the younger Blomfield argued that architecture was a product of 'continuous growth'[197] which expressed the 'instinct of the nation and the race'.[198] Yet his conclusions were somewhat different.[199] Whilst Jackson had regarded the revival of Roman forms as 'the end of the old native traditional liberty',[200] Blomfield praised the neo-classicists for responding to the needs of modern life.[201] These differing analyses begged a question. Jackson described the early Renaissance as the last truly vernacular style, and used it as his model.[202] Blomfield praised the Baroque 'Grand Manner' and advocated its adoption.[203] To some extent, this reflected nothing more than a difference in age and the changing whims of fashion. Jackson and his generation had chosen the early English Renaissance. Blomfield and his contemporaries favoured the 'High Game' of the late Renaissance.[204] But it also suggests a more important problem—and one that both Blomfield and Jackson had to address. To what extent should history influence theory? Should the example of the past determine present practice?

Following Fergusson, T. G. Jackson argued that there was an insuperable difference between archaeology and architecture, past practice and present

[190] Jackson, *Renaissance of Roman Architecture*, vol. iii., p. vi.
[191] Jackson, *Byzantine and Romanesque*, vol. i, p. xx.
[192] Jackson, *Gothic Architecture*, vol. i, p. 216.
[193] Jackson, *Byzantine and Romanesque*, vol. i, p. 162; vol. ii, p. 172.
[194] Jackson, *Gothic Architecture*, vol. i, p. 250.
[195] Jackson, *Renaissance of Roman Architecture*, vol. i, pp. 24, 147; vol. ii, pp. 211, 213.
[196] Watkin, *Architectural History*, 96–102.
[197] Blomfield, *French Architecture*, vol. i, p. vii.
[198] Blomfield, *Architecture in England*, 66.
[199] Jackson, *Renaissance of Roman Architecture*, vol. ii., pp. v–vi; *Architectural Record* 40 (1916), 282.
[200] Jackson, *Renaissance of Roman Architecture*, vol. ii, p. 213.
[201] Blomfield, *Architecture in England*, 396.
[202] Jackson, *Renaissance of Roman Architecture*, vol. i, p. 147.
[203] Blomfield, *The Mistress Art*.   [204] Crook, *Dilemma of Style*, 220–1.

life.[205] History might act as an inspiration, but mere copyism must be avoided.[206] A slavish imitation of the past had been the great mistake of both classicists and neo-goths.[207] A new style would only emerge in an atmosphere of freedom, with artists escaping the 'shackles' and 'fetters' of antiquarian architecture,[208] and working 'with freedom of design, independence of precedence, conformity to conditions of climate, material, habit, convenience, and the general requirements of England and Englishmen. These', he wrote, 'are the motives with which our forefathers worked and by which they evolved the Gothic art of the past. It is only by working in the same spirit as they, not by copying the mere letter of what they did, that we may hope to rival them in the future.'[209] For Jackson, then, history was important, but as an inspiration, not as a pattern for future development.[210] This was a position which he adopted relatively early on in his career as a writer. In 1887, William Emerson had seen in Jackson's study of Dalmatian art 'the starting point of our future architecture in this country . . . a much better *point de départ* than the mixture of Gothic and Classic to which we are becoming accustomed'. Far from being flattered, though, Jackson utterly repudiated any such suggestion. 'With regard to the use which may be made of the study of Dalmatian architecture', he replied, 'I am sure that there is nothing which we can directly copy, nor do I think in any style of art that this is the proper thing to do.' Rather, his Dalmatian developments were simply an encouragement, which 'ought to give us some hope with regard to the art of our own time'.[211] In the book itself, he was willing to go a little further, and he rejoiced in the 'happy mixture of Gothic and Classic forms which is so suggestive to us moderns who must of necessity be eclectic'.[212] Nonetheless, in no sense was this an acceptance of historical imitation. Indeed, it was precisely the reverse.

In Jackson's later works of history this argument was subtly expanded upon. The model of historical development which he had evolved led him to adopt a variant of the argument by analogy that others had made in the 1870s. In this, however, he was more careful than his colleagues. Unlike Stevenson there was no naïve sense that history could repeat itself, nor that one style was fated to follow another. Unlike Emmett, he did not seize upon a single period as the basis for all future development. Unlike Champneys, he held his nerve. But the cyclical pattern of growth and decay that Jackson had perceived in history had an obvious application to current questions. He came to see the late nineteenth and early twentieth century as a transition period, one of many throughout history. The lesson of the past was that 'revival after depression always began by the

---

[205] Fergusson, *History of Architecture* (2nd ed.), vol. i, p. xv; Jackson, *Reason in Architecture*, viii.
[206] *Guardian* 1902, 155.   [207] Jackson, *Life and Travels*, 102–3.
[208] Jackson, *Reason in Architecture*, 12–14.   [209] *Times*, 10 Oct. 1901, 10.
[210] *Builder* 61 (1891), 461; see also Jackson, *Reason in Architecture*, 12–14.
[211] RIBA, *Proceedings* 3 (1887), 361–2, 367.   [212] Jackson, *Dalmatia*, vol. ii, p. 275.

attempt to revive an older art, with the result that when art did revive it was always something new'.[213] This had already happened, and now architects must prepare themselves for this new style. It would evolve of its own accord; it had done many times before. 'The bringing in of a new style is no concern of ours', he wrote. 'If it comes it will come of itself, as it always has done, and we shall awake to the fact that it has come without observation.'[214] History, then, gave him hope for the future.[215] A belief in the possibility of progress, based on a theory of organic evolution, sustained him despite his doubts. 'No conscious seeking for novelty will help us', Jackson argued. 'It is from the demands of utility that the best suggestions for advance in architecture have come in the past, and to them we must look in the future.'[216] Something was bound to turn up, he seemed to say, it always had done before. The demands of modern life; the needs of modern people; the spirit of the modern world: all these would, if given the chance, generate an authentic modern architecture.

It was here, of course, that history and theory, scholarship and polemic, were united. As Jackson himself saw it, the study of history simply confirmed his assertion that 'we must be satisfied with recording our eclectic age in eclectic buildings of our own'.[217] In that sense, indeed, the division between his historical and his more obviously controversial works is an artificial one. In fact, all his books, be they serious history or entertaining travel writing, reflected their opinionated author's strong beliefs. Jackson was never happier than when he was condemning 'classic dogma',[218] exposing 'Vitruvian hypocrisy',[219] or damning the intolerance of Inigo Jones.[220] Equally Graham Jackson's strong sense of historical development led him to articulate a very clear set of ideas about modern architecture. This was more than mere prejudice. History, he believed, taught that only an architecture which grew unselfconsciously out of the real demands of a society and a true understanding of its building materials, would last or be valid. The organic evolution he had learnt from Choisy gave hope for the future after all.

This, then, was the conclusion that Jackson came to—and it was a popular and persuasive conclusion too. His writings had made him one of the most public experts on art in England. His views on architecture and on history were known throughout the world.[221] When he attacked professional art critics, the *Times Literary Supplement* felt compelled to respond with a front-page defence.[222] Over fifty years, he had carved out a place for himself as an important commentator on art and architecture. In offering a scholarly approach both to art history and architectural theory, he had superseded his elders, outlasted his

[213] Jackson, *Byzantine and Romanesque*, vol. i, p. xx.   [214] *Guardian* 1902, 155.
[215] *Times*, 7 Feb. 1905, 5.   [216] Jackson, *Renaissance of Roman Architecture*, vol. iii, p. 210.
[217] *Times*, 20 Jan. 1885, 10.   [218] Jackson, *Architecture*, 295.
[219] Jackson, *Umbria*, 33.   [220] Jackson, *Renaissance of Roman Architecture*, vol. ii, p. 156.
[221] *Times*, 20 Aug. 1887, 4; 10 April 1889, 16; 13 March 1896, 8; 28 Dec. 1904, 5; 30 Jan. 1905, 10; 7 Feb. 1905, 5; 11 Aug. 1911, 3; 30 June 1913, 8; 7 Sep. 1917, 5; 17 Feb. 1919, 3; 11 July 1922, 15.
[222] *Times Literary Supplement*, 14 June 1917, 277.

contemporaries, and influenced many younger writers. Yet in many respects his conclusion was paradoxical. A new style, he wrote, 'must flow from us unconsciously . . . for art to be self-conscious is fatal'.[223] Yet how could an architect learn to be unselfconscious? Jackson's answer was to abandon theory and to transform existing practice. This solution would not be found in thinking or writing, he declared, but in making and doing. In the final analysis, Jackson came to believe that a solution would be found through a new way of working. That new way, he claimed, was the arts and crafts movement, a development which embodied all his hopes for an architecture truly born of its time and of its place.

---

[223] Jackson, *Renaissance of Roman Architecture*, vol. iii, p. 216.

2

'The Unity of Art'[1]
Jackson and the Arts and Crafts

T. G. Jackson's commitment to craftsmanship was more than mere theory. It was demonstrated in every work he undertook. As C. R. Ashbee observed, he became the first architect in large professional practice to commit himself wholeheartedly to the work of the arts and crafts movement.[2] His hopes of transcending style by transforming architectural activity, of 'combining the three arts' and thereby 'restoring our dead architecture to life', drove his career.[3] Nor was this expressed in Jackson's buildings alone. Rather, whilst seeking a more profound reform of contemporary design, he became involved in art education, in the campaign against professional registration, and in a range of organizations committed to improving art and society. It was in this role, indeed, that Jackson became one of the two or three most important leaders of the architectural profession in the late nineteenth century.[4] But this also brought controversy and dispute. Negotiating his place within this public space was to prove all too problematic. The arts and crafts movement was by no means a homogenous whole. It was often divided and could appear contradictory or confused. Moreover, aspects of his own work were potentially unacceptable to his allies. The restoration of ancient buildings, for example, was to become an especially important focus of dissatisfaction. Nonetheless, Jackson remained a pivotal figure in the arts and crafts movement and a real source of inspiration for many younger architects. He had written of the need for a new unity of art. Throughout his professional practice he sought to show that it could be achieved.

Although ferociously loyal to certain institutions—his school, his college, and his club, in particular—Jackson was not a natural joiner.[5] Some saw this as arrogance; others explained it as eccentricity; Graham Jackson himself believed

[1] Gerald Horsley, 'The Unity of Art', in R. Norman Shaw and T. G. Jackson, eds., *Architecture: a profession or an art* (London, 1892).   [2] NAL, 86/DD/10, 11, C. R. Ashbee, 'Memoir', 282.
[3] T. G. Jackson, *Modern Gothic Architecture* (London, 1873), 185.
[4] Reginald Blomfield, *Memoirs of an Architect* (London, 1942), 65.
[5] Although he was, appropriately, a mason.

that his youthful shortsightedness had made him shy.[6] Whatever the cause, the effect in one respect was clear. He shunned the professional bodies that provided a social network for other architects. Jackson was not a member of the Royal Institute of British Architects (RIBA), or of the Society of Architects, or of the Architectural Association. This inevitably limited his influence, as members of these groups were only too keen to assert. After Jackson had delivered a paper to the RIBA, for example, William White pointed to the presidential throne and exclaimed 'Ah, Mr. Jackson, you have great influence, but how much greater would it be from that chair.'[7] His suggestion, though, was dismissed. Jackson ignored all these arguments and remained aloof.[8] It is, then, a measure of how important he considered the claims of craftsmanship to be that he was prepared to abandon this independence and join the arts and crafts movement. Jackson, indeed, was to go still further. He was to find a place at the heart of this campaign. Gone was the splendid isolation, and in its stead came an active agitator, a signer of petitions, and a prominent member of high-profile campaigns.

Talk of a single, unified arts and crafts movement, it must be made clear, understates the diversity that this apparently simple label conceals.[9] There were arts and crafts architects, glaziers, textile-makers, furniture-designers, cerami-cists, and people working in a whole host of other media.[10] Nor were these widely varying projects united by a single philosophy or programme. The movement incorporated both utopian socialism and commercial enterprise, and stretched from Ashbee's idealistic Guild of Handicraft to Queen Victoria's money-making tapestry and stained-glass concern.[11] In part this simply reflected the intellectual confusion of those involved. The return to supposedly traditional craftsmanship proved to be a hopelessly debatable ideal. As those who have subsequently written on the movement acknowledge, its thinking was not clear and its approach was often woolly.[12] Moreover, this complexity could be seen to reflect a fundamental fragmentation within the movement: not diversity, but division. Linda Parry, indeed, has declared that she is loath to use the 'all-embracing yet nebulous' term 'arts and crafts'. In the absence of a more

---

[6] Blomfield, *Memoirs*, 67; *Architects' Journal* 60 (1924), 763; T. G. Jackson, *Recollections: the life and travels of a Victorian architect* (London, 2003), 36.   [7] Jackson, *Life and Travels*, 191.

[8] See Jackson's indignant response to the mistaken addition of FRIBA to his name: Bod. Dep. C.590 (649), Jackson to Percy Manning (1896).

[9] For this see especially Gillian Naylor, *The Arts and Crafts Movement* (London, 1990).

[10] Peter Davey, *Arts and Crafts Architecture* (London, 1995); A. Charles Sewter, *The Stained Glass of William Morris and His Circle* (2 vols.; New Haven and London, 1974–5), vol. i, pp. 88–9; Linda Parry, *Textiles of the Arts and Crafts Movement* (London, 1988), 7–11; Mary Greensted, *Gimson and the Barnsleys* (Stroud, 1980); Jon Catleugh, et al., eds., *William De Morgan Tiles* (London, 1983); Elizabeth Cumming and Wendy Kaplan, *The Arts and Crafts Movement* (London, 1991), ch. 3.

[11] Alan Crawford, *C. R. Ashbee: architect, designer and romantic socialist* (New Haven and London, 1985); S. K. Tillyard, *The Impact of Modernism* (London and New York, 1988), 4.

[12] Alan Crawford, 'The Arts and Crafts Movement', in Crawford, ed., *By Hammer and By Hand: the arts and crafts movement in Birmingham* (Birmingham, 1984), 23–4.

exact alternative, though, she continues to deploy it.[13] Unfortunately, there is no useful substitute—as the Victorians themselves acknowledged. Although aware of the inadequacy of the description, they were clear that a movement existed, however unwieldy and inchoate it might appear.[14]

In essence, the complexities and contradictions of the arts and crafts movement were a product of its genesis. Nineteenth-century Britons were peculiarly conscious of their artistic inferiority. A select committee of 1835 declared that English industrial design was declining in attractiveness and excellence.[15] The 1851 Great Exhibition taught Owen Jones that 'We have no principles, no unity; the architect, the upholsterer, the paper-stainer, the weaver, the calico-printer, and the potter, run each their independent course; each struggles fruitlessly, each produces in art novelty without beauty, or beauty without intelligence.'[16] Many turned to a wider criticism of contemporary society in their attempt to solve this pressing problem. The idea of a return to craftsmanship was hardly new, and a dislike of industrialization was widely shared.[17] These two themes had, of course, been powerfully articulated by Augustus Pugin[18] and Thomas Carlyle[19] from the 1820s onwards, and were reformulated by Ruskin in subsequent years.[20] It was on this ideology that a revival of the crafts in the 1850s and 1860s was built. Architects like Norman Shaw and Philip Webb sought to utilize local materials and rekindle traditional skills.[21] Designers like William Morris attempted to rediscover lost techniques and reform existing practices.[22] It was this revival which created the arts and crafts movement.

William Morris, in particular, drove the process forward. As a patron, as a writer, and as a businessman, he was at the vanguard of this mid-century revival of craftsmanship. It was for Morris that Philip Webb built Red House, Bexleyheath (1859–60), and it was for Red House that Morris and his circle produced a complete decorative scheme—carving, painting, and weaving the furnishings with their own hands.[23] As a result, it was as much a manifesto as it

[13] Parry, *Textiles*, 7.

[14] T. J. Cobden-Sanderson, *The Arts and Crafts Movement* (Hammersmith, 1905), 3.

[15] Quentin Bell, *The Schools of Design* (London, 1963), 51–73.

[16] Owen Jones, 'An Attempt to Define the Principles which should Regulate the Employment of Colour in the Decorative Arts', *Lectures on the Results of the Great Exhibition of 1851* (London, 1853), 253–300, at 256.

[17] Alan Crawford, 'Sources of Inspiration in the Arts and Crafts Movement', in Sarah Macready and F. H. Thompson, eds., *Influences in Victorian Art and Architecture* (London, 1985), 155–60.

[18] A. N. W. Pugin, *Contrasts* (1836; Leicester, 1973).

[19] Thomas Carlyle, *Signs of the Times* (London, 1829); *Past and Present* (London, 1843), bks. III and IV.

[20] John Ruskin, *Collected Works*, ed., E. J. Cook and A. Wedderburn (39 vols.; 1910–15), esp. vol. 10, pp. 184–352.

[21] Andrew Saint, *Richard Norman Shaw* (New Haven and London, 1976), 321; W. R. Lethaby, *Philip Webb and His Work* (London, 1935), 119–37.

[22] Fiona MacCarthy, 'The Designer', in Linda Parry, ed., *William Morris 1834–1896* (London, 1996), 35–6.   [23] Edward Hollamby, *Red House* (London, 1991).

was a home.[24] Nor did William Morris live there long. The demands of his business soon called him back to London. In 1861 he founded Morris, Marshall, Faulkner & Company, a firm that was intended to bring this craftsmanship to a much wider audience. From 1874 Morris ran the company alone, and made it into a hugely successful and highly important arbiter of taste. Through Morris and Company, the arts and crafts entered the homes of hundreds.[25] Its products were expensive and exclusive, however; handcrafted and made with the best available materials, they could scarcely fail to be. His message nonetheless reached a wider audience in other, different ways. Through his lectures, letters, articles, and books, Morris's conception of craftsmanship was broadcast to thousands who could not afford his wallpaper, stained glass, or furniture. Again and again, he talked-up the 'revolution . . . against the utilitarianism which threatens to destroy the arts'.[26] Drawing—repeatedly—on Ruskin's writings,[27] he urged his contemporaries to 'rebel against the tyranny compounded of utilitarianism and dilettantism, which for the greater part of this century has forbidden all life in Art'.[28] It was a popular message and it was to prove highly influential. By 1880, the revival of craftsmanship had become the goal of a generation.[29]

As Jackson himself acknowledged, 'It would be difficult to over-estimate the influence [Morris] . . . had on English decorative art.'[30] Or, indeed, the influence he had on artists. Almost all of those who became arts and craftsmen in the 1880s were to some extent following Morris's lead. In their search for social and artistic reform, William Morris and John Ruskin had both turned to the medieval world—and especially to the medieval guilds. Morris celebrated the guild system in a number of lectures;[31] Ruskin founded the portentously-titled Guild of St George.[32] So it should come as no surprise that from 1880 onwards this was the model chosen to promote the arts and crafts. In 1882, A. H. Mackmurdo founded the Century Guild and 1884 saw the creation of the Art-Workers' Guild. C. R. Ashbee established the Guild of Handicraft in 1888—and these were just the first. There was also the Hearth and Home Art Guild (1891), the Guild of Arts Craftsmen (1899), the Clarion Handicraft Guild (1901), the Working Ladies Guild (1902), and many other local and regional

---

[24] George Jack, 'An Appreciation of Philip Webb' (1915), in Alistair Service, ed., *Edwardian Architecture and Its Origins* (London, 1975), 18–20.
[25] Charles Harvey and Jon Press, *William Morris: design and enterprise in Victorian Britain* (Manchester and New York, 1993), 38–88.
[26] William Morris, *Gothic Architecture* (London, 1893), 4–5.
[27] Mark Swenarton, *Artisans and Architects: the Ruskinian tradition in architectural thought* (London, 1989), 71–3.
[28] William Morris, *Collected Works*, ed., May Morris (24 vols.; London, 1910–15), vol. 22, p. 421.
[29] Peter Stansky, *Redesigning the World: William Morris, the 1880s, and the arts and crafts* (Princeton, 1985), 8, 28–30, 124, 265. [30] Jackson, *Life and Travels*, 223.
[31] Morris, *Works*, vol. 2, pp. 296–317; *Art and Its Producers* (London, 1901), 6.
[32] John Dixon Hunt, *The Wider Sea: a life of John Ruskin* (New York, 1982), ch. 22.

organizations.[33] They differed in their aims and in their membership. But they were united in their inspiration. As Mackmurdo had put it in the founding charter of the Century Guild, they sought 'to emphasize the *Unity of Art*; and by thus dignifying Art in all its forms . . . to make it living, a thing of our own century, and of the people'.[34] There are two elements here. In the first place, Mackmurdo was stressing the essential unity and equality of all the arts—from architecture to needlework. In the second, he was articulating the great hope of the Guilds that through a growth of craftsmanship and respect for material, tradition, and function, the 'artist' would replace the 'tradesman' as the judge of beauty and utility.[35] This was Morris's call, and it was finally being heeded.

Predictably, the ways in which this ambition was realized differed widely. Ashbee's Guild ended its existence deep in the Cotswolds, where he had taken his followers and founded an arcadian community.[36] The Clarion Guild, by contrast, was based on the sales of a popular magazine.[37] Others appreciated the aesthetic without accepting its ideological implications. William Morris, indeed, came to feel that he was doing nothing more than 'ministering to the swinish luxury of the rich', and his self-criticism was also echoed in the attacks of others.[38] Norman Shaw believed him to be at best 'a great man who somehow delighted in glaring wallpapers'; and at worst a money-grubbing hypocrite.[39] Graham Jackson took delight in the contradiction of a revolutionary socialist who insisted on defending his own intellectual property.[40] Personal attacks, however, could be ignored. More importantly, as Ashbee pointed out in his unpublished memoirs, the arts and crafts movement was from the first split straight down the middle. On one side was Morris, and those who had been born in the 1830s. They had experienced the revival of the 1860s and were the inspiration for the arts and craftsmen of the 1880s.[41] On the other were those born in the 1850s and 1860s, of whom the founders of the Century Guild are a good example. In 1882 Mackmurdo was thirty-one, Selwyn Image thirty-three, Herbert Horne was only eighteen.[42] These were the men 'who stood for that Guild Socialism of which the Art Workers' Guild is the aesthetic wing'. Whilst the older men 'may have conducted workshops, admired the Middle Ages, talked Socialism . . . they were individualists first, not Guildsmen. They looked at their craft from the point of view of the individual designer,—not as one of a group whose craft is a common trust.'[43] Ashbee exaggerated, of course,

[33] Lionel Lambourne, *Utopian Craftsmen: the arts and crafts movement from the Cotswolds to Chicago* (London, 1980).   [34] In Stansky, *Redesigning the World*, 99.
[35] Mackmurdo in Naylor, *Arts and Crafts Movement*, 117.   [36] Crawford, *Ashbee*.
[37] Tillyard, *Impact of Modernism*, 15.
[38] In E. P. Thompson, *William Morris: romantic to revolutionary* (New York, 1976), 250.
[39] Saint, *Shaw*, 258; Davey, *Arts and Crafts Architecture*, 36.
[40] Jackson, *Life and Travels*, 223.   [41] Saint, *Shaw*, 321.   [42] Naylor, *Arts and Crafts*, 117.
[43] NAL 86/DD/10,11, Ashbee Memoir, 259.

but the point still stands. The arts and crafts movement was, perhaps more than anything else, critically divided by age.

One of the 'Great masters of painting, architecture, and sculpture' that Ashbee included in the older generation was T. G. Jackson. Although an inspirational figure for the younger men (and they were, at first, mainly men),[44] his involvement in the arts and crafts movement was, to begin with at least, indirect. This was a function of his age. For although Jackson was clearly committed to the revival of craftsmanship, his commitment grew out of the 1850s and 1860s rather than the 1880s or 1890s. As a pupil in G. G. Scott's office, Jackson was introduced to unity of the arts. His letter of admission to Spring Gardens made this clear. 'Of old,' wrote Scott,

painting and sculpture were subordinate to Architecture so far as this, that their highest object was to enrich it. In these days they have so thoroughly severed themselves that Architecture has too generally become a profession rather than an art. The aim of those whose heart is in the Cause is to put an end to this divorce and to enlist in the architectural cause those who are artists at heart.[45]

These were prophetic words for T. G. Jackson. Uniting the arts and healing the division between artist and professional became his vocation—and this was in 1858, before his career had even begun. Once in Spring Gardens, Jackson was required to turn his hand to a variety of arts. To begin with he invented gargoyles and weathercocks, and created an iron floor-grating which was used in a large number of churches.[46] Soon, he was trusted with more prestigious work. The breakfast room of the Midland Grand Hotel was evidently drawn in perspective by him,[47] and Jeremy Cooper is no doubt correct to suspect that Jackson was responsible for its furniture and fittings.[48]

Jackson thus emerged from his pupilage with experience of almost all aspects of architectural design. Like G. E. Street, another of Scott's pupils, he was determined to use this hard-won skill. Whilst Gilbert Scott had delegated detailed design, his protégés were determined to produce it themselves.[49] Street, indeed, exercised such an all-consuming dominance over each of his buildings that his assistants complained he would even not let them design a keyhole.[50] Jackson could be similarly obsessive: even on holiday in Croatia, he corrected tracings and checked budgets.[51] Two early experiences reinforced this dedication to craftsmanship. The first was Jackson's visit to Italy in 1864. The same trip which confirmed his apostasy from Gothic Truth ironically augmented other lessons he had learnt in Spring Gardens. Italy taught him 'the close union of the three arts, Architecture, Sculpture and Painting', and he came

---

[44] Isabelle Anscombe, *A Woman's Touch: women in design from 1860* (London, 1986), ch. 1.
[45] In Jackson, *Life and Travels*, 53.   [46] Ibid., 65.
[47] Joanna Heseltine, ed., *The Scott Family: a catalogue of the drawings collection of the R.I.B.A.* (Amersham, 1981).
[48] Jeremy Cooper, *Victorian and Edwardian Furniture and Interiors* (London, 1987), 91.
[49] *Builders' Journal* 11 (1900), 309.   [50] Lethaby, *Webb*, 75.
[51] NAL, 86/SS/69, T. G. Jackson, 'Diary of a Journey from London to Bosnia, 1893', 13 Oct. 1893.

back from his travels 'resolved that architecture pure and simple should not absorb all my attention, but that I would devote myself also to the decorative arts'.[52] Life as a young fellow of Wadham had its impact too. Unable to support himself by architecture alone, Jackson turned to less monumental enterprises. He designed furniture, embroidery, glassware, and a variety of other products, and in so doing attempted to realize 'that pattern of an all-round artist which has always been my ideal and in the attainment of which lies . . . the hope of English art'.[53]

In his work as an architect and as a designer Graham Jackson remained loyal to these early principles. His practice, indeed, was founded upon them. He employed few assistants and took on few pupils; but he had a loyal and long-lived staff who understood the way in which he wished to operate. His chief clerk, Alfred Rickarby, was with him for over forty years. Edwin Long was employed as a clerk of works for a similar length of time—though without adopting Rickarby's 'semi-clerical garb'.[54] Jackson trusted his workers absolutely. Mockford, the clerk of works at projects as varied as Brasenose College,[55] Eltham Palace,[56] and Bishop's Waltham Church, was recommended to clients as a man of absolute integrity, who 'does more than any ordinary clerk of works'.[57] This loyalty was mutual. At Brighton College, Mockford was so quick to reject sub-standard work that the builder claimed he was being driven out of business.[58] Jackson's relationship with a number of his sub-contractors was similarly close. He worked well with Farmer & Brindley, the celebrated marble masons, and with Powell's, the Whitefriars' glassmakers. A Mr Childs from Farmer & Brindley worked with Jackson for over thirty years.[59] His colleague, Mr Maples, was Jackson's head carver for more than two decades. 'I regularly formed him', the architect recalled, and 'could always trust him to follow out the start I used to give him at the beginning of each work.'[60] Nor was any need felt for a formal contract with his firm.[61] Familiarity and mutual confidence made conventional business practices redundant.

Supported by a network of loyal workers, Jackson exercised a dominant influence over every project, and every aspect of every project, that his office undertook. He tried to control every part of any scheme, 'leaving nothing to others but mere mechanical draughtsmanship'.[62] Work with craftsmen was also conducted on Jackson's terms. His stonemasons, for example, were expected to follow exact specifications, with a new and full-scale drawing or model made out for each detail.[63] They were 'free men within those limits', as Jackson put it. Despite the fact that this undermined the autonomy of his

---

[52] Jackson, *Life and Travels*, 87.   [53] Ibid., 92.   [54] *Times*, 20 July 1912, 6.
[55] BNCA, Uncat. Corresp., New Building (1883–7).
[56] NA, CRES 35/1516 Eltham Palace 1896–1900.
[57] HCRO, 30M77/PW38 Bishop's Waltham Church, Jackson (25 Feb. 1897).
[58] BCA, 154/7 Correspondence 1884, Griffiths (16 May 1884), Jackson (23 May 1884).
[59] *Hertford College Magazine* 5 (1912), 127.   [60] Jackson, *Life and Travels*, 120.
[61] CUA Geol 8/8 Geological Museum Syndicate 1897–1902, Jackson (14 Feb. 1901).
[62] Jackson, *Life and Travels*, 109.
[63] BNCA, Uncat. Drawings of grotesques. *Hertford College Magazine* 5 (1912), 127.

18. Athelstan Riley's piano (1890–2).

craftsmen, he believed that this was necessary. Certainly, it ensured 'consistency and harmony' throughout his work.[64] Even the smallest details, from the key escutcheons upwards, were Jackson's concern. Many of these—his stove fronts, for example—were used time and again; Messrs. Barnard & Bishop kept standard designs for his sole use.[65] Much work, though, was also provided to order. This could be as inexpensive as the door handle designed for the Royal Academy, or as valuable as the Inner Temple's silverware.[66]

In all cases, though, the same fundamental principles were followed. Jackson was committed to good craftsmanship and to use of the best material. At Hertford College Chapel, for example, he used a dozen different types of marble in the pavement of the sanctuary: Irish stone from Cork and Connemara; Verde Antico from the ancient quarries of Cassambali; Rosso Antico cut from the residue of a statue of Byron, and many more.[67] This made his work expensive. A piano designed by Jackson in 1890 cost many hundreds of pounds and was built in mahogany and ivory, purple wood stained a deep dark green, gesso, satinwood, mother-of-pearl, and tortoiseshell.[68] It was embellished with fine veneer

[64] Jackson, *Life and Travels*, 87.
[65] TCA, Uncat. Records of New Buildings, Jackson (20 June 1887).
[66] RA Library, Uncat. Drawings by Jackson.   [67] HCA, Uncat. Drawings.
[68] It was originally designed for Athelstan Riley (for whom see Ch. 5) and is now on display in Salt's Mill, Saltaire, West Yorkshire.

19. St John's Church, Hampstead (1881–7).   20. The organ case at Radley College (1893–5).

and intarsia work, with great sprays of leaves—foliage in gold on a ruby ground—inlaid in the surface. 'I drew the whole of the ornament full size myself', recalled Jackson, 'for it was not a matter in which anyone could help me.'[69] Nor was its importance confined to its decorations. It was functionally appropriate too. The supports alone, claimed the *Builder* bathetically, 'ought to make a revolution in piano-legs'.[70]

This emphasis on craftsmanship and on using the finest of materials was found in all Jackson's works. Although this was to be his only piano, there were organ cases at Blenheim Palace, Hampstead Church, and Radley College that exhibit the same obsessive attention to detail.[71] In Oxford he housed organs at Brasenose, Corpus Christi, Hertford, Oriel, and Wadham Colleges; whilst his case in the Sheldonian Theatre was especially admired.[72] 'Beautiful alike in outline, detail, and colour, it . . . seems little short of perfection', as one critic put it. Importantly, it was also seen to suit its surroundings, harmonizing with

[69] Jackson, *Life and Travels*, 195.

[70] *Architect* 45 (1891), 101; *Builder* 64 (1893), 15; *Gentlewoman* 8 (1894), 658.

[71] *Architect* 41 (1889), 41; Andrew Freeman, *English Organ Cases* (London, 1921), 72; *Builder* 64 (1894), 351, 352.

[72] BNCA, B.13.2. Working Drawings (1892); Jackson, *Life and Travels*, 152; *Builder* 87 (1904), 274; Jackson, *Life and Travels*, 152; T. G. Jackson, *Wadham College, Oxford* (Oxford, 1897), 174–5.

Wren's building quite 'splendidly'.[73] When Graham Jackson was able to provide
the decoration as well, the results could be even more spectacular. His piano, for
example, was just the 'finishing touch' to a much wider scheme.[74] Jackson's
decorations for the home in which the instrument was housed included a min-
strels' gallery embellished with a frieze by George Frampton (1893). There were
De Morgan tiles, Dutch strap-work, and Corinthian pillars in the library. The
chapel was panelled with cedar, the drawing-room hung with embossed Spanish
leather. Carved alabaster, patterned marble, oak panelling, and decorated plaster
ceilings were found throughout the house.[75] Everything, from the piano hinges
to the postman's bell, was designed by hand and by Jackson.[76]

Of course Jackson was not alone in this attention to the detail of design. He
was not even alone in designing expensive pianos: Burne-Jones had decorated
a far more famous Broadwood Grand in 1884.[77] Nor was he the only architect to
design furniture, fixtures, or fittings. William Burges' extraordinary Cardiff
Castle (1869–71) and Castell Coch (1876–81) make Jackson's efforts seem
almost half-hearted.[78] Other architects also sold their products on the open market. Jackson's contemporaries G. G. Scott, junior, G. F. Bodley, F. W. Davenport,
and Thomas Garner founded Watts & Company in the early 1870s.[79] It is still
producing church furnishings to this day. Unlike many other architects, however, Jackson's commitment to a revival of craftsmanship was expressed in print
as well as in practice. Like William Morris, his writings made his thought
available to those who could not afford his buildings or his decorations.
Moreover, he became actively involved in the ambitions and organizations of an
important group of younger workers. This combination of designing, writing,
and agitation gained him a large audience. Many came to feel with William
Lethaby that Jackson's thinking 'could hardly be bettered'.[80] The result was a
greater and more direct influence on the arts and crafts movement than that of
almost any of his generation.

As a result of his age, however, there were always differences between Jackson
and his allies. He did not help to establish any of the organizations that mobilized
the movement of the 1880s and 1890s. Initially at least, these were the enterprises of much younger men, many of them the students of Richard Norman
Shaw. For although Arthur Mackmurdo's Century Guild was founded first, it
was the Art-Workers' Guild of Edward Prior, Ernest Newton, Mervyn
Macartney, Gerald Horsley, and William Lethaby that proved to be the more
influential.[81] Believing that 'Art and Architecture were drifting asunder', they
wished to establish a forum for 'Handicraftsmen and Designers in the Arts', to

[73] Freeman, *Organ Cases*, 73.   [74] Jackson, *Life and Travels*, 192.
[75] *Builder* 48 (1885), 898; *Gentlewoman* 8 (1894), 657–8; *Studio* 1 (1893), 255.
[76] RA Library, Uncat. Drawings.   [77] *Builder* 55 (1888), 242–3.
[78] J. Mordaunt Crook, *William Burges and the High Victorian Dream* (London, 1981).
[79] Gavin Stamp, 'George Gilbert Scott, junior, 1839–1897' (Ph.D., Cambridge, 1978), 278.
[80] Lethaby, *Webb*, 83.   [81] Naylor, *Arts and Crafts*, 119–22.

21. The organ and Chapel extension at Oriel College, Oxford (1883–4).

22. The chancel of Northington Church (1887–90).

bring them back together. In 1884 they found 55 interested people; ten years later there were 182 Guildsmen—a mixture of painters, sculptors, and craftsmen.[82] But whatever their differing backgrounds, they shared a common ambition: the revival of craftsmanship and the unification of the arts.[83] For all these men the Art-Workers' Guild was a place to discuss contemporary aesthetics, to share insights, and to learn new techniques. Debates were confidential and unreported.[84] For many, like Massé, the Guild was 'a haven of refuge in the hurly-burly of Nineteenth-Century Art'.[85] It was profoundly influential and

[82] E. S. Prior, 'The Origins of the Guild' in H. J. L. Massé, *The Art-Workers' Guild* (Oxford, 1935), 7, 12, 14.
[83] John Brandon-Jones, 'W. R. Lethaby and the Art-Workers' Guild', in Sylvia Backemeyer and Theresa Gronberg, eds., *W. R. Lethaby 1857–1931* (London, 1984), 25.
[84] John Brandon-Jones, 'Architects and The Art-Workers' Guild', *Journal of the Royal Society of Arts* 121 (1972–3), 192–206, 196.   [85] In Massé, *Art-Workers' Guild*, 2.

much loved. It was also, as Jackson put it, 'the realization of what I had pleaded for'. He was elected a member in 1889.[86]

Many of the other organizations which also pressed for an artistic revival grew out of the Art-Workers' Guild. The Arts and Crafts Exhibition Society, indeed, was so closely associated that it shared the same address. Founded in 1888, its objective was to take the message of the movement out to the masses. It aimed, as Stella Tillyard has observed, to achieve for the craftsman the same status as the fine artist, and it sought to do this by holding regular exhibitions and public lecture series on the revival of craftsmanship.[87] The Society was remarkably successful, and by 1916 it was exhibiting at the Royal Academy, the home of the fine arts itself.[88] Once again, though, this was an organization run by the younger generation.[89] In the first catalogue, Walter Crane attempted to associate the Society with William Morris and his philosophy of design.[90] Given his importance to its members, this was an entirely appropriate gesture, but it was also disingenuous. Morris had in fact refused to participate. 'The public don't give a damn about the Arts and Crafts', he had exclaimed when asked to join the Society, and he had consequently refused to exhibit or to lecture.[91] The success of the first exhibition changed his mind, however. At the second show, in 1889, he gave a talk on Gothic Architecture; in 1893 he edited a collection of the best lectures given, entitled—significantly—Arts and Crafts Essays.[92] Jackson was also a late joiner.[93] But by 1890 he had contributed an introduction on intarsia to the catalogue: an article which was later included in Morris's collection.[94] This was more than a demonstration of Jackson's literary ability. It also reveals his importance to the movement as a whole.

This significance was emphasized in a wholly different environment, too. The National Association for the Advancement of Art and Its Application to Industry, established in 1887, was the ideal environment for Jackson's skills, and for his message. Based on the British Association for the Advancement of Science, this was intended to be a forum for artistic debate, dispute, and collaboration.[95] In this respect at least it resembled the Art-Workers' Guild.[96] Two factors distinguished the organizations, however. In the first place the National Association was a public arena; it published transactions of its

[86] T. G. Jackson, Recollections (B. H. Jackson, ed.; Oxford, 1950), 218.
[87] Tillyard, Impact of Modernism, 3.   [88] ACES, Catalogue 11 (1916).
[89] Cobden-Sanderson, Arts and Crafts Movement, 5, 14–18.
[90] ACES, Catalogue 1 (1888), 7.   [91] Lambourne, Utopian Craftsmen, 32.
[92] ACES, Catalogue 2 (1889), 16.
[93] He was a member from 1893 to 1910: see ACES Catalogues 3–9.
[94] ACES, Catalogue 3 (1890), 67–77; Arts and Crafts Essays (London and New York, 1893), 330–44.
[95] Walter Crane, An Artist's Reminiscences (London, 1907), 324. Gillian Naylor has also noted a similarity to the French Union Centrale des Beaux-Arts Appliqués à l'Industrie (Naylor, Arts and Crafts, 161). The collapse of the Social Science Association removed the sole forum for the discussion of similar issues. See Lawrence Goldman, Science, Reform and Politics in Victorian Britain: the Social Science Association 1857–1886 (Cambridge, 2002).   [96] Blomfield, Recollections, 69–71.

proceedings.[97] Secondly, and importantly, it was a far grander organization than any Guild. Its first president was Sir Frederick Leighton, and his vice-presidents included three earls: Derby, Pembroke, and Wharncliffe. Even with this weight of establishment support, though, it was not a long-lived project. The Association lasted for only three meetings—at Liverpool (1888), Edinburgh (1889), and Birmingham (1890). Nonetheless, whilst it survived, it was 'an artists' tournament' in which the 'Arts and Crafts Banner was well to the fore', as Walter Crane recalled.[98] William Morris, Walter Crane, Basil Champneys, Rowand Anderson, Cobden-Sanderson, and many other Guildsmen entered the fray. Jackson, too, thrived in this intellectually demanding environment. In 1888 he spoke on art education,[99] and at the 1890 meeting he was president of the architectural section.[100] This was no small achievement. Architecture, as William Morris lectured the Association, was 'the foundation of all the arts'.[101] At the Birmingham Conference Jackson was thus at the heart of the arts and crafts endeavour: acknowledged as a leader and valued as an advocate.

His position was precarious, however. It was always difficult to reconcile this role with the realities of professional practice. Ironically, indeed, Jackson's very success made the implementation of his ideals more difficult. He found it almost impossible to keep up with the sheer volume of work that he attracted—and little wonder. A record of his visit to Oxford on 11 March 1884 shows that it was planned to the last minute; not a second could be wasted. His itinerary ran as follows: beginning at nine-thirty, he inspected a house in the Botanic Gardens; at noon, he viewed work on the cricket pavilion in the University Parks; between 1 p.m. and 2 p.m. he lunched at Beam Hall, which he was restoring; at 2 p.m. he visited the President of Corpus Christi; a tour of his buildings at Trinity was next at 2.30 and at 4.30 he returned to London.[102] This hectic pace left little room for error or inefficiency. And despite his hard work Graham Jackson was rarely efficient. 'I fear he is not always very business like', wrote one client in 1902. In order to get the simplest detail dealt with 'I have had to write 3 times'.[103] This was as frustrating to the contractor as it was to the customer. 'Matters are not properly and sufficiently described', wrote the builder of Brasenose in some despair; he was losing money as a result.[104] Jackson's combination of disorganization and total (if remote) control was potentially disastrous. Certainly, mistakes were made. At Trinity College, Oxford, for example, Jackson was horrified to find that the bedrooms were far smaller than expected. In the

---

[97] NAAA, *Transactions* 1888, 1889, 1890. There were plans to hold an 1891 meeting in Nottingham (NAAA, *Transactions* 1889, p. xvi). This appears not to have happened.

[98] Crane, *Reminiscences*, 324–5.   [99] NAAA, *Transactions* 1888, 193–202.

[100] NAAA, *Transactions* 1890, 78–93.   [101] Morris, *Art and Its Producers*, 34.

[102] OUA, UC/FF/305/1/3 Botanic Gardens 1880–8, Jackson (10 March 1884).

[103] CUA, Geol. 9/35/59 Chawner (30 June 1902).

[104] BNCA, New Building I, Uncat. Papers, George Dobson (12 Feb., 8 March 1890).

architect's absence, the builders had simply misconstrued the plan.[105] Had
Jackson followed his own advice—had he been on site and in place—this would
never have happened.

Jackson's own descriptions of his office practice were still more surprising,
particularly for a doyen of the arts and crafts movement. He mocked 'the high
stools, the drawing-boards, the dusty piles and rolls of paper'. He dwelt on the
horrors of post-time which 'drives us into a frenzy to get off arrears of correspondence that cannot be postponed any longer'. He described, in other words, a
working environment far removed from his ideal. Far removed, indeed, from the
practices of the arts and crafts.[106] In this respect, at least, Jackson was closer to
his older colleagues than to his younger allies. The resemblance to G. E. Street
is, once again, attractive. Certainly, Harry Hems' depiction of Street's chaotic
practice in Cavendish Place seems superficially similar. There Street was to be
found

standing at his desk knocking off large detail drawings—and beautiful drawings too—at
a rate of a dozen or more an hour, but in spite of that and all his wonderful energy and
ability, Mr. Street was always behind. The most vexatious delays were constantly occur-
ring 'all over the shop' on Mr. Street's jobs, because the foreman or the clerk of works in
charge was 'waiting for details'. Mr. Street, as a rule, large as was his practice drew all
details with his own hand in pencil.[107]

In one respect this comparison is helpful. It makes the point that any architect
who insisted on controlling every part of his office's work could only do so by
sacrificing efficiency or scale. G. E. Street was always late; Philip Webb—who
sought the same kind of authority—built very little.[108] But to pursue this
analogy, and to suggest that Jackson was no different to Street, is a mistake. For
Jackson was operating in a very different environment, and to a very different set
of priorities. An association with Street, indeed, implies that Jackson was in
some sense disengaged from the arts and crafts movement. Nothing, in fact,
could be further from the truth.

In reality, it is not to Street, but to one of Street's pupils, that we must look for
a closer analogy. William Morris encountered the same problems in the minor
arts that Jackson found in architecture. Both men recognized that the current
system was inadequate, but were unsure how to change it. How could one reconcile profit with principle; abstract belief with real life? Morris resolved his
dilemma in the same way as Jackson, by creating a clear distinction between the
artist and the workman. Although Morris's workers were better treated than
most, they had little opportunity to influence design and were predominantly

[105] TCA, Uncat. Records of New Buildings, Jackson (10 Dec. 1884). Jackson swiftly moved to
rectify the error, and the rooms were subsequently built to the correct size.
[106] *Builder* 72 (1897), 334–7.
[107] *Builders' Journal* 11 (1900), 309. This is also quoted in Andrew Saint, *The Image of the
Architect* (New Haven and London, 1983), 69.
[108] His philosophy of art is elegantly summarized in Lethaby, *Webb*, 119–37.

occupied with performing laborious and largely repetitive tasks. What William Morris invented they merely executed—and at an hourly rate.[109] This, he argued, was inevitable. The circumstances of society meant that 'our art is the work of a small minority composed of educated persons, fully conscious of their aim of producing beauty, and distinguished from the great body of workmen by the possession of that aim'.[110] Jackson agreed. 'There is no school of workmen nowadays capable of filling in the details on a general design given them by an architect', he claimed. Whilst this remained the case, there was no alternative to drawing out every aspect of a building.[111] Only education (for Jackson) or revolution (for Morris) could change this.[112] Thus, although both men recognized the inadequacy of their current practice, they could see no realistic alternative. This was not hypocrisy, but it did set them apart from the more zealous of their younger followers.[113]

On one issue, indeed, Graham Jackson was critically separated from both Morris and the wider movement. Jackson had a very wide and hugely varied restoration practice. He restored and rebuilt much of Oxford; and worked on projects throughout England and Wales. There were country houses, like his Renaissance remodelling of the long gallery and chapel at Castle Ashby (1880); or the Queen Anne addition to Catton Hall, Derbyshire (1907); or the Jacobean restorations of Longleat (1911).[114] Nor does the list end here. There were still more prestigious projects: the chapel at Blenheim Palace (1888), the halls at Eltham Palace (1900–2) and Greenwich Hospital (1906–9), and the gateway at Nottingham Castle (1906–11).[115] These domestic commissions were outnumbered by ecclesiastical work: from Malden, begun in 1863, to Bromley, begun in 1883, to Mold, completed in 1923; from Denbighshire to Suffolk; and from Lancashire to Kent.[116] Much of this work was highly important. At Stamford he restored a tower so grand that Sir Walter Scott used to doff his hat to it.[117] In Great Malvern, Jackson saved the Priory from serious structural weaknesses.[118] The restoration of Bath Abbey lasted thirty years (1899–1906; 1922–4).[119]

---

[109] MacCarthy, *Morris*, 452–6.

[110] William Morris, *Arts and Crafts Essays* (London and New York, 1893), viii.

[111] *Builder* 72 (1897), 336.

[112] For Jackson's involvement in educational reform, see below. For Morris see Harvey and Press, *Morris*, 154–63.   [113] Cobden-Sanderson, *Arts and Crafts Movement*, 14–20.

[114] Gervase Jackson-Stops, 'Castle Ashby, Northamptonshire', *Country Life* 179 (1986), 310–15, at 315; Arthur Oswald, 'Catton Hall, Derbyshire', *Country Life* 127 (1960), 566–9, at 569; Jackson, *Life and Travels*, 270.

[115] RA Library, Uncat. Manuscripts (17 Sept. 1888); NA, CRES 35/1516 Eltham Palace 1896–1902; NA, ADM 169/362; *Builder* 100 (1911), 510.

[116] St John's (1863–76): SHC, 2508/2; St Peter and St Paul (1883–4): LPL ICBS 8827; St Mary's (1921–3): RA MSS. For a complete list of works see Jackson, *Life and Travels*, 266–300.

[117] NMR 15555 St Mary's, Stamford.

[118] Anthony Charles Deane, *Great Malvern Priory Church* (London, 1926), 30–1.

[119] Neil Jackson, *Nineteenth-Century Bath Architects and Architecture* (Bath, 1991), 176–8. See also *Builder* 77 (1899), 328; 80 (1901), 351; 88 (1905), 603; 90 (1906), 238; 104 (1913), 596; 23 (1922), 733; *RIBA Journal* 32 (1924–5), 49–50.

Nottingham Castle
Proposed adaptation of
the Gateway to purposes
of the Museum.

T.G. Jackson. R.A.
Oct. 30. 1902.

Present condition
of the Gateway.

23. The gateway to Nottingham Castle (1906–11).

Holy Trinity, Coventry (1915–19), was of such significance that its repair was carried out despite the first world war and at a cost of £9,000.[120] In many respects, the extent of Jackson's experience in fact remains unclear. The loss and dispersal of his papers has meant that the list of his works is incomplete. Records of refitting at Montacute (?1915), for example, are now unavailable. Although attributed to Jackson, the remodelling of the house 'is [now] almost a matter of conjecture'.[121] The glimpses we do get, however, offer a broadly accurate picture. Whether assisting Gilbert Scott or in his own right, Jackson was one of the most prolific and respected of the late-nineteenth-century restorers.[122]

He was trusted because of his sensitivity to ancient work. From the first Jackson was determined to treat buildings with more appreciation than

---

[120] *Architect* 95 (1916), 223; *Times* 15 Jan. 1915, 11; 26 May 1919.
[121] *RIBA Journal* 32 (1924–5), 50; Malcolm Rogers, *Montacute House* (London, 1991), 31.
[122] Martin S. Briggs, *Goths and Vandals* (London, 1952), 214–17; Jane Fawcett, 'A Restoration Tragedy: cathedrals in the eighteenth and nineteenth centuries', in Jane Fawcett, ed., *The Future of the Past* (London, 1976), 98.

preceding generations had shown.[123] At Chessington Church in 1865, he made his position clear. 'I will only say that too much stress cannot be laid on the *duty* of those who are as it were trustees of the public for our old buildings to keep every stick and stone in its place that can be preserved',[124] he wrote to his client—and he remained true to these principles.[125] As late as 1911, the local Antiquarian Society praised Jackson for his work at Nottingham Castle; congratulating him 'upon the careful manner in which he has carried out the alterations, retaining everything of antiquarian interest'.[126] He was also employed for his expertise. At Rushton Hall in Northamptonshire both he and Alfred Gotch were commissioned to provide a 'careful nurturing of the old house of the Treshams and Cockaynes'. Gotch was of course a much-published writer on the English Renaissance. Jackson was similarly well qualified to act 'in sympathy with the original work'.[127] His client clearly agreed with another well-placed critic that Graham Jackson's 'authority on archaeological and architectural questions is pre-eminent'.[128] His reputation for knowledge and sensitivity was, thus, well developed—and well deserved. Certainly, the vicar of Christchurch Priory felt that commissioning T. G. Jackson would 'be a guarantee that everything will be carried out in a thoroughly careful and conservative spirit, and that no ancient work will be interfered with'.[129] Few would have disagreed.

Christchurch was just one of the many important projects Jackson accepted as architect for the diocese of Winchester. Appointed in 1899, it was a plum job for an ambitious builder. Stretching from Dorset to Surrey, Winchester was one of the largest and richest of the English sees, and the appointment gave Jackson a real opportunity. He built in Bournemouth and Basingstoke, Lyndhurst and Laverstoke, and in churches all across the diocese.[130] Much of this was minor work, but there were some larger schemes as well. At Aldershot, for example, he built St Augustine's (1906–7) and more than doubled the size of St Michael's (1910–12).[131] At Curdridge, he effectively refounded St Peter's (1888; 1894).[132] Nor was his work purely parochial: there were some projects of national importance too. The restoration of St Thomas's in Portsmouth (1902–4: now Portsmouth Cathedral), for example, cost over £10,000.[133] The church was collapsing and

[123] J. Mordaunt Crook, 'T. G. Jackson and the Cult of Eclecticism', in H. Searing, ed., *In Search of Modern Architecture* (New York, 1982), 109–10.

[124] SHC, 2473/2 Chessington Church, Jackson (18 Feb. 1865).

[125] e.g. HCRO 55M81 W/PW21 Hyde Church, Report (12 Nov. 1900).

[126] *Builder* 100 (1911), 510.   [127] *Country Life* 29 (1909), 495.

[128] HCRO 21M65/88F/12/I Christchurch Priory, Chancellor of the Diocese of Winchester (13 Oct. 1911).   [129] HCRO 21M65/88F/12/II Christchurch, leaflet (28 Feb. 1912).

[130] Bournemouth: St Michael: chapel (1920), HCRO 21M65/58F/7; 44M86/PW32–4 and St Peter: chapel and vestry (1905–6), HCRO 21M65/60F/6. Basingstoke: St Mary: new nave (1912), *Buildings of England: Hampshire.* Lyndhurst: Hargreave Memorial (1919): RA MS. Laverstoke, St Mary: war memorial chapel (1919).   [131] LPL ICBS 10683; HCRO 21M65/57/5.

[132] HCRO 21M65/107F/1.

[133] E. K. Barnard, *From Parish Church to Portsmouth Cathedral, 1900–1939* (Portsmouth Papers 52, 1988).

24. St Peter's Church, Curdridge (1888; 1894).

Jackson saved it.[134] His expertise allowed him to underpin, restore, rebuild, refit, reseat, and strengthen the building. His sensitivity ensured that 'St Thomas's came through it all unspoilt.'[135] This, though, was nothing compared to his labours at Winchester Cathedral (1905–12).[136] At a cost of £130,000 Jackson rescued the building from imminent collapse. Called in by a panicking cathedral architect, he found that the twelfth-century extensions had been built on a great beech raft, resting on marshy ground. The raft was sinking, and the force of this subsidence now threatened the whole structure.[137] Jackson's approach, to say the least, was 'rather experimental'.[138] He underpinned the building, pumping out water and

[134] Edward S. Washington, 'Vicar Grant and his successors, 1868–1924', in Sarah Quail and Alan Wilkinson, eds., *Forever Building: essays to mark the completion of the cathedral church of St Thomas of Canterbury, Portsmouth* (Portsmouth, 1995), 77–82.

[135] Henry T. Lilley and Alfred T. Everitt, *Portsmouth Parish Church* (Portsmouth, 1921), 159–63.

[136] For which, see T. G. Jackson, 'Winchester Cathedral, an account of the building and of the repairs now in progress', *Transactions of the St Paul's Ecclesiological Society* 6 (1910), 217–36; Frederick Bussby, *Winchester Cathedral 1079–1979* (Southampton, 1979), 255–78; Keith Walker, 'The twentieth century and the future', in John Crook, ed., *Winchester Cathedral Nine Hundred Years, 1093–1993* (Chichester, 1993), 335–6; Diana Holbrook, 'The Restoration of Winchester Cathedral by Thomas G Jackson, 1905–12', *Transactions of the Association for Studies in the Conservation of Historic Buildings* 11 (1986), 48–71. There is also a large collection of material in the cathedral archives.   [137] *Times*, 22 Oct. 1907, 8.

[138] *Times*, 12 April 1906, 11.

replacing it with concrete.[139] The walls were grouted and tie-rods inserted. The nave was buttressed; the chapter-house restored; and the crypt re-vaulted. Thus was the cathedral saved.[140] It marked, as Jane Fawcett puts it, 'a new era in architectural first aid'.[141] Jackson, moreover, was proud of his restraint. 'We might . . . have done more,' he wrote, 'I am sure we could not have done less.'[142] This could have been the motto for all his restorations.

Nonetheless, despite this hard work, knowledge, and concern, Jackson was to find these endeavours constantly criticized by his arts and crafts allies. It was his misfortune to work at a time in which any restoration, however limited, was likely to be the subject of attack. This debate was not new, of course. From 1789 onwards, James Wyatt suffered perpetual abuse for his restoration work. For more than a decade John Carter ran a one-man crusade to stop 'Wyatt the Destroyer' in his track.[143] The mid-1840s saw yet another furious debate, driven by Edward Freeman's devastating critique of contemporary practice.[144] In 1850, George Gilbert Scott waded in, with his *Plea for the Faithful Restoration of Our Ancient Churches*. He argued for limited, or in his terms, 'conservative' restoration and claimed this was the aim of all his work.[145] Nonetheless, his assertion that 'even entire rebuilding . . . may be effected *conservatively*', gives some clue to his thinking.[146] For Scott and his allies, it was possible to return a building to its original form. A church, for instance, would be more authentic—even if entirely rebuilt—so long as the restorer had followed the presumed intentions of its first builders.[147] From the 1860s onwards, however, a growing group of critics was to attack this approach.[148] John Ruskin, amongst others, made a strong distinction between design and material; between the original and its copy. He argued that it was impossible for a building to revert to its original appearance. Worse still, by altering the fabric of the structure, restorers actually made it less authentic rather than more.[149] Soon it was suggested that any alteration to a building, however minor, destroyed its integrity. Intervention was only desirable to prevent collapse.[150]

---

[139] Francis Fox, *Sixty-Three Years of Engineering* (London, 1924), 126–39. The heroic work of William Walker, the diver charged with carrying the concrete underwater, is told in Ian T. Henderson and John Crook, *The Winchester Diver: the saving of a great cathedral* (Crawley, 1984).

[140] *Building News* 116 (1919), 116–17.

[141] Fawcett, 'Restoration', in Fawcett, *Future of the Past*, 98.   [142] *Times*, 13 July 1912, 7.

[143] J. Mordaunt Crook, *John Carter and the Mind of the Gothic Revival* (London, 1995), 27, 33–41. For a defence of Wyatt's work, see Antony Dale, *James Wyatt* (Oxford, 1956), 7–9.

[144] E. A. Freeman, *Principles of Church Restoration* (London, 1846), 10–11, 17.

[145] Briggs offers a defence of Scott's work: *Goths and Vandals*, 170–202; see also Gavin Stamp, 'Sir Gilbert Scott and the "restoration" of medieval buildings', *AA Files* 1 (1981–2), 89–97.

[146] G. G. Scott, *Plea for the Faithful Restoration of Our Ancient Churches* (London, 1850), 29.

[147] C. E. Miele, 'The Gothic Revival and Gothic Architecture: the restoration of medieval churches in Victorian Britain' (Ph.D., New York University, 1992), 25, 84–5, 139, 184–8, 292–7, 532–5.

[148] Chris Miele, 'Real Antiquity and the Ancient Object: the science of Gothic architecture and the restoration of medieval buildings', Vanessa Brand, ed., *The Study of the Past in the Victorian Age* (Oxford, 1998), 103–24.   [149] Ruskin, *Works*, vol. 8, pp. 221–44.

[150] George Aitchison, 'What principles should govern the restoration of ancient buildings or their preservation as memorials?', *Transactions of the National Association for the Promotion of Social Science* 1877, 712–20.

This distinction, between restoration and preservation, was hugely influential on the arts and crafts movement.[151] Believing, as they did, that artists 'divine the Ideal of an age and express it', the arts and craftsmen argued that each building was a record of a particular moment in time.[152] To alter it was to deface a record of the past.[153] The contrast with Scott could not have been clearer, and when conflict came it was painful for both sides. The year 1877 was of particular importance: William Morris, George Aitchison, W. J. Loftie, Sidney Colvin, and many others launched an all-out attack on contemporary restoration—and particularly on Scott.[154] Though George Gilbert Scott gave as good as he got, this was an undoubtedly hurtful experience.[155] Few would not sympathize with Scott's anguish as he heard himself publicly denounced by one of his own pupils at the RIBA. His former student, J. J. Stevenson, echoed the complaints of all the arts and crafts architects. 'An old church', he declared, 'which has not been restored is an absolutely trustworthy historical document, a continuous record of English history.' To alter it in any way was to perpetrate 'the falsification of history'. Eschewing this, he argued that architects should simply avoid old buildings; 'Is it too much to suggest that we should leave them alone?' he asked.[156] This was controversial stuff, the 'gospel of despair and death', claimed Beresford Hope. It was also extremely naïve. Ancient work needed to be repaired; churches and houses had to be extended. Stevenson offered no practical way of doing this. As Scott himself asked, 'What is the use of giving advice which you know cannot by any possibility be followed?'[157]

Stevenson, though, was not the most extreme member of the movement, nor the most naïve. Sidney Colvin went still further. He argued that even repairs could be positively harmful; ruin was preferable to restoration. 'Better the fate of Melrose, Tintern, or Rievaulx', he wrote, 'than the fate of Worcester or Durham.'[158] Confronted by attitudes like this, Scott was never going to be able to convince his critics, nor were they likely to be satisfied by anything less than complete capitulation.[159] And their voice was growing stronger. For 1877 was also the year in which the anti-restoration movement was formally embodied. The *Athenaeum* of 10 March 1877 carried a letter from William Morris, calling for the establishment of an association 'To keep a watch on old monuments, to protest against all "restoration" that means more than keeping out the wind or weather, and, by all means, literary or other, to awaken a feeling that our ancient

---

[151] Miele, 'Gothic Revival', 84.   [152] Cobden-Sanderson, *Arts and Crafts*, 20.
[153] *Architectural Review* 4 (1898), 3–4, 50.
[154] Aitchison, 'Principles', 712–20; Sidney Colvin, 'Restoration and Anti-Restoration', *Nineteenth Century* 11 (1877), 446–70; W. J. Loftie, 'Thorough Restoration', *Macmillan's Magazine* 36 (1877), 136–42; William Morris, *Athenaeum* 1877, 326.
[155] G. G. Scott, 'Thorough Anti-Restoration', *Macmillan's Magazine* 36 (1877), 228–37.
[156] J. J. Stevenson, 'Architectural Restoration: its principles and practice', *RIBA Transactions* 1876–7, 219–35.   [157] *RIBA Transactions* 1876–7, 229–34.
[158] Colvin, 'Restoration and Anti-Restoration', 463.
[159] G. G. Scott, *Personal and Professional Recollections* (1879; Stamford, 1995), ch. v.

buildings are not mere ecclesiastical toys, but sacred monuments of the nation's growth and hope.'[160] It was in this way that the Society for the Protection of Ancient Buildings (SPAB) was born. Known by its allies as 'Anti-Scrape', it was thus an archetypally arts and crafts project.[161] Its members were Jackson's friends. But it was to cause him nearly as much trouble as it gave Gilbert Scott.

This was unfortunate; and all the more so because Jackson was no Scott. He himself criticized over-zealous restoration. J. L. Pearson, for one, received a rebuke for his proposed work at Peterborough Cathedral. 'Neither he nor anyone else in this age is qualified to add a fresh chapter to that stone book which should now be closed for ever', Jackson wrote.[162] His actions, too, reflected this belief. At Dursley in Gloucestershire, between 1866 and 1868, Graham Jackson restored the parish church. It was a hard job, which involved dismantling numerous walls and pillars. In line with his ideals, though, he aimed to maintain the integrity of the building. 'Stones were carefully numbered as they were removed, and replaced in the same situation which they had previously occupied: and when each column was set up again on its new foundation of concrete . . . it was, in fact, the column which the builders of the fifteenth century had erected restored rather than renovated', enthused one contemporary.[163] But even despite these efforts, disputes were inevitable. For although Graham Jackson was committed to the sensitive treatment of old buildings, he could not accept Colvin's Ruskinian argument that ruin was better than restoration. He shared the sense that buildings were records of the past, but he was also forced to acknowledge the needs of the present. 'The real truth', as the Secretary of the SPAB, Thackeray Turner, put it, 'is that Mr. Jackson is a "restoring" architect, and we are opposed to "restoration".'[164] This fundamental division was to have the most dramatic consequences for Jackson's career. Whilst a number of other architects were able to reach an accommodation with the SPAB, Jackson denied its claim to interfere in his work. By 1885 Bodley, Champneys, Ponting, Prior, G. G. Scott, junior, and Frederick Waller—amongst others—were submitting their work to the SPAB for approval. Eustace Balfour, Ernest George, John Honeyman, Temple Moore, J. D. Seddon, and Aston Webb in their turn kept the Society informed about their restorations.[165]

[160] William Morris, *Athenaeum* 1877, 326.

[161] Chris Miele, 'The First Conservation Militants', in Michael Hunter, *Preserving the Past: the rise of heritage in modern Britain* (Stroud, 1996), 20–7; ' "A small knot of cultivated people", William Morris and Ideologies of Protection', *Art Journal* 54 (1995), 73–9. More generally, see Chris Miele, ed., *From William Morris: building conservation and the arts and crafts cult of authenticity, 1877–1939* (New Haven & London, 2005).

[162] *Times*, 5 Jan. 1885, 10. For this, see Anthony Quiney, *John Loughborough Pearson* (New Haven and London, 1979), 186–98.

[163] John Henry Blunt, *Dursley and its Neighbourhood* (London and Dursley, 1877), 73.

[164] SPAB Archive, 128 (a) Winchester Cathedral, *Times* 7 Jan. 1908.

[165] Miele, 'Conservation Militants', 33. Although for Scott in particular see Gavin Stamp, *An Architect of Promise: George Gilbert Scott junior (1839–1897) and the late Gothic Revival* (Donington, 2002), ch. 7.

All this, to Jackson, was anathema.[166] Conflict, as a result, was inevitable—and often intense.

The crisis point in his relationship with the SPAB came with the restoration of St Mary the Virgin in Oxford.[167] Jackson's work in this, the university church, began in 1891. The tower was in a perilous condition, and Jackson's survey showed that it needed urgent restoration if it were not to prove dangerous. Two parts of the spire, in particular, caused concern. Both the statues and the pinnacles were in a worrying condition and, although they had been restored as recently as 1852, they were close to collapse. Jackson recommended that both pinnacles and statues be replaced. This was a big job; indeed it was estimated that it would cost nearly £9,000 to complete.[168] It was also to prove hugely controversial. Each of these elements—the statues and the pinnacles—had their defenders. The SPAB was particularly concerned about the statuary and on 23 December 1892, Thackeray Turner wrote on its behalf to Jackson. He appealed to the architect to retain the statues if at all possible. Graham Jackson was presumed to be an ally, and so the letter was especially mollifying. The Society, wrote Turner, 'are confident that you will agree, and they venture to hope that you will use your influence to prevent the threatened mischief'.[169] He could not have been more wrong.

Jackson was furious at this interference in his work. He replied in the most aggressive of terms, and—worse still—sent the correspondence to the *Times*. He wrote:

With the abstract principles your letter enunciates I quite agree, and I need hardly say I deplore the ruin of these interesting sculptures as much as you do—perhaps even more, because I know them better. But I can hardly advise the University, as you desire me, to let them remain and continue to shed their heads, hands, and other members, as they have latterly done, to the peril of the church and the passers by. Nor can I advise them to remove the statues and leave the niches empty. Nor need I doubt our ability to do as well as our predecessors of 40 years ago, whose work you mistake for genuine sculpture of the 14th century.[170]

This was slashing stuff, indeed. Jackson had accused the SPAB of ignorance, impracticality, and irrelevance. As Chris Miele has observed, these were criticisms with some justification.[171] But the Society could scarcely leave them unchallenged. For the next month, letters flew between numbers 9 and 14 Buckingham Street, the offices of Anti-Scrape and Jackson respectively, and through the pages of the *Times*.[172] The argument became increasingly intemperate, but Jackson was

[166] OUA, NW20/8 St Mary the Virgin 1891–6, Jackson (13 Jan. 1893).

[167] A detailed review of which is in T. G. Jackson, *The Church of St Mary the Virgin* (Oxford, 1897), 149–154, 160–1.

[168] OUA, UC/FF/197/1/1, St Mary's Church Misc. 1867–1927, Report (25 Nov. 1892).

[169] *Times* 28 Dec. 1892, 10.   [170] Ibid.

[171] Chris Miele, 'The Conservationist', in Parry, *Morris*, 75.

[172] *Times*, 3 Jan. 1893, 11; 5 Jan. 1893, 7; 9 Jan. 1893, 14; 10 Jan. 1893, 11. The SPAB report was printed: 17 Jan. 1893, 17.

The Spire and Pinnacles
as reconstructed in 1849-1850
from Mr Buckler's Design

ST MARY
THE VIRGIN
OXFORD.
Proposed repair
and reconstruction
of the Pinnacles.

25. St Mary the Virgin: the proposed restoration.

presumed to have won it. The SPAB, wrote one correspondent, 'have had more than one well-merited rebuff owing to their ill-timed interference; but never such a one as they have just received at the hands of Mr. Jackson'.[173] Nor was this opinion confined to outsiders. S. C. Cockerell, an SPAB stalwart, described at least one of Jackson's letters as 'so admirably done that I cannot see any possible reply that would be effective'.[174] After this, wrote the *Builder*, 'the SPAB will probably see the wisdom of letting Mr. Jackson alone'.[175]

Yet although Graham Jackson 'was supposed to have smashed the opposition', the battle continued.[176] William Morris was drawn into the fray, launching one of his 'most vigorous protests ever'.[177] Worse still, Jackson found himself confronting a revolt of the dons, led by Thomas Case, whose own house he had restored. Case was an active Oxford politician, increasingly conservative and convinced of his own amateur archaeological skills.[178] He was, in short, 'one of those knowing noodles of which Oxford always produces so many', as Morris put it.[179] Case became progressively more and more obsessed with the state of the pinnacles, rather than the statues. These had also been restored in the early 1850s and Case advocated replacing them with a conjectural combination of seventeenth- and fourteenth-century work.[180] It was an argument wholly irrelevant to the SPAB's defence of the statues.[181] Philip Webb, indeed, described Case's proposal as 'illogical [an idea] as . . . an Oxford don's might be expected to be!'[182] Nonetheless, it kept the issue alive. Jackson found himself confronting an opposition made up of his closest allies—the arts and craftsmen and the academics. The conflict fascinated Oxford, and was soon broadcast to a wider audience.[183] By the time Convocation, the university's ruling body, came to vote on the restoration, it had become an issue of national importance. The room was packed.[184] Morris was present, and Case's book on the pinnacles just published.[185] All was set for a dramatic confrontation.[186]

Certainly, the debate was impassioned. William Morris spoke up for his 'ragged regiment' of statues.[187] That argument, however, was now irrelevant. It

[173] SPAB Archive, Oxford St Mary, unattributed article (1893).
[174] SPAB Archive, Oxford St Mary, S. C. Cockerell to Turner (1893).
[175] *Builder* 63 (1892), 516.   [176] Jackson, *Recollections*, 235–6.
[177] Norman Kelvin, ed., *Collected Letters of William Morris* (4 vols.; Princeton, 1984–96), vol. iv, p. xxiv.
[178] E. B. Mowat, ed., *Letters to the 'Times' 1884–1922 Written by Thomas Case* (Oxford, 1927).
[179] Morris, in Kelvin, *Collected Letters*, vol. iv, p. 47.
[180] Thomas Case, *St Mary's Clusters* (Oxford, 1893), 163.
[181] SPAB Archive, Oxford St Mary, Thackeray Turner to G. T. Pilcher (31 May 1893).
[182] Kelvin, *Collected Letters*, vol. iv, p. 51.
[183] *Oxford Magazine* 11 (1892–3), 162, 170, 209, 243, 311, 340, 394, 416, 420, 430–1; suppl., 4; *Oxford University Gazette* 23 (1892–3), 183–4, 433–52, 511, 562; SPAB Archive, Oxford St Mary, *Morning Post* 7 June 1893, *Building News*, 13 Jan. 1893.
[184] *Oxford Magazine* 11 (1892–3), 420.
[185] Jackson, *Recollections*, 234–5; *Oxford Magazine* 11 (1892–3), 430.
[186] *Times*, 7 June 1893, 8.
[187] Jackson, *Recollections*, 235; Kelvin, *Collected Letters*, vol. iv, pp. 46–50.

was the pinnacles that dominated the discussion. Thomas Case, and others, dismissed Jackson's designs. Jackson himself defended his plans. He argued, as the *Times* reported, that whilst 'he had been guided by the principle that not a stone should be tampered with of whatever remained of the original design', the mid-nineteenth-century restorations had made this impossible. 'Where there was nothing to guide one', he maintained, 'archaeology would only hamper, and it was reasonable to aim at beauty.'[188] Evidently others agreed, for the vote reflected his judgement. Only nine people supported design A, which retained the 1852 version of the spire. Another eleven plumped for B, which returned the pinnacles to the version supposedly implied by a print of 1611. Two other proposals remained—both by Jackson. Plan D was approved by the architects Bodley and Garner; plan C was Jackson's own preference. Thirty-two people voted for D, and a hundred and two followed Jackson's advice and chose C. However, when a final vote was taken, there was no absolute majority even for this and a delegacy was set up to resolve the dispute.[189] Models of both Jackson's proposals, and of Case's conjecture, were put up on the tower, and plan D, Jackson's design as approved by Bodley, was selected.[190] The statues, too, were replaced, and new versions carved by George Frampton. Despite the hostility, and despite the debate, Jackson seemed to have won out in the end.

The aftershocks of this event, though, lasted for some time. Completion of work on the spire was the signal for yet more criticism. In 1896 the *Daily Chronicle* ran a series of attacks on Jackson's work at St Mary's.[191] In 1898 Jackson's book on the church served as the opportunity for Henry Wilson to condemn this 'effacement . . . of a social, racial document'.[192] More damagingly still, the rupture between Jackson and the SPAB was never to be healed. During the restoration of Winchester Cathedral, he found himself once again slighted by this 'well-meaning but somewhat hysterical society'.[193] The exchange of letters in the *Times* was similarly ill spirited, and the comparison with St Mary's quite openly made. Indeed, as Thackeray Turner made quite clear, the removal of the statues in Oxford was still seen as a proof of Jackson's bad faith.[194] Events in Oxford had poisoned the relationship between the architect and Anti-Scrape for good. Despite the *Builder*'s suggestion that the SPAB should 'leave Mr. Jackson alone for the future', the abuse continued.[195] As late as 1912, indeed, the SPAB was attacking Jackson's work in precisely the same terms and the controversy over St Mary's was to haunt T. G. Jackson for years to come.[196]

[188] *Times*, 7 June 1893, 8.   [189] *Oxford University Gazette* 23 (1892–3), 511.

[190] OUA, UC/FF/197/1/1, St Mary's Church Misc. 1867–1927, Report (25 Nov. 1892).

[191] SPAB Archive, Oxford, St Mary's, *Daily Chronicle* 21 May, 25 May, 30 May, 6 June 1896.

[192] *Architectural Review* 4 (1898), 3–4, 50.   [193] *Times*, 11 Jan. 1908, 11.

[194] SPAB Archive, 128 (a) Winchester Cathedral, *Times* 7 Jan. 1908.

[195] It went on to observe that the SPAB 'seems to have an unrivalled capacity for making itself disliked and for putting itself in the wrong'. SPAB Archive, 128 (a) Winchester Cathedral, *Builder* 11 Jan. 1908.   [196] *Times*, 21 Nov. 1912, 13.

Nonetheless, it could have been worse. At the height of the crisis, it had appeared that it would split the arts and crafts movement from top to bottom. Graham Jackson's involvement in the Art-Workers' Guild, in particular, had of course always been compromised by his restoration work. As Ashbee put it, his membership risked 'the possibility of a clash at any moment between the "profession" of architecture and the principles of the S.P.A.B.'.[197] The events of 1893 provided just such an opportunity. His appeals rejected by Oxford, William Morris turned to the Art-Workers' Guild for a defence of St Mary's statues. He hoped to commit the Guild to opposing their removal. There was 'great dread of what might happen', recalled Massé; 'no less indeed than the disruption of the Guild following the probable resignation of T. G. Jackson'.[198] He was too important to lose, though, and his loss would be too traumatic. Despite their differences over restoration, it was inconceivable that the Guild could expel someone so committed to its ideals, and so useful in conveying its message. A compromise was soon worked out, and the question was never put.[199] Thus Jackson's relations with Morris remained amicable, and in 1896 he became Master of the Art-Workers' Guild itself.[200]

Jackson's year as Master was especially important for the Guild. It came at a point in which the Guildsmen were beginning to question the purpose of their organization. Many, like Morris, hoped to make it a far more active public force. As early as 1889, the Guild had openly opposed work on St Mary-le-Strand and St Clement Danes.[201] Others now argued that they should seek to elect an Art-Workers' Guild Councillor to advocate craftsmanship and the preservation of ancient buildings on the London County Council.[202] Jackson as Master strongly opposed this move. Partly this was due to his hatred of party politics.[203] More importantly, though, he argued that this would damage the Guild. It would be, he declared, 'departing from the old lines on which it . . . [had] advanced to its present position of usefulness and success'.[204] Instead, he focused on education. Graham Jackson was acutely aware of the need to train the next generation of Guildsmen, and so he founded the Art-Students' Guild, which in 1901 became the Junior Guild. With Walter Crane as its first Master, it was created to teach 'the interdependence of one Art upon another' and thereby prevent students from 'stiffening into mere narrow practitioners running blindly into a groove'. It was, however, a call that went unheeded. The Junior Guild was not a success.[205]

---

[197] NAL, 86/DD/10,11 Ashbee Memoirs, 282.

[198] Massé, *Art-Workers' Guild*, 48. That the threat of Jackson's resignation was real is shown in Jackson MSS, 'Recollections', vol. ii, 468–9.

[199] Sir William Richmond was less fortunate in the dispute over his mosaics for St Paul's Cathedral. See Lynne Brown Walker, 'E. S. Prior, 1852–1932' (Ph.D., London, 1978), 159–60.

[200] Jackson, *Recollections*, 247; Kelvin, *Collected Letters*, vol. iv. p. 54.

[201] *Builder* 56 (1889), 378.   [202] Walker, 'Prior', 157.   [203] *Times*, 30 March 1914, 10.

[204] Massé, *Art-Workers' Guild*, 50.

[205] Jackson's nephew Hugh Arnold was one of the strongest supporters of the Junior Guild: Art-Workers' Guild, *Hugh Arnold* (London, 1916), 13.

Although it produced a number of future Masters, including H. M. Fletcher and Basil Oliver, by 1928 it was agreed to have 'outlived its purpose'.[206] Nonetheless, by resolutely opposing moves into the public sphere and by refocusing attention on its role as an educational organization, Jackson had set the Guild on the path it continues to this day. Its Junior branch may not have thrived, but the values it represented are still informing the society.

The Junior Guild was just one—and, indeed, the least successful—of Jackson's attempts to reform the training of artists and architects. It was part of a much wider movement for change. The 1890s saw a general rejection of the art teaching which had been in place for more than a generation. The 'South Kensington System' of training, which had been established by Henry Cole in 1852 came in for particular condemnation.[207] The ideals behind it were utilitarian, and the approach possessed a Gradgrindian moral force. 'Accuracy in addition and straight lines', claimed Cole, 'are a national want.'[208] His system was designed to satisfy this need, and by 1864 sixteen thousand students were following Cole's method.[209] Hubert von Herkomer, who experienced the South Kensington System, described the faithful copying of geometrically pure designs that it involved as a 'miserable agony'.[210] Certainly, it was not designed to inculcate originality. Less systematic approaches, however, were often no more satisfactory. Victorian architects, in particular, had few opportunities for regular instruction. There was pupilage, of course, but as has already been observed, this was often substandard. Eric Gill, for example, rarely saw his master and recalled that Caröe 'had no time to teach his pupils'.[211] Nor were classes at the Royal Academy much more use; as Lethaby recalled, 'It was good fun, but it was anarchy.'[212] A new way forward had to be found. Jackson's role in tracing the way ahead was critical, and has been almost universally undervalued.[213]

Jackson's interest in education can be seen throughout his life. Like many other architects, he had his own pupils.[214] Whilst building in Oxford, he organized talks for his workmen.[215] He himself gave lectures, travelling across the country from Leeds to London,[216] and including a series for the Royal Academy.[217] He was, indeed, offered the Professorship of Architecture by his

---

[206] Massé, *Art-Workers' Guild*, 3, 28.

[207] NA, ED 23/4, Report by Sir J. F. D. Donnelly (29 June 1896).

[208] Quoted in Stuart Macdonald, *The History and Philosophy of Art Education* (London, 1970), 228. See also Elizabeth Bonython and Anthony Burton, *The Great Exhibitor: the life and work of Henry Cole* (London, 2003), chs. 7 and 13.

[209] W. B. Stephens, 'The Victorian Art Schools and Technical Education: a case study, 1850–1889', *Journal of Educational Administration and History* 2/1 (1969), 13–19, at 13.

[210] In Macdonald, *Art Education*, 232.   [211] Eric Gill, *Autobiography* (London, 1942), 95.

[212] W. R. Lethaby, 'Richard Phené Spiers', *RIBA Journal* 3rd series 23 (1916), 334.

[213] Although see Quentin Hughes, 'Education and the Architectural Profession in Britain at the Turn of the Century', *Art and Design Education* 1 (1982), 135–44.

[214] A list is given in Jackson, *Life and Travels*, 303.   [215] Jackson, *Life and Travels*, 137.

[216] T. G. Jackson, 'The Commonplace of Architecture', *Builder* 48 (1885), 425–6, 441–3.

[217] Published, of course, as *Reason in Architecture* (London, 1906).

fellow academicians,[218] and although he turned it down, he continued to act as a visitor to the Royal Academy Schools.[219] He was an examiner there, too, and also for the National Competition of the Schools of Art.[220] The books, the letters, and the lectures, the visiting and the examining, were all part of a life-long commitment to education. But Jackson's involvement in the reform of art teaching came about in response to a specific set of circumstances. In the first place, there was the widely acknowledged failure of the existing system. Secondly, the alternatives appeared no more appealing. In particular, Jackson saw the proposed compulsory registration of architects as a real threat to his hopes of artistic change. From the end of the 1880s to the beginning of the 1900s, Jackson fought an occasionally lonely and often unpleasant battle against the RIBA and those who wished to 'make architecture a close profession like law and physic'.[221] The compulsorily registered architect of Jackson's nightmares would study architecture 'as a profession and not as an art . . . from text-books and authorities, just as a lawyer gets up law from Blackstone or Coke'.[222] This was the direct opposite of his vision of architecture as an art and of the 'architect's work [as] the direction of a variety of handicrafts'.[223] It was thus in defence of the arts and crafts movement that T. G. Jackson entered the field of educational theory.

Graham Jackson's commitment to 'art-architecture' and opposition to professionalization was challenged by an equally determined group of protagonists.[224] The Institute, as Jackson's generation called the RIBA, had first instituted a voluntary professional examination as early as 1863, although it had not been a success. Between its inception and 1881 the exam was held only a dozen times and only forty-six architects passed it. Determined to reverse this setback, the RIBA made the test a compulsory qualification for entrance to the Institute.[225] At the same time, important figures like William H. White, Secretary to the RIBA; Phené Spiers, the *Beaux-Arts* educated master at the Royal Academy Schools; and Arthur Cates, a member of the Institute's Executive Committee, began to press for professional architecture and for obligatory registration of all architects via the RIBA's qualifying test.[226] Similarly, in 1884, the Society

[218] Jackson, *Life and Travels*, 242.
[219] Between 1892 and 1908: Royal Academy, *Annual Report*, 1892–1908. He was also a visitor to the Architectural Association: John Summerson, *The Architectural Association* (London, 1947), 31.
[220] e.g. *Parliamentary Papers* 1900, vol. 19, pp. 59–60: with G. F. Bodley, Aston Webb, J. J. Stevenson, and John Belcher.   [221] NAAA, *Transactions* 1888, 202.
[222] *Nineteenth Century* 33 (1893), 408.   [223] NAAA, *Transactions* 1890, 84.
[224] For the background to this, see J. Mordaunt Crook, 'The Pre-Victorian Architect: professionalism and patronage', *Architectural History* 12 (1969), 62–78. For a wider context: W. J. Reader, *Professional Men: the rise of the professional classes in nineteenth-century England* (London, 1966), 117–18 and Harold Perkin, *The Rise of Professional Society* (London and New York, 1989).
[225] J. A. Gotch, 'The Royal Institute of British Architects', in J. A. Gotch, ed., *The Growth and Work of the Royal Institute of British Architects 1834–1924* (London, 1934), 25–31.
[226] RIBA *Transactions* 1883–4, pp. 66–73; *Proceedings* 1883–4, 93–111, 126–31.

of Architects was established to promote 'the Statutory Education and Registration of Architects'.[227] The aim of both these groups was clear: they wished to prevent the unqualified from practising as architects. But they recognized that only primary parliamentary legislation could achieve this change.[228] Campaigning, lobbying and, in the case of the Society of Architects, public speaking tours of Britain, were all used in an effort to effect reform.[229] It was this activity, and this publicity, that led them inexorably into a collision course with Jackson.

The first attempt at introducing a bill to register architects was made in 1887. It was opposed by the RIBA and by the representative bodies of the surveyors and the engineers. It was badly drafted and failed to satisfy even the most enthusiastic supporters of compulsory registration.[230] Nonetheless, Jackson saw the danger to come. He devoted a lecture at the Architectural Association to opposing the bill and attempted to persuade Norman Shaw to join his attacks. Both the *Builder* and Shaw thought that he took this threat far too seriously—and the proposal was indeed easily defeated.[231] Three years later, however, another bill was proposed, and the threat of its becoming law seemed all the more serious. Although the RIBA once again denied its support, the forces behind registration had grown much stronger.[232] This time, as Jackson recalled, 'Norman Shaw took it up hot'.[233] Nor did he exaggerate; Shaw's position was utterly changed. 'It must be war now, and no quarter', he wrote to Reginald Blomfield.[234] Shaw mobilized his pupils and allies and, at his invitation, Jackson and others were invited to discuss the crisis at Mervyn Macartney's house. The protest which they sent to the *Times* was drafted by Jackson, and signed by seventy leading artists and architects. The memorialists, as they became known, included Bentley, Butterfield, and Bodley; Brown and Burne-Jones; Alma Tadema, William Morris, Philip Webb, and three score of others. Even Phené Spiers opposed the move 'to make Architecture a close profession' through compulsory registration.[235] Jackson followed the memorial up with further letters to the *Times*; an enthusiastically received lecture at the Architectural Association; and—more importantly—by editing a book.[236]

Architecture, a Profession or an Art,[237] the volume which was issued under the names of both Graham Jackson and Norman Shaw, has been so often described

[227] Barrington Kaye, *The Development of the Architectural Profession in England* (London, 1960), 143; C. MacArthur Butler, *The Society of Architects* (London, 1926), 51.

[228] Lawrence Booth, 'The Institute and Architectural Education', *Builder* 52 (1887), 700–1.

[229] Butler, *Society of Architects*, 52.   [230] RIBA, *Proceedings* 1889, 339.

[231] *Builder* 53 (1887), 869, 873–5.   [232] Alfred Waterhouse in *Times* 9 March 1891, 10.

[233] Jackson, *Life and Travels*, 261.   [234] Summerson, *Architectural Association*, 32.

[235] Jackson, *Life and Travels*, 262–3; *Times*, 3 March 1891, 9.

[236] *Times*, 7 March 1891, 15; 12 March 1891, 3; 17 Nov. 1891, 3; T. G. Jackson, 'The Training of Architects to the Pursuit of Architecture', *Builder* 61 (1891), 460–3; Summerson, *Architectural Association*, 32.

[237] R. Norman Shaw and T. G. Jackson, eds., *Architecture, a Profession or an Art* (London, 1892).

that it may seem almost unnecessary to discuss it again.[238] But, in fact, the book has generally been misunderstood, and often misinterpreted. Nor has Jackson's contribution been fully appreciated. Although Andrew Saint quite rightly sees Norman Shaw as the 'ringleader of the protest' and the initiator of the campaign, he plays down the fact that Jackson was the editor of the book that the campaign produced, 'with full powers of revising and arranging' its contents.[239] And, as Saint reveals, it was an important book: 'the one significant manifesto of the late-Victorian art-architects and one of the rare British books to conduct a reasoned argument on a matter of architectural principle'.[240] It was introduced and concluded by Jackson, and contained essays by many of his closest allies. In addition to Norman Shaw and G. F. Bodley, the writers included Reginald Blomfield, Mervyn Macartney, Edward Prior, Basil Champneys, W. R. Lethaby, and J. T. Micklethwaite. These were men who shared Jackson's commitment to the arts and crafts movement, and who were distanced from Shaw's belief in the architect as an 'isolated designer of masterpieces'.[241] Gerald Horsley's essay on 'The Unity of Art' summed up their creed, and it was one they had learned from Jackson, not from Shaw.

The book was a *cause célèbre*. J. T. Emmett, in particular, saw it as 'the proclamation of a renovated architectural faith, and the first recommencement of sincere, artistic, building'.[242] The writers not only wished to oppose the creation of a 'close and self-elected corporation' or 'privileged caste' of architect-surveyors.[243] They hoped also to advocate a complete reform of architectural practice, based on the arts and crafts movement.[244] It was here that the book showed its greatest weakness, however. As Lord Grimthorpe was only too pleased to point out, the views of the memorialists, like those of all the arts and craftsmen, were often confused and inchoate. 'If the revival of architecture', he wrote 'is to depend upon such a series of unpractical, visionary, impossible essays and remedies as [Jackson] has now given us, it is indeed hopelessly sunk.'[245] Certainly, as Andrew Saint has noted, the book was not wholly successful: 'its critique was too shallow, its standpoint (from the highest echelon of architectural practice) too restricted'. Although the compulsory registration bill was abandoned in 1891, the RIBA became progressively more and more

---

[238] See especially, Mark Crinson and Jules Lubbock, *Architecture, Art or Profession?* (Manchester and New York, 1994), 62–4; Jenkins, *Architect and Patron*, 224; Kaye, *Architectural Profession*, 140–7; A. A. R. Powers, 'Architectural Education in Britain 1880–1914' (Ph.D., Cambridge, 1982), 33–44; Saint, *Image of the Architect*, 63–7.

[239] Saint, *Shaw*, 319; *Image of the Architect*, 64; Jackson MSS, 'Recollections' vol. ii, 443. See also Lord Grimthorpe, 'Architecture, a Profession or an Art?', *Nineteenth Century* 33 (1893), 73.

[240] Saint, *Image of the Architect*, 64.   [241] Saint, *Shaw*, 319.

[242] [J. T. Emmett], 'Architecture, a Business, a Profession, or an Art?', *Quarterly Review* 176 (1893), 40–72, at 40.

[243] Jackson, in Shaw and Jackson, *Architecture*, 214; *Nineteenth Century* 33, 411.

[244] Horsley, in Shaw and Jackson, *Architecture*, 195.   [245] *Nineteenth Century* 33, 634.

committed to the principle.[246] As soon as a majority of architects were members of the Institute, the legislation would be passed—as in 1931 it was.[247]

One essay, however, was of immediate and direct importance: T. G. Jackson's chapter 'On True and False Ideals in the Education of an Architect'. In it, Jackson confronted many of the problems that were ignored by other writers. He mocked the pretensions of the RIBA; challenged the idea that a written examination could diagnose architectural genius; and attacked the 'pretence of protecting the public' which merely concealed an attempt to raise the social standing of the architectural profession. Moreover, unlike most of his fellow memorialists, he recognized that the majority of buildings were not designed by architects. Creating a sharp distinction between registered architects and unregistered builders, Jackson argued, would perpetuate current problems. His goal was to make architects master-builders; to return them to craftsmanship. Compulsory registration was for him a barrier to the unity of art. Instead, reform of architectural education was needed. This, and this alone, could save British design. Jackson imagined a 'National School of Architecture, to which anyone connected with building could have access, whether he intended to be an architect, or a builder, or a craftsman in one of the arts connected with building'. They would be taught together by 'the best masters of the art', given practical experience and theoretical training.[248] It was, as Quentin Hughes and Godfrey Rubens have written, a profoundly important idea.[249] To be sure, Jackson was not the first to suggest such a thing: in 1864 Gilbert Scott had talked of a central school of architecture run by the RIBA and the Architectural Association.[250] But Graham Jackson's arts and crafts ethos had given the school a wholly different form. Here, both artists and craftsmen were to be on equal terms. The unity of art was to be embodied in a unified curriculum.

This National School of Art is easily dismissed as utopian, but in fact Jackson was to come close to realizing it in practice.[251] His opportunity came as the older systems broke down. From 1881 the Birmingham School of Art began the process of abandoning the South Kensington System.[252] In 1894 W. R. Lethaby founded the Central School of Arts and Crafts in London.[253] Here the students were to learn through practical experience, training in a workshop and handling materials and tools.[254] This was just what Jackson had hoped for, but his

[246] Harry Barnes, 'Registration', in Gotch, ed., *Growth and Work of the RIBA*, 70–4.
[247] Saint, *Image of the Architect*, 66–7.
[248] Jackson, in Shaw and Jackson, *Architecture*, 208–37.
[249] Quentin Hughes, 'Before the Bauhaus: the experiment at the Liverpool School of Architecture and its Applied Arts', *Architectural History* 25 (1982), 102–13, at 104–6; Godfrey Rubens, *William Richard Lethaby: his life and work, 1857–1931* (London, 1986), 203.
[250] Summerson, *Architectural Association*, 19.   [251] Powers, 'Architectural Education', 40.
[252] Hughes, 'Education and the Architectural Professional', 139; John Swift, *Changing Fortunes: the Birmingham School of Art Building 1880–1995* (Birmingham, 1996), 14–15.
[253] Theresa Gronberg, 'William Richard Lethaby and the Central School of Arts and Crafts', in Backemeyer and Gronberg, *Lethaby*, 16–18.   [254] Rubens, *Lethaby*, 188.

influence was (to say the least) unclear. Nor did either of these schools offer improved architectural training.[255] It was in Liverpool in 1894 that Jackson was to have his most palpable effect on art teaching, with the foundation of the School of Architecture and Applied Art.[256] As its name implies, this was the first time that all the arts, both 'major' and 'minor', had been united in one institution. Architecture was the pivot around which the course revolved.[257]

It was, in that sense, a far more radical experiment than had been attempted elsewhere. It was also exactly the model that Jackson had advocated: 'It is in the *rapprochement* of our architecture to the handicrafts—of the architect to the craftsman—that I see the only opening by which we are likely to make any sensible progress', he had written.[258] Now was the chance to see if this would work. The head of the new school was F. M. Simpson, a member of the Art-Workers' Guild, one of the Memorialists, and a protégé of Jackson's.[259] Indeed, it is clear that Jackson got Simpson the job.[260] He had evidently learnt from Jackson's writings on architectural education, and came to Liverpool committed to putting Jackson's ideals into practice.[261] The curriculum was thus devised in collaboration with the great architect himself, and with its insistence on practical training and experiencing all aspects of craftsmanship, it embodied Jackson's thought exactly.[262] The similarity between this and the architectural training he had proposed three years earlier was not lost on Jackson himself when he opened the Liverpool School in 1895. His 'Utopian Dream', he declared, had come true.[263]

Jackson's involvement in educational reform did not cease with the Liverpool experiment. He was also to take his ideas to the National Art Training School. This was at the heart of the South Kensington System, and as such it was the subject of continual criticism by those who opposed conventional art teaching.[264] After thirty years, change was overdue—and on its way. In 1896, the National School became the Royal College of Art (or RCA).[265] In 1898, Walter Crane, the arts and crafts designer, was appointed principal.[266] Finding its curriculum 'terribly mechanical and lifeless', he soon resigned his post.[267] But in

[255] T. G. Jackson, 'Architecture, a Profession or an Art', *Nineteenth Century* 33 (1893), 406; NAAA, *Transactions* 1888, 194.
[256] Lionel B. Budden, ed., *The Book of the Liverpool School of Architecture* (London, 1932), 33–4.   [257] Hughes, 'Education and the Architectural Profession', 138–9.
[258] T. G. Jackson, 'Presidential Address', NAAA, *Transactions* 1891, 84.
[259] Powers, 'Architectural Education', 66. Jackson nominated Simpson as ARA.
[260] Alan Powers, 'Liverpool and Architectural Education', in Joseph Sharples, Alan Powers, Michael Shippobottom, eds., *Charles Reilly and the Liverpool School of Architecture* (Liverpool, 1996), 4; Jackson MSS, 'Recollections', vol. ii., 504.
[261] Fred Simpson, *Architectural Education* (London, 1896).
[262] Macdonald, 'Schools of Arts and Crafts', 132; Hughes, 'Education and the Architectural Profession', 139; *Builder* 68 (1895), 370; *RIBA Journal* ii (1894–5), 635.
[263] T. G. Jackson, *Some Thoughts on the Training of Architects* (Liverpool, 1895), 37.
[264] Christopher Frayling, *The Royal College of Art* (London, 1987).
[265] *Studio* 9 (1896–7), 62.   [266] Isobel Spencer, *Walter Crane* (London, 1975), 166–7.
[267] Crane, *Reminiscences*, 457.

1900 real reform began. The newly established Board of Education appointed a Council of Advice on Art, and this Council took as its first priority the reorganization of the Royal College. There were four members, each representing a different art: Sir William Richmond for painting, Onslow Ford for sculpture, Walter Crane for design, and T. G. Jackson for architecture. With the appointment of these four men, the Art-Workers' Guild had made a clean sweep.[268] They acted quickly, dividing the College into schools of architecture, painting, sculpture, and design, under Beresford Pite, Gerald Moira, Edward Lanteri, and William Lethaby.[269] Each student was to be taught in a workshop and obtain practical experience of their subject. All students were to be required to study in each of the departments and gain some knowledge of each craft.[270] Walter Crane claimed the credit for this reform, and he has often been given it alone.[271] But Jackson played an important role too. He was clearly responsible for drafting much of the syllabus, and the curriculum reflected many of his own priorities.[272] In particular, the requirement that all students should undergo a period of training in the school of architecture, was clearly a Jacksonian innovation.[273] Making architecture the crux of all artistic education was what he had done at Liverpool. In this way he hoped 'to bring all the arts into union'.[274] Working with his arts and crafts colleagues, he was able to ensure that his goal would be reached.

More accurately, perhaps, at least Jackson was able to try. His achievements in Liverpool, at the Royal College of Art, and across the country were impressive. The Parisian *Ecole des Beaux-Arts* was inclined to defer to English models for the first time, following his reforms at the RCA.[275] The division of the College into separate departments was copied throughout England after the First World War.[276] The Liverpool School of Architecture, as both Hughes and Macdonald have observed, prefigured the Bauhaus by a quarter of a century.[277] But in all these cases, Jackson was forced to compromise and work with others who had very different ideas. Never was that made more clear than in the 1903–6 Board of Architectural Education. This was established by Aston Webb, the president of the RIBA, and was an attempt to reconcile the memorialists with the Institute and produce a national syllabus for architectural education.[278] It proved highly

---

[268] Macdonald, 'Schools of Arts and Crafts', 124.

[269] NA, ED 24/56A Royal College of Art 1871–1900, Memorandum (June, 1900); ED 9/11, Royal College of Art, Prospectus (1901).

[270] Frank P. Brown, *South Kensington and its Art Training* (London, 1912), 32.

[271] Crane, *Reminiscences*, 459; Frayling, *Royal College of Art*, 67.

[272] NA, ED 9/11 Royal College of Art, Minutes of Council of Advice on Art.

[273] Parliamentary Papers 1911, vol. 18: Reports, 549–609.

[274] Jackson, *Life and Travels*, 240.   [275] Brown, *South Kensington*, 32.

[276] Macdonald, 'Schools of Arts and Crafts', 125.

[277] Hughes, 'Before the Bauhaus', 107; Macdonald, 'Schools of Arts and Crafts', 132.

[278] Henry M. Fletcher, 'The RIBA and Architectural Education', in Gotch, ed., *Growth and Work of the RIBA*, 90–3.

successful. Many of those who had resigned from the RIBA in 1891 rejoined and others were quite willing to participate in discussions. Basil Champneys became Vice-Chairman whilst Reginald Blomfield was an honorary secretary. Other arts and craftsmen were similarly involved: Beresford Pite and Leonard Stokes from within the Institute, William Lethaby and Edward Prior from without.[279] Jackson feared that this new body would insidiously lead to registration, but nonetheless agreed to represent the Royal Academy in its deliberations.[280] Although his work for the Board has been largely ignored, it is clear that he was highly involved.[281] Moreover, as Godfrey Rubens has noted, the syllabus of 1906 which it produced reflected many of his ideas.[282] With its emphasis on practical experience, on pupilage, on the evolution of architecture 'through constructional and social conditions', it was very much a Jacksonian project.[283] But there were inevitable compromises. So much so indeed, that the curriculum can be seen as a catchall, certainly capable of uniting both arts and crafts and *Beaux-Arts* approaches, but only in a hollow consensus amounting to very little in practice.[284] It was not until 1911 that a clear programme of architectural training was conceived, and by then Jackson's influence and the Guild tradition were on the wane.[285]

Indeed, many of Jackson's successes were to be threatened or overturned. The Liverpool School of Architecture was always underfunded, and Jackson's craftsmen were soon swamped by paying students, pursuing hobbies rather than vocations.[286] Worse still, in 1904, Charles Reilly succeeded Simpson, and brought with him classical *Beaux-Arts* training. The arts and crafts were soon unwelcome in Liverpool.[287] Nor was the RCA an unmitigated triumph. The reforms were variously attacked as too sweeping,[288] and too limited.[289] In 1911 a Departmental Committee recommended that the Royal College be disbanded in favour of a more devolved system of training.[290] Here, though, there were strong defenders of the curriculum so newly established, and it was more or less retained.[291] Nonetheless, the loss of Liverpool and the challenge to the Royal College were signs of the times. Jackson and his approach were growing dated. And this proves a point. For in this case—as in so many others—his success was critically linked to the growth of the arts and crafts movement. As it declined, so

[279] RIBA Archive, 'Special Committee Minutes' 4 (1899–1908), 98.
[280] Blomfield, *Memoirs*, 105.
[281] Powers, 'Architectural Education', 86–7; RIBA Archive, 'Special Committee Minutes' (1899–1901), 4, 106, 119.   [282] Rubens, *Lethaby*, 214.
[283] RIBA *Kalender* 1905–6, ix–xv.   [284] Crinson and Lubbock, *Architecture*, 74–5.
[285] Reginald Blomfield, *RIBA Journal* 3rd Series 18 (1910–11), 767–70.
[286] Hughes, 'Education and the Architectural Profession', 141.
[287] See Sharples *et al.*, *Charles Reilly*.
[288] Martin A. Buckmaster, 'Further Remarks on Art Teaching in Secondary and Other Schools', *Art Workers' Quarterly* 4 (1905), 70–3.
[289] C. R. Ashbee, *Should We Stop Teaching Art?* (London, 1911).
[290] Parliamentary Papers 1911, vol. 18, 549–609.   [291] *Daily Telegraph*, 27 March 1911, 8.

did his influence.[292] Not that he was a mere hanger on, of course. Jackson, as a writer, a practitioner, a leader, and a teacher, was in fact amongst the most important figures in the arts and crafts movement itself. But this could be a difficult position to sustain. The diversity and inconsistency of the movement and its commitment to abstract principles which were difficult to honour in practice, made leadership a challenging and impossible role. Nonetheless, Jackson fulfilled a need and Reginald Blomfield was not alone in his praise for this labour. 'We younger men', he wrote, 'were fortunate in having Shaw and Jackson as our leaders.'[293] Ultimately, Jackson's contribution was valued, even if it is forgotten today.

[292] Tillyard, *Impact of Modernism*, 35–6.   [293] Blomfield, *Memoirs*, 65.

3

'The Maker of Modern Oxford'[1]
Jackson and the Architecture of Progress

Amidst much pageantry, carefully choreographed by Lord Curzon, on 28 June 1911 T. G. Jackson was awarded an honorary doctorate by the University of Oxford.[2] It was a tribute by his *Alma Mater* to a man who 'might most rightly be called the . . . creator of modern Oxford', as the Professor of Poetry put it. Never one to underestimate his own value, Jackson accepted this affirmation of his importance with apparent equanimity.[3] And indeed, whilst the orator's comparison between Jackson and Vitruvius now seems more than a little over-stated, his importance to the University is undeniable. Even Nikolaus Pevsner, who found his work unpalatable, was nonetheless prepared to admit that once Jackson had 'set his elephantine feet' on the City, 'Oxford would never be the same again'.[4] Celebrated in his life as 'Oxford Jackson', he is recognized by more sympathetic critics as a hugely important figure in the architectural history of the city.[5] J. Mordaunt Crook, for one, is clear that 'the appearance of Oxford in modern times owes more to Jackson than to any one man'.[6] From his first major commission, the New Examination Schools (1876–83), to his last, at Hertford College (1923–6), Jackson did indeed dominate the architecture of the University. He brought with him a new approach and a new style. He transformed the image of Oxford.[7]

T. G. Jackson's success lay not just in what he was building. It was equally significant how and for whom he was designing. The architect, and the style in

---

[1] *Oxford Journal*, 13 Oct. 1900, 5.

[2] David Cannadine, *Aspects of Aristocracy* (London, 1994), 97–9.

[3] T. G. Jackson, *Recollections: the life and travels of a Victorian architect* (Sir Nicholas Jackson, ed.; London, 2003), 249.

[4] J. Sherwood and N. Pevsner, *The Buildings of England: Oxfordshire* (London, 1974), 59.

[5] Alastair Martin, 'Oxford Jackson', *Oxoniensia* xliii (1974), 216–21.

[6] J. Mordaunt Crook, 'T. G. Jackson and the Cult of Eclecticism', in H. Searing, ed., *In Search of Modern Architecture* (New York, 1982), 107.

[7] The standard accounts of Oxford's architecture in this period are both by Peter Howell, 'Oxford Architecture 1800–1914', in M. G. Brock and M. C. Curthoys, eds., *The History of the University of Oxford* vol. vii (Oxford, 2000), 729–80 and 'Architecture and Townscape since 1800', in R. C. Whiting, ed., *Oxford: studies in the history of a university town* (Manchester, 1993), 53–84. An exemplary introduction to Oxford architecture as a whole is provided by Geoffrey Tyack, *Oxford: an architectural guide* (Oxford and New York, 1998).

which he built, expressed a particular approach both to Oxford and to education. That indeed, was the secret of his success. Jackson, and the 'Anglo-Jackson' style, were taken up by Oxford's academic reformers and used to identify their projects, mark their colleges, and symbolize the reformed university. In the process of reform, architecture was used as a rhetorical device, signifying difference. The university for which Jackson first built in the early 1870s was celibate, monastic, and medieval. By the turn of the century, it had reformed, revived, and was reworking Renaissance motifs. Jackson's work symbolized this change. It represents part of a general movement of 'reforming architecture' now made famous as Mark Girouard's architecture of 'Sweetness and Light'.[8] As Deborah Weiner has shown of late-Victorian London, many institutions built in this period were designed to be read by their users as embodiments of a reforming ethos.[9] Jackson's work was no less symbolically significant in Oxford. He expressed the ideals of the progressives, and recast the idea of Oxford.[10]

The university which the observer would have seen in the late 1860s was very different from that which Jackson finally left in 1924. It was an apparently unchanging icon, with its 'mellow old Colleges, standing as they ever did and will—staunch old Tories'.[11] Embodied in that image was a sense of the buildings symbolizing immovable and incorruptible tradition within an ever-evolving world. Oxford was a Gothic town, 'whispering from her towers the last enchantments of the Middle Age'.[12] It was 'an oasis in a desert of change'.[13] The men who overthrew this Gothic ideal were Jackson's patrons. They were known as the party of progress, and they sought, as Goldwin Smith put it, to 'strike off the fetter of medieval statutes from [the University] and the Colleges, set it free from the predominance of ecclesiasticism, recall it to its proper work, and restore it to the nation'.[14]

Architecture was an important part of this change. After all, Smith blamed Oxford's conservatism on 'Celibate fellowships, mediaeval buildings and the statutes of mediaeval founders'.[15] Each of these had to change if Oxford was to reform and modernize. The acknowledged leader of this party of reformers was Benjamin Jowett, from 1871 the Master of Balliol College. He famously observed that 'I should like to govern the world through my pupils', and he came very close to achieving his goal.[16] Jowett's focus was on undergraduate teaching

[8] Mark Girouard, *Sweetness and Light: the 'Queen Anne' movement, 1860–1900* (Oxford, 1977).
[9] Deborah E. B. Weiner, *Architecture and Social Reform in Late-Victorian London* (Manchester and New York, 1994).
[10] See also William Whyte, 'Anglo-Jackson Attitudes: reform and the rebuilding of Oxford', *The Victorian* 12 (2003), 4–9.   [11] *Oxford Journal*, 14 Oct. 1871, 6.
[12] Matthew Arnold, *Essays in Criticism* (London and Cambridge, 1865), xviii.
[13] *Oxford Journal*, 14 Oct. 1871, 6.
[14] Evelyn Abbott and Lewis Campbell, *The Life and Letters of Benjamin Jowett* (2 vols., London, 1897), vol. i, p. 177.
[15] Goldwin Smith, 'Oxford University Reform', in *Oxford Essays* (1858), 265–87, at 266.
[16] Richard Symonds, *Oxford and Empire* (London, 1986), 24.

and on building Oxford into a nursery for Britain's future leaders. The university was to expand and extend its constituency to include people from all creeds and classes. Tutorial teaching, lecturing, examinations, and sport were to build future statesmen and scholars.[17] It was this group that created modern Oxford, and to this caucus that Jackson pledged his allegiance. 'My sympathies', he recalled, 'were all with the party of progress.'[18] As a fellow of Wadham he was involved in precisely those reforms which Jowett advocated;[19] as an architect he embodied these reforms in stone. Together, the party of progress destroyed the calm of the university, leaving the curiously nostalgic radical William Tuckwell to bemoan that 'The Oxford of today is not the Oxford of my youth.'[20] And that, indeed, was the point.

Change came slowly, however. The party of progress was forced to contend with other, competing visions of Oxford. One came from a former ally of Jowett's: Mark Pattison, the Rector of Lincoln College from 1861. He gradually became convinced of the necessity for research to predominate within the university. Oxford was to be an oasis of the intellect: a beacon of light in a darkening world.[21] There was little room for undergraduates in Pattison's vision of Oxford—and, indeed, he defined the difference between himself and Jowett in precisely these terms: a distinction of 'Science and Learning *v.* School Keeping'.[22] Pattison was joined by C. E. Appleton, a Fellow of St John's College, A. H. Sayce, a Fellow of The Queen's College, and several others in arguing repeatedly for the 'Endowment of Research'.[23] Together, these 'Researchers' or 'Educationalists', were to prove persistent and effective propagandists, and able opponents of the party of progress.[24]

This academic battle was further complicated by the existence of a third group of combatants. The 'Non-Placet Society', as it came to be called, was opposed to almost all change.[25] Its members were united by a distaste for what they believed was 'Progress: falsely so-called'. Pattison was condemned as a 'troglodyte', and Jowett damned as a 'Poseur' and 'ruthless seeker after notoriety' who 'represented all we disliked'.[26] Their leader was the reactionary James Bellamy, from 1871 the President of St John's College; a 'Conservative of

[17] Geoffrey Faber, *Jowett: A Portrait with Background* (London, 1957).
[18] T. G. Jackson, *Recollections* (B. H. Jackson, ed.; Oxford, 1950), 105.
[19] WCA, 2/4, 'Convention Book 1829–1944', 162, 173.
[20] Bod., MS Top. Oxon. b.164, William Tuckwell, 'Reminiscences of Oxford' (1900), 243–5.
[21] Mark Pattison, *Suggestions on Academical Organisation* (Edinburgh, 1868). See also, John Sparrow, *Mark Pattison and the Idea of a University* (Cambridge, 1967), 194.
[22] V. H. H. Green, *Oxford Common Room: a study of Lincoln College and Mark Pattison* (London, 1957), 260.
[23] J. H. Appleton and A. H. Sayce, *Dr. Appleton, His Life and Literary Relics* (London, 1881), 10–20; Diderick Roll-Hansen, *The Academy 1869–1879, Victorian Intellectuals in Revolt* (Copenhagen, 1957), 57, 61, 73–90.   [24] A. H. Sayce, *Reminiscences* (London, 1923), 88.
[25] *Oxford Magazine* v (17 June 1887), 271.
[26] Charles Oman, *Memories of Victorian Oxford* (London, 1942), 210, 232, 239, 209, 234.

Conservatives' who had made St John's the 'centre of that cause'.[27] But the Non-Placet Society stretched throughout the university, and it proved a formidable obstacle to change. Clever, committed, and completely ruthless, the Non-Placets railed against reform and agitated against change. They saw them-selves as defenders of an unchanging university, the true Oxford, against an invasion by the Greekless, the Godless, and—worst of all—women.[28]

As if these competing parties did not make university government difficult enough, Oxford's complex system of decision-making made consensus vital and hard to achieve. Every college, ruled by its self-elected fellows in an autonomous Governing Body, was a law unto itself. Even within the University, power was split between several competing—and often conflicting—institutions. Legislation originated with the Hebdomadal Council. This comprised the Chancellor (who never attended), the Vice Chancellor (whose term of office lasted four years and who was chosen from amongst the heads of colleges), two Proctors (who served for a year at a time and were appointed by each college in turn), and eighteen elected officials, chosen by a body called Congregation. Congregation itself was made up of all Oxford MAs living within a mile and a half of Carfax, a crossroads at the centre of the city. Its job was to approve legis-lation proposed by Council. Once this was done, the statutes passed to Convocation for final clearance. Any MA, whether resident or not could vote at Convocation. And whilst amongst the residents, as a reformer smugly explained, 'Liberalism has become co-extensive with intelligence',[29] Convocation remained the last bastion of the backwoodsmen.[30] Disagreement was always possible, and rarely avoided. Oxford men, as Leslie Stephen once observed, always seemed to be indulging in 'battles royal'.[31]

Some of the key crisis points for the university, and the parties contending within it, came with the construction of buildings. They were seen by particip-ants in the debate as symbols of the competing ideas of Oxford. This tendency became more pronounced as the battle of the styles intensified. Thus Pugin's plans for a rebuilt Balliol were rejected on the grounds of his Roman Catholicism, whilst the erection of the Martyrs' Memorial (1841–3) represented an attempt by orthodox Oxford to dish the Tractarians and damn the papists.[32] Similarly, the University Museum (1855–60), resplendent in its radical Ruskinian Gothic treatment, was condemned as a 'cockatrice's den' by one

[27] Ernest Barker, *Age and Youth* (London, 1953), 42.
[28] R. B. Mowat, ed., *Letters to the 'Times' 1884–1922 Written by Thomas Case* (Oxford, 1927), 22, 31–4, 53, 81.
[29] [Charles Alan Fyffe] 'Study and Opinion in Oxford', *Macmillan's Magazine* 21 (1870), 184–92, at 186.   [30] W. Reginald Ward, *Victorian Oxford* (London, 1965), 291.
[31] [Leslie Stephen], *Sketches from Cambridge by a Don* (London and Cambridge, 1865), 137.
[32] Howard Colvin, *Unbuilt Oxford* (New Haven and London, 1983), ch. 7; Andrew Atherstone, 'The Martyrs' Memorial at Oxford', *Journal of Ecclesiastical History* 54 (2003), 278–301.

divine and shunned as unduly scientific by others. Never properly funded, many details of the building remain uncompleted to this day.[33] But this only makes the point more clearly. The University Museum was recognized as a symbol of a new kind of university—and was always treated as such.[34] In Oxford, architecture was never neutral and never was this clearer than with the building of the New Examination Schools.[35]

The New Schools were fervently supported by the party of progress, and determinedly opposed by both other parties. The Researchers regarded examinations as an 'instrument of mere torture', and viewed lecturing as 'incompatible with research'.[36] The Non-Placet Society saw the emphasis on examination and on lecturing as synonymous with 'the Modern University', and, as such, as thoroughly bad.[37] Only the party of progress was committed to the idea of New Schools. They were a requirement if the university was to expand and to examine increased numbers of students. As the size of the student body rose, and the requirements of the Bodleian Library grew greater, space within the Old Schools Quadrangle was at a premium. To allow their project to succeed, the progressives resolved that New Schools should be built.[38] Disregarding Lord Westbury's helpful advice that the Bodleian's books should be wheeled to the Parks and burnt, as early as 1862 Hebdomadal Council had accepted the progressives' argument.[39] Three years later, in 1865, the site of the Angel Hotel on the High Street was acquired by the University and, after two years of debate, Hebdomadal Council resolved that this would be the ideal place for the New Schools.[40] G. E. Street, the diocesan architect, and T. N. Deane, designer of Christ Church's Meadow Building (1862–6), were invited to compete for the contract. Most Victorian architectural competitions were badly run, but it took a particular genius to produce the debacle that Oxford was to witness.[41] Between 1867 and 1869 a Committee of Council failed to resolve on

[33] J. B. Atlay, *Sir Henry Wentworth Acland: a memoir* (London, 1903), 210, 207; H. W. Acland, *The Oxford Museum* (London, 1859), 28; H. M. and K. Dorothea Vernon, *A History of the Oxford Museum* (Oxford, 1909), 67–8, 75–85.   [34] Acland, *Oxford Museum*, 13–19.

[35] See also, William Whyte, ' "Rooms for the Torture and Shame of Scholars": the New Examination Schools and the architecture of reform', *Oxoniensia* 66 (2001), 85–103. Roland Wilcock, *The Building of Oxford University Examination Schools, 1876–1883* (Oxford, 1983); James Bettley, 'T. G. Jackson and the Examination Schools', *Oxford Art Journal* 6/1 (1983), 57–66; and especially Colvin, *Unbuilt Oxford*, 141–7 are also useful.

[36] Pattison, in A. J. Engel, *From Clergyman to Don: the rise of the academic profession in nineteenth-century Oxford* (Oxford, 1983), 143; A. H. Sayce, 'Results of the Examination System at Oxford', [C. E. Appleton, ed.], *Essays on the Endowment of Research* (London, 1876), 124–48, at 139.

[37] Oman, *Memories*, 239.

[38] Lawrence Stone, 'The Size and Composition of the Oxford Student Body, 1580–1909', in Stone, ed., *The University in Society vol I* (London, 1975), 3–110, at 65–70; Curthoys, 'The Examination System', 340–9; Edmund Craster, *The History of the Bodleian Library 1845–1945* (Oxford, 1952), 61.

[39] Abbott and Campbell, *Jowett*, vol. ii, p. 133; OUA, HC 3/1/1, 'Minutes of Committees of Council 1857–1873', (10 Nov. 1862) 23–4.

[40] The process of acquisition is dealt with in Wilcock, *Examination Schools*, 7.

[41] Roger H. Harper, *Victorian Architectural Competitions* (London, 1983), xiii–xviii; Joan Bassin, *Architectural Competitions in Nineteenth-Century England* (Ann Arbor, 1984), 3, 16.

26. T. N. Deane, Examination Schools (1872).

the rival merits of the two designs. It finally selected Deane, but only to tell him to redraft his designs.[42] The architect eventually produced two alternative plans and on 6 December 1870 they were finally presented to Convocation. Both were rejected. Some three years after the competition had first started, it had ended in anticlimax. Deane's designs were disregarded. Success was years away.[43]

Two years later, in 1872, the liberals tried again. This time the MAs were involved at an earlier stage, and a joint Delegacy between Council and Convocation was convened.[44] It took a year to organize the competition, and the list of competitors was a curious and perhaps ill-advised one. Deane and Street were reinvited, and to their names were added Blomfield, Waterhouse, and John Oldrid Scott. Street and Waterhouse declined to compete.[45] Blomfield and Deane were soon rejected by the Delegacy—leaving Oldrid Scott the clear winner, and his scheme was swiftly accepted by Council.[46] However, despite

[42] OUA, HC 3/1/1, (6 Feb. 1867) 102; (11 Feb. 1869) 211. Bod., G. A. Oxon. 4° 119 (2), 'New Examination Schools, by One of the Committee' (1870), 1.

[43] *Oxford University Gazette* 1 (1870–1), 1.

[44] OUA, 1/2/2, 'Minutes of Hebdomadal Council 1866–1879', 317 (8 June 1872); *Oxford University Gazette* 3 (1872–3), 247–8.

[45] Whether from loyalty to Deane, fear of rejection, or both is unclear. Jackson, *Life and Travels*, 110; *The Builder* 31 (1873), 452; C. J. Faulkner, in John Brandon-Jones, 'Letters of Philip Webb and his Contemporaries', *Architectural History* 8 (1964), 52–72, at 61.

[46] OUA, HC 1/2/2, 341 (15 May 1873).

27. J. O. Scott, Examination Schools (1876).

offering to make 'any modification, either in plan or design, or even style, that . . . may appear desirable',[47] Scott was defeated in Convocation. On 23 May 1873 his plans received only twenty votes in favour and fifty-four against.[48]

For the second time, the plans of the party of progress had been frustrated. The progressives had been lackadaisical in organization and incompetent in their management of Convocation. A coalition had grown up against the New Schools sufficiently strong to prevent their creation. As St John Tyrwhitt was forced to acknowledge,

> When spending money is the subject of its deliberations, a Convocation of residents invariably divides itself into the party who ask for money for the prescribed purpose, and those who want it for other purposes. There may be added to these a floating balance of gentlemen who habitually oppose any vote of money whatever.[49]

As a leading liberal and advocate of the New Schools, Tyrwhitt's acuity was born of frustration. This was indeed precisely what had happened. The Researchers wished to build a new university library. Pattison and Professor Rolleston even

---

[47] Bod., G. A. Oxon. b. 138 (86), J. O. Scott, 'New Examination Schools' (5 June 1873), 2–3.

[48] *Oxford University Gazette* 4 (1872–3), 191.

[49] Bod., G. A. Oxon. c. 33 (181), R. St John Tyrwhitt, 'A Letter to the Vice-Chancellor' (18 May 1875).

commissioned an engineer to prove that a Bodleian built in the Parks would 'fulfil every required condition for a great University Library'.[50] The Non-Placet Society remained implacably opposed to the Schools. At the same time, the party of progress found itself divided over the buildings proposed. The committed reformer G. W. Kitchin found himself unable to support Deane's designs of 1870.[51] C. J. Faulkner, a powerful progressive within the university, was co-author of the pamphlet which destroyed Scott's proposals of 1873.[52] It took all of Jowett's effort to unite the progressives, frustrate the conservatives, and draw in the Researchers. But eventually he succeeded. In early 1875, the Bodleian Curators abandoned the idea of moving.[53] By splitting the opposition and enticing Pattison's allies across, the party of progress ensured the success of their programme.

On 20 April 1875, after a year of slow progress and frequent disappointments, a new Delegacy was accepted by Convocation. For the first time the progressives were organized and confident of victory. The party of progress captured the Delegacy. Charles Launcelot Shadwell, a progressive Proctor, organized at least two of the nominations—those of W. W. Jackson and John A. Godley.[54] It seems likely that he facilitated others. Certainly, it is true to say that not a single person opposed to the New Schools was even nominated.[55] Council elected three reformers: Dr Liddell, Dean of Christ Church;[56] Professor H. J. S. Smith, Jowett's greatest friend and ally;[57] and the Vice-Chancellor, James Sewell, Warden of New College and, incidentally, the first man to propose the building of the New Schools.[58] Convocation elected Edward Moore, R. St John Tyrwhitt, George E. Thorley, William W. Jackson, Alfred Robinson, and G. W. Kitchin— now convinced of the need for new Schools. All these men were progessives. They were also rather more knowledgeable about contemporary aesthetics than their predecessors. 'The University may feel confident in the good taste and business capacity of this delegacy', enthused the *Architect*, 'and it is to be hoped that their labours will not be as thankless and unfruitful as those of the former delegacy.'[59] Thanks to the superior organization of the party of progress this hope was to be fulfilled. Oxford was to get its New Schools.

Despite the disasters of the previous years, the Delegacy narrowly resolved to hold another competition. As Howard Colvin observes, 'nearly every eminent Victorian architect' found himself on the initial list of competitors, which

[50] Douglas Galton, in *Oxford University Gazette* 5 (1873–4), 290.

[51] *Oxford Journal*, 10 Dec. 1870, 5.

[52] The pamphlet, signed C.J.F., C.A.F., E.J.P, was clearly the work of three liberal Fellows of University College: Faulkner, C. A. Fyffe, and E. J. Payne. No copy now exists, but it is condensed and criticized in Scott, 'New Examination Schools'.   [53] Craster, *Bodleian Library*, 131–3.

[54] Bod., G. A. Oxon c. 33 (34), Letter from W. W. Jackson to Shadwell.

[55] *Oxford University Gazette* 5 (1874–5), Supplements to No. 188.

[56] Henry L. Thompson, *Henry George Liddell: A Memoir* (London, 1899), 198–200.

[57] Abbott and Campbell, *Jowett*, vol. ii, p. 238.

[58] Hastings Rashdall and Robert S. Rait, *New College* (London, 1901), 227–30; OUA, HC 1/2/1, 380 (17 Nov. 1862).   [59] *Architect* 13 (1875), 289.

included both George Gilbert and John Oldrid Scott, G. E. Street, Norman Shaw, Alfred Waterhouse, T. N. Deane, T. G Jackson, Basil Champneys, G. F. Bodley, John Prichard, R. C. Carpenter, Philip Webb, and—later— E. M. Barry.[60] Deane and Oldrid Scott were reinvited, and (after a ballot) Norman Shaw, E. M. Barry, and G. E. Bodley were asked to compete.[61] Both Shaw and Barry refused to enter, and in their place were invited Basil Champneys and T. G. Jackson.[62] Uniquely, Jackson had built nothing in Oxford. He was responsible only for 'a number of unimportant alterations' at his own college, Wadham.[63] Nonetheless, Jackson's selection was not accidental. He had been the author of a widely-admired, if ultimately unsuccessful design for a bell-tower at Christ Church.[64] He was a fellow of Wadham, and had been a university examiner.[65] As an academic reformer, he was on familiar terms with the party of progress: George Thorley, the Delegate who proposed Jackson for the job, was Sub-Warden of Wadham and would be his best man.[66]

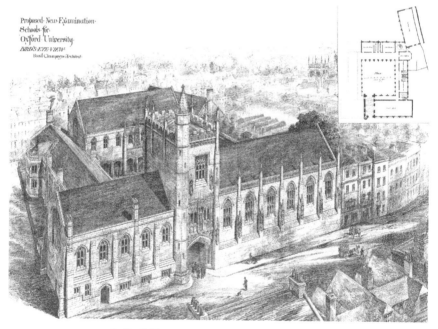

28. Basil Champneys, Examination Schools (1876).

[60] Colvin, *Unbuilt Oxford*, 143; OUA, UC 3/1, 'New Schools Delegacy Minute Book', 15 and 19 May 1875.   [61] Ibid., 19 May 1875.
[62] Ibid., 29 May and 1 July 1875.   [63] *Oxford Journal*, 24 Oct. 1874, 7.
[64] *Architect* 14 (1875), 161.
[65] Albeit in drawing, *Oxford University Gazette* 5 (1874–5), 106.
[66] Jackson, *Life and Travels*, 110 and 144.

Jackson's close relationship with the progressives was not enough to guarantee victory, of course. His initial position on the reserve list of architects indicated some doubts about his ability. These were soon overcome. On 15 March 1876 the Delegacy met to consider the entrants' designs. No votes were cast for either Deane or Scott. Basil Champneys came third, with one vote. Bodley's plan gained two supporters. But Jackson gained an absolute majority, with six votes.[67] Once approved by Council, his plans were presented to an unusually well-attended Convocation. On 15 June 1876, by 106 votes to 16, and then 87 to 8, the designs were accepted.[68] The greatly increased attendance at Convocation reflected both the importance of the issue and the success of the progressives in marshalling their supporters. Jowett, in the previous October, had explained that he was 'trying to get the Liberal Party together here', and this result showed he had succeeded.[69] The surprise came from the fact that such a relative unknown had won, and had triumphed despite his decision to build in a non-Gothic style. This was, after all, almost 'the most important building in the chief street of Oxford'.[70] All of Jackson's fellow competitors, indeed every

29. Jackson, Examination Schools, Oxford (1876–83).

[67] OUA, UC 3/1, 15 March 1876
[68] OUA, HC 1/2/2, p. 437 (29 May 1876); *Oxford University Gazette* 6 (1875–6), 441–2.
[69] Abbott and Campbell, *Jowett*, vol. ii, p. 96.   [70] *Architect* 15 (1876), 364.

Oxford architect since the Martyrs' Memorial, had built in a medieval manner. This was the accepted Oxford approach.

Basil Champneys had selected the 'English third pointed' as a period 'thoroughly characteristic of Oxford', and 'by a close study of examples of this phase of architecture in Oxford itself' had sought to 'impart to the design a specially local character'.[71] G. F. Bodley also aimed to 'erect a building that would be in harmony with the ancient buildings of Oxford'. In his case, this meant selecting 'strictly English Gothic of the fifteenth century', which, he averred, would harmonize with 'the best examples of your beautiful collegiate buildings'.[72] Jackson alone eschewed the Gothic Revival. Ironically, his design more closely resembled Bodley's usual style than anything he had done previously. There were hints here of the new London School Board building (1872–9) begun by Bodley and Garner just four years before.[73] There was also a close resemblance to Hartshorne's and Somers Clarke's unbuilt Polish mansion, which had been such a hit in the Royal Academy Exhibition of 1871.[74] More than this, though, the Schools were an *omnium gatherum* of Jackson's past life. Both Somers Clarke and Bodley were pupils of Sir Gilbert Scott—and there was indeed much of Spring Gardens to be found here. There were also details derived from Jackson's tour of the continent, from his arts and crafts interests, and even from the great houses he had visited as a child. Indeed, he claimed that it was a haunting vision of Kirby Hall that inspired the idea for the Schools.[75] Certainly, the exterior shows the influence of great Elizabethan mansions like Haddon and Hardwick, Kirby and Knole. The quadrangle, with its pedimented windows, putti, and frontispiece, derived details from Oxford, East Anglia, Venice, and beyond. Inside, the inspiration is Italian: with elements from Ravenna, Siena, Florence, and Rome.[76] Even the Clipsham stone used was new to the city. Jackson was committing heresy, and instead of being burnt, he was to be beatified.

This would not have been possible had the party of progress not been confident of success. Their optimism allowed Jackson to design a modern building which reflected their commitment to progressive thought. Faulkner, as his letters to Philip Webb show, did not oppose the Schools in principle—indeed, he stood as a candidate for the 1875–6 Delegacy. Rather, by attacking Scott in 1873, he had sought to ensure that the design chosen was the best example of modern architecture possible. His friend and ally, Charles Fyffe, made their objections clear. He believed that Scott's design was a complete failure: 'Not a feature but was a reduction, and a parody of something else in Oxford.' Not only was the

---

[71] Bod., G. A. Oxon. c. 33 (182), Basil Champneys, 'Oxford Examination Schools Competition: Report' (1876), 3–7.

[72] Bod., 8° 164 (9), G. F. Bodley, 'New Examination Schools for the University of Oxford' (1876), 4–5.   [73] *Builder* 30 (1872), 489; 33 (1875), 704.

[74] *Builder* 29 (1871), 339.   [75] Jackson, *Life and Travels*, 111.

[76] Jackson's plans are in the Bodleian: Bod., MS. Top. Oxon. A.19.

architecture banal, it was also inappropriate. 'The elevation towards the High-Street embraced with many other elements that of a church. It did not harmonise with the other academical buildings of the High-Street but faintly only with St. Mary's [the University Church].'[77]

Jackson succeeded by convincing men like Fyffe and Faulkner that his work was modern, original, and progressive. His approach tallied completely with that of the progressives. Just as the party of progress wished to 'strike off the fetter of medieval statutes' and free the university from 'the predominance of ecclesiasticism', so Jackson's architecture of progress sought to release Oxford's buildings from 'the yoke of mediaevalism', and revive a domestic, secular, and Renaissance style.[78] He was not unique in this. E. R. Robson, the architect of the London School Board, argued for the abandonment of 'church-architecture' for non-denominational schoolhouses. 'In its aim and object', he wrote, modern school architecture should 'strive to express civil rather than ecclesiastical character'.[79] He achieved this by abandoning a Gothic in favour of a 'Queen Anne' revival style.[80] Just as this symbolized change in London, so Jackson's

30. Examination Schools, quadrangle.

[77] *Oxford Journal*, 31 May 1873, 4.
[78] T. G. Jackson, *Modern Gothic Architecture* (London, 1873), 56.
[79] E. R. Robson, *School Architecture* (1874; Leicester, 1972), 321.
[80] Girouard, *Sweetness and Light*, 64–9; Weiner, *Architecture and Social Reform*, 1–5, 67–71, 81–6.

neo-Jacobean expressed an ideal in Oxford: it embodied the ambitions of the party of progress. Gothic—once a symbol of reform in the city—had become synonymous with reaction. The Renaissance had come of age.

Confident though the progressives were, they were not foolhardy. Nor would Jackson jeopardize his first major commission. It was vital, as Tyrwhitt recognized, to produce a design 'which will have some chance of Common Room approval'.[81] And in some respects, Jackson was being far from reckless in abandoning the Gothic Revival. He was correct to suspect that 'the majority of the Residents rather welcomed the rupture with strict Gothic precedent'.[82] In short, he had taken a calculated risk. Even within Oxford, tastes were gradually moving away from the Revival. In the villas of North Oxford, the 'Mediaeval' was being abandoned in favour of the 'Old English'.[83] St John Tyrwhitt had in 1864 commissioned a High Victorian Gothic house at 62 Banbury Road.[84] Nine years later, in 1875, he was recommending that the New Schools should be based on the 'South or Meadow-front of Merton College'.[85] This was pure early Renaissance, and Jackson was inspired by it throughout his life. But Tyrwhitt was, like Faulkner and Fyffe, at the cutting edge of contemporary aesthetics.[86] Jackson's real success with the residents who were not reformers rested rather more on his rhetorical than on his architectural skills. He defended his designs in terms of their fitness for Oxford. 'My object', he declared, 'has been to give the buildings a collegiate character which would harmonise with the traditions of Oxford.' He had consequently chosen 'that late eclectic form of Gothic of which Oxford and Cambridge contain examples so many and so well worked out in detail that they almost constitute an academical style themselves'.[87] It was this putative 'academical style' that Jackson and his allies sold the university.

There were critics, of course. Those opposed to the programme of the party of progress correctly saw in the Schools a symbol of all that was wrong with the reforms in Oxford. Ruskin, growing increasingly unhappy with the University to which he had returned, exploded in anger at the sight of the Schools. He refused to enter the building whilst it was under construction, and once built, he did nothing but decry it.[88] This was clearly more than a defence of the ill-used Deane.[89] In the first place, Ruskin attacked the Schools in aesthetic terms. They were built, he claimed, 'in a style as inherently corrupt as it is un-English'.[90] But he also went further, abandoning simple stylistic criticism. In that sense, Ruskin

---

[81] Tyrwhitt, 'Letter'.   [82] Jackson, *Life and Travels*, 120.

[83] Tanis Hinchcliffe, *North Oxford* (New Haven and London, 1992), 113–14.

[84] E. O. Dodgson, 'Notes on Nos. 56, 58, 60, 62 and 64 Banbury Road', *Oxoniensia* xxxii (1967), 53–4.   [85] Tyrwhitt, 'Letter'.

[86] R. St John Tyrwhitt, *Greek and Gothic: progress and decay in the three arts of architecture, sculpture, and painting* (London, 1881).

[87] Bod., G. A. Oxon. c. 33 (184), T. G. Jackson, 'Proposed New Examination Schools for the University of Oxford', (1876).   [88] Jackson, *Life and Travels*, 120.

[89] Although cf. Brooks, *Ruskin and Victorian Architecture*, 262.

[90] John Ruskin, *Collected Works*, E. J. Cook and A. Wedderburn, eds. (39 vols.; London, 1903–9), vol. 33, p. 313.

was not so much condemning the progress of architecture as damning the architecture of progress. He abjured these 'rooms for the torture and shame of . . . scholars' and disparaged the decision to charge students 'for the ornamentation of their inquisition chambers'.[91] In an unlikely alliance, Ruskin was joined by E. A. Freeman in slighting the Schools. Ostensibly a 'conservative reformer', Freeman found the university to which he had returned as Regius Professor of History in 1884 a less than congenial place.[92] He saw Jackson's recently completed building as 'an amazing piece of architectural perversity'.[93] But if it was stylistically suspect, this was nothing compared to its moral failings. In particular, he fiercely objected to the celebrations held on its inauguration. 'There was formerly some regard to the proprieties of things and places', he wrote, 'now a ball in a college hall is a common thing; and we have seen a new University building solemnly opened by dancing.'[94]

For both men, Jackson's work was synonymous with a changed and alien Oxford: a feminized Oxford filled with women who have brought with them 'a foolish imitation of London ways, London hours, and much that was unknown in the simpler days of old'.[95] Freeman associated the 'fantastic and incongruous building' with a university which was now 'thoroughly bad'.[96] Ruskin similarly linked the New Schools and their new style with new women. He condemned the university for building 'ball rooms instead of lecture rooms'.[97] Jackson's choice of a domestic model facilitated this juxtaposition. Together, Ruskin and Freeman focused on the ephemeral uses of the Schools, and used a symbol of decadence, femininity, and frivolity to undermine the value of Jackson's building.[98] It was seen not just as corrupt but as a corrupting architecture. The New Schools, and the style in which they were built, were part of a programme with which the conservatives could never agree.

Jackson, 'by combining all styles of architecture [had] shown to this generation a new form of beauty', as Curzon later put it.[99] It was an approach that became instantly popular, at least with those who shared his progressive agenda. Within five years of the completion of the Schools, Freeman was forced to admit that Magdalen College and New College were 'the only two bodies who have not bowed the knee to Baal', and adopted the architecture of progress.[100] All over the city, colleges were striking 'Anglo-Jackson' attitudes. Part of this was the inevitable effect of the Schools. As he himself acknowledged, they were the

[91] John Ruskin, *Collected Works*, vol. 33, p. 363; vol. 37, p. 477.

[92] W. R. W Stephens, *The Life and Letters of Edward A. Freeman* (2 vols.; London, 1895), vol. 1, p. 147.

[93] E. A. Freeman, 'Oxford After Forty Years: II', *Contemporary Review* 51 (1887), 814–30, at 816.

[94] E. A. Freeman, 'Oxford After Forty Years: I', *Contemporary Review* 51 (1887), 609–23, at 613.

[95] Ibid., 609.   [96] Freeman, 'Oxford After Forty Years: II', 816.

[97] Ruskin, *Works*, vol. 33, p. 476.

[98] For the gendering of Victorian buildings: George L. Hersey, *High Victorian Gothic: a study in associationism* (Baltimore and London, 1972), 23–4, 49, 60.   [99] Jackson, *Life and Travels*, 249.

[100] E. A. Freeman, 'Architecture in Oxford', *The Architect* 38 (1887), 363.

31. Examination Schools, entrance hall.

32. Examination Schools, plan.

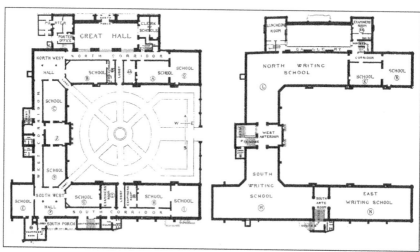

means by which he was transformed from the 'unknown Mr. Jackson' to 'Jackson of course!' in such a short time.[101] His influence depended yet further on the network of progressives which had supported his plans for the Schools. He was commissioned because he was a member of the party of progress, and because he was capable of translating their ideas into architecture. At their most obvious, Jackson's uniquely helpful connections with the university were exemplified in his own college. It was as a fellow of Wadham that Jackson received his first academic commission: refurbishing the Warden's Lodgings. He was not even above proposing work at Governing Body Meetings, and only the poverty of the college prevented a Jackson quadrangle being added along Holywell Street.[102] To the very end of his life, restoration work at Wadham was inevitably done by Jackson, who also designed glassware, furniture, embroidery, and the library bookplate. He was less conveniently placed at other colleges, but his success was no less dependent on a mixture of personal contact and ideological alliance, as he himself recognized.[103]

As the work at the Examination Schools progressed, Jackson's relationship with the progressives became increasingly close. Extraordinarily, he was responsible solely to the Curators of the University Chest, a group dominated by reformers. As such, he was given an incredible level of latitude to decorate the building,[104] and this trust was soon repeated in the colleges—and by the same people. The Delegates who selected Jackson in 1876 were amongst his keenest advocates from the first. Even Jackson's University Cricket Pavilion (1880–1) arose from Jowett's ambition to establish 'Cricket for the University' in the parks.[105] Likewise, when it was agreed that a building should be erected for the Non-Collegiate students (1886–8), only one name was even considered as architect: T. G. Jackson.[106] He was an appropriate choice. The Non-Collegiate Delegacy was intended to provide inexpensive education for those excluded from Oxford by the high cost of college living.[107] It was, thus, a critical part of the reformers' transformation of Oxford. Moreover, it was not simply a progressive project; it was also designed in a self-consciously 'modern' style. True, the *Oxford Magazine* sneered at the contrast between its rubble walling and the ashlar of the neighbouring New Schools, suggesting that if this was intended 'by some occult symbolism to signify the relation of the Non-Collegiate students to the University', then 'it is neither fair nor courteous to

---

[101] Jackson, *Life and Travels*, 105, 148.

[102] WCA, 2/4, pp. 162–3 (19 June 1874); C. S. L. Davies, 'Decline and Revival, 1660–1900', in C. S. L. Davies and Jane Garnett, eds., *Wadham College* (Oxford, 1994), 46.

[103] Jackson, *Life and Travels*, 72; *Recollections*, 164.

[104] Roland Wilcock, 'The University Chest, 1868–1914', Brock and Curthoys, eds., *History of the University*, vol. vi, p. 438.   [105] Abbott and Campbell, *Jowett*, vol. ii, p. 214.

[106] OUA, UC 3/1, 29 May 1886.

[107] Alan Bullock, ' "A Scotch University Added to Oxford"? the Non-Collegiate Students', in Brock and Curthoys, eds., *History of the University*, vol. vii, pp. 193–208.

33. The Cricket
Pavilion in the Parks
(1880–1).

34. Non-Collegiate
Building (1886–8).

35. Trinity College, Oxford, Jackson Building (1883–8).

hint that the relation is that of the rough to the polished, or the semi-detached to the incorporated.'[108] In reality, though, the arts and crafts influenced re-working of Jacobethan themes marked the Non-Collegiate building out as a part of a much wider movement. The same was true of the Cricket Pavilion, although— as befitted its site and purpose—it had other inspirations. This was Jackson's version of the 'Queen Anne' Revival—the 'Architecture of Enjoyment'.[109]

The apotheosis of this approach, and of Jackson's role as the architect of progress, came with his new buildings at Trinity College (1883–8).[110] Stylistically and symbolically, this project embodied all that Jackson aimed to achieve, and (as he himself acknowledged) formed his most successful Oxford commission.[111] This is not simply because the design was popular, although it was said that the work 'beats Botticelli'.[112] Nor was the cost of the work its most significant feature, although the expenditure of over £21,000 at a time of 'falling rents and general depression' was exceptional.[113] Much more importantly, Jackson's buildings were the embodiment—indeed, the central feature—of an attempt to reform and revitalize the college. The choice of Jackson, and the use of his style, were thus of critical importance. The New Building and the President's Lodgings symbolized the radical transformation of the college hoped for by John Percival, President of Trinity. Percival, Jowett's choice as

---

[108] *Oxford Magazine* 5 (1887), 218.   [109] Girouard, *Sweetness and Light*, 186–207.
[110] See also Clare Hopkins, *Trinity: 450 years of an Oxford college community* (Oxford, 2005), ch. 9.
[111] Jackson, *Life and Travels*, 154.   [112] *Oxford Magazine* 4 (1886), 162.
[113] TCA, Uncat. Records of the New Buildings, 'Final Statement' (23 May 1888); Letter from J. Percival (Jan. 1887).

President, was 'an extreme liberal', and arrived at Trinity in 1879 resolved to reform the college, and the university.[114] Such was his impact on the ethos of the undergraduates that the Bursar found himself forced to apologize to the college wine merchant, embarrassed by a sharp reduction in the level of consumption.[115] A key part of Percival's project was to improve discipline by increasing the accommodation available; thus reducing the number of students living beyond college control in lodging houses.[116] The instrument of his ambitions was T. G. Jackson.

Plans for new buildings were first mooted as early as 1880, but it was not possible to start work on them until 1882. Building actually began in 1883.[117] At no point was it suggested that anyone but Jackson should even be consulted. His first elevation, which was photographed and sent to old members as part of the fund-raising campaign, was revised, but essentially contains the basis of the building as eventually constructed. The aim was to create 25 to 30 sets of rooms together with 'a Lecture Room, Undergraduates' Library and Magazine Room, such as the best Colleges have already added to their buildings'.[118] If the aims of the project were thus defiantly progressive, and inspired by a leading liberal, the style in which they were accomplished was yet more so.[119] Working closely with the President and Fellows, Jackson was persuaded to make his design even more idiosyncratic and showy. The college expressed itself 'content to wait till we can get the ideal front', and quickly ensured that the gables of the building should receive additional decoration, whilst insisting that the President's Lodgings be made larger and grander.[120] The neo-Renaissance style closely associated these buildings with the Schools and the party of progress. This was not simply a monument to the reforming ideals of Percival, although it would not have happened without his drive, or the year's salary he donated to pay for it.[121] It was also a triumphant monument to the Oxford progressives as a whole, and to Jackson's ability to express their ideals in his buildings.

This pattern was repeated all across Oxford. As at Trinity, Jackson was commissioned by liberals to symbolize their success and express their identity. His work at Corpus Christi (1884–5) is a perfect example. The college was notoriously liberal: Jowett's ally H. J. S. Smith was a Professorial Fellow; John Matthias Wilson, President from 1872–81 was one of the leading university reformers.[122] His successor Thomas Fowler, President from 1881 to 1904, was

[114] William Temple, *Life of Bishop Percival* (London, 1921), 64–6.
[115] Jeremy Potter, *Headmaster: the life of John Percival, radical autocrat* (London, 1998), 160.
[116] TCA, Records of the New Buildings, 'Appeal Letters', 1880–7.
[117] TCA, Col. Govt. III A.4, 'Order Book D (1852–1884)', 314 (16 Oct. 1880); 329 (15 June 1882); 342 (15 Oct. 1883). [118] Bod., c. 287. 48, 51, 'Proposed New Buildings' (1882).
[119] TCA, I/C/3, Jackson Building: plans and elevations; I/C/4, President's Lodgings.
[120] TCA, Uncat. Records, Letter to Jackson (14 March 1883); Letter from Jackson (2 June 1884); Report by Jackson (14 March 1885). [121] Temple, *Percival*, 86–7.
[122] Thomas Fowler, *History of Corpus Christi College* (Oxford Historical Society xxv; Oxford, 1893), 377.

36. President's Lodging, Trinity College, Oxford, (1883–8).

37. New Building, Corpus Christi College, Oxford, from Merton Street (1884–5).

similarly progressive.[123] Jackson was clearly Fowler's choice as architect. Even before the college had decided to build, Fowler had written to Jackson inviting him to lunch in order to discuss the prospect.[124] Against some determined opposition, Fowler defended Jackson's Merton Street elevation as originally conceived, and successfully piloted his designs through the Governing Body.[125] The result was another Renaissance-inspired building for undergraduates: an *aedes annexae* ornamented with aedicules.

A no less progressive or idiosyncratic approach was adopted at Balliol in 1892. Jackson's house, the King's Mound, was initially intended to be a part of a putative Balliol Hall and represented Jowett's attempt to widen access to the college by providing cheaper accommodation for poorer undergraduates. The project foundered on the indifference of the fellows, but Jowett ensured the success of his plan to build a grand tutor's house in Holywell in the most direct way.[126] He simply paid for the building and chose the architect himself.[127] To ensure 'that the house might be worthy of the College', suggest Jowett's biographers, 'he insisted on securing the services of Mr. Jackson'.[128] Working in close harmony with the Master, with A. L. Smith and his wife (for whom the house was intended), Jackson produced what Jowett believed was 'a great work for the College'. It was certainly further proof of Jackson's involvement in the process of university reform.

It should also come as no surprise that Jackson built at Somerville. This was the archetypal project of the party of progress. Founded in 1879, the college was established to provide women's education and, unlike the more respectable Lady Margaret Hall, this was to be non-denominational instruction. The list of supporters of the college reads like a roll-call of Oxford progressives. The founding committee alone included T. H. Green, Mrs Humphry Ward, G. W. Kitchin, and (as President) John Percival, the head of Trinity.[129] It was a remarkably successful venture for the reformers. In 1880, Somerville was able to acquire the freehold of its site. In 1881 it was incorporated as a college under the Companies Act. Rising student numbers soon necessitated new accommodation.[130] It was thus in an atmosphere of some triumph that Jackson was called in to erect the first new building of this flourishing new college. His name was proposed by Miss Smith, sister of Jowett's friend H. J. S. Smith, and his designs were swiftly

[123] V. H. H. Green, *The Commonwealth of Lincoln College, 1427–1977* (Oxford, 1979), 476.
[124] CCCA, B/14/1/1 Misc. Papers From the President's Lodgings, Fowler to Jackson (14 Nov. 1883).
[125] CCCA, B/14/1/1 J. W. Oddie to Fowler (8, 10, 17 March 1884); B/4/1/8, 'College Minute Book, 1881–1897' (2 Feb., 1 March 1884), 60, 67.
[126] Jackson, *Life and Travels*, 162; John Jones, *Balliol College: a history* (2nd ed; Oxford, 1997), 220, 235–6.   [127] BalCA, 'English Register, 1875–1908', 24 April, 5 March 1892.
[128] Abbott and Campbell, *Jowett*, vol. ii, p. 345.
[129] SCA, 'Minutes of Council, 1879–1908' (28 Feb. 1879) 9.
[130] SCA, 'Log Book, 1879–1907', 2; 'Reports and Calendars, 1879–1899', Report (Oct. 1897–Oct. 1880).

38. Corpus Christi College New Building, from the garden.

39. The King's Mound in Mansfield Road, Oxford (1892–3).

40. Jackson's extension to Somerville College, Oxford (1881–2).

commissioned, approved, and executed.[131] Although only an extension—and a small one at that—the building employed many of Jackson's familiar tropes, and as such stood as a strong statement of confidence and distinction.[132] Basil Champneys at Lady Margaret Hall adopted a reticent and reserved approach. Jackson's work at Somerville was, by contrast, closer to Champneys' work at Newnham. Both colleges were secular, both were controversial, and both were defiantly progressive. At each, the 'Queen Anne' revival served as a symbol of social change. Inexpensive though it was, Jackson's Somerville extension was clearly part of the architecture of progress.

T. G. Jackson was chosen to work at Somerville because it was a progressive college, run by reformers, who expressed themselves in a reformist style. The link

[131] SCA, 'Minutes of Council' (19 Feb.; 22 March; 10, 21 June; 16, 22 July 1881), 81, 83, 89, 91, 93.

[132] Although cf. Margaret Birney Vickery, *Buildings for Bluestockings* (Newark and London, 1999), 92–5.

between Jackson's work and a feminized Oxford had already been made. His commission to build the High School for Girls in 1880 confirmed the association identified by Freeman.[133] Additionally, Jackson's domestic themes perfectly suited Somerville, which had abandoned the old staircase arrangement for colleges in favour of a supposedly more proper approach, which placed the students in self-contained houses. It took a particular sensitivity to produce a design that incorporated both cushioned window seats inside, and 'Flower-balconies' without.[134] Jackson's reputation as the architect of progress was also helpful to the college in a more material sense. Somerville could not afford to build without the donations of the party of progress. Those who gave included W. W. Jackson, T. H. Green, G. W. Kitchin, John Percival, and others who had commissioned or would employ Jackson as their own architect.[135] His name and his style were guarantees of both the legitimacy and importance of the project. They provided a focus for fund-raising amongst a particular group of individuals. For, above all else, it was Jackson's personal relationship with the party of progress which gave him work at the college. He was working for people who had supported his career since its inception. As the first Principal of Somerville, Miss Shaw-Lefevre, recalled in 1911, the result was 'the best bit of building we have'.[136] It was also a powerful example of the party of progress in action. At Somerville, as at Trinity, Balliol, Corpus Christi, and elsewhere, Jackson was dependent on and used by a small but important network of reformers. They made his career, as he remade Oxford.

More than this, the success of the progressives ensured that Jackson's architectural imagination became formative for the whole university—even for those colleges where reform was apparently anathema. As Oxford was reshaped, so Jackson's style became more than just the outward and visible sign of an inward and spiritual change. It became the university style itself. To some extent, of course, this was inevitable. The sheer scale of the Schools was bound to have an impact. It was, after all, by far the largest project undertaken by the university in the nineteenth century. Indeed, as early as 1877 Jackson found himself commissioned by Merton to propose a new quadrangle opposite the college. This project, although never built, is indicative of the possibilities in Jackson's approach and the potential for his work to transcend narrow party divides.[137] For although the college was not immune from what its Warden called the 'restless spirit of progress within the university', it was certainly not at the vanguard of

---

[133] Hinchcliffe, *North Oxford*, 154.   [134] SCA, 'Log Book', 20.

[135] SCA, 'Reports and Calendars, 1879–99', Report: 1881–2, 12–15.

[136] Pauline Adams, *Somerville for Women: an Oxford College, 1897–1993* (Oxford, 1996), 42.

[137] MCA, Uncat. Plans; Colvin, *Unbuilt Oxford*, 148. Eventually, the annexation of St Alban Hall negated the need for new buildings. See MCA, 1.5a 'College Register 1877–1914' (11 June 1878, 3 June 1879, 21 Feb. 1881), 21, 39, 67; Bernard W. Henderson, *Merton College* (London, 1899), 170.

reform.[138] Merton's proximity to the Examination Schools, and the growing sense that Jackson was becoming the leading university architect, clearly had an impact.

It was an impact felt further away as well. The Grove Building at Lincoln College (1880–3) was both a symbol of progressive triumph and of Jackson's growing importance within the university more generally. Perhaps most importantly, it represented the impotence of Mark Pattison and the self-confidence of the college itself.[139] Jackson almost certainly owed his commission at Lincoln to Thomas Fowler, the Sub-Rector, who was to be his patron as President of Corpus Christi. By the 1870s it was the progressive Fowler, rather than the researching Pattison, who ran Lincoln. As an old member recalled, Fowler blithely disregarded the ailing Pattison's views: 'We take no notice of the Rector', he would say; 'send your application to me.'[140] Jackson was the only architect considered for the building. He was Fowler's candidate—and he won. At the same time, coming so soon after the end to the abortive plans to create a Brasenose-Lincoln College, it was a powerful sign of 'the College's confidence in its future'.[141] The building in that sense was a symbol of Lincoln's desire to go it alone and to retain its position within the university. The choice of T. G. Jackson as architect was undoubtedly important for this. With its pedimented windows, Jacobean doorways, and Gibraltar stone dressings, the Grove building was irrevocably linked with Jackson's other projects, and with his work as chief architect for the university.

The high point for Jackson in his role as arbiter of the university style came with the foundation of Hertford College. In 1874 the ailing and impoverished Magdalen Hall was re-endowed and re-named Hertford College.[142] This new institution needed new buildings—and Jackson was just the man to do it. Once again, he built both as architect of progress and as the university architect. The college was acutely conscious of its medieval roots—claiming somewhat dubiously to be a successor to the thirteenth-century Hart Hall—and it was particularly concerned to establish its precedence over Keble College, which was founded in 1868 as the culmination of the Oxford Movement. Built in a variegated brick by Butterfield, Keble aggressively asserted its independence from a supposedly corrupt university. Hertford, as a second and, despite its ancient origin, officially younger Anglican foundation, risked slighting comparisons with Keble.[143] Jackson's Catte Street frontage (1887–9) thus not

---

[138] George Charles Brodrick, *Memories and Impressions, 1831–1900* (London, 1900), 3–4; Mallet, *Oxford*, vol. iii, pp. 396–7.

[139] LCA, 'Order Book, 1872–1889' (24 July 1877–11 June 1881), 142, 158, 162–3, 328, 250, 270, 275–6. Unfortunately the plans and elevations (catalogued as II/2) have been lost by the college.

[140] Green, *Commonwealth of Lincoln*, 490.   [141] Green, *Oxford Common Room*, 298–301.

[142] See also William Whyte, 'Unbuilt Hertford: T. G. Jackson's contextual dilemmas', *Architectural History* 45 (2002), 347–62.

[143] Andrew Goudie, ed., *Seven Hundred Years of an Oxford College* (Oxford, 1984), 43–7; OUA, HC 1/2/3, 'Hebdomadal Council Minutes, 1879–96' (27 Nov., 4 Dec. 1887), 92, 94.

41. The Grove Building at Lincoln College (1880–3).

42. The Staircase and Hall at Hertford College, Oxford (1887–9).

only complemented the existing buildings by William Garbett (1818–22), but acted as a clear statement of difference between Hertford and Keble. Other work in the college, between 1888–1926, offered a similar contrast with the neo-Gothic of still newer establishments like Non-Conformist Mansfield and Manchester Colleges.[144] At the same time, Jackson's designs also allowed Hertford to claim a place amongst the modern colleges within the university.

Thomas C. Baring, who had refounded Hertford, was 'one of those conscientiously grumpy characters who are always assumed to have a heart of gold but give few grounds to support such an assumption'.[145] Baring was in fact a reactionary curmudgeon. Opposed to almost all change, he loathed the reform movement sweeping through Oxford. His benefaction was intended to create a college which retained the old clerical restrictions abolished in all other colleges. As an exclusively Anglican institution, it would have been easy for Hertford to become a bastion of reaction. This was avoided, however. Henry Boyd, Principal from 1877 to 1922, although not a radical, was an educational reformer.[146] Amongst his colleagues were convinced liberals, like G. A. Godley, previously private secretary to Gladstone, who was recommended as a Delegate for the Schools by W. W. Jackson.[147] The college was thus self-consciously concerned to expand and to innovate: to escape, indeed, the double-edged legacy of T. C. Baring. T. G. Jackson's designs showed that they were doing so. Even in what appear purely aesthetic details, Jackson reconciled competing ideals: antiquity and modernity; tradition and progress. The staircase in the old buildings—Pevsner's 'bastard child of Blois'—for example, is a tribute to the 'freedom of the Middle Ages; unfettered . . . by the Classic dogma'.[148] In this case, as in others, the application of Jackson's theory perfectly satisfied the demands of his clients. Before he had been commissioned, a guide to Oxford had declared that 'When finer buildings represent the College, a brilliant future may be confidently expected' for it.[149] Thirty years later, it was clear that Hertford had been 'brought into quiet architectural significance by Mr. Jackson'.[150] What more could the college require?

This reconciliation of the demands of both progressive and establishment rhetoric was to prove increasingly important to Jackson's career. His first work for Brasenose, commissioned in 1880, is built in a style similar to both the New Schools and Hertford; its closest relative is the west elevation of Jackson's building at Trinity.[151] In the later (1886–90; 1907–11) High Street frontage, however,

[144] HCA, Bound Volume of plans and elevations, 1888–1913.
[145] Philip Ziegler, *The Sixth Great Power: Barings 1762–1929* (London, 1988), 192.
[146] HCA, 4/1/1, 'Minutes of Governing Body, 1874–1929', 517–18 (10 March 1922); *Hertford College Magazine* 11 (1922), 3.
[147] Goudie, *Oxford College*, 46–7; Bod., G. A. Oxon. c.33 (34).
[148] Pevsner, *Oxfordshire*, 139; T. G. Jackson, *Architecture* (London, 1925), 295.
[149] Algernon M. M. Stedman, *Oxford: its social and intellectual life* (London, 1878), 29.
[150] *Journal of the RIBA* 3rd Series xix (1912), 291.
[151] BNCA, B.14.2. Working Drawings of New Buildings.

43. Hertford College Chapel (1903–8).

Jackson's approach is subtly changed and exuberantly embellished. This building is in a style so varied in inspiration and individual in approach that Crook has
dubbed it 'Gothic Survival Revived'.[152] Had Jackson got his way, it would have
been still more striking. To top off the tower, he proposed a crown steeple. This
putative 'adornment to the High Street', resembled the entrance to Marischal
College, Aberdeen, and would have transformed the townscape.[153] After a
furious debate, though, the steeple was abandoned.[154] Jackson had gone too far.
But his overall vision was accepted. The frontage was built in 'pure Gothic',[155]
whilst the north elevation, within the quadrangle, was continued in 'the style
which, for college work, Mr. Jackson has made his own'.[156] In other words, the
front of the building was Gothic, and the back was a Cotswold Renaissance. To
some extent this is to be expected. It was always Jackson's policy that 'considera-
tion should be had for neighbouring buildings'. Street architecture, he believed,
was social architecture. As a result, 'it ought to conform to those rules of convention by which men in society are governed'.[157] This is in part what he was doing
at Brasenose: responding to his context, to the college's position next to the
university church. But there was more to it than that.

It would be flippant to suggest that in this confusion of styles we can find the
ethos of the college: the ability to hold 'a middle place, without at any time
descending into mediocrity'.[158] However, it is evident that Jackson's work at
Brasenose, although different from that at other colleges, does share a similar
rhetorical scheme. Brasenose was by no means the exclusively conservative
college described by its biographer John Buchan. It may perhaps have
'laboured always to produce the type rather than the individual' amongst its
undergraduates, but its fellowship was far more interesting.[159] Indeed, the fear
of the students that the Governing Body was intending to turn Brasenose away
from sport and towards more intellectual activities was expressed in a series of
near-riots in the mid-1890s.[160] This was the college of the aesthete Walter Pater,
the artistic Humphry Ward, and the antiquary Falconer Madan. It was rich,
reforming, and the first college to introduce research fellowships.[161] Its
Governing Body asked William Morris for architectural advice and members
hung his paper in their rooms.[162] It was for this reason that Jackson was
commissioned to build in his usual style within the quadrangle. However, not
only was Brasenose an aesthetically engaged institution, it was also building on

[152] Crook, *The Dilemma of Style: architectural ideas from the picturesque to the post-modern*
(London, 1987), 152.
[153] BNCA, Folder 502, Uncat. Letters, Jackson to Butler (18 Jan., 26 Feb. 1887).
[154] *Oxford Journal*, 15 Oct. 1887, 5.   [155] *Brazen Nose* i, No. 5 (Nov. 1911) 186.
[156] E. W. Allfrey, 'The Architectural History of the Buildings', *Brasenose Quartercentenary
Monographs* iii (Oxford, 1909), 60.
[157] T. G. Jackson, 'Street Architecture', *Journal of the Society of Arts* liii/108 (23 Dec. 1904).
[158] John Buchan, *Brasenose College* (London, 1898), 143.
[159] John Buchan, 'Nine Brasenose Worthies', *Brasenose Quartercentenary Monographs* xiv
(Oxford, 1909), 4.   [160] Janet Adam Smith, *John Buchan: a biography* (London, 1965), 58.
[161] Engel, *From Clergyman to Don*, 260–5.
[162] BNCA, SB (Uncat.), New Buildings 1881–1911 (8 March 1887); D819, Building Accounts,
'Summary of Building Accounts, 1881–1887', 3.

44. New Buildings and Bridge at Hertford College (1901–16).

45. The New Quadrangle at Brasenose College (1880–90).

'the famous "High", the glory of Oxford', and a site even more significant than that of the Schools, as Jackson himself acknowledged.[163] The fellows consequently demanded a building which would be both imposing and fitting for its position. The building was thus a compromise between conservative

[163] T. G. Jackson, 'The High Street of Oxford, and Brasenose College', *Magazine of Art* 8 (1889), 332–40.

46. The High Street frontage to Brasenose College (1886–90, 1907–11).

47. Jackson's proposed frontage to Brasenose College, complete with crown spire (1889).

48. Brasenose College quadrangle.

and liberal, architect and client, Gothic and Renaissance. Jackson as a progressive, and an ally of William Morris, could be trusted to build within the college precincts; Jackson, as a don, and as the university architect, could be relied upon for the High Street frontage. It was for the architect 'a labour of love'.[164] For the college it was a tremendous responsibility. Employing Jackson reduced that risk, and produced a building which was widely admired.[165]

The High Street frontage to Brasenose remained an exception to Jackson's usual stylistic approach, however. In general, even despite the downturn in architectural work across Oxford from the mid-1890s onwards,[166] Jackson was able to rely upon old friends for new work and to build in his usual style. This is certainly the case with his designs for the Radcliffe Science Library (1898–1901) and the Electrical Laboratory (1908–10). Both buildings were paid for by the Drapers' Company who chose the architect and approved his design.[167] These projects were part of a much wider programme of educational charity, which included a Physiological Laboratory at Cambridge (also by Jackson), a University of South Wales, Queen Mary College in London, and the People's

[164] BNCA, 502, Jackson to Butler (8 Feb. 1890).
[165] Jackson MSS, 'Recollections', vol. ii., 419, Butler to Jackson (13 Oct. 1889).
[166] *Oxford Magazine* 13 (1894), 3.
[167] A. H. Johnson, *History of the Worshipful Company of Drapers* (5 vols.; Oxford, 1914–22), vol. iii, pp. 488–9.

49. Radcliffe Science Library, Oxford (1897–1901).

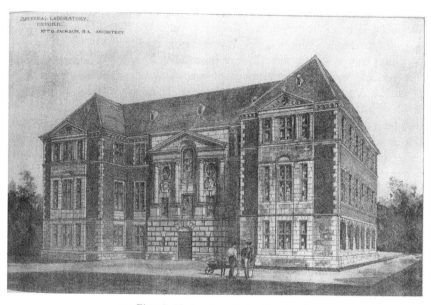

50. Electrical Laboratory, Oxford (1908–10).

Palace on the Mile End Road.[168] As this list suggests, the Drapers' Company was strongly committed to social and educational reform. It had predictably enough also employed Jackson to restore and refurbish Drapers' Hall.[169] Additionally, the Master of the Company who oversaw the initial proposal was Henry Boyd, Principal of Hertford. Little wonder that the Drapers' donations were dependent on Jackson and contingent on his designing both the Library[170] and Laboratory.[171] As befitted their progressive origin, the two buildings were built in a progressive style. The Radcliffe Science Library shows Jackson revisiting some old Renaissance themes. The Electrical Laboratory, in a bold, red-brick 'Wrenaissance', perfectly reflected the 'gas-lit, pitch-pine and terra-cotta atmosphere' which the Drapers' Company exuded.[172] Together, these buildings, his last original commissions in Oxford, represent the culmination and quintessence of his career. They show him as the architect of choice for the reformers, and the arbiter of the university style. Other architects would write in vain for the chance to design the Electrical Laboratory. As so often, Jackson had got there first.[173]

The result of this phenomenal success was to remake the image of Oxford. But whilst Jackson's façades were innovative and bold, his planning was highly conventional.[174] The late nineteenth century saw a wide variety of approaches to college building in Britain and America. In the United States, universities ranged in type from Harvard's campus to Bryn Mawr's colleges, via Smith's individual cottages.[175] Even in Britain, there was some diversity. Although the first campus university, Birmingham, was not begun until 1901, there were variations on the existing theme throughout the country.[176] At Newnham College, Cambridge, Basil Champneys abandoned the quadrangular form in favour of a more picturesque disposition of buildings. His dining hall, library, and accommodation blocks were arranged around a garden.[177] At Newnham, too, Champneys rejected the staircase system which had been used at Oxford and Cambridge for centuries, and placed his rooms along corridors.[178] Nor was this an innovation limited to the women's colleges. Champneys' work at

[168] Tom Girtin, *The Triple Crowns: a narrative history of the Drapers' Company, 1364–1964* (London, 1964), 340, 353, 360–1.   [169] Johnson, *Drapers Company*, vol. iii, p. 443.
[170] OUA, HC/1/1/46–51, 'Hebdomadal Council Papers, January 1897–December 1898' (26 May 1897), 47, 31.   [171] *Oxford University Gazette* xxxix (1908–9), 89.
[172] Girtin, *Triple Crowns*, 340.
[173] OUA, UC/FF/77/1, Electrical Laboratory, Letter (8 July 1908).
[174] For a comparative account of the evolution of the collegiate plan, see Konrad Rückbrod, *Universität und Kollegium Baugeschichte und Bautyp* (Darmstadt, 1977).
[175] Paul Venable Turner, *Campus, an American Planning Tradition* (Cambridge, Mass., and London, 1984) and Helen Lefkowitz Horowitz, *Alma Mater: design and experience in the women's colleges from their nineteenth-century beginnings to the 1930s* (New York, 1984).
[176] Eric Ives, 'A New Campus', in Eric Ives, Diane Drummond, and Leonard Schwarz, eds., *The First Civic University: Birmingham, 1880–1980* (Birmingham, 2000), 111–30.
[177] David Watkin, *The Architecture of Basil Champneys* (Cambridge, 1989) 9–20.
[178] Ibid., 10.

Newnham and at Mansfield simply followed William Butterfield's lead. At Keble as early as 1868 Butterfield had built a whole college with corridors.[179] There was, then, the possibility for change even in the ancient universities.

Jackson, however, ignored these innovations.[180] He remained committed to the quadrangular form and to the staircase system.[181] Even at Trinity, which may seem like an attempt at an embryo campus, it is clear that Jackson simply intended to erect an open quadrangle.[182] It was all extremely conventional, highly traditional, and fundamentally uninventive. Indeed, from the plan alone, it is all but impossible to identify Jackson's additions to existing buildings. In part, of course, this simply reflected his lack of interest in planning. Still importantly, though, this unoriginality clearly satisfied his reforming (but far from revolutionary) clients. Those colleges like Keble, Mansfield, and Newnham which abandoned conventional plans were all in some respect atypical. Keble was a Tractarian hothouse; Mansfield, a dissenting seminary; Newnham—of course—was for women.[183] Jackson's patrons had no wish to be associated with them. Just as Hertford's style had linked it with the mainstream of university reform, so its quadrangular planning marked it out as an authentically Oxonian institution. Thus, whilst Jackson's plans may not have been elegant, they were obviously sufficient.

For it is clear that his work more than satisfied his clients. Jackson, as the progressives recognized, may not have been an original planner but in other respects he was an inventive architect. Above all else, he was the author of a new style—a new style for the new Oxford. Returning to Oxford in 1886, Goldwin Smith found a place with which he was now proud to be associated. 'The improvement in education and in all that relates to the proper objects of the place', he enthused, 'has been immense.' This was explicitly represented in his mind with the changed direction in Oxford architecture. 'I am glad to see', he wrote, 'in the case of the Examination Schools and Trinity, a departure from that narrow addiction to the medieval which reigned under Neo-Catholicism and Scott.'[184] His response to two of Jackson's buildings was repeated by reformers at colleges throughout Oxford. For Jowett, H. J. S. Smith, Thomas Fowler, John Percival, and the party of progress more generally, 'Anglo-Jackson' was a focus for their identity and a symbol of their triumph.

The party of progress made Jackson the university architect, and work for the university made him the authority on Oxford architecture as a whole. Many of

[179] Howell, 'Oxford Architecture', 745.   [180] *Architecture* 2 (1897), 84.
[181] Although for some eighteenth-century alternatives to this tradition, see H. M. Colvin, 'Architecture', in L. S. Sutherland and L. G. Mitchell, eds., *History of the University of Oxford, vol. v: the eighteenth century* (1986), 831–56.   [182] TCA, Uncat. Records, Drawing (1880).
[183] Geoffrey Rowell, ' "Training in simple and religious habits": Keble and its first Warden', in Brock and Curthoys, *History of the University*, vol. vii, pp. 171–92; Elaine Kaye, *Mansfield College, its Origin, History, and Significance* (Oxford, 1996). See also Vickery, *Buildings for Bluestockings*.
[184] Goldwin Smith, 'Oxford Old and New', *Oxford Magazine* iv (1885–6), 229.

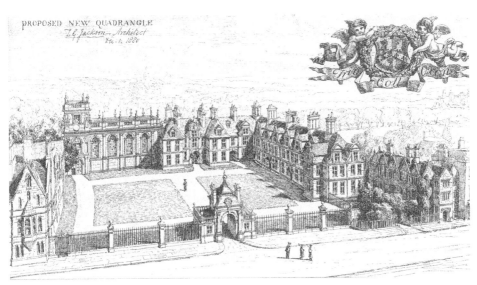

51. Trinity College, Oxford, as planned, with an open quadrangle.

the most prestigious projects in the city owed a debt to Jackson: the boys'
grammar school (1880–1) and girls' high school (1879–80);[185] the Oxford
Military College (1877) and the Acland Memorial Hospital (1896–7).[186] As late
as 1913 he was commissioned to design an old people's home.[187] And Jackson
had an indirect importance, too. His style became extremely influential,
inflecting—and even infecting—the work of other architects, both domestic and
municipal. 'We of the University' observed the *Oxford Magazine* in 1894,
'cannot complain if the houses in the North of Oxford are modelled upon the
ponderous magnificence of the New [Examination] Schools.'[188] Moreover, in
the shape of the town hall, as Nikolaus Pevsner noted, the architect H. T. Hare
simply gave to 'Oxford town' what Jackson had given to 'Oxford gown' for the
previous fifteen years.[189] With its fancy Flemish gables, its turrets and tourelles,
its Ipswich windows and its exuberant ornamentation, its influences were all too
clear. 'Mr Jackson', declared the *Magazine* 'has set his mark on modern Oxford,
and the new [municipal] buildings belong at least to the style with which he has
made us familiar.'[190]

[185] V. E. Stack, ed., *Oxford High School, Girls' Public Day School Trust 1875–1960* (Oxford,
1963); Bod., MS Top. Oxon. D.650, J. L. Marler, 'History of the City of Oxford High School for
Boys 1877–1925' (n.d.).
[186] Bod., G.A. Oxon. 4° 272, Misc. Papers relating to Cowley and G.A. Oxon c.317 (24), 'The
Story of the Acland Home' (n.d.).   [187] This was never built. *Builder* 104 (1913), 597.
[188] *Oxford Magazine* 13 (1894–5), 90.
[189] Sherwood and Pevsner, *Oxfordshire*, 302. See also Wendy Norbury, 'Oxford Town Hall: planning, building and financing the Oxford municipal buildings of 1897', *Oxoniensia* 65 (2000),
133–59.   [190] *Oxford Magazine* 13 (1894–5), 157.

Jackson's impact on the town was also seen in his work as a restorer. Although the great challenges of his career happened elsewhere—in Winchester, Portsmouth, Coventry, and Bath—Oxford was nonetheless a significant part of Jackson's restoration practice. His work at St Mary's has already been discussed, but this was just one of several churches that received his care: eighteenth-century All Saints' and twelfth-century St Peter's in the East were both restored as well.[191] Nonetheless, the bulk of Jackson's commissions came from the university. They ranged from minor repairs to major restructuring, and included buildings from every period in Oxford's history: Gothic, classical, and eclectic. He repaired Wren's Sheldonian Theatre (1890–2, 1909–10), Gibbs's Radcliffe Camera (1880), Wyatt's Radcliffe Observatory (1899–1903), as well as the more ancient work of older, often anonymous architects.[192] This included the mannerist Old Ashmolean (1896–8) and medieval Beam Hall (1884–5); Jacobean Wadham (1906–7) and Tudor Frewin Hall (1887–94).[193] With each project, Jackson's reputation and importance grew. Indeed, when repairs were needed to the Sheldonian there was no question of who would do them. 'When you say "our architect" ', wrote the Vice Chancellor to the Provost of Worcester in 1909, 'doubtless you mean T. G. Jackson.'[194] It was a refrain repeated across the city. Occasionally, in fact, his skills as a restorer overshadowed his ability as an architect. At Merton College, Jackson was responsible for a series of repairs to the chapel, sacristy, and library (1879–1901).[195] Yet in 1903, when Merton decided to build new accommodation, they turned to Basil Champneys.[196] The same thing happened at Oriel. Here he extended the chapel and built a new organ case (1883–4). But it was J. J. Stevenson and Champneys who got the bigger jobs.[197] This was far from normal, though. Far more typical was Jackson's work at Corpus Christi (1884–5), Lincoln (1891), and Brasenose (1892–5), where he was responsible for both important restorations and major extensions to the colleges.[198]

The most significant of the major restoration works was at the Bodleian Library. This was truly the task of a lifetime.[199] First commissioned to repair the building in 1877, his last contract was completed in 1915.[200] Even at the age of seventy-seven, he was still clambering up scaffolding to inspect decaying

[191] ORO, PAR 189/11/F4/6 and PAR 213/11/C2/1.

[192] OUA, ST 26 and UC/FF/197; Jackson, *Life and Travels*, 272.

[193] OUA, UC/FF/304/1/2–3; CCCA, B/4/1/9; *Oxford Journal* 13 Oct. 1906, 5; 12 Oct. 1907, 6; *Oxford Architectural and Historical Society Proceedings* NS 6 (1894), 38–47.

[194] OUA, ST 26, Herbert Warren (29 Jan. 1909).

[195] MCA, 1.5a College Register 1877–1914; Letter Book 1883–6, 957, 961; Letter Book 1886–90, 554, 76, 294, 401, 439, 643; Letter Book 1898–1902, 506, 525, 546.

[196] MCA, 1.5a, College Register 1877–1914, 357.

[197] OCO, Locked Case C, B I (I) 1265 (1898); ETC A8/4 Champneys Correspondence.

[198] OCCCA, B/4/1/9 College Minutes 1881–97, 81, 89, 98, 103; BNCA, B.13.2, Working Drawings: organ case and antechapel; *Oxford Journal* 12 Oct. 1895.

[199] Craster, *History of the Bodleian Library*, 140–3 gives details of the 1878–84 restoration alone.

[200] OUA, UC/FF/304/1/1 Bodleian (1876–89), Agreement (16 June 1877); OUA, UC/FF/304/6/3 Bodleian (1915–17), Certificate (1 May 1915).

LINCOLN COLL:
—OXFORD.—

'ROPOSED RESTORATION
OF THE HALL.

T.G.JACKSON.
ARCHITECT.
March
1891.

52. The interior of Lincoln College Hall, showing Jackson's restoration of the roof (1891).

masonry.[201] By then of course he was restoring his own work, done some forty years before.[202] This was comprehensive stuff: he rebuilt pinnacles and resurfaced stone, reglazed windows, and re-erected fallen statues. Not a spirelet escaped his attention.[203] Typically, though, he aimed to make any restoration as limited as possible. His work on the main gateway at the Botanic Gardens (1891) is a case in point. This was one of Nicholas Stone's great triumphs, built between 1632 and 1633 with 'all that unclassical profusion' which marks his porch to the University Church.[204] In 1891 it was in need of repair. Jackson was called in and counselled caution. 'The whole is indeed in a state of progressive decay', he wrote, 'but I should not recommend any very extensive renewal.' The result was the most limited of repairs—a pattern he followed at the Bodleian.[205] It was an advanced position to take, but many thought it worked. Certainly, his allies found the library 'well restored'.[206]

Not all his work was universally popular, of course. His methods and materials were the subject of sustained criticism by those outside Oxford. Jackson's decision to use Clipsham stone, in particular, was both radical and controversial. The native Headington stone had proved all too fragile, and from the Examination Schools onwards, Jackson insisted on importing the harder-wearing and rather more expensive Rutland stone he knew from his childhood in Stamford.[207] He chose well—it remains the first choice for Oxford architects to this day—but the effect was striking.[208] Oxfordshire stone is grey; Clipsham stone is yellow. Gradually, but inexorably, Oxford changed colour. It was not, for some, a popular change. The patching of the Bodleian Library with this alien stone so distressed Ruskin that he could not bear to look at it. He refused to walk within sight of the library.[209] Nor was William Morris any more keen to lose the 'grey streets' which were such an 'abiding influence and pleasure' for him.[210]

Nor was this his only criticism. Morris, of course, led the attacks on Jackson's work at St Mary's. He was similarly important in the campaign to save Trinity College's cottages. Jackson's initial proposal for the Broad Street front to Trinity had included the creation of a new porter's lodge and formal entranceway. This necessitated the demolition of an assorted collection of cottages. Morris was outraged. He claimed that they were 'in their way as important as the more majestic buildings to which all the world makes pilgrimage'.[211] The fellows were apparently impressed, and Jackson was forced to

[201] OUA, UC/FF/304/6/1 Bodleian (1913) Jackson (10 March 1913).
[202] OUA, UC/FF/304/3/1 Bodleian (1912) Jackson (21 Oct. 1912).
[203] OUA, UC/FF/304/5/2 Bodleian (1904–27) Jackson (17 May 1912).
[204] *Buildings of England: Oxfordshire*, 267.
[205] OUA, UC/FF/305/2/1 Botanic Garden (1885–91) Jackson (30 April 1891).
[206] Max Müller, *My Autobiography* (London, 1901), 216.
[207] *Times*, 3 June 1882.   [208] W. J. Arkell, *Oxford Stone* (Oxford, 1947), 110.
[209] Müller, *Autobiography*, 216.
[210] Quoted in J. W. Mackail, *The Life of William Morris* (1899; 2 vols. in 1; London, 1995), vol. 1, p. 49.
[211] *Architect* 34 (1885), 327.

retain the row of old wooden buildings, and abandon his plans for a gateway derived from the entrance to Worcestershire's Westwood Park.[212] In its place came a copy of the college's garden gate. Not everyone was pleased: the *Oxford Magazine* suggested that 'even that must have looked ugly when it was new'.[213] William Morris, however, was delighted, and paid tribute to Trinity on 'having preserved the quaint and characteristic houses near its gates, and thus offering a contrast to its ambitious neighbour Balliol'.[214]

It was a shrewd attack. For the fellows of Balliol were beginning to doubt the wisdom of their earlier building campaigns. The 'tea-tray gothic' of Butterfield's chapel (1856–7) and Waterhouse's Broad Street front (1867–71) soon seemed old-fashioned.[215] Jowett himself particularly disliked the chapel, whilst Waterhouse's work was cruelly caricatured by late-Victorian aesthetes: 'C'est magnifique, mais ce n'est pas la gare.'[216] In 1911, an attempt was made to change all this.[217] Walter Morrison, an old Balliol man and a millionaire philan-thropist, tried to build a new chapel. At the college gaudy, the Master had criticized Butterfield's work. The next day Morrison offered to pay for its replacement. The college accepted his cheque for £20,000 and his suggestion that Jackson should get the job.[218] The fellows of Balliol wished to replace Butterfield's chapel with an exact copy of its sixteenth-century predecessor. The Master was understandably anxious to 'find an architect sufficiently conscientious to sink himself, and really to work on the old lines'.[219] Jackson was the ideal choice—although he found the honour 'rather awkward'.[220] After all, he had been Butterfield's choice to complete his chapel at Rugby School only thirteen years before. Nonetheless, he was convinced that the college was resolved on the project, and drew up his plans.[221] He rejected the idea of an exact copy, and offered a chapel which was inspired by, rather than modelled on, the original.[222] Morrison accepted the suggestion, and the college seemed satis-fied.[223] But Butterfield's chapel was soon to be saved.

On 10 October 1911 Walter Morrison wrote to the Master. 'A storm is brew-ing, and it looks as if the only benefit which will come of my innocent action is an extended knowledge of human nature.'[224] He was only too right. The decision to destroy the old chapel was greeted with horror by many. Certainly, the debate

[212] An association suggested by Howard Colvin in his *Unbuilt Oxford*, 151.

[213] *Oxford Magazine* 4 (1886), 180.

[214] Norman Kelvin, ed., *Collected Letters of William Morris* (4 vols.; Princeton, 1984–96), vol. 4, p. 158.   [215] Compton Mackenzie, *Sinister Street* (2 vols.; London, 1913–14), vol. ii, p. 646.

[216] Jones, *Balliol College*, 207. The quotation is from Geoffrey Tyack, *Oxford, an Architectural Guide* (Oxford, 1998), 228.

[217] See also Peter Howell, ' "The Disastrous Deformation of Butterfield": Balliol College Chapel in the twentieth century', *Architectural History* 44 (2001), 283–92.

[218] BalCA, English Register 1908–24.   [219] BalCA, D.10.16/A (4 July 1911).

[220] Jackson, *Life and Travels*, 249.   [221] BalCA, Architects' Plans and Designs, 6 (1911).

[222] BalCA, MBP 317, Report (1911).   [223] BalCA, D.10.16/C (12 Oct. 1911).

[224] BalCA, D.10.16/A.

53. Carfax Tower, Oxford (1896–7)

was fierce: Curzon, Asquith, Edmond Warre—all the luminaries of Balliol had their say. The fellowship was split, with dons arguing both for and against.[225] The old members, too, were divided—though a majority wished to retain Butterfield's work.[226] Embarrassingly, the issue became a national concern. Norman Shaw and Basil Champneys wrote to the *Times* to oppose the recon-struction of the chapel. Selwyn Image wrote to Balliol to argue that 'the profes-sional resentment . . . against any architect who undertook its destruction and rebuilding would be very great indeed'.[227]

Just as at St Mary's, the arts and crafts anti-restorers were ganging up on one of their own. The peculiarity of the case was this: they were defending a building few of them liked. C. F. Bell's letter was characteristic of this attitude. He found the chapel 'Unpleasing, repulsive even', but could not countenance its

[225] BalCA, D.10.16/B.   [226] Jackson, *Life and Travels*, 249–50.
[227] BalCA, D.10.16/B.

demolition: Butterfield's work was simply too important.[228] Embarrassed by the attacks and the attention, the governing body of Balliol dropped Morrison's proposals and abandoned Jackson's plans. It had been an edifying spectacle for no one. As the Master of Balliol admitted to Jackson, 'It is nothing amiss with your plans which to me at least seem very beautiful.'[229] The objections to any change were simply too great. Jackson accepted his setback at Balliol without any rancour. 'I quite expected there would be a good deal of opposition', he wrote to the Master. 'P.S. I have paired with the Dean of Winchester on the question of Greek or no Greek tomorrow.'[230] As his reference to debates in Convocation makes plain, he could afford to be phlegmatic. His position in Oxford was without any serious rival. He might fail at Balliol, but he would succeed elsewhere.

Fundamentally, Jackson was called upon precisely because he could satisfy the very particular needs of his Oxford patrons. This was as true of his restorations as it was of his other projects, as the case of Carfax tower makes plain. The church of St Martin, Carfax, was knocked down as part of a road improvement scheme in 1896.[231] Its tower, marking the end of the High Street, is all that now remains. Jackson was commissioned to strengthen and restore it—despite being the third choice for the job. The reasons for his success give a good guide to his appeal for the people of Oxford. The original architect had been H. T. Hare, who was at the same time building the new Oxford Town Hall. He proposed to restore the tower 'in a very elaborate fashion', which—like his civic building—would include 'a considerable amount of Renaissance decoration'.[232] Public opinion was outraged, and the vicar talked of betrayal.[233] Amid the cacophony of abuse, Hare was abandoned in favour of G. F. Bodley. Bodley rejected the Renaissance, arguing for restoration 'in the manner of the ancient masonry', and advised on the construction of an elaborate belfry stage.[234] These plans were also attacked and condemned as 'rebuilding for rebuilding's sake'.[235] The lesson appeared to be—as the local paper put it—that only someone able 'to enter into the spirit in which an old Oxonian looks on the tower' would be able to do the job.[236] Jackson was called into action, and proposed a much less radical treatment.[237] He was 'against interfering with the features of the tower more than is actually necessary for its actual repair'.[238] The result was approved and carried out. This was no longer 'a tower of Babel, but a tower of peace and concord'.[239]

Perhaps the *Oxford Times* exaggerated. Certainly, a visitor to the tower today would find its description absurd, though Carfax remains a symbol of Jackson's

[228] BalCA, D.10.16/B.   [229] BalCA, D.10.16/C.   [230] Ibid.
[231] Carteret J. Fletcher, *A History of the Church and Parish of St. Martin, Carfax, Oxford* (Oxford, 1896), v, 83–5.   [232] *Oxford Magazine* 15 (1896–7), 4.
[233] Fletcher, *St. Martin*, 89–91.
[234] Bod., GA Oxon c. 204, 'Carfax Church', 51a (1897).   [235] *Oxford Times*, 23 Jan. 1897.
[236] *Oxford Journal*, 17 Oct. 1896.   [237] Bod., GA Oxon. C. 204, 64–7.
[238] Bod., GA Oxon. C. 204, *Oxford Times*, 20 March 1897.   [239] Ibid., 10 July 1897.

success. Standing at the heart of Oxford, it is equally important to both city and university.[240] It embodies Jackson's status not just as the 'Maker of Modern Oxford', but also 'the restorer of old Oxford'.[241] In short, it exemplifies his dominant influence on the city's buildings; the way in which Jackson became 'our Oxford architect', as the university journal put it.[242] The success of the party of progress, the growth of the university, and Jackson's own ability had placed him in an unrivalled position. Both as an architect and as a restorer, he came to define Oxford. His buildings embodied the reformed university. His career reflected the new Oxford. At the Commemoration of 1911, Curzon called Jackson the 'artifex oxoniensissime': the most Oxford of artists.[243] It was a fitting tribute to the maker of modern Oxford, a man who had changed the way that Oxford looked—and how it saw itself.

---

[240] It remains the case that undergraduates must reside within six miles of Carfax during term.
[241] Jackson, *Life and Travels*, 255.   [242] *Oxford Magazine* 16 (1897–8), 351.
[243] Jackson, *Life and Travels*, 249.

4

'In the Shadow of Anglo-Jackson'[1]
Jackson and the Public Schools

Few now remember John Calcott Horsley (1817–1903).[2] Whilst other nineteenth-century artists have been reclaimed by the critics, Horsley's career is largely forgotten. Yet, before he was twenty he had earned the praise of the *cognoscenti* for his *Rent Day at Haddon Hall* (1836). By the time he died, he had been elected a Royal Academician, and served as Treasurer to the Academy. He painted for the new Palace of Westminster, the Prince Consort, and Queen Victoria.[3] His was a long and distinguished life, but it is remembered—when it is remembered at all—for two curiosities. The first is his brief but bitter campaign, waged within the pages of the *Times*, against nude modelling. It was this that won him his nickname Clothes Horsley.[4] The second is rather more significant: Horsley was the man who made Norman Shaw's career. In 1864 J. C. Horsley and family moved to Cranbrook in Kent; here they employed the young and unknown Shaw to extend and rebuild their home. Almost immediately, Shaw's career took off.[5] Thus it is as patron rather than painter that Horsley takes his place in history. It is also how he entered Jackson's life. Twenty years later, T. G. Jackson was also called to Cranbrook. Horsley, 'growing old', but still 'full of life and energy', was a governor of the local school, which was expanding and wished to expand still further.[6] Jackson was commissioned to build 'Big School', an edifice which still dominates the site, and reflected the ambitions of headmaster and Horsley alike.[7] By choosing Shaw for his home and Jackson for his school, J. C. Horsley was leading the way.[8] In the last thirty years of the nineteenth century, Jackson and Shaw

---

[1] J. Mordaunt Crook, 'T. G. Jackson and the Cult of Eclecticism' in H. Searing, ed., *In Search of Modern Architecture* (New York, 1982), 102–20, 117.

[2] Even T. S. R. Boase ignores him almost utterly in his *English Art, 1800–1870* (Oxford, 1959), 210, 214–15, 254, 288–9.

[3] J. C. Horsley, *Recollections of a Royal Academician* (London, 1903).

[4] He was also immortalized in Whistler's comment, 'Horsley soit qui mal y pense'. See Alison Smith, *The Victorian Nude* (Manchester and New York, 1996), 227–34.

[5] Andrew Saint, *Richard Norman Shaw* (New Haven and London, 1983), 32–6.

[6] T. G. Jackson, *Recollections* (Basil H. Jackson, ed.; Oxford, 1950),190–1.

[7] Nigel Nicolson, *Cranbrook School* (London and Ashford, 1974), 19.

[8] Horsley and Jackson remained friends: Bod. MS Eng. c.2236 fol. 33, Jackson to Rosamund Horsley (1903).

can be said to have dominated scholastic and domestic architecture respectively. Cranbrook is a microcosm of late-Victorian taste which chose, when it could, a public school by Jackson and a country house by Shaw.

Nor is this observation simply hindsight; contemporaries also acknowledged its truth. Beresford Pite in his obituary of Jackson recalled that from the mid-1870s, 'if Norman Shaw, in domestic work, made the running with Queen Anne, Jackson's Jacobean led the way in Collegiate building'.[9] T. G. Jackson, and his style, were certainly successful. He was in demand from schools throughout England, and his clients included Eton and Harrow, Radley and Rugby, Uppingham and Westminster, as well as those which simply hoped to reach the top. 'Generations of . . . schoolboys', as J. Mordaunt Crook observes, 'have grown up in the shadow of Anglo-Jackson.'[10] And to work at these schools was no small achievement for Jackson was following the greats of the previous generation. He inherited the mantle of his master, Scott, at Brighton, followed Burges at Harrow, and succeeded Street at Uppingham. He replaced Sir Arthur Blomfield at Eton and at Rugby he completed Butterfield's chapel, following this with a Speech Room commemorating the great Dr Temple. Each of these schools had different wants and different needs; each had different histories and different futures. But all were united by a need for adequate buildings and suitable symbolism. For their identity as public schools was critically linked to their architecture. Jackson was commissioned by those schools which recognized the importance of this link and could afford to commission the best. 'No one can mistake one of Mr Jackson's schools for anything but a school', wrote one admirer.[11] It was precisely this ability to build appropriate architecture that was valued. It was this that took Jackson to Cranbrook—and elsewhere.

The demand for good architects was quite clear. 'As the number of schools which now rank as "public schools" has much increased', wrote a Charterhouse classics master in 1906, 'so the competition between them has naturally much increased also, and it has far too often taken the form of expenditure on buildings and the like.'[12] By the turn of the century, this had become a truth almost universally acknowledged. The previous fifty years had seen a massive growth in fee-paying education: a growth which was reflected in the provision of ever grander architecture. New schools needed new buildings, and old schools had to keep up.[13] It was a tremendous opportunity for an ambitious architect. But it also presented

---

[9] *Builder*, cxxvii (1924), 753.   [10] 'T. G. Jackson and the Cult of Eclecticism', 117.
[11] *Architectural Review* 1 (1896–7), 159.
[12] T. E. Page, 'Classics', in [T. E. Page, ed.], *The Public Schools from Within* (London, 1906), 4.
[13] William Whyte, 'Building a Public School Community, 1860–1910', *History of Education* 32 (2003), 601–26. See also Malcolm Seaborne, *The English School: its architecture and organisation 1370–1870* (London, 1971) and, with Roy Lowe, *The English School: its architecture and organisation 1870–1970* (London, 1977); Malcolm Seaborne, 'The Architecture of the Victorian Public School', in Brian Simon and Ian Bradley, eds., *The Victorian Public School* (Dublin, 1975); R. A. Low, 'The Organisation and Architecture of Schools in England, 1870–1939' (Ph.D., Birmingham, 1977); N. G. Hamilton, 'A History of the Architecture and Ethos of the School Chapel' (Ph.D., Bristol, 1985).

real problems. The public schools required their buildings to fulfil a number of functions. They were intended to influence behaviour; both to control and to inspire their inhabitants. School buildings and their surroundings, wrote one contemporary, 'have the power to mould character'.[14] Equally, and importantly, public schools operated in a highly competitive environment and they had to sell themselves. It was precisely because their new buildings 'please the popular eye and look well in an illustrated paper', that they were built.[15] Furthermore, architecture was used as a means of identification and to assert an identity. The architecture of the London Board Schools, argues Deborah Weiner, 'was one of the tools by which the newly emergent institutions defined their goals and were, in turn, understood by the public'.[16] This was true for the public schools too. In a period of dramatic change and deep insecurity, buildings became all important.

This was undoubtedly a time of uncertainty for the public schools. 'It would indeed be difficult to name any educational institution in the country which has undergone so much active change in recent years', wrote T. E. Page.[17] And more than anything else, this change meant the creation of a public school community. The 'strong tie of brotherhood between our great Public Schools', was, as the headmaster of Harrow put it in 1899, 'a comparatively recent' development.[18] Nonetheless, it was a tangible, observable fact by then. The start of this process can be seen in the 1860s, coinciding with the establishment of two government enquiries into secondary education. The Clarendon Commission was appointed in 1861 and instructed to investigate nine schools: Eton, Westminster, Winchester, Charterhouse, St Paul's, Merchant Taylors', Harrow, Rugby, and Shrewsbury.[19] Their status as the nine public schools of England was enshrined in a subsequent act of parliament. In 1864 the Taunton Commission was set up and began its enquiry into other endowed schools.[20] The distinction between the two groups was far from clear. Nor was the impact of the two commissions revolutionary. The Commissioners could do little more than encourage reform, and counsel change.[21] But this often unwanted attention reflected a growing consensus. Even within the schools, there was a demand for change, for reform, and for a new approach to elite education.[22]

This shift was stimulated by the ever-closer links between different public schools. Some of these were institionalized. The Headmasters' Conference, which

[14] Edward Allen Bell, *A History of Giggleswick School* (Leeds, 1912), 202.
[15] Page, 'Classics', 4.
[16] Deborah E. B. Weiner, *Architecture and Social Reform in Late-Victorian London* (Manchester and New York, 1994), 2. See also Karl Otto, ed., *School Buildings* (London, 1966), vol. 1, p. 9.
[17] Page, 'Preface' to *Public Schools*, xiv.
[18] H. Montague Butler, *Public School Sermons* (London, 1899), 7.
[19] Colin Shrosbree, *Public Schools and Private Education* (Manchester and New York, 1988) gives the best account of the Clarendon Commission.
[20] David Ian Allsobrook, *Schools for the Shires* (Manchester and New York, 1986) chs. 8 and 9.
[21] Shrosbree, *Public Schools*, 2–3.
[22] Although cf. Edward C. Mack, *Public Schools and British Opinion since 1860* (London, 1941), 104–5, 117 for an alternative analysis of the period.

provided an increasingly important forum for debate and analysis, was founded in 1869.[23] Others, however, were less formal. Masters and headmasters moved between schools, taking with them the traditions they had absorbed. Two institutions proved to be particularly important in this respect: Winchester and Rugby. Winchester had a good right to call itself the oldest public school in existence, and its traditions guaranteed an atmosphere of respectable antiquity. At Glenalmond, for instance, Wykehamist slang was enforced and the boys wore surplices to chapel. 'Mainly', as the Warden explained, 'because they formed one of the links which bound us to Winchester and gave us the semblance of an old foundation.'[24] Even Thomas Arnold, the reforming headmaster of Rugby, brought Wykehamical traditions to the school. 'I envy Winchester its antiquity', he wrote, 'and am therefore anxious to do all that can be done to give us something of a venerable outside, if we have not the nobleness of old associations to help us.'[25] Curiously, though, Arnold's interpretation of Winchester life was to prove more influential than the original.[26] Through the work of men like A. C. Tait and E. W. Benson, Edward Goulburn and Frederick Temple, Henry Hart and Henry Walford, the models established at Rugby were soon found in Sedburgh, Birmingham, Wellington, and even Tractarian Lancing.[27] Under C. J. Vaughan, Rugby came to Harrow, and the ideal soon became intercontinental.[28] In 1877, indeed, a 'Public School' in Natal appointed a headmaster whose only claim to the position was that he had been educated at Rugby, and whose main contribution to the school was the importation of Rugby football and the prefect system.[29]

Gradually, competition and co-operation created an ideal type. This was not quite the 'deadening conformity' that some writers have seen taking hold of the public schools, but it is evident that a clearer definition of the public school soon evolved.[30] Schools—if they were to be public schools—were required to offer certain facilities, and to pursue particular goals. A public school was likely to be a boarding school: 'the boarding school element is the key-stone of the public school arch', as one writer put it in 1901.[31] St Paul's and Merchant Taylors' remained the lonely exceptions to this rule, and few desired—or could afford— to follow their example.[32] Similarly, the organization of the school was standardized: prefects, fagging, and corporal punishment were all instituted. By 1900 one writer even assumed that the creation of a system of prefects 'would be

---

[23] Alicia C. Percival, *The Origins of the Headmasters' Conference* (London, 1969).
[24] G. St. Quintin, *The History of Glenalmond* (Edinburgh, 1956), 22, 27.
[25] A. P. Stanley, *The Life and Correspondence of Thomas Arnold* (10th ed.; London, 1877), vol. i, p. 137.   [26] Ibid., vol. i, p. 104.
[27] David Newsome, *Godliness and Good Learning* (London, 1961), 100–93.
[28] E. D. Laborde, *Harrow School, Yesterday and Today* (London, 1948), 52.
[29] J. R. de S. Honey, 'The Victorian Public School', (D. Phil., Oxford, 1969), 164.
[30] John Roach, *Secondary Education in England* (London, 1991).
[31] J. G. Cotton Minchin, *Our Public Schools, their Influence on English History* (London, 1901), 413.
[32] Shrosbree, *Public Schools*, 27.

almost sufficient to mark the year 1853 as the real date at which Bradfield College became a public school'.[33] Even more importantly, the curriculum was dominated by the study of Latin and Greek. At Sherborne, for instance, classics took up 60 per cent of the timetable in 1865.[34] A gradual broadening of the curriculum modified this to some extent, but even the weakest pupils were expected to learn Latin, and entrance to Oxford or Cambridge was dependent on a knowledge of Greek.[35] Sporting activity took up much of the rest of a pupil's time. Athleticism was believed to be vital for the boys' health and moral well-being.[36] 'If boys were encouraged to be manly, energetic, and enthusiastic at their games', wrote one contemporary, 'they would be trained to become healthy and ingenuous throughout their whole school life; failing this course, there will arise an unmanly precocity in self-indulgence, betting, smoking, and drinking.'[37] There was also more symbolic importance to sport. Public schools only played sports against comparable establishments. Shared games also implied an equal status.[38]

This, then, was the public school system as it evolved in the last half of the nineteenth century. The schools came to resemble each other, and a community of inter-related institutions grew up. By the turn of the century, a collective identity had emerged. Masters were urged 'so to educate boys that, when they leave school, they are not Eton, Harrow or Rugby boys, but only public-school boys'. Parents were advised to choose a school which, be it new or old, was 'subservient to the public school system'.[39] The 'nine public schools' acknowledged in 1867,[40] had become—for one writer at least—240 just twenty years later.[41] This was almost certainly an over-estimation. Nonetheless, modern research suggests that the public school community between 1880 and 1902 consisted of around a hundred schools: with a core group of fifty acknowledging each other's status.[42] Even the youngest foundations could develop all the facilities of a public school. Thus it was that Rossall, founded in 1844 as the 'effort of a soi-disant Roman Catholic hotel-keeper and speculative squire, to develop a new watering-place',[43] developed archetypally public school characteristics in the 1870s.[44] Soon there was a house system, prefects, games, scholarships, a prep-school, chapel, hall, and training

---

[33] Arthur F. Leach, *A History of Bradfield College* (London, 1900), 70. See also Rupert Wilkinson, *The Prefects: British leadership and the public school tradition* (London, 1964).

[34] A. B. Gourlay, *A History of Sherborne School* (Sherborne, 1871), 128, 180.

[35] Cotton Minchin, *Our Public Schools*, 95–6.

[36] J. A. Mangan, *Athleticism in the Victorian and Edwardian Public School* (Cambridge, 1981). For the ways in which this represented a change in ideal, see Newsome, *Godliness and Good Learning*.

[37] Clement Dukes, *Health at School Considered in its Mental, Moral and Physical Aspects* (London, 1887), 196.   [38] Honey, 'Victorian Public School', 245.

[39] Dukes, *Health at School*, 22.

[40] E. E. Bowen, 'On Teaching by Means of Grammar', in F. W. Farrar, ed., *Essays on a Liberal Education* (London, 1867), 198.   [41] Dukes, *Health at School*, 19.

[42] J. R. de S. Honey, *Tom Brown's Universe* (London, 1977), 264, 268.

[43] Leach, 'Bradfield', 3.

[44] John Frederick Rowbotham, *The History of Rossall School* (Manchester, 1894).

corps.[45] Little wonder that by 1891 it had joined Rugby, Winchester, Westminster, and Eton in the 'Public School News' column of the *Cambridge Review*.[46]

The public school community was built upon similarity. Nonetheless, differences did remain. Three broad and by no means stable categories were acknowledged by contemporaries. At the top of this unofficial hierarchy came the Clarendon Schools: the nine institutions investigated by the Royal Commission of 1861. These were, on the whole, older, richer, and more prestigious. They were, however, also threatened by the growth of newer schools. Shrewsbury's position as one of the great Public Schools was always doubtful, and even Rugby, Westminster, and Eton could find themselves 'outstripped by younger competitors'.[47] These competitors were the endowed schools investigated by the Commission of 1864. The headmasters of Uppingham, Wellington, and others were outraged to find themselves excluded from the Clarendon nine—and well they might be.[48] Many of the innovations which were to become universal across the public school community were initiated by this second group of institutions. The idea of a 'Modern Side', teaching a predominantly non-classical curriculum, was pioneered in schools like Marlborough (1854) and Wellington (1866).[49] In 1869 the first school mission was founded at Uppingham. It was soon copied throughout the public school system.[50] Not all institutions could afford the risk of innovation, however. An important third group was made up of schools whose public school status was highly suspect, and whose future was unclear. Many of them were short-lived. Both Wimbledon College and All Saints', Bloxham, to name just two, were established in the empty shells of previously failed schools.[51] Others were later absorbed into the state sector.[52] These schools were a world away from Eton, Uppingham, and the more prestigious establishments, but they could rise. As late as 1850 the boys of Rugby were refusing to play Marlborough, excusing themselves on the grounds that 'We don't play private schools'.[53] This, though, was soon to change, as Marlborough adopted the prefect system, fagging, and compulsory games.[54] Just such a translation was the ambition of all. Indeed, the public school community was built upon it.

---

[45] W. Furness, ed., *The Centenary History of Rossall School* (Aldershot, 1945), 8.

[46] *Cambridge Review* 12 (1890–1), vii.

[47] See Shrosbree, *Public Schools*, ch. 5 and [Page, ed.], *Public Schools from Within*, 199.

[48] T. W. Bamford, *The Rise of the Public Schools* (London, 1967), 182.

[49] J. R. Taylor, H. C. Brentnall, and G. C. Turner, eds., *A History of Marlborough College* (London, 1923), 182; David Newsome, *A History of Wellington College* (London, 1959), 134.

[50] Malcolm Tozer, ' "The readiest hand and the most open heart": Uppingham's first mission to the poor', *History of Education* 18/4 (1989), 323–332.

[51] Anthony Poole, *A History of Wimbledon College* (Wimbledon, 1992), 1–13; *History of All Saints' School, Bloxham* (2nd edn; Bloxham, 1925), 4–7.

[52] Some were of respectably ancient foundation, and have since left the state sector. See, for example, D. M. Sturley, *The Royal Grammar School, Guildford* (Guildford, 1980).

[53] Tony Money, *Manly and Muscular Diversions* (London, 1997), 85.

[54] Taylor et al., *Marlborough*, 183.

Both the similarities and differences inherent in this system were expressed in its architecture. Buildings, as one writer put it, 'make up the outward and visible home of the School life', and as the schools changed, so did their buildings.[55] The Taunton Commissioners of 1864 were quite clear about the importance of architecture. They asserted that

Next to a good master there is nothing more important for a school than a good site and buildings. Health, order, dignity, good teaching and good learning are all intimately concerned with the aspect and accommodation of the school itself . . . a grammar school should occupy a worthy position among the buildings of the town.[56]

As this implies, both the functional and symbolic aspects of architecture were stressed. 'Health, order, and dignity' were just as important as 'good teaching and good learning' in public school buildings. Certain sorts of accommodation, however, were regarded as fundamental. Self-evidently, the first requirement of any school was a place to teach. Traditionally, this role was fulfilled by the 'School Room', or 'Big School': a single room in which all pupils were taught. By the late nineteenth century, however, this pattern was seen as old-fashioned and the continental class-room system was increasingly widely adopted.[57]

This, though, was just part of a general trend towards specialization. Schools acquired libraries and laboratories, music rooms, drill halls, armouries, theatres, and other impedimenta. By the turn of the century it was observed that 'It would be hard to find a single public school of recognized position that has not a laboratory', and engineering workshops were considered part of the 'necessary plant of a Public School'.[58] Sports, too, required specialized provision. Fields were purchased and prepared; gymnasia, pavilions, and changing rooms were built—and the expense could be crippling. Glenalmond was very nearly bankrupted by the cost of its fives courts alone.[59] But these additions were considered essential. Just as important was the provision of residential accommodation for sleeping, reading, and eating. Studies and dining halls were by no means universal, but boarding houses were very widely adopted. So all-pervasive was the boarding ideal, indeed, that even day-boys came to acquire houses: at Rugby, there was 'Town Boys Hall', whilst at Clifton the admission of Jewish pupils was marked by the foundation of 'Jews' House'.[60] The 'crowning building' of any school, however, was the chapel.[61] A college without a chapel, one enthusiast claimed, was like 'an angel without wings'.[62]

[55] R. H. Hardy, *Public School Life: Rugby* (London, 1911), 32.
[56] *Report of the Schools Inquiry Commission* (21 vols.; 1868–70), vol. i, p. 276.
[57] Seaborne, *English School . . . 1370–1870*, vol. 1, p. 267.
[58] T. Nicklin, 'Laboratories', in Page, *Public Schools*, 81; Leach, *Bradfield*, 22.
[59] William Rankin, 'Trinity, Glenalmond', *Anglican World* 7/2 (1967), 38.
[60] J. B. Hope-Simpson, *Rugby since Arnold* (London, 1967), 148; Jeremy Potter, *Headmaster: the life of John Percival, radical autocrat* (London, 1998), 44–6.
[61] P. R. Egerton quoted in, *All Saints' School, Bloxham*, 27.
[62] Quoted in Newsome, *Godliness and Good Learning*, 1.

The motivations behind these buildings were not purely poetic, of course. There was a clear commercial case for attractive architecture. The first head-master of Lancing, for example, was quite sure that his school was held back by its buildings. It was, he declared, 'below all other schools of its rank and cost in the machinery which the parents of boys, rightly or wrongly, consider essential to a well-ordered school'.[63] Similarly, the headmaster of King's College School blamed its decline on 'the insignificant nature of our Strand entrance'. He went on to complain that 'All our rivals have during the last ten years vastly improved their school accommodation and equipment whilst K.C.S. is as badly housed and as poorly equipped as it was thirty years ago.'[64] Buildings were also intended to influence their inhabitants. The classic statement of this view was made by Edward Thring, headmaster of Uppingham. 'Whatever men say or think', he declared, *'the almighty wall is, after all, the supreme and final arbiter of schools.'*[65] There were two elements to his analysis. In the first place, the architec-ture had to be 'honest', in a Ruskinian sense. 'The rooms should tell no lie', he wrote, 'but speak the truth, the honourable truth, about work done in them.'[66] Secondly, and importantly, he maintained that architecture had the power to shape behaviour. 'The mere force of fine surroundings', Thring believed, 'would make the low views and meannesses connected with lessons and learning drop off'.[67] Although rarely articulated so clearly, these beliefs undoubtedly underpinned public school building. And so, in addition to its role as advertise-ment and inspiration, architecture was also used to combat disobedience, bad behaviour, and vice.[68] In an age of alarm about 'school boy morality', buildings were a crucial battleground.[69] Badly-designed schools, it was feared, would allow 'boys to get together for immoral purposes, unseen and undetected'. Ill-planned dormitories, it was suggested, could allow pupils to call out 'obscene remarks and be undetected'.[70]

In many different ways, then, buildings were important to the public schools. But their relative wealth and success affected what they could build and who designed it. Harrow established a science block as early as 1874.[71] Oundle, by contrast, acquired laboratories only in 1914.[72] Not that the Clarendon Schools had a monopoly on architectural innovation. The first school gymnasium was

---

[63] Quoted in Brian Heeney, *Mission to the Middle Classes: the Woodard Schools* (London, 1969), 32.
[64] Thomas Hinde, *A Great Day School in London: a history of King's College School* (London, 1995), 39.   [65] Edward Thring, *Addresses* (London, 1887), 75.
[66] Ibid., 73.
[67] George R. Parkin, *Edward Thring: headmaster of Uppingham School* (2 vols.; London, 1898), vol. ii, p. 120.
[68] See also Alisdaire Hickson, *The Poisoned Bowl: sex and the public school system* (London, 1995), 16.
[69] [Social Purity Alliance], *Schoolboy Morality: an address to mothers* (London, 1888), 3, 11.
[70] Dukes, *Health at School*, 76–80.
[71] W. O. Hewlett, 'Harrow School Buildings', in Edmund W. Howson and George Townsend Warner, eds., *Harrow School* (London, 1898), 33.
[72] William George Walker, *A History of the Oundle Schools* (London, 1956), 532.

built at Uppingham in 1859.[73] Soon similar buildings were found throughout
the public school community, from Eton downwards. The choice of architect
was similarly important. Minor public schools competed for the best local men.
Thus James Wilson built for Colleges in Cheltenham, Taunton, and Bath,[74] and
Charles Hansom was commissioned by both Clifton and Malvern.[75] Richer
schools looked further afield. Scott and Burges worked for Harrow; Butterfield
for Rugby; Street for Uppingham, and elsewhere. There was aspirational building too: progress by association. The Clarendon Schools of Charterhouse, Eton,
and Shrewsbury all commissioned the respectably establishment architect Sir
Arthur Blomfield, as did the rising stars of Malvern, Oundle, and Repton. But
his work for schools in Croydon and Chester can only be explained as wishful
thinking; an unsuccessful attempt to break into the public school community by
building big.[76]

This was a role that Graham Jackson was often required to fulfil. His connections and associations were of the utmost importance to the schools he served.
Even so, they were constrained by their resources, and some schools were simply
unable to afford him. The £11,000 boarding house he proposed for Victoria
College, Jersey, in 1897, proved to be nearly twice as much as the school could
countenance. The governors were forced to commission the art master's son,
who produced a new plan for £4,000 less.[77] Yet Jackson's success elsewhere was
in fact in many ways dependent on his expense. A Jackson building represented
an investment; a promise of growth, expansion, and ambition. His links with
Oxford were an important part of this architectural association. As one writer
implied, it was as 'the Oxford architect *par excellence*' that the public schools
commissioned him—at least at first. They saw the changes in the university style
and simply 'followed suit'.[78] Later on, institutions were less interested in
Oxford, and more influenced by the wider public school community. But the
rhetorical importance of Jackson's work remained the same. He was commissioned by schools at all levels of the public school hierarchy, and the results were
inevitably different in each case. Nonetheless, the motivations of his clients were
essentially the same. Each school wished to stress its membership of the public
school community, to keep up with the competition, and to influence the behaviour of its pupils. Jackson's career was based upon his ability to satisfy each and
all of these aims.

---

[73] Newsome, *Godliness and Good Learning*, 220.

[74] M. C. Morgan, *Cheltenham College: the first hundred years* (Chalfont St Giles, 1968), 14; Roger
Dixon and Stefan Muthesius, *Victorian Architecture* (London, 1985), 270.

[75] Ralph Blumenau, *A History of Malvern College* (London, 1965), 6.

[76] Richard A. Fellows, *Sir Reginald Blomfield: an Edwardian architect* (London, 1985), 170–1.

[77] D. J. Cottrill, *Victoria College, Jersey* (London and Chichester, 1977), 53–4. He was also
beaten to the commission for Cheltenham College Chapel in 1893 by an Old Cheltonian,
H. A. Prothero and A. S. Owen, *Cheltenham College Chapel* (Cheltenham, 1928), 8.

[78] Humphry Ward, *History of the Athenaeum, 1824–1925* (London, 1926), 330.

As in Oxford, though, it was reform rather than revolution that made Jackson's career. Whilst the style in which he built was often self-consciously modern, he once again offered no real innovations in his plans. From the smallest to the largest projects, Jackson's preference was always for the conventional and the collegiate. Of course, he was not alone in this. Basil Champneys' first board schools showed a similarly unadventurous approach to style and reticence in planning. His Harwood Road School (1873), for example, pioneered the 'Queen Anne' Revival in its elevation, whilst retaining an old-fashioned form of plan.[79] Moreover, Jackson's clients clearly had no wish for a break with the planning of the past. They evidently accepted his suggestion that the Oxford tradition was appropriate for the public schools.

Nonetheless, in at least one case, Jackson's old-fashioned planning was to lose him work. In 1893 Christ's Hospital resolved to leave its cramped and inadequate accommodation in London and build a new school in Horsham. The Council of Almoners invited a group of architects to compete for the job. Major figures like Jackson, T. E. Collcutt, Aston Webb and Ingress Bell, Edward Paley and Hubert Austin, all accepted the invitation.[80] The winners were Webb and Bell.[81] This was a deep disappointment for Jackson, who subsequently refused permission for his designs to be reproduced.[82] It was not a surprising result, however. In part, Jackson's failure was due to the unique status of Christ's Hospital, which was an academic charity, not a public school, and presumably had no wish to look like its more conventional competitors. The Hospital was proud to be 'without parallel in this country', and chose architects who would express this in stone.[83] Jackson's designs, so obviously inspired by Christ Church, Oxford, would have tied the school into a system which it had explicitly rejected.[84] More importantly, though, his plans were regarded as deficient. Webb and Bell had rejected the quadrangular form in favour of a series of separate blocks arranged round a campus. It was, declared the *Builder*, 'unquestionably the best plan submitted', providing a good architectural effect and 'the best sanitary conditions'.[85] Jackson's quadrangles, by contrast, were condemned. Although 'pleasant in architectural effect', they were damned as insanitary, impractical, and old-fashioned.[86] Fortunately for Jackson, however, this proved to be an isolated disappointment. In the main, his clients seem to have been satisfied with his planning, however unimaginative it might have

---

[79] Frank Kelsall, 'The Board Schools: school building 1870–1914', in Ron Ringshall, Margaret Miles, and Frank Kelsall, eds., *The Urban School: buildings for education in London, 1870–1980* (London, 1983), 13–28, at 19.

[80] G. A. T. Allan and J. E. Morpurgo, *Christ's Hospital* (London, 1984), 75–6.

[81] See Ian Robert Dungavell, 'The Architectural Career of Sir Aston Webb (1849–1930)' (Ph.D., London, 1999), ch. 4.   [82] *Builder* 66 (1894), 456.

[83] Allan and Morpurgo, *Christ's Hospital*, 10.

[84] Jackson redrew his entry and exhibited it at the Royal Academy. See *Builder* 68 (1895), 376.

[85] *Builder* 66 (1894), 455. See also, *British Almanac and Companion* 1895, 287–9.

[86] *Builder* 66 (1894), 457.

54. Jackson's abortive plan for Christ's College, Horsham (1895).

been. In fact, that very conventionality proved to be an important secret of his success.

There was nothing inevitable about his achievement, of course. Indeed, Jackson's first school was a world away from Eton and the others. It proved to be a dead end, both stylistically and in terms of its type. It was a small village school in a small Kentish village called Otford. In this part of the county Jackson was a local man. Indeed, it is still as a 'well-known Kentish architect' that he is remembered in local guidebooks.[87] Jackson's client was the vicar, R. B. Tritton. Perpetual curate from 1845 to 1868, when he succeeded to the newly created living of Otford, Tritton was an undistinguished man with a good eye for architecture. In 1862 he had called in G. E. Street to restore the church.[88] Exactly ten years later, in 1872, Jackson was invited to design the village school. It was undoubtedly welcome work for the impoverished fellow of Wadham, but it was not a career-making move. Jackson's later success was built on expensive work in a post-Gothic Revival style for the liberal elite of the Victorian educational system. Otford School was the complete reverse. It was an elementary church school, run by the—exclusively Anglican—National Society. As in so many villages, spurred on by the threat of secular school boards set up by the 1870

[87] Elizabeth Ward, *A Short Guide to the Centre of Otford* (Otford, 1994), 17.
[88] Dennis Clarke and Anthony Stoyel, *Otford in Kent: a history* (Otford, 1975), is a model parish history; see 209–10, 215, 216, 254, 273.

Elementary Education Act, Otford was seeking to retain denominational teaching by building a better school.[89]

Typically, church schools were built in a form of Gothic, reflecting an association with the Established Church.[90] Still more problematically for Jackson, Otford was far from wealthy. Well into the twentieth century its parishioners drank out of a pond.[91] The result was a plain, brick-built box, polychromatic, and with a few Gothic details. The schoolmaster's house next door is a simple vernacular cottage in white-painted brick. It is certainly not one of Jackson's most impressive buildings, and it is the only elementary school he ever built, but it does give some suggestion of future directions. Jackson's sensitivity to his locality is evident. The hipped roofs of both school and house are typically Kentish, whilst the choice of materials is eminently suited to Otford. At the same time, his use of colour and decorative detail prefigures the playfulness of later work. Above all else, it was the distinction between school and schoolhouse, the scholastic and domestic, which was the key feature of the future. Given the desire to have honest architecture fit for its purpose, this was a distinct achievement. It marked a satisfactory—if scarcely mould-breaking—start to Jackson's life as an educational architect.

It was Oxford rather than Otford, however, that began his life of building for public schools. Jackson's success in the city after the building of the New Examination Schools was soon seen in educational architecture far beyond the university. The first of his projects was at the Oxford Military College at Cowley, founded in 1877. 'Being neither civil nor military, under a military governor who did not teach and a headmaster who had no authority it languished and expired' in a short time.[92] As in the case of most other military colleges, almost no interest has been shown in its short existence.[93] Nonetheless, in its time it was an intriguing attempt to create a new kind of school. The aim was to equip the sons of officers with the sort of education they would require in the army. The onus was on the practical rather than the classical. Science, modern languages, modern history, and militarism dominated the curriculum.[94] Given the preponderance of Greek and Latin at most first grade schools, this was a radical move. Unsurprisingly, it was one made by the party of progress in Oxford. G. W. Kitchin was joined by the muscular Christian Socialist Thomas Hughes

[89] Between 1870 and 1877, the National Society established places for an additional 1,069,712 children. John Hunt, *Education in Evolution* (London, 1971), 224.

[90] Seaborne, *English School . . . . 1370–1870*, pp. 211–12; Seaborne, 'E. R. Robson and the Board Schools of London' in History of Education Society, *Local Studies and the History of Education* (London, 1972), 63–82, at 74.

[91] Albeit one that is—as a particularly important example of its type—now Grade II listed.

[92] T. G. Jackson, *Recollections: the life and travels of a Victorian architect* (Sir Nicholas Jackson, ed.; London, 2003), 150.

[93] See Trevor Hearl, 'Military Academies and English Education: a review of some published material', *History of Education Society Bulletin* (1968), 11–21.

[94] Bod., G.A. Oxon. 4° 272, Misc. Papers relating to Cowley, Pamphlet (1880).

55. Oxford Military College (1877–81).

on the founding council, whilst Humphry Ward was director of studies.[95] With this provenance, the employment of Jackson as architect was all but inevitable. For this new kind of school, he built in a new kind of style (1877–81).[96] There are details here from Spain and Italy and the Netherlands, but also from English manor houses like Sutton Place or Layer Marney. The uncompleted central court was more parade ground than quad, and the richly ornamented pilasters and other details strike a jaunty note, strikingly dissimilar to the Oxford fron-tispiece he planned. In its rejection of Gothic the school symbolized its aban-donment of the old ways, and embraced an association with Oxford's liberals. It was a link that was retained throughout its short existence.[97]

More successful, though no less typical, was work for the two Oxford High Schools founded in this period. Both were liberal projects. Both chose Jackson. The first was the High School for Girls, founded in 1875 as part of the Girls' Public Day School Company.[98] Like Somerville, this was a quintessentially

[95] Bod., G.A. Oxon. 4° 272, Prospectus (1877).   [96] *Architect* 18 (1877), 72.
[97] See *The Trumpeter* vol. i (1886–8), vol. ii. (1889–91).
[98] Founded 'to supply education of the highest class, and to occupy for Girls the position taken in the education of Boys by the great Public Schools'. Bod., B.160/39, Girls Public Day School Company Prospectus (1905); see also, V. E. Stack, ed., *Oxford High School, Girl's Public Day School Trust 1875–1960* (Oxford, 1963).

56. Oxford High School for Girls (1879–81).

progressive project. Education for women was the goal of many in the party of
progress. Without education for girls it was simply not possible. The foundation
was funded by many familiar figures. H. J. S. Smith, T. H. Ward, T. H. Green,
R. St John Tyrwhitt, Benjamin Jowett, and John Percival all bought shares.[99]
The ubiquitous Kitchin gave lectures on the principles animating the school.[100]
After two years renting the Judge's Lodgings in St Giles', during which time the
Assizes had driven them out on several occasions, it was resolved to build a
school of their own. The choice of architect was simple. Jackson began building
in 1879 and was finished by 1880. The school owes most of its character to the
bold terracotta pilasters and cornice which Jackson designed. This was a clear
case of architecture in the service of advertising. 'It has been mentioned to me',
wrote Graham Jackson, 'that the Oxford Committee & those interested in the
School wish the building to have some architectural character.' The 'terracotta
enrichments' and 'architectural features'—such as a lantern and rubbed-brick
window aprons—were his response.[101] They also linked the building with its
neighbour: J. J. Stevenson's vibrant redbrick and terracotta house for
T. H. Green.[102] This was, to some extent, liberalism by association. More than

[99] OHSA, Scrapbook of Material Relating to the Foundation, List of shareholders (n.d. ?1877).
[100] Bod., G.A. Oxon. B.160/38, Advertisement (1876/7).
[101] OHSA, Scrapbook, Jackson to Mrs Max Müller (13 May 1879).
[102] Tanis Hinchcliffe, North Oxford (New Haven and London, 1992), 154–5.

that, with its flamboyant pseudo-Spanish flavour, it announced a total rejection of Gothic conservatism. Better still, it was fit for its purpose and, with its ornamental features, stylistically suited for girls.[103] The links between Jackson, the new Oxford and new women made by Freeman had been triumphantly proved.

The defining progressive project of the period, however, was the City of Oxford High School for Boys.[104] Inspired by T. H. Green, the City High School was intended to be the bridge by which local boys could enter the university, 'without reference to social conditions or religious belief'.[105] Green, as a town councillor and university politician, was the driving force behind the school, and with him came the party of progress.[106] Sewell and Jowett and H. J. S. Smith subscribed £50; Kitchin and Fowler gave £10. The Warden of Wadham donated £52 and W. W. Jackson sent 7 guineas. Green himself gave £200, and was joined on the governing body by H. J. S. Smith.[107] A competition to choose the architect of this thoroughly progressive project was held in 1880. Jackson won. He beat two local men, both of whom had conceived Gothic schools. One, by Wilkinson, was rejected, 'not having complied with the instructions' which strictly limited the cost of building.[108] The other, severely Revivalist structure by Frederick Codd was simply not appealing enough to win the vote.[109] Codd's subsequent cry of plagiarism was utterly incorrect.[110] Jackson won with a building compared by contemporaries to the New Examination Schools, built 'in the early form of the English Renaissance'.[111] It was a suitable style for the school: expressing a new vision of Oxford. For Green saw his creation as part of a 'ladder of learning', leading those 'from the humblest well-disciplined home to the universities'.[112] It was only too appropriate that the indigent scholar should be able to progress up this ladder with a Jacksonian backdrop: from the City High School to the New Examination Schools, he would be framed by the architecture of progress.

Unsurprisingly, these Oxonian connections remained important for commissions outside the city too. Jackson's new school at Sandwich, in particular, was

[103] *Oxford High School Magazine*, vol. i (April 1881), 232–4.
[104] Bod., MS Top. Oxon. D.650, J. L. Marler, 'History of the City of Oxford High School for Boys, 1877–1925' (19??), 11.
[105] Bod., G.A. Oxon. C.111, 'The Proposed Foundation of a High School for the City of Oxford' (1877), 4.
[106] R. L. Nettleship, *Memoir of Thomas Hill Green* (London, 1906), 181–2; Melvin Richter, *The Politics of Conscience: T. H. Green and his age* (Bristol, 1996), 359.
[107] Bod., G.A. Oxon. B.160, List of donations 1879 and 1880; Bod. Lib. G.A.fol. A.139, 'City of Oxford High School for Boys, Scheme and Deed of Trust' (1878),10.
[108] *City of Oxford High School Magazine* vol. xlviii (July 1956), 62.
[109] I. H. Taylor, 'Sir T. G. Jackson and the High School', *City of Oxford High School Magazine* 58 (1966), 45–50.   [110] *Building News* (1880), pp. 237, 340 (20 Feb. and 19 March 1880).
[111] Bod., B.160/23 'City of Oxford High School for Boys' (1880).
[112] Bod., G.A. Oxon. 8°659/6, T. H. Green, 'The Work to be Done by the New Oxford High School' (1882), 9.

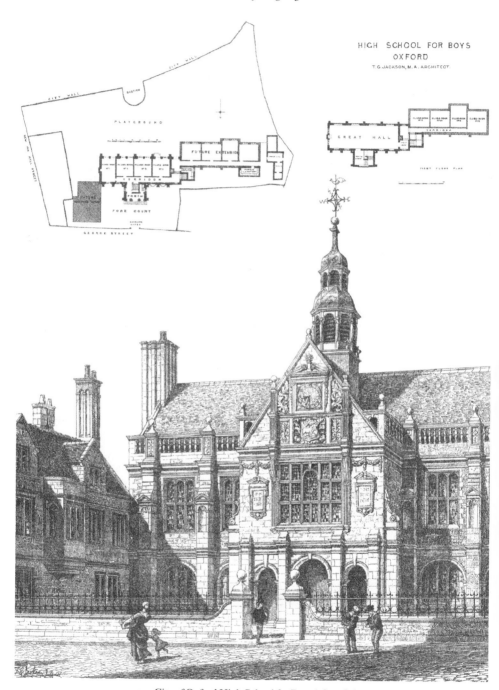

57. City of Oxford High School for Boys (1879–81).

58. Sir Roger Manwood's School, Sandwich (1894–5).

essentially an Oxford project. Certainly, it could not be described as a truly public-school commission. Sir Roger Manwood's was in fact a brand new grammar school, founded out of an existing educational endowment which the Charity Commissioners had threatened to sequestrate. The Governors were ambitious, however, and had big plans for their new school. It was this ambition, and their Oxford connections, that brought Jackson to Sandwich in 1895. Lincoln College was one of the school's patrons, and the bursar of Lincoln sat on its governing body. Jackson's work for the college was a guarantee of his ability and his association with Oxford was intended to prove inviting to putative parents. For although new, the school was intended to offer a 'public school' education for the 'Sons of Gentlemen'. Manwood's was one of the many institutions intending to leap the queue for public school status, and it intended to do this with impressive facilities and all the appurtenances of a higher-class education. Thus the school soon gained a *Calendar* (1897), an old boys' association (1899), a school magazine (1900), and a cadet corps (1902).

Most important, however, were its buildings. This impoverished academy was willing to spend over £5,000 on the accommodation considered appropriate for a public school. Jackson's work, indeed, was the central feature of Manwood's advertising campaign, with the school selling itself on the promise of 'Excellent buildings (from plans by T. G. Jackson, R.A.)'.[113] The headmaster's house, dormitory, classrooms, and projected hall were formed into what became known as 'the quadrangle'.[114] Oxford and the essence of the public school had come to Kent: the buildings were even illustrated in the *Public School Magazine*.[115] Nonetheless, this was not a wholly successful translation. Sandwich, like many

---

[113] RMSA, BL 12 (Prospectus, 1897), BL 13 (Advertisements).
[114] W. J. Brown, *So Far . . .* (London, 1943), 29.   [115] *Public School Magazine* 2 (1898), 379.

other schools of its status, failed in its attempt to become a public school. It was too small, too poor, and too late in entering the game. Jackson's hall was never built. The old boys' club never took off, and the frequent exhortations on the value of 'public school spirit' seemed to have little effect. But the project was entirely typical. This school's hope of stressing its Oxford links through its choice of architect were repeated elsewhere. So too was the effort to attract parents with expensive, showy, and 'suitable' architecture.[116]

He was to be a little more successful at another Kentish school. Cranbrook was a rather older institution, and already close to public school status when Jackson arrived in 1882. Here, of course, it was an artist rather than an academic that commissioned him, but the intention was the same. Cranbrook was on the way up, and Jackson was intended to propel it still further. As headmaster, Charles Crowden had spent thousands at the school since his appointment in 1866. He had built fives courts, a gymnasium, and laboratories, and 'had transformed the little Cranbrook grammar school and *almost* propelled it into a future of "public school" independence'.[117] Jackson's 'Big School' was to be the crowning part of this bid for greater status.[118] Entirely typically, then, it was as 'Oxford Jackson' that Horsley brought him to Crowden's aid. A link with the ancient universities was proof of public school status, and Cranbrook was keen to stress this. Indeed the school promoted itself with a photomontage, which included the arms of both universities and of all the colleges at which the masters had studied.[119] Jackson's open quadrangle was suitably collegiate, and bore comparison with his concurrent work at Trinity College. Cranbrook was doing everything right—but everything was actually about to go wrong. The school's endowment was limited and in 1888, the governors refused Crowden's request for yet further expansion. Infuriated, he resigned and took himself off to Eastbourne College. In his seven years there Crowden spent £20,000 pounds on new buildings. Yet even in Eastbourne, he could not have it all his own way. In 1895 he resigned and used his last speech as headmaster to outline the further buildings required to make Eastbourne College a true public school.[120]

As this case makes plain, the gap between aspiration and achievement could only be bridged by money. Buildings were a vital part of a school's claim to membership of the public school community—but they were expensive. Indeed, that was partly the point. This was, as it were, a case of conspicuous construction. After all, only the best schools could afford the best buildings.

---

[116] John Cavell and Brian Kennett, *A History of Sir Roger Manwood's School, Sandwich* (London, 1963), 68–89.

[117] Peter Allen, 'Biographical Sketch: the Reverend Dr Charles Crowden, headmaster 1866–88' (unpublished article, 1992); Duncan H. Robinson, *Cranbrook School* (Cranbrook, 1971), 10–12.

[118] *Builders' Journal*, 13 Jan. 1897; CSA, Uncat. Material: Jackson, Report (July 1883); 'The Opening of the New Buildings' (1885); Robinson, *Cranbrook*, 12.

[119] CSA, Box of Material 1866–88, photomontage (1887).

[120] V. M. Allom, *Ex Oriente Salus: a centenary history of Eastbourne College* (Eastbourne, 1967), 49–69.

59. Cranbrook School (1884–5).

Difficulties inevitably arose when schools built beyond their means. In this respect, as in others, Jackson's work at Brighton College is the acme of his projects for the struggling minor public schools.[121] All the elements present in Sandwich and Cranbrook were made manifest—and indeed magnified—at Brighton. There was also the added embarrassment that Jackson's work bankrupted the school. In the three years between 1884 and 1887, over £33,000 was spent on new buildings; an extravagance that the college quite simply could not afford.[122]

It had all seemed worth it at the time, of course. Jackson, as an Old Brightonian, and as a great Oxford architect, was highly prized by the school.

---

[121] See *Public School Magazine* 3 (1899), 241–53.
[122] Martin D. W. Jones, *Brighton College, 1845–1995* (Chichester, 1995), 79, 94.

Association with Oxford was particularly important for Brighton. Threatened by the success of competitors like Cranbrook and Eastbourne, and keen to enter the ranks of the 'Great Public Schools', Brighton needed to stress its superior educational connections. Graham Jackson, indeed, had to restrain the headmaster from improperly appropriating the arms of Oxford and Cambridge for the

60. Brighton College, Proposed Entrance (1884–7).

school.[123] This was prevented but there was no copyright on quadrangles.[124] Jackson's plans involved a massive extension to Gilbert Scott's original Schoolhouse, providing a frontage to the street and a conventionally collegiate plan. Had the money been available, an even more impressive set of buildings would have been erected, including a vast hall and chapel.[125] The fact that Brighton College still holds original drawings of Jackson's work in Oxford suggests that the association was deliberately sought by the school. Certainly, it was hoped that the result would prove enticing for future parents. As Jackson himself put it, a 'quadrangle of stately proportion', would certainly impress 'any one who should come to see the College with the idea of sending a boy there'.[126]

This use of architecture for advertising influenced all the decisions made by Brighton College. As one helpful correspondent put it, 'At present, the great competition between schools is in *appliances* such as boarding houses built for the purpose . . . Parents think much of these things—they see them at one place and expect them everywhere'.[127] Even Jackson's cricket pavilion (1883) was driven by the search for competitive advantage. How else to explain the College's systematic survey of other public school pavilions before it settled on a design of its own?[128] Likewise, the levelling of the playground (1882–3) was influenced by the governors' conviction that 'It is of the greatest importance to the prosperity of the College that its approaches and neighbourhood should be as attractive as possible.'[129] These were all extremely costly: nearly £10,000 was spent on the pavilion and sports fields alone. But the prize was great. As the headmaster put it, Jackson's work was the means by which Brighton would 'take its place among the great public schools'.[130] Of course, this hope was to be frustrated. Brighton's bankruptcy in 1895 put an end to this attempt. It could not, however, kill the school's ambition. Jackson was called back by the College in 1919 to build a war memorial chapel. Even here, though, expense limited effect. The original appeal had been intended to raise £20,000—'the lowest sum asked for by any public school', it was stressed.[131] In fact, only £9,000 was accrued, and Jackson's work was restricted to extending the existing chapel (1922–3).[132] Brighton's insistence on commissioning the elderly and expensive architect is significant, however. Even in its poverty, the school was keen to keep up, if it could.

These three south-eastern schools were lucrative projects for Jackson. They were not, and could never be, prestigious. Moreover, they represent his dependence on Oxford for further work. Whether it was direct personal contact (as at Sandwich) or indirect association (as in Cranbrook), his undertakings in

[123] BCA, 154/5, Griffith Papers 1881–2, Jackson to Griffith (7 Dec. 1882).
[124] Seaborne and Lowe, *English School since 1870*, 41.
[125] BCA, Uncat. Plans and elevations (1882–7); *Builder* 48 (1885), 796–7.
[126] BCA 154/4, Jackson, Report (25 March 1882).
[127] BCA 131 Madden Papers 1874–88, Henry Latham (18 June 1883).
[128] BCA 154/2–6.   [129] Quoted in Jones, *Brighton College*, 82.
[130] Ibid., 73.   [131] Ibid., 177.   [132] BCA, Uncat. Plans (1919–22).

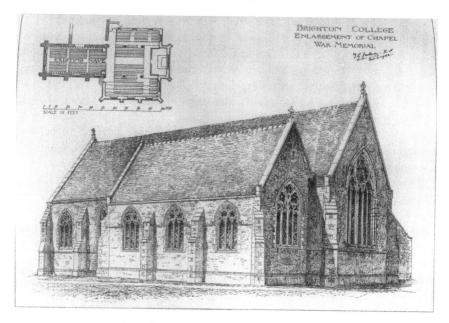

61. Brighton College, Chapel Extension (1922).

the university were the source of other educational commissions. Alone, this could only limit his appeal. There was, however, another focus to his public school work; one that was to prove far more useful. Just as Jackson had been used by Oxford to signify change, so several of the Clarendon Schools employed him to symbolize their own reform. Determined to sustain their position, Jackson's architecture was the ideal instrument to demonstrate their modernity, their success, and their relevance. His work began in Harrow. Here he built Church Hill House (1877–8; demolished 1921), a massive extension to a smaller, older boarding house. It was a tremendous advertisement for the school's transformation. 'Nothing', wrote E. M. Butler in 1898, 'shows more glaringly the different conception held now and formerly of what schoolboys require', than the contrast between the old building and Jackson's additions.[133] It was a propitious time to build. The Clarendon Commission investigations had led to a re-writing of the school's statutes.[134] Jackson's client, J. A. Cruikshank, was at the vanguard of these reforms and wanted his architect to build a new and better Harrow.[135]

    In particular, the architectural context made Jackson's job quite clear. The existing house was old and dilapidated. His extension was quite the reverse.

[133] E. M. Butler, 'The Houses', in Howson and Warner *Harrow School*, 51.
[134] E. D. Laborde, *Harrow School Yesterday and Today* (London, 1948), 52–9.
[135] *The Harrovian*, vol. iv, No. 8 (18 Oct. 1891), 89.

62. Church Hill
House, Harrow
School (1877–8).

The contrast between the 'airy and beautifully proportioned dining-hall' which
Jackson built, and the 'old one, half under-ground, which received no sun and
very little light', was obvious to all.[136] Even more significant was the building's
relationship to its newly-built neighbour: a speech room, erected in 1874 to celebrate the school's tercentenary. Cruikshank had initially been one of the leading
proponents of this project. He soon changed his mind. The architect forced on
the school was William Burges, whose monumental muscular Gothic building
was universally loathed by the masters of Harrow.[137] It was described by one as

[136] Butler, 'The Houses', 51.
[137] J. Mordaunt Crook, *William Burges and the High Victorian Dream* (London, 1981), 245–6.

both a moral danger and a 'breach of faith'.[138] Cruikshank himself resigned as treasurer of the fund-raising committee.[139] Thus, when in 1876 he succeeded to a boarding house next to Burges' speech room, he had already made his views quite clear. The choice of Jackson to rebuild and extend the house in 1878 was a conscious one. It was, in a sense, an attempt to recapture the architectural initiative for the reformers—and it worked. Jackson produced a piece of strikingly modern architecture. True, it was built in brick to harmonize with its surroundings, but in all other respects it was a glaring innovation. This was the 'Harrow Renaissance'.[140] What better way of commemorating it than to build in a revived Renaissance style? Church Hill House had a *piano nobile* for the dining hall, complete with Venetian windows.[141] In a school dominated by Gilbert Scott and bullied by Billy Burges it was an extraordinarily bold move. The result was 'one of the finest pieces of architecture on the Hill'.[142]

Jackson's use as an architect of reform did not end with Harrow. At Westminster, in 1895, he was called on to be a midwife at the school's rebirth. It had suffered in the nineteenth century from declining repute and diminishing numbers. Despite its place amongst the Clarendon nine, it had been 'outstripped by younger competitors', as inertia obstructed reform.[143] In particular, Westminster was believed to be 'condemned' to decline 'by the benumbing influence of its existing site'.[144] Jackson was one of many who recognized that a bad location had made a worse reputation.[145] Westminster was one of the few great schools which remained in central London. Merchant Taylors' moved in 1875.[146] St Paul's began the first of several relocations in 1884.[147] Christ's Hospital moved to Horsham in 1891, having discussed the move since 1869.[148] Even King's College School sought to avoid decline by leaving the Strand and moving to Wimbledon.[149] Only Westminster stayed, shackled to its old buildings.[150] Decrepit and smoke-besmirched, they stood as a symbol of the school's slump in status.[151] None of the houses was adequate, and many were simply substandard.[152]

In particular, writers identified three buildings, built by Robert Furze Brettingham in 1789, as emblematic of Westminster's mediocrity. 'All three',

[138] In Edward Graham, *The Harrow Life of Montague Butler* (London, 1920), 224–6.
[139] J. A. Cruikshank, 'Dr. H. Montague Butler', in Howson and Warner, *Harrow School*, 119.
[140] Percy M. Thornton, *Harrow School and its Surroundings* (London, 1885), 302–9.
[141] *The Architect* 14 Nov. 1890; *Building News* 5 July 1878.
[142] *The Harrovian* vol. xlii, No. 1 (2 March 1929), 3.   [143] *Public Schools from Within*, 199.
[144] Cotton Minchin, *Our Public Schools*, 217.   [145] Jackson, *Life and Travels*, 219–20.
[146] F. W. M. Draper, *Four Centuries of Merchant Taylors' School, 1561–1961* (London, 1962), 183–5.
[147] Michael F. J. McDonnell, *A History of St. Paul's School* (London, 1909), 419, 428; A. N. G. Richards, *St. Paul's School in West Kensington, 1884–1968* (London, 1968), 6–10.
[148] G. A. T. Allen and J. E. Allen, *Christ's Hospital* (London, 1984), 70–6.
[149] Hinde, *King's College School*, 43–8.
[150] Lawrence E. Tanner, *Westminster School* (London, 1951), 73.
[151] Cotton Minchin, *Our Public Schools*, 214.   [152] Shrosbree, *Public Schools*, 16.

63. Rigaud's House, Westminster School (1896–7). Jackson's addition is to the right.

observed a commentator in 1881, 'are dismal specimens of late eighteenth century architecture'; they were even believed to contribute to a sense of melancholy in the schoolyard.[153] As chance would have it, one of the houses, Rigaud's, burnt down in 1895, and W. G. Rutherford, the reforming headmaster, called in Jackson. For £10,000 Rutherford got an entirely new house—and a new image for Westminster.[154] The rebuilt Rigaud's (1895–6) was defiantly decorative, abandoning the late eighteenth century to seek inspiration from Wren. It still stands as an incongruous and individual part of the school.[155] As such, it was an appropriately assertive structure. Rutherford's commitment to reform was unquestioned. From his appointment as headmaster in 1883 onwards, and amidst much controversy and criticism, he dragged the school into the modern world.[156] Jackson's new house was an embodiment of this aggressive approach: Rutherford and reform were memorialized in Rigaud's. Westminster was keeping pace with its younger competitors—and Jackson was thus the ideal man for the job.

At Eton, too, Graham Jackson was valued not so much for his links with Oxford, as for his ability to respond to the college's quite specific needs.

[153] Cotton Minchin, *Our Public Schools*, 229.
[154] John D. Carleton, *Westminster School, a History* (London, 1965), 119, 134.
[155] 'The house does not harmonize with its surroundings.' (Lawrence E. Tanner, *Westminster School: its buildings and their associations* (London, 1923), 63.)
[156] Tanner, *Westminster*, 76–8; Carleton, *Westminster*, 72–80.

On occasion this meant commissions that were intended to symbolize change. Not all his work here was reforming, however. His underpinning of the lower chapel (1900) called on his skills as an engineer and as a well-known expert on church restoration.[157] Equally, his boat house (1900–3), cricket pavilion (1901–3), and racquets courts (1902–3) represented little more than the expansion of an already extensive sporting establishment.[158] The Lawson Memorial Museum (1904) was more obviously important: built as a poignant tribute to a boy who had perished in a boarding house fire.[159] It was not, though, the start of anything innovative, but rather the completion of an existing project.[160] The most significant of his commissions were nevertheless clearly linked to educational reform. His science schools (1902–4) and music rooms (1903–5; 1908–9) marked a new beginning for the college.[161] Eton was falling behind its younger rivals, and was urgently broadening its curriculum. As in Oxford, a change in architect reflected a change in ethos; a move away from 'Ye bigot spires, ye Tory towers, | From progress ever free', and towards something new, something modern, something rather more progressive.[162] In particular, Jackson's buildings marked an attempt to introduce new subjects and to bring science to all Etonians.[163] The difference between Eton and its competitors was its wealth, of course. In total, the science schools and music rooms cost the College nearly £11,000.[164] But this expenditure also reflected the importance of Graham Jackson's work. Eton needed to change, and to show that it had changed. Once again, even the Clarendon schools had to run to keep up.

The threats to Eton, Westminster, and the other Clarendon nine did not come from schools like Brighton or Cranbrook, of course, and still less from Sandwich. After all, Jackson's laboratories and music rooms at Eton had cost more than twice what the governors of Sir Roger Manwood's spent on an entire school. The challenge to the 'Great Public Schools' came rather from the broad band of ambitious middle-ranking institutions. As has already been noted, not all of these were prepared to spend money on an expensive—if nationally recognized—architect. Nonetheless, two of the most obviously flourishing schools did choose Jackson. They were seeking to confirm their place amongst

---

[157] ECA, Coll/B5/64, Lower Chapel Records.

[158] ECA, Coll/B5/224, Playing Fields (1900–3); Coll/B5/303, Racquet Courts (1902); R. A. Austen-Leigh, *An Illustrated Guide to the Buildings of Eton College* (3rd ed.; Eton, 1921), 133.

[159] ECA, Coll/B5/306, Lawson Museum papers (1903).

[160] Austen-Leigh, *Eton College*, 149.

[161] ECA, Coll/B5/299/2, Papers relating to the Science Schools (1902–4); Coll/B5/304, Papers relating to the Music Schools (1903); Coll/B5/305, Papers relating to the Music Schools (1903–9).

[162] *Pall Mall Gazette*, 17 Nov. 1882, 4.

[163] Science had been taught to some since 1869. H. C. Maxwell-Lyte, *A History of Eton College, 1440–1910* (London, 1911), 529. But for a criticism of the teaching see ECA, Coll/B5/299/1 H.E.R. to Warre (10 Aug. 1898).

[164] ECA, Coll/B5/299/2, Cost of science buildings at Eton (n.d. ?1904); Coll/B5/305, Music Schools (1904), Go/115 Finance Committee (1905–11).

the public school community, and Jackson proved the perfect vehicle for this goal. A combination of his links with Oxford and his ability to embody reform in the buildings he designed proved immediately appealing to both Radley College and Uppingham School. Each school was expanding and wished to grow further. Both were challenging the Clarendon nine. Jackson enabled them to express this in their architecture. Perhaps more than any other public schools, they are monuments to his achievement. Certainly, they made his name outside Oxford.

Initially, however, it was precisely these Oxford connections that secured Jackson his work at Radley. He was first employed by H. L. Thompson, Warden of the college between 1888 and 1896. A 'strong liberal', Thompson had been Censor of Christ Church and a member of the party of progress in Oxford.[165] As the vicar of Iron Acton he had commissioned Jackson to restore his church (1878–9)[166] and once appointed to Radley he again employed the architect.[167] Graham Jackson's first job was far from radical. His sanatorium (1890–1) was admittedly successful. It was described by no less a figure than Sir James Paget as 'the best school infirmary in England'. But it was scarcely eye-catching.[168] Soon, though, Jackson was to transform the face of the school. It had been originally founded at Radley Hall, a Georgian mansion by William Townsend (1676–1739), and remains an unassuming if attractive country house: red brick, with stone quoins, stringcourses, and a cornice.[169] Jackson's job was to extend this and provide new accommodation. His chapel (1893–5), dormitory, cloister (1890–1; 1893), and hall (1909–10) were all part of that process. The result was to make Radley look like an Oxford college. Georgian was out and Gothic was in. A quadrangle was built and, had the money been there, the school would have gained a 'College gateway with tower above' and a huge 'Great Hall'.[170] Even without these, though, the perpendicular of both hall and chapel formed a striking counterpoint to the existing house.

It was a deliberately startling change. For Jackson's collegiate Gothic was intended to symbolize a new school. Radley had made its name as home for the children of the Tractarian rich. Its founder, William Sewell, had intended it to resemble 'a family in which noblemen's sons might live as in their own father's house'.[171] Radley Hall provided just such an environment. It was an idiosyncratic approach, of course. Sewell had rather alarmingly claimed that everything

---

[165] Catharine Thompson, 'Memoir', in H. L. Thompson, *Four Biographical Sermons* (London, 1905), 1–50.   [166] Jackson, *Recollections*, 150, 162, 173.
[167] W. W. Jackson was also a trustee of the college; see A. K. Boyd, *The History of Radley College, 1847–1947* (Oxford, 1948), 147.   [168] Jackson, *Recollections*, 246.
[169] M. T. Cherniavsky and A. E. Money, *Looking at Radley: an architectural and historical survey of the earlier buildings* (Radley, 1981), 9–26.
[170] RadCA, Misc. Drawings, plan (18 Oct. 1889); Uncat. MSS 1889–1913, Architect's Report (11 June 1890).
[171] In Christopher Hibbert, *No ordinary place: Radley College and the public school system* (London, 1997), 35.

64. Radley College Chapel (1893–5).

65. The interior of Radley College Chapel.

from 'the organisation of the School to the choice of the carpets' was based on the Athanasian Creed.[172] Seeking to make Radley a rather more orthodox member of the public-school community, Thompson used Jackson to build a more conventional college. Inevitably, conservative figures within the school opposed this attempt. They deprecated the loss of Radley's 'homelike and picturesque appearance'.[173] But that, of course, was the intention. Thompson was unmoved—and he was ultimately victorious. Under him (and with Jackson's help) Radley 'became a public school'.[174] Naturally, this was more reform than transformation. Even the masters acknowledged the need for a suitable chapel, arguing that 'Radley should not be left behind other schools in such a matter as this', and urging that any such building should 'not be inferior to those recently built by other schools of our standing'.[175] Equally, the choice of style was multifunctional. The college needed the support of those 'sympathetic to its religious aims' if it were to sustain the expense.[176] The polychromatic perpendicular chosen had hints of high-church Selwyn College, Cambridge, and even of Keble College, Oxford. In other words, Jackson's work was entirely fitting.[177] It was certainly successful, and he was invited back to build the hall and, later, the war memorial archway (1921–2).[178] These were eminently public-school projects and proof, indeed, of Radley's membership of the public school community.

Uppingham, too, was an increasingly important member of this exclusive system, and an institution determined to escape its unconventional past. Some of Jackson's work here was quietly understated. The refitting of the library (1890–1) was a work of restoration rather than radical change.[179] This, however, proved to be the exception. As Jackson himself put it, he was employed at Uppingham 'to do in fact what I had done for Brasenose at Oxford'.[180] Had the school been able to afford his fancy gables for the Tercentenary Building (1888–91), it would have looked even more Oxonian.[181] As it was, with the Victoria Buildings (1896–7) Jackson created a quadrangle with a grand High Street frontage.[182] It could not have been more collegiate. Once again, though, this went beyond mere fashion. Uppingham was being rebuilt by its new Headmaster, E. C. Selwyn. Indeed his work amounted to a refoundation. He had inherited a school which had grown great under the charismatic Edward Thring. It had done so, however, despite Thring's opposition to the conventions of public-school life and his contempt for the Clarendon schools, obsession with prizes, athleticism, and the Arnoldian ideal on which that community was

[172] William Sewell, in Boyd, *Radley*, 99.   [173] RadCA, Letter to Warden (9 May 1891).
[174] T. D. Raikes, *Sicut Columbae: fifty years of St. Peter's College, Radley* (Oxford and London, 1897), 145, 177.   [175] RadCA, Letter from Masters (9 May 1891).
[176] RadCA, Appeal Letter (?1891).   [177] Although, see *The Radleian*, 19 Oct. 1893, 51.
[178] RadCA, Misc Drawings, Gateway (7 Feb., 9 Nov. 1921); E. Bryans, *Sicut Columbae: a history of S.Peter's College, Radley, 1847–1922* (Oxford, 1925), 211–12.
[179] *Builder* 59 (1890), 189; 63 (1892), 128. The internal porch is clearly derived from that at Broughton Castle. See *Country Life* 67 (1930), 126–34.   [180] Jackson, *Life and Travels*, 192.
[181] USA, Uncat. Drawings; *Builder* 58 (1890), 11–12.   [182] *Builder* 74 (1898), 419.

66. War Memorial
Gateway, Radley
College (1921–2).

67. Uppingham School
Library (1890–1).

68. The Tercentenary Building, Uppingham (1888–91).

built. Under his rule the school remained exceptional.[183] Selwyn, who had married into the Arnold family, rejected this inheritance, and brought Rugby to Uppingham.[184] Such was the change that his headmastership is known by Thring's admirers as the great betrayal.[185] The whole paraphernalia of public-school life—philathleticism and school colours, rifle drill and limited science, compulsory chapel and obligatory sport—were introduced. Jackson's plans were a key part of this.[186] Selwyn and his architect had 'turned Thring's unique school into a conventional public school'.[187] It had changed what it did, and it had changed how it looked. Uppingham was a place reformed.

Success at each level of this educational community, from the least to the greatest, made Jackson one of the quintessential public-school architects. His work at two very different schools makes this plain. One was rather grand; the other was certainly not. At Rugby, in many ways the very model of the modern public school, it was with the express approval of William Butterfield that T. G. Jackson extended and completed the school chapel as a memorial to a master in 1898.[188] Ten years later he was to build a monument to an even more important figure. The Temple Speech Room (1906–9), named after a past headmaster and Arnold's heir, was large enough to seat the whole school.[189]

[183] Cormac Rigby, 'The Life and Influence of Edward Thring' (D. Phil., Oxford, 1968).
[184] Bryan Matthews, *By God's Grace . . . a history of Uppingham School* (Maidstone, 1984), 117–22.   [185] Rigby, 'Edward Thring', 299, 373–4.
[186] USA, Minute Book 1875–1894 (17 Feb., 1 June 1888) 265, 268. Thring had always insisted that the school should not expand (Matthews, *By God's Grace*, 121).
[187] Malcolm Tozer, 'Physical Education at Thring's Uppingham' (M.Ed., Leicester, 1974), 238; see also 215–48.
[188] Hardy, *Public School Life: Rugby*, 39–40; H. T. Rhoades, *A Handbook to Rugby School Chapel* (Rugby, 1913); Jackson MSS, 'Recollections', vol. ii., Butterfield to Jackson (5 June 1896).
[189] *The Meteor* xliii, 15 July 1909, 94; J. B. Hope Simpson, *Rugby since Arnold* (London, 1967), 147.

Together, these two buildings formed the symbolic heart of Rugby—and, by implication, a focus of public school identity. The same could not be said of Aldenham, a very minor public school in Hertfordshire.[190] Yet even there Jackson's role as public-school architect *par excellence* was quite clearly stated. This was a job designed to draw attention to the school, and the governors were willing to pay for the best. Jackson's boarding house (1905–6) cost £8,383— nearly twice as much as they were willing to spend on the headmaster's house and over £1,000 more than the Board of Education had advised.[191] But the school evidently believed that it was worth it. It was keen to stress its status. As the records show, Jackson was employed because the governors admired his 'similar works' at Eton and Uppingham. Such was his success that they even attributed work at Repton to him.[192] The comparison was ludicrous for the tiny school; Aldenham was making a category error. But it was an understandable mistake. Jackson's influence was everywhere, and his work was well known. Aldenham was just his latest conquest. Nor would it be his last.

It is at Giggleswick in North Yorkshire that Graham Jackson's most striking work can be seen. This curiously underrated school chapel (1897–1901) is an important monument in its own right. As N. G. Hamilton has commented, it is 'one of the most original and most neglected creations of late Victorian and Edwardian church architecture'.[193] It was also, as Jackson himself acknowledged, a uniquely complete and coherent project unfettered by expense or outside interference.[194] As such, it offered him the crowning triumph of his public school career. Graham Jackson was commissioned by the millionaire philanthropist Walter Morrison, a governor of Giggleswick and Liberal MP for Skipton.[195] The school was a good one, based on the public-school model— though with a modern curriculum. With boarding houses, a focus on athletics, and even (from 1897) an Old Boys' Club, it had all the equipment of a good public school.[196] All, that is, apart from a chapel. Morrison resolved to amend

---

[190] R. J. Evans, 'History', in Edmund Beevor, G. C. F. Mead, R. J. Evans, and T. H. Savory, *The History and Register of Aldenham School* (London, 1938), lvi–lxxxv. See also *Public School Magazine* 7 (1901), 81–9.

[191] London, Guildhall, MS 18411/2, Aldenham School Minute Book 1893–1913, 110, 178, 183, 187, 200, 212.

[192] Ibid., (21 March, 7 April 1904), 178, 180. Jackson never built at Repton. They had confused him with Sir Arthur Blomfield. See Alec MacDonald, *A Short History of Repton* (London, 1929), 205–6.   [193] Hamilton, 'School Chapel', 219.

[194] Jackson, *Life and Travels*, 230. See also Noel Proudlock, *Giggleswick School Chapel* (Leeds, 1997).

[195] W. R. Mitchell, *Walter Morrison: a millionaire at Malham Tarn* (Settle, 1990).

[196] Edward Allen Bell, *A History of Giggleswick School* (Leeds, 1912), 153, 165, 171–9, 184–95.

69. The Victoria Building,
Uppingham School (1896–7).

70. The Temple Speech Room,
Rugby School (1906–9).

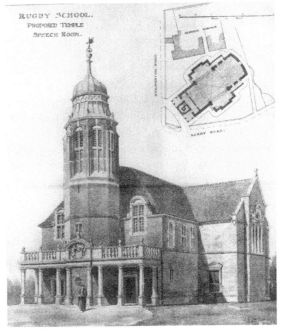

71. Giggleswick School.

this lack. Desiring 'to increase the prosperity of the School', he wished to equip it properly, and had concluded that 'a chapel was part of the proper plant of every large school'.[197] Here his university connections came into play.[198] He went to Jackson, whom, he recalled, 'I considered our best man, partly owing to my admiring the new Buildings at Trinity'.[199] In addition to the chapel, Morrison offered to pay for a new pavilion and gatehouse. The whole scheme was presented to the governors in March 1897, and it was gratefully accepted.

Morrison had made it known that no expense was to be spared on the chapel.[200] He had only two requests: firstly, that nothing should be left for anyone to do after Jackson had finished; secondly, that the chapel should have a dome.[201] Over four years an extraordinary edifice was erected—the 'crowning glory' of Giggleswick, as the *Public School Magazine* put it.[202] Jackson was in complete control, and his every wish was granted by an indulgent patron. The result was remarkable: a synthesis of Greek and Gothic elevation and plan.[203] Partly, this was no doubt due to the success of Lethaby and Swainson's 1894 *Sancta Sophia*, a book which inspired the short-lived Byzantine revival of the

---

[197] In *Giggleswick School Chronicle* 6 (Oct. 1897), 163.
[198] Morrison was educated at Eton and Balliol. He graduated in 1857 with a First in Greats.
[199] BalCA, D.10.16, Chapel (7 July 1911).
[200] GSA, Uncat. Chapel Papers, Box 2, Analysis of building accounts (22 April 1902).
[201] Jackson, *Life and Travels*, 230.   [202] *Public School Magazine* 9 (1902), 207.
[203] Crook, *Dilemma of Style*, 184.

72. The Gatehouse at
Giggleswick School
(1901–2)

73. Giggleswick School
Chapel (1897–1901).

74. The Dome of Giggleswick School Chapel.

1890s. Partly, it reflected Morrison's interest in the archaeology of the Near East.[204] Partly, too, it was the product of Jackson's exploration of Byzantine architecture.[205] Most importantly, though, it was an opportunity for Jackson to experiment and to prove—as Gilbert Scott had always argued—that 'domes and Gothic architecture are not incompatible'.[206]

The chapel was consecrated in 1901. Significantly, it was opened by Edmond Warre, Headmaster of Eton. It is his speech that sums up the source of Jackson's achievement. The chapel, he said,

seems to me to be a parable in wood and stone of the education that should, in our Public Secondary Schools, edify, build up, and train the youth of our country. For does it not lay under contribution, in artistic design, in construction, in material, the old and the new, the east and the west, the north and the south [?] . . . And out of all this variety and

---

[204] Palestine Exploration Fund, *Quarterly Statement* (1921–2), 55–7.

[205] The dome is illustrated in T. G. Jackson, *Byzantine and Romanesque Architecture* (2 vols.; Cambridge, 1913), vol. i, p. 40.

[206] Jackson, *Life and Travels*, 230. See also Crook, *Dilemma of Style*, 184.

diversity of conception and material has arisen, under the creative inspiration of the master mind, a structure which, like Jerusalem of old, is built as one 'that is at unity in itself'; and in this it also shadows forth what the result of a right education should be in the man and in the school.

It heralded, Warre claimed, a new future for Giggleswick. 'It has now before it, the future of an English Public School with good traditions and suitable buildings and the power of expansion and every prospect of success', he declared.[207] However overstated, this was in essence the goal of all Jackson's clients. His ability to respond to their needs—to use architecture as means of articulating their ideals and ambitions—explains his achievement. Jackson's connections with Oxford, his reforming beliefs, and his achievement all across the country made him the ideal public school architect for establishments at all levels of the system. As in Oxford, they were constructing a new community, whilst he built their new identity.

[207] GSA, B.C. Uncat. Material, Warre, 'Address at the Opening of New Chapel' (4 Oct. 1901).

5

'Cambridge At Last!'[1]
Jackson and the Architecture of Science

Jackson's public-school practice was undoubtedly important for him. It took him out of Oxford and widened his reputation. His contemporaries, however, were well aware that he might yet do more. 'He ought to have been an architect in the 17th century, at Rome', wrote John Willis Clark. 'What Palaces he would have built for Papal Nephews!'[2] Oxford had made his name, but it had also limited his appeal. Nor did work outside the city do much to shake this association, at least at first. Town halls, houses, and offices came and went, with seemingly little effect. What Jackson needed was another field of operation; another place to call his own. In the 1890s this opportunity presented itself. He finally came to Cambridge. Even here, of course, he remained 'Oxford Jackson', but he managed to escape the limiting consequences of this sobriquet. Work in Cambridge confirmed his place as a national figure and a force to be reckoned with.[3] By the turn of the century, Jackson had become the dominant architectural voice in elite education in Oxford, Cambridge, and beyond.

At times, this transformation seemed an impossible dream. Jackson's efforts to escape the limiting effects of Oxford appeared in the 1870s and 1880s to be doomed from the start. Even his work outside the city was the product of his Oxford success. In the most unlikely places, and for the most unlikely people, Jackson was required to apply an academic style to non-academic buildings. The result was not always popular; certainly, it did little for his reputation. In Tipperary, for example, Jackson built a town hall (1876–7). Although praised at the time, it was to remain his only municipal building—and the explanation for this is all too simple.[4] Tipperary town hall was an anomaly. Worse still, it became an embarrassing symbol of failure. Jackson's client was Arthur Hugh Smith-Barry, an Eton and Oxford educated progressive, and Liberal MP for County Cork from

---

[1] T. G. Jackson, *Recollections: the life and travels of a Victorian architect*, (ed., Sir Nicholas Jackson; London, 2003), 235.
[2] CUMAA, MM2/1/3 Correspondence re: New Museum 1907–13, J. W. Clark to Baron Anatole von Hügel (29 Aug. 1908). [3] *Cambridge Review* 21 (1899–1900), 35.
[4] *Building News* 35 (1878), 394.

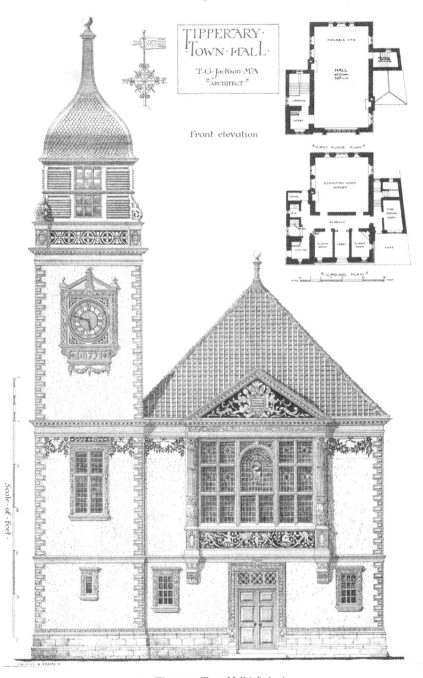

75. Tipperary Town Hall (1876–7).

1867 to 1874. He was a rich and reforming landowner,[5] whose family had dominated (and owned) Tipperary since the eighteenth century.[6] This personal patronage was, in itself, unusual. Most town halls were not commissioned by a single individual. Rather, in the majority of cases corporations held the purse strings and used town halls as symbols of civic pride.[7] The competition between cities like Bradford and Leeds, for example, found expression in the battle to build bigger and better town halls.[8] By contrast, Tipperary's new building was as much a symbol of the Smith-Barrys as it was of the town. This was to prove its undoing.

Not that Arthur Smith-Barry was an ogre. Under his rule, Tipperary had grown and thrived. The town was rich, profitable, and successful; by 1878 its butter market, the second largest in the United Kingdom, was worth an estimated £650,000 a year.[9] Still more importantly, Smith-Barry was a generous man. The town hall was the climax of a series of improvements he had financed, which included the enlargement of the market and a variety of charitable projects designed to ameliorate the lot of the poor.[10] At a cost of £3,000 the hall was worth a quarter of his Tipperary estate.[11] It was—in intention at least—a thoroughly progressive project. Which is where T. G. Jackson comes in. The choice of Jackson as architect was undoubtedly due to Smith-Barry's Oxford connections. Jackson was, after all, just beginning to make his name with work on the New Schools. Smith-Barry wanted a similarly modern building; a suitable symbol of his reforms in the town. And he got it. This was not the usual classical or Gothic municipal edifice to which the Victorians were accustomed. Rather, Jackson produced a 'Queen Anne' town hall. That was rare enough; but Jackson did not stop there.[12] His design was 'Queen Anne' with a twist, and without red brick. Instead he used rough-cast, terracotta, and sgraffito. It was a unique combination, and produced a building which is entirely *sui generis*. This, indeed, was the problem. Town councils were notoriously unadventurous, and unwilling to choose avant garde designs.[13] Jackson had brought progressive Oxford to reforming Tipperary, but in the absence of another, equally enthusiastic patron, this was likely to remain an isolated

---

[5] James S. Donnelly, *The Land and the People of Nineteenth Century Cork* (London and Boston, 1975), 168.

[6] He owned 21,000 acres in Ireland: over 8,500 were in Tipperary where he owned the town, licensing the market and levying duties on sales. He was, however, an absentee landlord, living in County Cork, London, and Cheshire. Denis G. Marnane, *Land and Violence: a history of West Tipperary from 1660* (Tipperary, 1985), 10–19, 67–9, 88–102.

[7] This was not, of course, new. See Robert Tittler, *Architecture and Power: the town hall and the English urban community c. 1500–1640* (Oxford, 1991).

[8] Asa Briggs, *Victorian Cities* (London, 1968), 153–83.

[9] Marnane, *Land and Violence*, 67.

[10] 'Mad Tipperary', *Irish Loyal and Patriotic Union Publications* 5 (Dublin and London, 1890), 25–8.

[11] T. Jones Hughes, 'Landholding and Settlement in County Tipperary in the Nineteenth Century' in William Nolan, ed., *Tipperary: history and society* (Dublin, 1985), 342.

[12] Colin Cunningham, *Victorian and Edwardian Town Halls* (London, 1981), 141–2.

[13] Ibid., 99.

example. His network of supporters was all-powerful in Oxford, but had little influence in the corporations of other towns.

Worse was to come, however. Tipperary town hall was soon synonymous with fear and failure. Far from becoming a symbol of liberalism, it became the embodiment of landlordism. The land war of the 1880s swept through Tipperary—and the town hall was at the heart of the battle. The 'refreshment room' for use 'during balls, concerts &c.'[14] was soon used for barracks rather than balls, as armed men were brought in to put down trouble and oversee evictions.[15] By 1890, Smith-Barry's tenants had turned their back on the town—and on its seat of government—and were building a 'New Tipperary' outside his jurisdiction and beyond his control.[16] A. H. Smith-Barry became a Unionist, an MP for an English seat, and was forced to travel through Tipperary defended by an armed guard. Jackson's building had become a tragic reminder of failure.[17] Already disowned by the people, it was quietly dropped by its patron. There is little wonder that Jackson was never again asked to build a town hall. His work in Tipperary had depended on Oxford connections. It had been the pet project of a single rich man. This in itself made it unusual, but the horrors of the 1880s made it unrepeatable. It soon became an embarrassment to all concerned and was abandoned and burnt out in the twentieth century.

A similar judgement awaited Jackson's greatest domestic commission: 2 Kensington Court (1883–5).[18] When first built, this was acknowledged as a tremendous triumph for the architect, and his client, Athelstan Riley. The house faces onto Kensington Road and was 'the admiring cynosure of the many wayfarers who pass along this thronging route of London traffic'.[19] It was extensively reported in journals, from the *Architectural Review* to the *Builder*; from the *Studio* to the *Gentlewoman*.[20] Yet it remains Jackson's only town house.[21] This was a disappointing response to such a striking building, but the explanation lies with the patron and project themselves. Riley, although educated at Eton and Oxford, was not a typical client for Jackson. 'I am', he wrote, 'an anti-Liberal.' 'I am a Christian man', he went on, 'and I have never yet known a man with really liberal principles who was *thoroughly* sound on matters of faith.'[22] The son of a

---

[14] *Building News* 35 (1878), 394.   [15] 'Mad Tipperary', 264.

[16] Denis G. Marnane, 'Fr. David Humphreys and New Tipperary', in Nolan, ed., *Tipperary*, 370–7. The town cost £40,000 and was deserted by October 1891. Donnelly, *Nineteenth Century Cork*, 375.

[17] *Irish Unionist Alliance Publications* I (Dublin, Belfast, and London, 1893), 33.

[18] 2 Kensington Court is now part of the Milestone Hotel, and I must thank Mr Michael Fernandez for allowing me access to it.   [19] *Architecture* 2 (1897), 85.

[20] *Architectural Review* 1 (1896–7), 142; *Builder* 48 (1888), 898; *Studio* 1 (1893), 225; *Gentlewoman* 8 (1894), 657–8.

[21] Though he made alterations to John Murray's houses in Albemarle Street and Dover Street. ITA, BUI/17, Hare Court, Jackson to Sub-Treasurer, 3 April and 4 Aug. 1894; Crook, 'Cult of Eclecticism', 119.

[22] LPL, Riley Papers, MS 2343 General Corresp. 1879–95, (47) Riley to unknown correspondent (13 July 1884).

76. 2 Kensington Court (1883–5).

barrister and grandson of the founder of the Union Bank, Riley was a rich man; certainly, he was never 'called upon to put his hand to the plough'.[23] After considering (and rejecting) ordination, he devoted himself to travel, music, and theology.[24] His was an idiosyncratic Anglo-Catholicism, which derived as much from the traditions of the Orthodox Church as it did from the Anglican: but it was deeply felt.[25] The chief tenet of his faith was clear: 'Liberalism and Catholicism are as distinct as ice from fire'.[26]

Why, then, did Riley choose Jackson? The answer, once again, must be Oxford. He was an undergraduate at Pembroke whilst the New Examination Schools were built, and remained in college whilst 2 Kensington Court was erected.[27] He continued to be closely associated with Oxford, being proposed as a Proctor for Pembroke in 1897, and standing unsuccessfully as a parliamentary candidate for the university as late as 1919.[28] At the age of twenty-five, he may have known few architects and have chosen Jackson by default. Perhaps more importantly, the situation of the house called for a fashionably modern designer. Kensington Court was developed by Jonathan T. Carr, instigator of Bedford Park, the model estate for aesthetes with which Norman Shaw had become so ineluctably associated.[29] By 1883 he had taken up with J. J. Stevenson, who was responsible for laying out and designing much of Kensington Court.[30] Plot 2 was bought by Riley in the sure and certain knowledge that it would be surrounded by some of the most fashionable buildings in London, for Stevenson's work at Kensington Court was in the vanguard of taste. Domestic, decorative, and utterly distinctive, it would later be guyed as 'Pont Street Dutch'.[31] Contemporaries found its combination of fancy gables, classical details, and pedimented windows deeply daring.[32] The choice of Jackson thus allowed Riley to be modern, stylish, and different. Standing out from the crowd was undoubtedly important for John Athelstan Riley.[33] But above all this, beyond Riley's naivety and his idiosyncrasy, we must come back to Oxford for Jackson's client liked to think of himself as an intellectual. Jackson's university experience and his Oxford associations provided the perfect environment for Riley's mind to

[23] Victor G. Plass, *Men and Women of the Time* (15th edn; London, 1899), 914.

[24] LPL, Riley Papers MS 2342, letter 20 Sept. 1881. He co-edited the *English Hymnal* in 1906. See Adam Fox, *English Hymns and Hymn Writers* (London, 1947), 44. Marcus Donovan, *After the Tractarians: from the recollections of Athelstan Riley* (Glasgow, 1933).

[25] Athelstan Riley, *The Anglican Theory of the Catholic Church* (London and Oxford, 1916), 8–9; *Eastern Christendom* (1930). [26] LPL, Riley Papers MS 2343/47 13 July 1884.

[27] Ibid.

[28] LPL, Riley Papers MS 2344, General Correspondence 1896–1902, A. T. Boston to Riley (12 Nov. 1897); MS 2353 Misc. Papers, 138 and 139 Election Address (1919). For the election see Charles Oman, *Memories of Victorian Oxford* (London, 1941), 147. Riley also contributed the chapter on Pembroke to Hanslip Fletcher, ed., *Oxford and Cambridge* (London, 1909), 141–6.

[29] *Survey of London*, vol. xlii, p. 67.

[30] W. J. Loftie, *Kensington, Picturesque and Historical* (London, 1888), 125.

[31] Girouard, *Sweetness and Light*, 227.

[32] Mark Girouard, 'The Architecture of John James Stevenson', *The Connoisseur* 184 (1973), 166–74, 185. [33] Riley, *Anglican Theory*, 8–9.

thrive. With its library, 'in a style highly reminiscent of Oxford Colleges',[34] its chapel, and its music gallery, the house was designed to bring a little bit of Oxford into London.

The result was unlike anything Jackson had built before or was to build again. Seemingly unfettered by restrictions of cost or taste, he produced an extraordinarily exuberant design of dubious origin and wanton ornament.[35] The front was a slender three bays long, with a shaped gable and four attenuated pilasters. To the side was a longer and more restrained façade with oriel windows to two floors and a recessed entrance. The whole house was enlivened with cut brick flourishes and terracotta details. Athelstan Riley's monogram was everywhere; accompanied by putti swinging on swags, or playing on pipes, or just reading and writing. The origins of these features are difficult to disinter. As with all of Jackson's houses, there is something of the Low Countries, visited and admired by both architect and client.[36] Other features derive from closer to home. In the moulded terracotta can be seen echoes of Layer Marney and Sutton Place.[37] Certainly, the chapel windows resemble Jackson's work for Brighton College, which drew on precisely these themes. Later additions were still more ornate. Around 1890 Jackson raised the rear section by a storey and a half, with a niche containing a statue of St Lawrence.[38] He also added a bay window to Riley's study, topped with a lead cap made up of a writhing mass of sea dragons: an idea taken from the spire of the Copenhagen Exchange,[39] visited by Riley in 1875.[40] It was a remarkable house, for an extraordinary man.

For Jackson's admirers and allies, however, it was not a success. 'In a careless moment', wrote Mallows, he had flirted 'with his true love's coquettish cousin from Flanders, with the result that his temporary perfidy is written large upon the building, and tends to lower it . . . to a level below that of his other work.'[41] Nor was he ever asked to repeat the experiment. In part, this simply reflected the reluctance of men with money to abandon their chosen classical, French, or Italianate idiom.[42] Without Riley's resources, 2 Kensington Court would not have been possible—and few of Jackson's progressive clients could afford such liberality. But more than this, the very eccentricity which led Riley to commission

[34] *Architecture* 2 (1897), 88.

[35] Crook, 'Cult of Eclecticism' calls it 'Franco-Flemish-Gothic', 112.

[36] LPL, Riley Papers MS 2355 Notes on travels: 1877. Riley remarks of Bruges, 'Charming old town . . . notice the curious gables of the houses'. He also admired Antwerp. See also London, Papers in the possession of J. Mordaunt Crook, Jackson to Collett (20 Aug. 1894), 'Amsterdam is as charming almost as Venice.'   [37] Loftie, *Kensington, Picturesque*, 125.

[38] Estimates the *Survey of London* vol. xlii, p. 72. It may be a little later: Riley's engagement book shows him meeting Jackson on 16 Oct. 1891 (LPL, Riley Papers, MS 2365, Engagement Book 1891). He is mentioned again on 5 Jan. 1893 (MS 2366, Engagement Book 1893) and 29 Jan. 1894 (MS 2367, Engagement Book 1894).   [39] *Survey of London* vol. xlii, p. 71.

[40] LPL, Riley Papers MS 2355 Notes on Travels (1875).

[41] *Architectural Review* 1 (1896–7), 142.

[42] J. Mordaunt Crook, *The Rise of the Nouveaux Riches: style and status in Victorian and Edwardian architecture* (London, 1999), 42, 45, 58–67, 167, 173–4.

77. The bay window at
Kensington Court (c. 1890).

Jackson diminished the architect's appeal. Even as the house was being built, Riley was becoming the leader of a bitter anti-liberal campaign. Always interested in education, in 1891 Athelstan Riley became a member of the London School Board. He was motivated by a desire to drive down its cost for rate payers, and a determination to enforce orthodox Anglicanism in its schools. Since 1871 teachers had been required to instruct pupils on the Bible, but had been forbidden from enforcing any denominational interpretation. It was an attempt at a compromise, reconciling Churchmen with dissenters and Christians with agnostics.[43] For Riley it was, of course, anathema.[44] He described the Board Schools as the 'greatest enemy of the Christian religion in the land', and his efforts at destroying the compromise paralysed the Board between 1893–4.[45]

[43] Hugh B. Philpott, *London at School, the story of the School Board* (London, 1904), 98–100.
[44] J. S. Laurie, *Rileyism and Bigotry versus Reason and Common Sense: an episode in the London School Board* (London, 1890), 12, 18.
[45] Quoted in Robin Betts, *Dr. Macnamara, 1861–1931* (Liverpool, 1999), 61. See also T. J. Macnamara, 'Three Years Progressivism at the London School Board', *Fortnightly Review* 74 (1900), 790–802, 791.

In the 1894 School Board elections 2 Kensington Court became a significant part of the campaign. For Riley's detractors, it was a symbol of his luxurious and 'artistic' life.[46] For Riley, it was a means of conveying his message. Progressives ridiculed the posters used to cover the façade. 'All passers-by', recalled Thomas Gautrey, 'were attracted by the sight of one of the finest mansions in Kensington being utilised as a bill-poster's station.'[47] Even interior design became an issue. Jackson's famous piano was the 'finishing touch to the house'.[48] It was a very expensive accessory. The comparison between this extravagance and Riley's determined opposition to the purchase of pianos for Board Schools was too good to miss.[49] The *Board-Teacher*, despite its admiration for Jackson's 'beautiful piano', cautioned Riley against 'surrounding yourselves with luxuries' whilst begrudging a few pennies for the poor.[50] The result of the election was disastrous for Riley, and he was soon abandoned by his less fanatical friends.[51] Isolated, but unabashed, he continued on the Board until 1897, by which time he was left in a minority of one. That election saw the victory of the Progressives and Riley's resignation.[52] Jackson's house, and even his piano, had become symbols of religious extremism and Athelstan Riley's unpopularity. Little wonder it was his only town house. Riley himself soon left London for Jersey, where he employed Reginald Blomfield to build him a mansion.[53]

So much for the house that Jackson built. Essentially, Kensington Court failed for two reasons. In the first place, Jackson had not sufficiently escaped his experiences in Oxford; he had not crafted a convincingly domestic idiom. At the same time, Jackson had altered his approach enough to alienate his previous champions. It was both something and nothing: an Oxford building strangely warped and changed. Fortunately, Jackson was to prove more assured—and more successful—in his academic commissions. As early as 1879, for example, he was called to St David's College, Lampeter. His clients here were old friends: the Principal, Francis John Jayne, was a Wadham man who had been recommended for the job by Benjamin Jowett.[54] Basil Jones, Bishop of St David's and patron of the college, had examined Jackson for his degree.[55] It was more than the old-boys' network that drew Jackson to Wales, however. His mastery of Oxford architecture was also a crucial motivation. For under Jayne Lampeter found itself drawn into the orbit of Oxford. It was Jackson's job to express this architecturally. St David's College was the bulwark of Anglicanism in the principality and it had performed dismally since its foundation in 1827.[56] Jayne, appointed in 1879, rightly sensed that reform, similar to that under way in Oxford, could

[46] Thomas Gautrey, '*Lux Mihi Laus*', *School Board Memories* (London, 1937), 60.
[47] Ibid., 107.   [48] Jackson, *Life and Travels*, 192.   [49] *Schoolmaster* 44 (1893), 147.
[50] Quoted in Betts, *Dr. Macnamara*, 84.
[51] *Schoolmaster* 46 (1894), 918; *Schoolmaster* 48 (1895), 1111.
[52] Philpott, *London at School*, 110.
[53] Jo Park, *Athelstan Riley, Patron of St. Petroc Minor, Little Petherick* (Truro, 1982), n.p.
[54] D. T. W. Price, *A History of St. David's University College, Lampeter* (2 vols.; Cardiff, 1977–90), vol. ii, pp. 134–5.   [55] Jackson, *Life and Travels*, 143.
[56] Price, *Lampeter*, vol. i, p. 46.

transform the fortunes of the ailing institution. As a result, new statutes were quickly promulgated. On 1 June 1880 Lampeter became the first college affiliated to Oxford. Three years later, it was affiliated to Cambridge.[57] St David's was not rich, and could not celebrate this change with monumental architecture. But for a church college, where divine service was said twice daily, the chapel was the locus of the institution's identity.[58] Jackson was commissioned to remodel it along conventional university lines. He took a parochial church and transformed it into a collegiate chapel, literally bringing Oxford to Wales by fitting stalls taken from New College.[59] St David's, claimed Bishop Jones, 'could now claim to be the eldest daughter of Oxford'.[60] Jackson had ensured that there would, at least, be a family resemblance.

Aesthetic associations with Oxford resulted in a commission at the Inner Temple too (1893–4). The visual similarity between the ancient universities and the Inns of Court is still today quite clear.[61] Individually, as a commentator noted in 1909, they present 'the engaging completeness of a collegiate Building . . . forming just such a Court or Quadrangle as delights the eye at Oxford or Cambridge'.[62] And, indeed, just like Oxford and Cambridge, the mid-nineteenth century saw Gothic becoming the almost universal architectural idiom at the Inns of Court. Thus, whilst in 1821 Charles Lamb could criticize Robert Smirke's medievalizing additions (1816–17) to the Inner Temple's 'fine Elizabethan Hall', whose 'collegiate aspect' had previously so delighted him, by 1866 the hall as a whole was destroyed to make way for Sidney Smirke's unmistakably Gothic replacement (1866–70).[63] Still further Gothic invasions were made by Smirke in 1876.[64] By this time, though, the Inns of Court were themselves being changed. They were coming not merely to resemble, but to emulate the universities. Indeed, reminded of their previous status as 'the third university of England', and conscious of the nation's failings in legal training, they were beginning to slough off their former lethargy and engage in the teaching and examination of students.[65] In part, this was a role forced upon them. The Royal Commission on Legal Education (1854–5) had found little legal education to investigate, and recommended the amalgamation of the Inns to form a legal university.[66] As it was, Oxford, Cambridge, and London soon took on this

---

[57] W. J. Lewis, *A History of Lampeter* (Ceredigion, 1997), 104.

[58] Price, *Lampeter*, vol. i, pp. 134–9; Alfred Ollivant, *Sermon Preached in the Chapel of St. David's College, Lampeter on the 24th June 1880* (Oxford and Cambridge, 1880), 6, 8, 12, 17.

[59] Jackson, *Life and Travels*, 137.   [60] *St. David's College Magazine* 1 (1880), 158.

[61] See Duncan McCorquodale, ed., *The Inns of Court* (London, 1996).

[62] Cecil Headlam and Gordon Home, *The Inns of Court* (London, 1909), 86–7.

[63] Charles Lamb, *Elia and the Last Letters of Elia* (London, 1912), 95–7.

[64] Frank Douglas MacKinnon, *Inner Temple Papers* (London, 1948), 51; J. H. Baker, *The Inner Temple* (London, 1991), 9–10; J. Mordaunt Crook, 'Sidney Smirke: the architecture of compromise' in Jane Fawcett, ed., *Seven Victorian Architects* (London, 1976), 50–65.

[65] J. H. Baker, *The Third University of England* (London, 1990), 3, 16, 21.

[66] William Holdsworth, *A History of English Law* (17 vols.; London, 1905–72), vol. 15, ed., A. L. Goodhart and H. G. Hanbury, pp. 234–9; E. M. Underdown, 'The Inner Temple', in E. Blake Odgers, ed., *Six Lectures on the Inns of Court and of Chancery* (London, 1912), 118.

responsibility.[67] But the need for change had been noted. Compulsory Bar Examinations were introduced in 1872.[68] The Council of Legal Education was established by the four Inns in 1883.[69] Significantly, these changes were symbolized in architectural terms. Between 1875 and 1878 E. M. Barry erected Temple Gardens, an elaborately carved French Renaissance building, commissioned jointly by the Inner and Middle Temples.[70] It was joined by the neo-Jacobean Garden Court Building, the work of J. P. St Aubyn, in 1881–5.[71]

Given this prevailing aesthetic and the talk, even as late as 1898, of refounding a legal university, it seems almost predestined that Jackson would be called in to build.[72] His association with John James Hooper, a member of the Inner Temple and prominent advocate of legal education, can only have helped.[73] Jackson had, after all, practically rebuilt his Somerset home just a few years before.[74] And indeed it was the neighbouring building to Hooper's chambers that Jackson was employed to work on. But in reality there was nothing inevitable about the commission. It came to him only after the Inner Temple's usual architect, Arthur Cates, had withdrawn through ill health.[75] Only then did the Benchers of the Temple alight on Jackson. The choice no doubt owed much to his other academic work. Indeed, the Inner Temple Archives hold a note from him providing a 'List of buildings of similar purpose to what is proposed'. He included his projects at Trinity, Brasenose, Hertford, Corpus Christi, Lincoln, Balliol, and the New Examination Schools, plus the (as yet unbuilt) Geology Museum at Cambridge. In addition, Jackson mentioned the 'New buildings' at Uppingham, Cranbrook, Radley, Brighton, and Harrow 'which to some extent involve similar arrangements'.[76]

His tactic worked. On 3 March 1893 Jackson was asked to produce plans for new buildings at 2–3 Hare Court.[77] He had been commissioned to build a collegiate building for a reforming and increasingly educational establishment. The result should surprise no one, although the design is distinctly different from anything built at the Inner Temple for over a hundred years.[78] Drawing on the rich legacy of seventeenth- and eighteenth-century red brick architecture around him, Jackson produced a consciously 'Queen Anne' edifice. As built, the

[67] J. H. Baker, *An Introduction to English Legal History* (3rd edn; London, 1990), 195.

[68] Baker, *Third University*, 16.   [69] Underdown, 'Inner Temple', 108.

[70] Mackinnon, *Inner Temple Papers*, 51.

[71] Jill Allibone, 'These Hostells being Nurseries or Seminaries of the Court . . .', in McCorquadale, ed., *Inns of Court*, 15.

[72] G. Pitt-Lewis, *The History of the Temple* (London, 1898), 90–3.

[73] Hooper was Vice-Chairman of the Joint Board of Examiners, Inns of Court (1877–84); Inner Temple Tutor in Constitutional and Legal History (1871–5); and a member of the Inner Temple since 1850. See also J. J. Hooper, *The Establishment of a School of Jurisprudence in the University of Oxford* (London, 1854), 3–9.   [74] See Ch. 6.

[75] ITA, BUI/17 Cates to Sub-Treasurer, 26 Jan. 1893.

[76] ITA, BUI/17 Undated note from Jackson.

[77] ITA, BEN/1.30 Bench table Orders 1892–6, 3 March 1893.

[78] Allibone, 'These Hostells . . .', 14.

78. Hare Court from the Inner
Temple (1893–4).

chambers were less elaborate than he had originally intended.[79] Nonetheless,
with its red brick and stone details; oriels and dormers; pilasters, pediments, and
rusticated quoins; cherubs, cartouches, and ignudi; and the rubbed brick door-
cases copied from its neighbours, it was an imposing and important building.[80]
Jackson had worked closely with his clients, who approved each feature bit by
bit.[81] The result was the only 'Queen Anne' revival building in the Inns of Court.
This was far removed from 'the style of the sixteenth century, before the admix-
ture of Italian architecture' preferred by Philip Hardwick for the Hall of
Lincoln's Inn (1843–5).[82] It was indeed its antithesis, and it represented a rejection of mid-Victorian attitudes.[83]

Neither Lampeter nor the Inner Temple, Tipperary nor Kensington Court,
provided the fresh start that Jackson needed. They were not followed by similar

[79] ITA, PLA/16 Hare Court: plans, drawings, elevations 1893.
[80] Simon Bradley and Nikolaus Pevsner, *London I* (2nd edn; London, 1997), 347.
[81] ITA, BEN/4.2 Committee Minutes 1892, Building Committee (28 April and 1 May 1893),
34–5; BEN/1.30 28 April 1893.   [82] Quoted in Headlam and Home, *Inns of Court*, 119.
[83] See ITA, BUI/17 Hare Court 1893–4, Letter from *St. James's Gazette* 28 Feb. 1893.

commissions: domestic, municipal, or legal. Even the growth of the civic univer-sities left his office undisturbed. Other architects got the jobs. In part this simply reflected rival patronage networks. Alfred Waterhouse, for example, owed his work at Manchester, Leeds, and Liverpool to his wide range of northern non-conformist patrons.[84] His son, Paul, succeeded him at Leeds, writing to the uni-versity that 'I realise that I must largely owe the enviable position into which you have put me not to any merits of my own but to the fame and ability of my good father.'[85] Similarly, local men were chosen at Bristol, Birmingham, Exeter, and elsewhere.[86] Even more importantly, poverty limited these colleges' choices. As the principal of Reading recalled: 'Beautiful and stately architecture was beyond our reach.'[87] So when a place like Firth College, Sheffield, wanted to build an interpretation of Clare College, Cambridge, it turned to a local architect, T. J. Flockton, rather than to a more prestigious (and more costly) national figure.[88] Jackson, as an expensive, elitist Oxonian did not stand a chance. As his work at the Inner Temple showed, the public-school commissions gave useful experience without significantly widening his appeal. He was still just Oxford Jackson.

From the last decade of the century, however, this was to change. In 1899 Jackson began a fifteen-year association with the University of Cambridge, initi-ated by the building of the Sedgwick Memorial Museum (1899–1904). As the *Cambridge Review* commented at the time, given his achievements elsewhere, 'it is not a little surprising to find that this is his first building at Cambridge'.[89] This was not, it must be said, through want of trying. Jackson was first called into Cambridge some seven years earlier, in 1892.[90] He was then just the latest in a series of architects charged with designing the new geological museum, intended to commemorate the life and work of Adam Sedgwick. By 1914, when he completed his final project, the new Physiology Department, Jackson had seen off competition from numerous others and his work had come to define the new, more scientific Cambridge. His was a vital role in the 'unparalleled growth . . . of buildings devoted to the advancement of natural sciences in our

[84] Colin Cunningham and Prudence Waterhouse, *Alfred Waterhouse, 1830–1905: biography of a practice* (Oxford, 1992), 23, 127.

[85] Quoted in P. H. J. H. Gosden and A. J. Taylor, eds., *Studies in the History of a University 1874–1974* (Leeds, 1975), 155.

[86] J. W. Sherborne, *University College, Bristol 1876–1909* (Bristol, 1977), 12; B. W. Clapp, *The University of Exeter* (Exeter, 1982), 7.

[87] W. M. Childs, *Making a University: an account of the university movement at Reading* (London, 1933), 56.

[88] Arthur W. Chapmen, *The Story of a Modern University: a history of the University of Sheffield* (London, 1955), 18. Malcolm Seaborne in his introduction to E. R. Robson, *School Architecture* (1874; Leicester, 1972), 34, suggests that Robson was also involved.

[89] *Cambridge Review* 21 (1899–1900), 35.

[90] CUA, Hughes Papers, Geol 8/6, Minutes of Geological Site and Building Syndicate 1891–5, 2 March 1892.

country'.[91] At the same time the buildings which he produced were acknowledged as amongst the best pieces of modern architecture then built.[92]

That it had taken until 1892 for Jackson to come to Cambridge is unsurprising. Just as his first commissions in Oxford owed much to personal connections, so Cambridge turned to men it knew when seeking designers. Thus it was that Cambridge architecture was dominated by a small group of people; first, from 1850 onwards, by Salvin and Scott.[93] Later, came Waterhouse, and in the last twenty-five years of the century a group of artists divided up the spoils between them—including G. G. Scott, junior, J. J. Stevenson, G. F. Bodley, and Basil Champneys.[94] From the first, personal connections had proved important for securing commissions, and from Salvin to Champneys, architects showed that friends could also be clients. Alfred Waterhouse, for example, owed many of his commissions to friends and family. He was the 'natural choice' as architect of Girton (1873–84) precisely because his brother-in-law was heavily involved in its finances. Additionally, and helpfully, his Manchester patrons were also major benefactors of the college.[95] By contrast, Jackson was associated with Oxford and socially unknown at Cambridge. He was consequently shut out of the university and—in the absence of a competition—unable to break in.

This was despite the change in Cambridge architecture that occurred in the last three decades of the nineteenth century. As in Oxford, the Gothic Revival which had dominated the city was abandoned in favour of other, later, more eclectic styles.[96] The great symbol of this change was Newnham College, built to provide non-denominational education for women. Here, eschewing all neo-medieval pretensions, Basil Champneys chose 'Queen Anne'.[97] Between 1873 and 1910, he created an entirely new kind of college: rambling and domestic, with broken pediments and oriels, dormers and bay windows; all in red brick and white-painted wood.[98] It marked a total rejection of Gothic Revivalism and indicated a new approach to architecture. Champneys, of course, was never the dominant figure in Cambridge that Jackson was in Oxford.[99] Indeed Cambridge never really produced an equivalent to Oxford Jackson and Newnham was never really copied by other colleges. But it did reflect a wider change in the image of the university. As Peter Searby has noted, from 1870 onwards the Gothic stranglehold was loosened and variety became the keynote of

---

[91] A. E. Shipley, *'J'*, *a memoir of John Willis Clark* (London, 1913), 342.

[92] *Builder* 127 (1924), 748.

[93] Jill Allibone, *Anthony Salvin: pioneer of Gothic Revival Architecture* (Cambridge, 1987), 137–8.

[94] John Willis Clark, *A Concise Guide to the Town and University of Cambridge* (6th ed.; Cambridge, 1919); Nikolaus Pevsner, *Cambridgeshire* (2nd edn, Cambridge 1970); Tim Rawle, *Cambridge Architecture* (London, 1993).   [95] Cunningham and Waterhouse, *Waterhouse*, 70–1.

[96] Rawle, *Cambridge Architecture*, 58–60.

[97] Although see Margaret Birney Vickery, *Buildings for Bluestockings* (Newark and London, 1999), chs. 1–2.   [98] Girouard, *Sweetness and Light*, 70–6.

[99] David Watkin, *The Architecture of Basil Champneys* (Cambridge, 1989).

Cambridge architecture. There was now room for Gothic Girton and 'Queen Anne' Newnham, for Wrenaissance Pembroke and for Waterhouse's chateau-like Caius.[100]

This change in style, as at Oxford, reflected a reform of the university.[101] In the last thirty years of the nineteenth century Cambridge underwent a period of intensive reform and extensive expansion.[102] In 1871 parliament abolished religious tests. In 1872 a Royal Commission was established which recommended major changes to the character of Cambridge.[103] Reform came from within as well.[104] In 1873 Eton lost its exclusive rights to King's College, as the first open scholarship was awarded and the first non-Etonian elected as a Fellow.[105] Across the university, numbers rose and new subjects were created: Moral and Natural Sciences in 1851; Law in 1858; Theology in 1874; and History a year later.[106] There was a vast expansion in the physical and natural sciences,[107] and, as we have already noted, women came to Cambridge, to Girton (1869) and to Newnham (1871).[108] By 1900, J. W. Clark was able to celebrate a university 'accommodating itself with flexibility and readiness to requirements the most diverse, appointing new teachers in departments of study the most remote . . . flinging open doors to all comers, regardless of sex, creed, or nationality, and thronged with students'.[109] Cambridge was becoming a centre of real scientific excellence, with its 'go-ahead laboratories' believed to be far in advance of the 'mere collection of mediaeval survivals . . . that Oxford is'.[110]

This process was not uncomplicated, of course, nor universally accepted. As late as 1882 Selwyn College was established, in conscious imitation of Keble, as an exclusively Anglican foundation. Appropriately, it was built by Arthur Blomfield in a polychromatic Gothic (1882–95).[111] Nor did the adoption of the new styles necessarily indicate complete commitment to reform. Waterhouse's

---

[100] Peter Searby, *A History of the University of Cambridge: vol. iii, 1750–1870* (Cambridge, 1997), 43.

[101] A. G. L. Haig, 'The Church, the Universities and Learning in Later Victorian England', *Historical Journal* 29 (1986), 187–201, at 193.

[102] Christopher N. L. Brooke, *A History of the University of Cambridge: vol. iv, 1870–1990* (Cambridge, 1993), 2–90; Sheldon Rothblatt, *The Revolution of the Dons: Cambridge and society in Victorian England* (London, 1968), 228.

[103] D. A. Winstanley, *Later Victorian Cambridge* (Cambridge, 1947), 57–89; 264–70.

[104] R. St. John Parry, *Henry Jackson O.M.* (Cambridge, 1926), 26.

[105] L. P. Williamson, *A Century of King's, 1873–1972* (Cambridge, 1980), 4.

[106] Brooke, *History of Cambridge University*, 83. Between 1870 and 1900 the undergraduate population rose from 2,000 to 3,000 (p. 41).

[107] Elisabeth Leedham-Green, *A Concise History of the University of Cambridge* (Cambridge, 1996), 162.

[108] Although they were not, of course, to receive degrees from the university until 1948.

[109] John Willis Clark, *Old Friends at Cambridge and Elsewhere* (London and Cambridge, 1900), 13.

[110] *Granta* 17 (1903–4), 225. As early as 1853 commentators were noting Cambridge's scientific advantage over Oxford. J. Garbett, *University Reform* (London, 1853), 19; Janet Howarth, 'Science Teaching in Late-Victorian Oxford: a curious case of failure?' *English Historical Review* 102 (1987), 334–71.

[111] W. R. Brock and P. H. M. Cooper, *Selwyn College: a history* (Durham, 1994), 49–51.

work was popular at both progressive Pembroke and conservative Jesus.[112] Blomfield was employed by clerical Selwyn and reforming Emmanuel.[113] Moreover, the reforms of the period were far from uncontroversial. Even those broadly in favour of reform had objections to particular changes. In fact, given the need for any reform to negotiate a subject-specific Syndicate, the Council of the Senate, and finally the Senate itself, inertia often seemed the natural state of the university—as Jackson's experiences were to show. Change was only possible because there were people prepared to fight for it.

Although it was believed that, in contrast to Oxford, there were 'no sharply-defined camps' in Cambridge, the university was in fact riddled with factionalism.[114] Different groups fought for differing visions of change, whilst others hoped to resist all sorts of reform.[115] In 1908 this situation was satirized and accurately anatomized by F. M. Cornford in his now famous *Microcosmographia Academia, or A Guide for the Young Academic Politician.*[116] Cambridge, he suggested, had five main parties: Conservative Liberals, Liberal Conservatives, Non-Placets, Adullamites, and Young Men in a Hurry. Both the Conservative Liberals and Liberal Conservatives dwelt 'in the Valley of Indecision'. Aware that something ought to be done, they would accept some change, 'only not anything that anyone now desires'. The Non-Placet was 'a man of principle'; his one principle being opposition to change. The Young Man in a Hurry was 'inexperienced enough to imagine that something might be done before very long' and foolish enough 'even to suggest definite things'.[117]

Most important for Jackson's future, however, were the Adullamites. Although less of a party than an attitude of mind, they were a relatively cohesive group.[118] For Cambridge, wrote Cornford, they are 'dangerous, because they know what they want'. And what they wanted was 'all the money there is going'. These were the scientists: the builders and symbols of the new scientific university. They needed money to build laboratories, and to equip them. With the support of other reformers—men like Sidgwick, Augustus Austen Leigh, Henry Jackson, and John Peile—the scientists had been remarkably successful in their endeavour.[119] In the 1850s there had been no specialist provision for

[112] Aubrey Attwater, *Pembroke College Cambridge: a short history* (Cambridge, 1936); Arthur Gray and Frederick Brittain, *A History of Jesus College, Cambridge* (London, 1979).
[113] Sarah Bendall, Christopher Brooke, and Patrick Collinson, *A History of Emmanuel College, Cambridge* (Woodbridge, 1999).
[114] F. J. A. Hort, quoted in Brooke, *History of Cambridge University*, 9.
[115] Gordon Johnson, *University Politics* (Cambridge, 1994), 9–11, 36, 42–3, 48–53.
[116] Cambridge, 1908; republished as part of Johnson, *University Politics*, 85–110.
[117] F. M. Cornford, 'Microcosmographia Academia', in Johnson, *University Politics*, 85–110, at 95–6.
[118] The different attitudes and social background of the scientists are explored in Roy Macleod and Russell Moseley, 'The "naturals" and Victorian Cambridge: reflections on the anatomy of an elite 1851–1914', *Oxford Review of Education* 6 (1980), 177–95.
[119] William Austen Leigh, *Augustus Austen Leigh* (London, 1906); Brooke, *History of Cambridge University*, 34, 59, 61.

science beyond 'a small table, such as two people might take their tea at', which was brought into the Arts School three times a week during the summer term so that Professor Stokes could teach physical optics.[120] By 1921, Cambridge had a 'finer set of laboratories . . . than any other University in the Empire'.[121] In the process, the Adullamite party had grown in size and in importance. They held 'a Caucus from time to time to conspire against the College System'. Disguised, as Cornford joked, with 'blue spectacles and false beards' and saying 'the most awful things to one another', they had by the 1890s become powerful enough to draw thousands of pounds from the university and to raise still more from elsewhere. Their success was to be expressed in Jackson's architecture. The Adullamites managed both to obtain all the money there was going and to get an acknowledged expert to embody their triumph in their buildings.[122]

That the first of these monuments should be the Sedgwick Memorial Museum was entirely fitting. Adam Sedgwick had been a convinced academic reformer and a highly successful scientist. Elected Woodwardian Professor of Geology at the age of thirty-three, Sedgwick had taken the job with no prior knowledge of the subject he would be teaching. Hard work and determination soon made him one of the heroes of the 'golden age' of geology, and a great Cambridge figure.[123] In his own university he was regarded 'as one of the greatest men of science of the century'.[124] There was consequently only a short interval between his death in 1873 and the establishment of an appeal to erect a memorial in his name. This, it was resolved, would be a Geological Museum; a replacement for the cramped and inadequate Woodwardian Museum whose collection Sedgwick had done so much to build up. By 1878 the appeal committee held £12,000 and the requirements of Sedgwick's energetic successor, Thomas McKenny Hughes made the need for a new museum even more urgent.[125] It was all the more unfortunate, therefore, that it would take another twenty-six years for the memorial to be built. In 1880 Sir Arthur Blomfield, already working for Corpus Christi, Emmanuel, and Trinity, was chosen as architect by the syndicate set up by the University.[126] He was the obvious choice for the job—and had even given £10 to the Sedgwick appeal.[127] His plans were soon abandoned,

[120] Quoted in Brooke, History of Cambridge University, xx–xxvi.
[121] Arthur E. Shipley, 'Historical Introduction', to Alan E. Munby, Laboratories: their plannings and fittings (London, 1921), xiii.   [122] Cornford, Microcosmographia, 97, 93.
[123] Archibald Geikie, The Founders of Geology (2nd edn, 1905; New York, 1962), 421–2; Horace B. Woodward, History of Geology (London, 1911), 49, 58; Roy Porter, 'Gentlemen and Geology: the emergence of a scientific career, 1660–1920', Historical Journal (1978), 809–36, at, 817–18, 821–3, 829.
[124] Cambridge Review 17 (1895–6), 37; John Willis Clark and T. McKenny Hughes, The Life and Letters of the Reverend Adam Sedgwick (2 vols.; Cambridge, 1890), vol. ii, p. 37.
[125] CamUR 8 (1877–8), 566.
[126] CUA Hughes Papers, Geol 8/5, Geological Museum Syndicate Minutes 1879–86 (1 June 1880), 8.
[127] CUA, CUR 110, University Registry vol. 110, Sedgwick Memorial Museum, p. 4c (25 March 1873).

however.[128] There was neither the room nor the money for a suitable memorial or an adequate museum.[129] Despite his generosity, Blomfield had lost his chance. Despite its need, Geology had lost its building.

In 1882 a new idea arose. This was to combine the geological museum with the chemistry laboratories, and to ask G. F. Bodley to build them.[130] The chemical department was 'ill-housed and inconveniently arranged'.[131] Bodley was one of Cambridge's favourite architects: here he built All Saints' Church, and worked for King's and Queens', and for Christ's and Jesus Colleges.[132] It looked like the perfect match. But something went seriously wrong. Bodley was known to be strong-willed. 'I don't fancy', wrote the Professor of Chemistry to McKenny Hughes, 'that Bodley would be sufficiently tractable to carry out instructions.'[133] As a result, it was decided to have a limited competition between three invited architects. The committee, however, could not resolve on whom to choose. Blomfield and Bodley were both on the initial list, to which were added J. J. Stevenson, Basil Champneys, G. G. Scott (junior), C. S. Luck, and F. C. Penrose. No resolution was made. The syndicate quite simply could not decide between the candidates.[134] As a result, the concept of a competition was abandoned and after a succession of votes, J. J. Stevenson emerged as architect.[135] This was eminently satisfactory for the chemists, but disastrous for the geologists. They were unhappy with the choice of site and with the architect. There was also disagreement about the 'character of the building'.[136] Their squabbling made it impossible to proceed and it was resolved to build the chemical laboratory alone. Seeking to do justice to 'its association with a university and its prominent position', Stevenson built in the style 'of some of the most characteristic of the old Cambridge buildings'. He clearly meant the seventeenth-century Third Court of St John's (1669–71).[137] Geology may have escaped a building 'less fertile in imagination than Jackson's', but it was still without its museum.[138] The geologists had lost their best opportunity yet.[139] The syndicate had to be reconstituted, and the process was begun anew. Stevenson was reappointed architect in February 1885; by November he had

[128] CUA, Uncat. Drawings, Sedgwick Museum, A. W. Blomfield (21 June 1880); CUA, Hughes Papers, Geol 8/5, Minutes, 31 May 1882.   [129] CamUR 2 (1881–2), 645.
[130] CUA, Hughes Papers, Geol 8/5 Minutes, 9 June 1882.
[131] Shipley, 'Introduction' to Munby, Laboratories, xiii.
[132] Michael Hall, 'The Rise of Refinement: G. F. Bodley's All Saints', Cambridge, and the return to English models in the Gothic architecture of the 1860s', Architectural History 36 (1993), 103–26.
[133] CUA Hughes Papers, Geol 8/2, Rough Notes, Liveing to Hughes, 15 June 1883.
[134] The votes were: Blomfield: 6, Stevenson: 5, Champneys: 4, Scott: 4, Luck: 4, Penrose: 3, Bodley: 1. CUA Hughes Papers, Geol 8/5 Minutes, 9 Nov. 1883.
[135] Ibid., Minutes, 21 Nov. 1883. Blomfield and Stevenson both received 4 votes; 30 Nov. 1883, Stevenson: 6, Bodley: 3, Neutral: 2.   [136] CamUR 15 (1884–50), 656.
[137] CUA, Hughes papers, Geol 8/5 Minutes, 23 Dec. 1884.
[138] Pevsner, Cambridgeshire, 206.
[139] As James Mayo recalled: CUA Hughes Papers, 8/10 Sedgwick Museum flysheets 1896, Mayo to Hughes (23 Nov. 1896).

produced new plans.[140] Tenders were taken, but problems with the site led to the abandonment of the project.[141] A new site was suggested, and plans again drawn up in 1887.[142] Once more, amidst much acrimony, these were rejected.[143] By 1890 there had been two architects, at least twice as many plans, six syndicates, and there was still no museum.[144]

The geologists were not without hope, however. There was, after all, £20,000 in the memorial fund.[145] In 1891 Professor Hughes wrote to the vice chancellor asking for a syndicate made up of '4 Geologists and other members of the Senate who have not declared opinions adverse to the . . . Geological Department'.[146] His wishes were granted, and a syndicate of like-minded men elected. Their first priority was to select a site. Lack of space had frustrated every previous attempt. This time, though, they were able to claim a large and well-placed piece of land, adjacent to other laboratories on the Old Botanical Garden Site.[147] It was a positive start, and the subsequent syndicate, now chaired by the vice chancellor John Peile, resolved to choose a fresh architect.[148] Peile was 'a prominent member of the party of progress in the University', and he and his allies were to be crucial to the museum's success.[149] Jackson and Bodley were suggested by Professor Middleton; to which names were added J. J. Stevenson, R. W. Edis, R. H. Carpenter, and Sir Thomas Deane. Bodley received one vote, Stevenson three, but Jackson was the obvious winner with six.[150]

The reasons for this victory are unclear. It is evident, however, that once again Jackson's Oxford associations were to be useful outside his Alma Mater. Certainly it seems likely that Jackson's success with the equally intractable Examination Schools had a part to play. Moreover, by this period Cambridge was suffering from something of an architectural inferiority complex. As early as 1865 an American student had found it 'of all the provincial English boroughs the most insignificant, the dullest and the Ugliest'.[151] Nor were matters improving. As the vice chancellor was later to put it, 'the University could not afford always to be cheap and ugly [and] constantly inferior to Oxford in the new buildings which it was erecting'.[152] Who better to improve the architecture of Cambridge than Oxford Jackson? His work was modern, progressive, and

[140] CUA, Hughes Papers, Geol 8/3 Rough Notes 1884–8, 1 and Geol 8/5 Minutes, 5 and 13 Nov. 1885.
[141] CUA, Hughes Papers, Geol 8/3 Rough Notes, pp. 34–9; *CamUR* 17 (1886–7), 516: the Syndicate reported it could not make a decision until a site was resolved upon. It recommended the Downing Site (see below).
[142] CUA, Uncat. Drawings (Sedgwick Museum), J. J. Stevenson (16 June 1887).
[143] *CamUR* 18 (1887–8), 195.   [144] Shipley, *Clark*, 329.
[145] Willis Clark and Hughes, *Sedgwick*, vol. ii, p. 484.
[146] CUA, Hughes Papers, Geol 8/9 Rough Notes 1890–1, 14 March 1891.
[147] *CamUR* 22 (1890–1), 1106.
[148] The Syndicate consisted of progressives and Adullamites: Liveing, Hughes, Middleton, J. W. Clark, Ewbank, Morgan, Grant, Marr, Henn, Harker. CUA, Hughes Papers Geol 8/6, Minutes 1891–5, 2 March 1892.
[149] H. M. Kempthorne, in Ann Philips, ed., *A Newnham Anthology* (Cambridge, 1979), 1.
[150] CUA, Hughes Papers, Geol 8/6 Minutes 1891–5, 2 March 1892.
[151] William Everett, *On the Cam* (Cambridge, 1865), 11.   [152] *CamUR* 27 (1896–7), 290.

widely liked. Jackson's designs were soon completed and, after some modifications, 'generally approved'.[153] Nonetheless, despite the large majority that supported his plans, lack of funds postponed their execution. 'At least the site and design are now approved', said the vice chancellor with some relief, 'and further delay will be unnecessary, so soon as the augmentation, already secured, of the income of the university begins to be sensibly felt'.[154] Working drawings and tenders were ordered.[155] The Adullamites, it seemed, had succeeded. Sedgwick was to have his memorial and Hughes his new museum.

Life, much less university politics, is never that simple. The tenders showed that the building would cost too much, and neither Hughes nor the memorial committee would accept a diminution of its size or grandeur.[156] 'I begin to fear', wrote Jackson, 'that by the time the first stone is laid I shall have been laid in my grave.'[157] At the same time, Hughes was also agitating for a better site across the road, far removed from the crowded conditions of the Old Botanical Gardens. It had been his ambition to buy this land from Downing College since the earliest days of the museum proposal.[158] Now, efficient whipping of the Adullamites made this dream a reality.[159] The Downing Site was purchased and the geology museum given the first plot on it.[160] New plans were drawn up and shown to the syndics in 1897. But costs had once again escalated. When it was proposed that expenses should be reduced by decreasing the size of the building, Hughes threatened to resign.[161] The Museum Syndicate, influenced by the wider interests of the university, voted in favour of the smaller Plan A, at £34,000. The Memorial Committee, dominated by Adullamites, insisted on Plan B which would cost £36,500.[162] Cambridge was, once again, plunged into debate about the museum. 'Are you in favour of A or B?' asked the *Review*. 'That is the question everyone is just now asking his friends.'[163] In the end, good organization, and the judgement of experts, won out. On 16 February 1899, by 96 votes to 58, the more expensive Plan B was adopted.[164] Twenty-six years after Sedgwick's death, his memorial was finally to be built.

Jackson's museum had a three-fold purpose. It was vital that it should be a building 'architecturally important and beautiful, worthy of our great geologist'.[165]

---

[153] CUA, Uncat. Drawings (Sedgwick Museum), Jackson 27 April 1892; *CamUR* 23 (1892–3), 215–19, 308–15, 601–2, 669, 804.; Jackson, *Life and Travels*, 205.　　[154] *CamUR* 24 (1893–4), 11.

[155] Ibid., 237.　　[156] *CamUR* 25 (1894–5), 430, 27; (1896–7), 213.

[157] CUA, Hughes Papers, Geol 8/7 Syndicate 1895–6, Jackson to Alfred Harker 4 Feb. 1896.

[158] Ibid., Geol 8/5 Minutes, pp. 2–4; Geol 10/21 Downing Site: letters, 15 April 1885; *CamUR* 13 (1882–3), 847.

[159] Hughes Papers, Geol 8/10 Flysheets 1896, A. E. Shipley, printed postcard, 10 June 1896.

[160] J. W. Clark, *Endowments of the University of Cambridge* (Cambridge, 1904), 25–8; *CamUR* 27 (1896–7), 643. Downing, in real need of ready money, was forced by circumstance to alienate its land: land on which Wilkins had planned to build a propylaeum for the college. See Stanley French, *The History of Downing College, Cambridge* (Cambridge, 1978).

[161] *CamUR* 27 (1896–7), 643.　　[162] *CamUR* 28 (1897–8), 1071–4.

[163] *Cambridge Review* 20 (1898–9), 206.　　[164] Ibid., 222; *CamUR* 29 (1898–9), 573.

[165] Hughes Papers, Geol 8/4, Rough Notes 1887–9, J. W. Clark (9 May 1887).

At the same time, it was to be a working department of geology; a 'dual institution', made up of 'a great museum' and 'a school of science for over 200 students'.[166] With the foundation of the Cavendish Laboratory in 1873, the university had pioneered the research institute.[167] The Cambridge School of Geology was, in its own field, equally important.[168] Hughes' awareness of this importance, of the need for expansion and the necessity of expressing this in the museum building, had delayed construction for over twenty years. He simply would not accept an inferior building or an insignificant site. The wait, though, was worth it. On its opening in 1904, the Sedgwick Museum was described as 'the most spacious, the most stately of all the scientific Museums in the University'.[169] It was an appropriate home for geology and a fitting tribute to Hughes and his Adullamites. Inevitably, given the changes of site and of opinion, the building was different from that first envisaged by Jackson. His original plan of 1892 was revised two years later, and the result was a highly idiosyncratic and freely ornamented structure in brick with stone dressings, topped by a lantern to the centre and a spire to the west.[170] The ground floor was arched with recessed windows framed by polychromatic brick. There was a loggia to the first floor, gables to the second, and dormers to the third. These joined Jacobean pilasters and parapets, stone string courses, and friezes of flora and fauna. He added classical details too: Corinthian pilasters and windows with pediments.[171] This was an exuberant eclecticism indeed, and it perfectly reflected the needs of its promoters, as Hughes was happy to confirm.[172] The wider university community also accepted it as a 'building of great dignity and beauty' and 'a worthy memorial to Sedgwick'.[173]

Nevertheless, it was not this, but another building that was constructed. The museum of 1899 was on a corner site, with greater room to grow. Although Hughes proposed simply to cut the plans in half and arrange the parts at right angles to each other,[174] Jackson was able to persuade him to begin afresh with an entirely new proposition.[175] Again, he suggested red brick with stone dressings; Hughes and his allies being quick to observe that 'it would be appropriate to a memorial building that it should have some ornamental features'.[176] Jackson was more than willing to take them up on this suggestion. Once again, as in so much of his work, it was in the ornamentation rather than in the plan that he showed

[166] Hughes Papers, Geol 9/39 Corresp. with Jackson, T. McKenny Hughes to Jackson 1898.
[167] Egon Larsen, Cavendish Laboratory (London, 1962), 14.
[168] Roy Porter, 'The Natural Science Tripos and "the Cambridge School of Geology"', History of Universities 2 (1982), 193–216, at 193, 200–9; Brooke, History of Cambridge University, 157–9.
[169] Shipley, Clark, 332.
[170] The original stone building was too expensive to consider. CUA, CUR 110, (26 May 1897), 73.   [171] CUA Uncat. Drawings (Sedgwick Museum), Jackson, 1892–4.
[172] Hughes Papers, Geol 8/9 Rough Notes 1890–1, 26 April 1892.
[173] Cambridge Review 14 (1892–3), 117, 136.
[174] CUA Uncat. Drawings (Sedgwick Museum) 1896.
[175] Hughes Papers, Geol 12/4 Letters from Jackson 1895–8, 26 May 1898.
[176] CUA, CUR 110 (26 May 1897), 79.

real imagination. The architect, indeed, had very little responsibility for the layout of the museum. From first till last, the planning had been in the hands of Hughes and his colleagues. Jackson had, as he himself acknowledged, 'followed your plans pretty nearly'.[177] Yet if his plans were borrowed, his treatment of the façade was highly original. In particular, the choice of materials showed Jackson's usual resourcefulness.[178] The majority of the bricks were from Cranley, and brought a deep purple colour to Cambridge. The quoins were of bright red Castle Hedingham bricks, with voussoirs of a more sober brick from Bracknell. Exterior stone was from Clipsham and interior from Ancaster. The chimney pieces were of Portland, whilst Purbeck was used for the stairs. The building was as varied as the materials from which it was made.[179]

The Downing Street front is similar in many respects to the designs of 1892: recessed windows behind arches to the ground floor; mullioned and transomed windows to the first and second; with dormers and a fancy gable to the third. But it is, on the whole, plainer—despite some very striking features.[180] There is the entrance: a Venetian window with the university arms supported by a sloth and an iguana. Next to this is a carving of a woolly mammoth. The south side is broken up by a led-capped tower, with a pedimented and pilastered window. The main entrance is at first floor level, approached up a double staircase guarded by bison and bears.[181] The pediment of the door is supported by half-pillars with sheep and pterodactyls in the capitals.[182] Jackson's *jeux d'esprit* undoubtedly came at a cost—although he believed the building to be cheap.[183] There had, it was agreed when the museum was rated, 'been extravagance'. Jackson was 'an eminent architect', the experts acknowledged, 'but not a cheap one'.[184] The building undoubtedly reflected this. But perhaps the cost was worth it. 'Skilfully designed and carefully executed', said T. McKenny Hughes, 'it will allow us to display the finest educational collection in the world.'[185]

Jackson's museum, when opened in 1904, was adjudged a success. He had managed to reconcile the competing needs of the department and the university, the Adullamites and the others. Even those who objected to geology were satisfied with Jackson's designs. The dissenting Syndics of 1892, who opposed elements of the proposed museum, were forced to admit that Jackson's plans would 'lead to the creation of a worthy memorial to Professor Sedgwick'.[186] James Mayo, although possessing 'no liking for the science of geology', found

[177] Ibid., (8 Feb. 1898).   [178] *Cambridge Graphic* 17 Feb. 1900, 10.
[179] CUA, Uncat. Drawings (Sedgwick Museum) 1897.
[180] The cost of the masonry was a constant concern: e.g. CUA Hughes Papers, Geol 8/6 Minutes, Jackson to Hughes 28 Sept. 1895.
[181] CUA Hughes Papers, Geol 9/39, (23) Jackson to Hughes, 6 Jan. 1902.
[182] Ibid., Geol 9/14, Jackson to Hughes, 27 Aug. 1900.
[183] Ibid., Geol 14/6, Rating of the Museum (1) Jackson to Hughes 27 Dec. 1904.
[184] CUA, Hughes Papers, Geol 14/6, *Cambridge Chronicle*, 6 Feb. 1905.
[185] *Order of Proceedings and Description of the Buildings Opened by Their Majesties the King and Queen* (Cambridge, 1904), 39.   [186] *CamUR* 23 (1892–3), 308–9.

that Jackson's was a 'beautiful museum' and was glad 'to take the opportunity of erecting such a fine building'.[187] And it was of course the case that over three-quarters of the Senate supported Jackson's more expensive building in 1899.[188] This success inevitably led to other work. The purchase of the Downing Site had not only helped the geologists. A whole range of other disciplines saw it as a tremendous opportunity to expand. But the university was determined any growth should be organized and orderly. The Old Botanical Gardens Site reflected its spasmodic development. As Peile put it, 'The existing museums were heterogeneous, erected at different times and with no unity of design . . . and no one could regard the effect of the whole with satisfaction.'[189] Jackson took up the challenge and his solution was no less effective for being highly conventional. He began by setting out the Downing Site. It was to be an open quadrangle, with the Sedgwick Museum enclosing the north-west corner.[190] The remainder of Jackson's time in Cambridge was to be filled with the partial completion of the court.

The first of these new buildings was for law, assigned to the site in 1897.[191] The need for a new library and school had been acknowledged for years, and in 1891 the Law School Buildings Syndicate had recommended that they should be built to adjoin the university library.[192] This was a prime site, and Oscar Browning declared that the suggestion to build there was 'one of the most important' ever discussed by the university.[193] Unsurprisingly, the proposal was rejected: law was a small and relatively novel tripos and it could neither afford nor was believed to deserve such a place of honour. The Downing Site was a poor second place, but the lawyers were soon reconciled to it.[194] They were helped by a bequest from Rebecca Flower Squire, after whom the library was named. Squire had hoped to leave her money to Oxford, to found scholarships and fellowships in divinity and law, and a law library as well. The difficulty was that her will specified certain conditions for the awards—in particular, giving preference to members of her own family. In a rare burst of righteousness, Oxford rejected this conditional offer, and Cambridge—happily unburdened by such moral qualms—stepped in to the breach.[195] With both a site and the prospect of funds, they needed only an architect. It was important that he was good. In 1892 writers had predicted a law school 'whose gaunt and obstructive ugliness shall symbolize the popular misconception of the Faculty that dwells therein'.[196] The building had also to harmonize with the neighbouring Sedgwick Museum. It was necessary, the Syndicate acknowledged, to ensure 'a certain amount of unity of design in the architecture which was to form henceforth rather an important feature in the public buildings of the university'.[197] The obvious choice was T. G. Jackson.

---

[187] *CamUR 23* (1892–3), 313.   [188] *Cambridge Review* 20 (1898–9), 222.
[189] *CamUR 27* (1896–7), 290.
[190] *CamUR 35* (1904–5), 715; CUA, Uncat. Drawings (Sedgwick Museum), undated tracing.
[191] *CamUR 27* (1896–7), 1131.   [192] *CamUR 22* (1890–1), 1005.
[193] *CamUR 23* (1891–2), 554.   [194] *CamUR 26* (1895–6), 319, 508.
[195] F. H. Lawson, *The Oxford Law School, 1850–1965* (Oxford, 1968), 96–7.
[196] *Cambridge Review* 13 (1891–2), 294.   [197] *CamUR 30* (1899–1900), 912.

79. The Squire Law School, Cambridge, from Downing Street (1901–5).

The choice may have been obvious, but it was not immediate. The Professor of Law, E. C. Clark, favoured Ferguson, who had built at Aberystwyth College and for the Earl of Carlisle. Jackson's name was suggested together with that of W. C. Marshall, architect of the Engineering Department (1893–4). It is clear that the cost of Jackson's work was a worry to the lawyers. They suggested

80. The Squire Law School, south front (1901–5).

'that enquiries should be made as to the impression produced in Oxford by Mr. Jackson during the erection of buildings of which he was the architect, with special reference to the accuracy of his estimates'.[198] Clearly (if perhaps surprisingly) the impression was a good one. Jackson was given the commission. The law library was to form the grand entrance to the Downing Street Site, and his original conception of it was influenced by the gateway to the Bodleian Quadrangle, with a frontispiece and shaped gables.[199] An alternative design showed a towered gateway similar to Jackson's entrance to Uppingham.[200] The library and law school as built between 1901 and 1905 was somewhat different. Although embellished with carving—a figure of justice, an Alma Mater Cantabrigia, complete with flowing milk—it was a relatively simple structure. The building was five bays long, framed to Downing Street by two cupolled towers. The ground floor was arched: two for windows and three for the gateway, and within was a rib-vaulted space. High windows, mullioned, transomed, pedimented, and to the street gently bayed, dominated the building.[201] It was topped off with dormers and a lantern. On the south side was access to the school itself, through a tower containing stairs. In the fittings of the library no

[198] CUA Min. VI 43, Law School and Law Library Building Syndicate, Minutes 1819–1905, 29 May 1899.   [199] CUA, PII/30 Proposed Plans for Downing Site, Long Elevation.
[200] CUA, Uncat. Drawings (Sedgwick Museum), 15 April 1897.
[201] In line with the best contemporary advice: F. J. Burgoyne, *Library Construction: architecture, fittings and furniture* (London, 1897), 14, 26.

expense was spared, and indeed its luxury was to become impractical with time.[202]

These buildings have not remained popular. Dirty, disregarded, and unloved, the museum and library now form a rather dismal, featureless frame to Downing Street. Nonetheless, Jackson's work was undoubtedly valued by his contemporaries. The 'whole pile', wrote one, 'is an imposing one, exhibiting many of the graceful and scholarly features of Mr. Jackson's work'.[203] This was of course the intention. The library formed an imposing entrance to the quadrangle; an entrance, indeed, which was fit for a king. For in 1904 the Sedgwick and the Squire were visited by Edward VII, on the first tour of Cambridge by a reigning monarch for fifty-seven years.[204] The climax of the day was the opening of the Sedgwick, but the Squire was not forgotten.[205] 'The inauguration of these new schools of Learning and Science', observed the vice-chancellor, 'marks an epoch in our academic history.'[206]

Jackson's role in this new age had been crucial. The importance of his work to the university makes modern disregard for it difficult to understand. Even Pevsner misdates it all. Late-Victorian Cambridge and late-nineteenth-century science are both areas ripe for rediscovery. Until more research is carried out on both areas, however, Jackson's impact will continue to be under-rated. The complexity of his relationship with the university has frightened others: it was said at the time that it 'would require a course of lectures to give an adequate history' of the building of the Sedgwick Museum.[207] Amidst the babble of contending syndicates, it is easy to get lost. Yet Jackson's work is important, and it did not stop with these harbingers of change. In fact he became still more significant. The north-west corner of the Downing Site remained empty. It was allocated to the Museum of Archaeology and Ethnology, a department which to all intents and purposes did not exist.[208] The university's collection of artefacts, though, was outgrowing its accommodation.[209] The new museum was to be more than a mere collection, it was to be a research centre, the home of a Cambridge School of Archaeology and Ethnology.[210] This was the heroic age of museum archaeology and anthropology, and Cambridge's few specialists were at the forefront of modern thinking.[211] It was all the more galling, therefore, that

[202] J. D. Pickles, 'The Haddon Library, Cambridge', *Library History* 8 (1988), 1–9, 4.

[203] *Times*, 27 Feb. 1904, 6.   [204] *Cambridge Review* 25 (1903–4), 197.

[205] Ibid., 226. Also opened were W. C. Marshall's Botany School and E. S. Prior's rather more interesting Pathology Building (1900–4).   [206] *CamUR* 34 (1903–4), 561.

[207] *Cambridge Review* 20 (1898–9), 34.

[208] *CamUR* 27 (1896–7), 1131; CUMAA, MM2/1/2, Fundraising Leaflet, 26 Nov. 1903.

[209] Bod., GA Camb. 4° 30 (8), 'An Account of the Proceedings at the Opening of the Museum of Archaeology' (Cambridge, 1884), 1–2, 12.

[210] David Murray: *Museums: their history and their use* (3 vols.; Glasgow, 1904), vol. I, p. 259; Henry Balfour, 'The Relationship of Museums to the Study of Anthropology', *Journal of Anthropological Institute* 24 (1904), 16–19.

[211] William C. Sturtevant, 'Does Anthropology Need Museums?', *Proceedings of the Biological Society of Washington* 82 (1969), 619–49, at 622–4; George W. Stocking, 'Essays on Museums and

Oxford should possess the Pitt Rivers, and Cambridge a cramped and inadequate museum.[212] Given the site and the purpose of the project, the decision to appoint Jackson was almost axiomatic. In 1900 he began to prepare sketch plans.[213]

The novelty of the subject and the poverty of the museum meant that the years 1900 to 1907 were preoccupied with fund-raising. The curator of the museum, Baron Anatole von Hügel, devoted himself to writing letters and begging for money.[214] A renewed effort to generate cash began in 1908 and was accompanied by detailed plans and exact tenders for the museum.[215] In 1910 construction began on the first building and was completed in 1912. Another, smaller, section was begun in 1913 and added to in 1914,[216] when the war intervened and the building was never finished. Nothing was added until 1948, by which point Jackson's design was outdated both in terms of style and cost.[217] Nevertheless, the museum as actually erected is still a striking structure, which comfortably completes the courtyard.[218] Unsurprisingly, however, its plan was scarcely exciting. Even his clients recognized that. 'I do not think Jackson has put much ingenious scheming into his plans', wrote W. H. Macready, 'and I doubt whether we shall get him to do so. It is a pity that we have not got an Architect who takes an interest in doing this'.[219] The style, nonetheless, was somewhat new, and different from his other work in Cambridge. 'The details', wrote a critic, 'are reminiscent of the 17th century, of the 16th, of Lombardy, and of other periods and places, and yet welded into a style which is as characteristic of the author as one of his own beautiful drawings.'[220] The museum was a tribute to von Hügel's success, but more than this, to the ambitions of archaeology and anthropology within the university. The career of A. C. Haddon makes this plain. Appointed as the first ever lecturer in Anthropology in 1895, he led the expedition to the Torres Strait which founded English anthropological field-work between 1898 and 1899.[221] In 1904 a Board of Anthropological Studies was established. By 1909 he was Reader in Ethnology.[222] This was a subject whose time had come. The museum was thus

Material Culture', in Stocking, ed., *Objects and Others* (Madison and London, 1985), 7–8. For a contrasting view see Edmund Leach, 'Notes on the Mythology of Cambridge Anthropology', *Cambridge Anthropology* 9 (1984), 1–12.

[212] CUMAA MM1/2/12, Reports of Antiquarian Committee 1875–99; *CamUR* 29 (1898–9), 598, 727–30.   [213] CUMAA MM2/1/1, Minute Book 1899–1913, 15 March 1900.
[214] A. C. Haddon, 'Baron Anatole von Hügel', *Man* 28 (1928), 169–71, at 170.
[215] CUMAA MM2/1/4 Fundraising 1907–14; MM2/1/9 Notes 1909–17; MM2/1/1 Minutes, 8 Feb. 1909.
[216] CUMAA MM2/1/17 Memorandum from Board of Anthropological Studies (June 1917); MM2/1/1 Minutes, 8 April 1913.   [217] Information from Dr Robin Boast, CUMAA.
[218] *CamUR* 39 (1908–9), 922.
[219] CUMAA, Box 123 MM2/1/3 Correspondence 1907–13, W. H. Macready (22 Dec. 1908).
[220] *Cambridge Review* 35 (1913–14), 450.
[221] Anita Herle and Sandra Rowse, eds., *Cambridge and the Torres Strait* (Cambridge, 1998); J. W. Burrow, *Evolution and Society* (Cambridge, 1966), 68.
[222] A. Hingston Quiggin, *Haddon the Head Hunter* (Cambridge, 1942), xi, 95–142.

81. Cambridge Museum of Archaeology and Ethnology (1910–15).

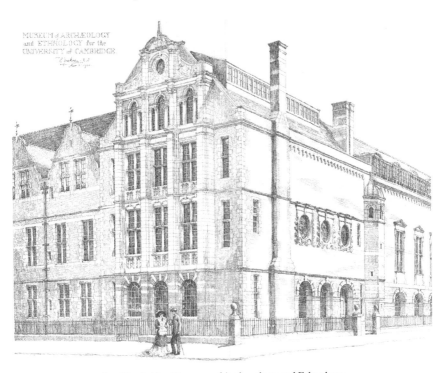

82. Cambridge Museum of Archaeology and Ethnology.

both a totem and a trophy: a symbol of achievement and a statement of intent.[223] Haddon's acceptance by the university was asserted and expressed by Jackson's designs.

By the time the museum was built, however, its plans were fourteen years old—and, to some extent, they looked it. Graham Jackson's last projects within Cambridge show him trying to keep up with the times. So much so, in fact, that his Physiology Department (1910–14) is erroneously identified by Pevsner as a building designed after the First World War.[224] The department was built in variegated brick, with a central pedimented feature, and shallow oriels to the side. Its Queen Anne inspiration is unsurprising given Jackson's clients. For, like the Electrical Laboratory in Oxford, this was a philanthropic gesture by the Drapers' Company, which chose the architect and approved the plans.[225] The need for the new laboratories was clear. Cambridge had the largest and best Physiology Department in the country.[226] Yet it was squeezed into evidently inferior accommodation, with researchers required to work in the coal cellar for lack of room elsewhere.[227] Jackson's building transformed their situation. As the Master of the Drapers' Company observed, 'Its erection by Sir Thomas Jackson, so well known in Cambridge, is a guarantee of its beauty and stability.'[228] Its five storeys gave room to grow, whilst the plan and fittings—determined by Langley, the head of department—made it amongst the most modern in the world.[229] It was, wrote his obituarist, 'a fitting recognition of the distinction and activity of the school of workers which Langley was leading'.[230]

As an annexe to the Physiology Department Jackson added the Psychology laboratory, paid for by its director, C. S. Myers.[231] This was a small building, now completely hidden by extensions,[232] although it apparently possessed 'a dignity' in its day.[233] With its three floors of laboratories, it was one of the best-equipped psychological departments in the world.[234] And its very existence is important in itself. Psychology was in many respects just finding its feet as a discipline. It was first formally established in England only in 1897, with the foundation of laboratories in London and Cambridge.[235] More than this,

[223] Cambridge Archaeology was similarly successful: by 1927 of the 10 teachers of archaeology in the country, half were based in Cambridge. Glyn Daniel, *Cambridge and the Back-Looking Curiosity* (Cambridge, 1976), 15.
[224] DHA, MB/F.9, Finance Committee Minutes 1909–16, 42, 46, 47, 167; Pevsner, *Cambridgeshire*, 208.   [225] DHA, MB62 Assistants' Minutes 1908–14, 128, 175.
[226] Gerald L. Geison, *Michael Foster and the Cambridge School of Physiology* (Princeton, 1978), 6, 309.
[227] 'John Newport Langley', *Proceedings of the Royal Society (Series B)* 101 (1927), xxxiii–xli, at xxxix.   [228] *CamUR* 44 (1913–14), 1203.
[229] Munby, *Laboratories*, 106–8; J. N. Langley, 'University of Cambridge Department of Physiology', *Methods and Problems of Medical Education* (New York, 1925), 8–13. I owe this reference to Chris Ratcliffe.   [230] 'Langley', *Proceedings of the Royal Society*, xxxix.
[231] F. C. Bartlett, 'Cambridge, England: 1887–1937', *American Journal of Psychology* 50 (1937), 97–110, 107.   [232] *Builder* 104 (1913), 597.   [233] *Cambridge Review* 35 (1913–14), 450.
[234] *Cambridge Review* 34 (1912–13), 78.
[235] L. S. Hearnshaw, *A Short History of British Psychology* (London, 1964), 135.

83. Cambridge Physiology Department (1910–14).

though, the building operated as a symbol of the Adullamites as a whole. Although attached to Physiology, the Psychology laboratory had originally been planned as part of the Museum of Archaeology.[236] The development of each of the departments was inter-related, as were the people involved. W. H. R. Rivers is a useful example of this.[237] He first came to Cambridge in 1893 as lecturer in the physiology of the sense organs. In 1897 he established the first psychological laboratory in Cambridge, and in 1898 he joined Haddon on the anthropological expedition to the Torres Strait. Until his death in 1922, he worked comfortably in all these areas, producing work of real importance for each of his subjects.[238] Like his colleagues, he was determined to make physiology, psychology, and anthropology real professions, hard sciences, and recognized parts of the university.[239] The role of Jackson's work in this process was no less important for being implicit.

[236] CUMAA MM2/1/3 Correspondence 1907–13, C. S. Myers to von Hügel (17 Aug. 1908); MM2/1/5 Tracings of Draft Plans (1908).

[237] Now of course better known from Pat Barker's *Regeneration* trilogy (London, 1991–5).

[238] Richard Slobodin, *W. H. R. Rivers* (New York, 1978); B. J. Mack, 'W. H. Rivers: the contexts of social anthropology' (D.Phil., Oxford, 1975), Ian Langham, *The Building of British Social Anthropology: W. H. R. Rivers and his Cambridge disciples* (Dordrecht and London, 1981), 69–90.

[239] W. H. R. Rivers, 'The Unity of Anthropology', *Journal of the Anthropological Institute* 52 (1922), 12–25; C. S. Myers, 'The Influence of the late W. H. R. Rivers', in Rivers, *Psychology and Politics* (London, 1923), 154–80; G. Elliot-Smith, 'Dr Rivers and the new vision in ethnology', in Rivers, *Psychology and Ethnology* (London, 1926), xiv–xviii.

The Adullamites, joked Cornford, 'inhabit a series of caves in Downing Street'.[240] It was T. G. Jackson, more than any other man, who had built these troglodytic habitations. His success, despite the 'good deal of contentious feeling' which surrounded the science buildings, owed much to his ability.[241] He was able to integrate new subjects into the university without compromising the requirements—aesthetic or practical—of the scientists. His achievement was acknowledged in 1910, with the award of an honorary degree by Cambridge.[242] It was a ceremony held in the Senate House that he had illuminated and altered in 1899 and 1909.[243] As in Oxford, he had been championed by a party, but accepted by the university as a whole. His work in Cambridge thus reflected his ability and established him, finally, as arbiter of the academic style. 'The buildings of Oxford and Cambridge are representative of their age in an almost unique sense', wrote a commentator in 1914. 'Among modern architects in this respect, no one has had the same chance as Sir Thomas Graham Jackson.'[244] His work may have been limited to elite education but within that field it was without parallel in importance. In reforming Oxford and scientific Cambridge, in Lampeter, the Inner Temple, and the public schools, the architect of choice became—and for thirty years remained—Sir Thomas Graham Jackson.

---

[240] Cornford, *Microcosmographia*, 95.   [241] Jackson, *Life and Travels*, 205.
[242] *CamUR* 40 (1909–10), 1318.
[243] *CamUR* 30 (1898–9), 591–2; CUA, University Register 46.1, Senate House (1900–23), 50, 55–55a.   [244] *Cambridge Review* 35 (1913–14), 450.

6

'An Intellectual Aristocracy'[1]
Jackson, his Clients, and their World

The twentieth century began on 1 January 1901. Twenty-one days later, the Victorian era ended.[2] Celebration turned to mourning; anticipation turned to retrospect. Even the prostitutes were clad in black, and the street-sweepers carried crepe on their brooms. It was an occasion, all agreed, which must be marked. Victoria, who had made the commemoration of death a way of life, now demanded her own memorial.[3] With almost indecent haste, a committee was convened and architects invited to compete; Jackson joined the list. This was not his first attempt at Imperial memorial—in 1881 he had unsuccessfully submitted a design for the Tsar Alexander II Church in St Petersburg—but it was undoubtedly the most important. And indeed this event deserves more than a footnote in his biography. Jackson's participation in the Victoria Memorial contest reflected his ambition, his desire to enter the world of great public architecture. The invitation to compete for this most important of memorials also illustrates the way in which Jackson had indeed entered the front rank of the profession.[4] But, more than this, Graham Jackson's failure in the competition is highly significant. It revealed that, despite his ambition and despite his importance, he was unable to escape the arena in which he had made his name. Although he could break out of Oxford, he could do no more than that. He was condemned to be known as the architect of elite education. Jackson's dominance of this one field undermined his success in others. He was the chosen instrument of a particular group made up of teachers, writers, and thinkers. This section of society, the new intellectual aristocracy, were Jackson's chief clients and they made his career—but in so doing they also limited it.

---

[1] Benjamin Jowett, quoted in Evelyn Abbott and Lewis Campbell, *Life and Letters of Benjamin Jowett* (2 vols.; London, 1897), vol. ii., pp. 212–13.

[2] Asa Briggs, 'The 1890s: past, present and future in headlines', in Asa Briggs and Daniel Snowman, eds., *Fins de Siècle* (New Haven and London, 1996), 192–4.

[3] John Wolffe, *Great Deaths: grieving, religion, and nationhood in Victorian and Edwardian Britain* (Oxford, 2000).

[4] See Ellen Christianson, 'Government Architecture and British Imperialism' (Ph.D., Northwestern University, 1995), 42–6, 96; E. and M. Darby, 'The Nation's Memorial to Victoria', *Country Life* 164 (1978), 1647–50; John Plunkett, 'Remembering Victoria', *The Victorian* 1 (1999), 4–9; M. H. Port, *Imperial London* (New Haven and London, 1998), 24–5; Tori Smith, ' "A Grand

Association with schools and universities undoubtedly curtailed Jackson's prospects. This was clear in the case of the Victoria Memorial. Here, the rather more versatile Aston Webb was chosen, and his proposal (suitably amended) was eventually carried out. At the heart of the project was a statue of Victoria by Thomas Brock. It was the setting for this sculpture that the architects—Webb and Jackson, Thomas Drew, Ernest George, and Rowand Anderson—were asked to design. From the start, this was a project enmeshed in argument and rich in irony. The competition was too limited, claimed the *Times*; the memorial was ill-conceived and badly sited, asserted others.[5] Most agreed, though, that Webb's solution was appropriate and well chosen—and therein lies the irony.[6] Just as the Byzantine-loving Prince Consort was immortalized in Gilbert Scott's Gothic, so his wife was to be commemorated in a classical style.[7] Although built

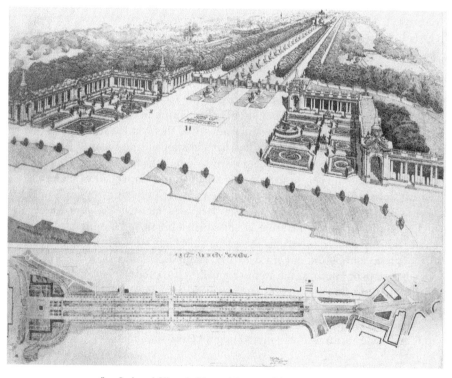

84. Jackson's Victoria Memorial competition entry (1901).

Work of Noble Conception": the Victoria Memorial and Imperial London', in Felix Driver and David Gilbert, eds., *Imperial Cities* (Manchester and New York, 1999), 21–39.

  [5] *Builder* 80 (1901), 229, 384.
  [6] H. M. Cundall, 'Queen Victoria Memorial', *Art Journal* 24 (1904), 198–201.
  [7] Chris Brooks, ed., *The Albert Memorial* (New York and London, 2001).

to remember Victoria, and eventually opened by George V, the memorial was archetypally Edwardian. Victoria was gone, and the Gothic Revival was undoubtedly dying. In Webb's imperial, classical, and thoroughly modern treatment, Brock met baroque in a brilliant display. The twentieth century had begun—and Jackson had missed his chance.

Yet this was never inevitable. Even the *Builder* could not 'but express the greatest admiration for Mr. Jackson's design', although it felt forced to note that the architect's 'brilliantly executed' accompanying watercolour was 'somewhat too profusely peopled with nurse-maids'.[8] But nonetheless he lost, and a superfluity of nannies is scarcely a sufficient explanation for this setback. There are other, more important, failings to be considered. In the first place, Jackson's planning was predictably poor. Despite an excursion to Berlin to assess the grandiose townscapes of the German Empire, his old weakness undermined his effectiveness. Whilst Webb 'won his position on the ground of superiority of plan', Jackson's design was fiddly and fussy and failed to resolve the complex problem of linking the Mall with Whitehall.[9] Nor was the choice of style his own. The government appears to have expected only classicism. Certainly, all the entrants offered neo-classical treatments: the Renaissance in Italy and the Low Countries from George and Anderson; French neo-classic from Drew; Italian Baroque from Jackson; and all of these and more from Webb.[10]

For T. G. Jackson, whose training was Gothic, whose preferences were Jacobean, and who genuinely believed that classicism represented 'the tyranny of the schools', this change of style was too great and too late in life.[11] He was in his late sixties—still with twenty years of work ahead of him, but growing increasingly intransigent in his attitudes. Jackson was learning a new language, and had not really perfected the grammar. The result might have been 'very favourably received', but it was scarcely convincing.[12] He had failed to perform in the Grand Manner: it was a continual problem; as Crook puts it, 'monumentality was never Jackson's strong suit'. The great public prizes would always go to 'rival architects with a greater sense of mass and a greater capacity for large-scale planning'.[13] And this is true, so far as it goes, but it is possible to go still further. Above all this—above the poor planning, infelicities of style, and lack of conviction—there was another impediment to Jackson's success: the judges looked at his work and thought not of empire, but of Oxford.

---

[8] *Builder* 80 (1901), 438. These nurse-maids are a common trope in Jackson's own illustrations.

[9] *Builder* 81 (1901), 377; *Architectural Review* 10 (1901), 203.

[10] J. Mordaunt Crook, *The Dilemma of Style: architectural ideas from the picturesque to the post-modern* (London, 1989), 214–15.

[11] T. G. Jackson, *Reason in Architecture* (London, 1906), 12.

[12] T. G. Jackson, *Recollections: the life and travels of a Victorian architect* (ed., Sir Nicholas Jackson; London, 2003), 241.

[13] J. Mordaunt Crook, 'T. G. Jackson and the Cult of Eclecticism', in H. Searing, ed., *In Search of Modern Architecture* (New York, 1982), 102–20, at 112.

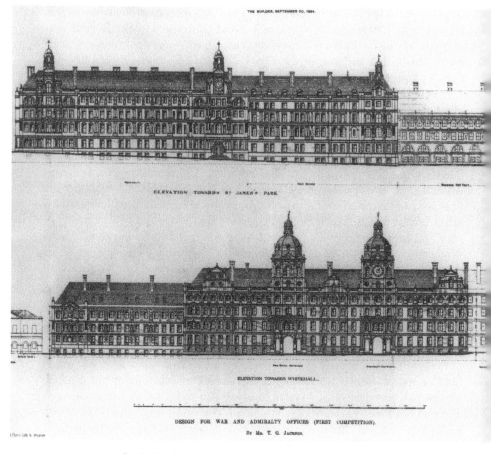

85. Jackson's Admiralty Building competition entry (1884).

This was a pattern repeated throughout Jackson's career and he lost some of the most prestigious competitions of the period. In each, he submitted designs that were admired; in all of them, he failed to satisfy the requirements of the judges. His first attempt, an entry to the 1884 Admiralty buildings competition, could not even make the shortlist. He was in good company: some of the most eminent architects of the day were amongst the excluded. The winners were the previously obscure Yorkshire firm of Leeming and Leeming. But, then, as Michael Port observes, the designs of the leading architects could scarcely be described as appropriate.[14] Jackson's in particular, although exhibiting 'architectural refinement', was simply too pretty for its own good. 'We should very much

[14] Port, *Imperial London*, 182.

86. Jackson's Imperial Institute competition entry (1887).

doubt', the *Builder* commented, 'if it would generally be taken by visitors for the
War Office. It is a good deal too quiet and domestic-looking.'[15] Jackson had the
same problem in 1887 at the Imperial Institute, where he was at least invited
to compete—joining Rowand Anderson, A. W. Blomfield, T. E. Colcutt,
T. N. Deane, and Aston Webb with Ingress Bell.[16] The terms of the competition
were 'cruelly vague', though Colcutt's winning design was admired by most.[17]
Jackson's entry was beautiful and refined but nonetheless looked like a college.[18]
Despite all the hard work, his entry was disregarded.

That Jackson continued, in spite of these high-profile humiliations, is testa-
ment to his ambition. But carry on he did—and he remained a runner-up. In
1890, the government agreed to fund the expansion of the South Kensington
Museum, and a competition was held to find the architect for this presti-
gious project. As competitors for the contract, the government nominated
T. E. Colcutt, Aston Webb, J. McVicar Anderson, and T. N. Deane. Alfred
Waterhouse, President of the RIBA, nominated Norman Shaw, William
Emerson, John Belcher, and, of course, T. G. Jackson. Shaw withdrew, and was

[15] *Builder* 47 (1884), 388.
[16] William Golant, *Image of Empire: the early history of the Imperial Institute* (Exeter, 1984),
5–10; *Imperial Institute* (London, 1956), 3, 8.
[17] *British Architect* (1 July 1887), 4; *British Almanac* 1888, 128.
[18] *Builder* 53 (1887), 3; *Survey of London* vol. 38, p. 222. Though see also G. Alex Bremner,
' "Some Imperial Institute": architecture, symbolism, and the ideal of empire in late Victorian
Britain, 1887–93', *Journal of the Society of Architectural Historians* 62 (2003), 50–73, at 58.

replaced by William Young.[19] The winner, with a certain inevitability, was Aston Webb. Waterhouse, the official assessor, produced detailed marking schemes which show that Jackson came fifth.[20] His proposal had been, as the *Builder* observed, 'rather nondescript and deficient in marked character'.[21] It certainly did not fit most people's idea of a museum—or, indeed, a public building more generally.

Jackson was unstoppable, however. Despite this setback, and his failure with the Victoria Memorial, he was still willing to enter the London County Hall competition of 1908. This was to be his final defeat and his last competition. He was beaten by the young and unknown Ralph Knott, an assistant of Aston Webb's.[22] In his design, Jackson's idiosyncrasies were allowed full rein. The majority of entries to the competition were in the Edwardian baroque which had become dominant in London local government architecture.[23] Jackson, by contrast, rejected this idiom in favour of his own approach. The result was not happy. As the *Builder* put it, his proposal 'would rather suggest a very large chateau than a municipal building—at least according to present ideas of what constitutes municipal character in architecture'.[24] Once again, Jackson had misjudged the market, and the consequence was another, very public rejection.

This litany of failures serves a purpose. It was more than merely disappointing that Graham Jackson lost these important competitions—it is in fact very telling. As the admiration of the periodicals suggests, these designs were not discreditable. They possessed 'a great deal of architectural charm'; they were 'fine and sumptuous', 'admirable', and 'full of beauty and refinement'.[25] These were not bad buildings, they were simply inappropriate. And this was not solely because of their appearance; their layout was suspect as well. The plan of the Imperial Institute, for example, was 'certainly a mistake for a building of this class'. 'It may be called a picturesque arrangement of plan', wrote the *Builder*, 'but ever since great buildings for state purposes have existed the world has thought that spaciousness and symmetrical arrangement are necessary conditions of dignity and monumental character; and the world is likely to go on thinking so.'[26] In this respect, Jackson's whole approach was misguided and even ill advised. His plan at South Kensington was similarly deficient in the 'long drawn out architectural vistas' which Waterhouse believed were an essential component of museum design.[27] Thus it was that in both artistic treatment and architectonic approach, Jackson failed to satisfy the requirements of his assessors. His proposals were simply inappropriate.

---

[19] John Physick, *The Victoria and Albert Museum: a history of its buildings* (Oxford, 1982), 184–5.
[20] Physick, *Victoria and Albert*, 197–8.   [21] *Builder* 61 (1891), 96.
[22] A. Stewart Gray, *Edwardian Architecture* (London, 1985), 230–1.
[23] English Heritage, *London's Town Halls* (London, 1999).   [24] *Builder* 94 (1908), 140.
[25] Ibid.; 81 (1901), 377; 66 (1894), 457.   [26] *Builder* 53 (1887), 3.
[27] Physick, *Victoria and Albert Museum*, 197.

Why was this so? How was it that a man so self-assured in Oxford should be so gauche in London? Why was he capable of transforming elite architecture, and yet a failure in other fields? Fundamentally, the problem was that Jackson's success in one sphere adversely affected his chances in others. The only reason that his Imperial Institute design 'looked like a college' was that it resembled his other works. The fact that the Anglo-Jackson style had become synonymous with educational architecture almost certainly limited his appeal. Much more than this, Jackson's failure to produce appropriate proposals reflected the circumstances of his success: it was a rather small, relatively homogeneous group of people which commissioned him in the public schools and ancient universities. He shared their values and they shared his taste. Jackson grew rich and successful as a result of this symbiotic relationship. But—to borrow a biological metaphor—like anything which relies upon a specific niche, outside that environment it was hard for him to thrive.

This reliance on a limited coterie of clients was not unique to T. G. Jackson. In the early nineteenth century Sir Robert Smirke had been the architect of choice for the stern, unbending Tories, including Robert Peel.[28] Earlier still, Sir John Soane had been taken up by Pitt the Younger, and his network of colleagues and clients.[29] A century before, Sir Christopher Wren had similarly relied on his high-church, high-Tory friends and family, whilst James Gibbs built his career on the patronage of Jacobites and Roman Catholics.[30] Among Jackson's contemporaries, Norman Shaw was repeatedly commissioned by Royal Academicians, Alfred Waterhouse relied on northern non-conformists, and William Butterfield benefited from a network of Tractarian clients.[31] Later in life, Jackson himself acknowledged how much he owed 'to the kindness of friends who recommended me to other friends'.[32] This was more than a passing tribute to his sponsors, however. In fact it underpinned his whole career.

Naturally, a network of clients took time to evolve. As a young man, Graham Jackson relied upon older friends and other allies. So it was that his first commission, Send vicarage in 1861, was from his tutor, C. R. Tate. Built in 1863, it was followed by related jobs at Ripley and Pyrford nearby. And, as Jackson himself acknowledged, his other work also 'fell into groups'. Some of these were simply geographical: wherever Jackson lived, he built—with his work required

---

[28] J. Mordaunt Crook, 'The Career of Sir Robert Smirke, R.A.' (Oxford D.Phil., 1961), 59, 355–8.
[29] Gillian Darley, 'Soane: the Man and his Circle', in Margaret Richardson and Mary Anne Stevens, *John Soane, Architect* (London, 1999), 16–25.
[30] Anthony Geraghty, 'Wren's Preliminary Design for the Sheldonian Theatre', *Architectural History* 45 (2002), 275–88, at 278; Terry Friedman, *James Gibbs* (New Haven and London, 1984), 8–13.
[31] Andrew Saint, *Richard Norman Shaw* (New Haven and London, 1976), 32–6; Colin Cunningham and Prudence Waterhouse, *Alfred Waterhouse* (Oxford, 1992); Paul Thompson, *William Butterfield* (London, 1971).
[32] T. G. Jackson, *Recollections*, (ed. B. H. Jackson, Oxford, 1950), 163–4.

in Hampstead and Stamford and Sevenoaks. 'Round about our home in Ewell', recalled Jackson, 'I restored and twice enlarged Malden Church, added an aisle to Chessington, built a village hall at Cheam and an addition to Cheam House for my friend Spencer Wilde.'[33] At Wimbledon he restored his own home, built the churches of St John (1865) and St Luke (1909), restored St Mary's (1920), erected one house (1908), extended another, and designed the war memorial (1921).[34] Jackson was often close to the client as well as the site. In Sevenoaks, for example, he was responsible for two houses and largely remodelled a third between 1873 and 1874.[35] One of these, Maywood, was built for a local Liberal politician, an ally of Jackson's and a tenant of the family into which Jackson was to marry.[36] Their association could not have been closer, nor their relationship more convenient.

With Jackson came his family, and with his family came commissions. Sevenoaks in particular is studded with Jacksonian projects: houses, a hotel, and a hospital. As early as 1854 his father, Hugh, had invested an inheritance of £10,000 in the provision of 'wholesome dwellings for artisans and labourers at fair rents', near their home in Hampstead.[37] This interest, which Jackson 'fully shared', led to the design of a further development in Sevenoaks. Alarmed at the 'mischievous sorting out of classes into distinct districts for rich and poor, which almost always has the effect of creating . . . two hostile camps', Jackson and his father secured land at the centre of town and built houses for the Kentish working classes.[38] They named the estate Lime Tree Walk, and between 1878 and 1882 twenty-four homes with a coffee-house and hotel were erected. Nor were the women of the Jackson family any less philanthropic. Jackson's sister, Emily, devoted her life to the care of children disabled by tuberculosis. Her career began in 1870. Thirty-one years later Graham Jackson began to build a new hospital, which opened in 1902.[39] Although the coffee-house closed between the two world wars, Lime Tree Walk and the Emily Jackson hospital are still serving the people of Sevenoaks. Arguably amongst his best works, they do indeed give 'one a good deal of respect for Jackson'.[40] More than this, they reveal the extent to which Jackson's relatives could also be his clients.

Jackson's family and friends were joined by less intimate acquaintances. Commissions came from his college and from further afield. His work at Thorne Coffin, near Yeovil, is a case in point.[41] Here he extended and practically rebuilt

---

[33] Jackson, *Recollections*, 114.   [34] Jackson, *Life and Travels*, 295–6.   [35] Ibid., 292–3.
[36] Christopher Rayner, *Sevenoaks Past* (Chichester, 1997), 103; John Dunlop, *The Pleasant Town of Sevenoaks* (Sevenoaks, 1964), 171.
[37] Jackson, *Life and Travels*, 31–2. He was later to add to the Hampstead dwellings himself.
[38] Ibid., 130.
[39] NMR 101356. Emily Jackson, *Children's Hospital for the Treatment of Hip Disease, Sevenoaks: its birth and growth* (Sevenoaks, 1910).
[40] John Newman, *Buildings of England: West Kent and the Weald* (2nd edn, London, 1976), 516.
[41] *Builder* 54 (1888), 396.

87. Lime Tree Walk, Sevenoaks (1878–9).

88. Thorne House, Yeovil (1877–88).

89. (*above left*) St Mary's Church, Lottisham (1876–8).

90. (*left*) St Peter's Church, Hornblotton (1872–4).

91. (*above*) Sgraffito work at Hornblotton

Thorne House between 1877 and 1888 for Judge James John Hooper. He was a Fellow of Oriel College and a former undergraduate at Wadham.[42] A bencher of the Inner Temple, Hooper was strongly committed to the reform of legal education generally, and in Oxford in particular.[43] Unsurprisingly, he and Jackson soon became 'great friends'.[44] Other friendships were still more fruitful. For Godfrey Thring, renowned hymnologist and brother of the more famous headmaster, Graham Jackson built the churches of Lottisham (1872), and Hornblotton (1872–4), and restored the church at Alford (1877–9). He also built

[42] Joseph Foster, *Man at the Bar* (London, 1885), 224.
[43] J. J. Hooper, *The Establishment of a School of Jurisprudence in the University of Oxford* (London, 1854), 3–9. [44] Jackson, *Life and Travels*, 128.

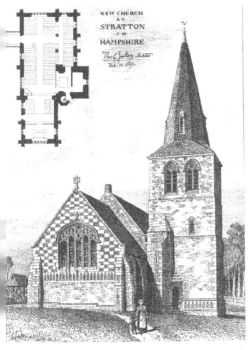

92. All Saints' Church, East Stratton (1885–90).   93. St John's Church, Northington (1887–90).

a house, Plonk's Hill, near Guildford (*c.* 1895), 'Jackson's in all but the name'.[45] Again and again, Jackson was able to capitalize on personal contacts. And all these individuals shared with Jackson a similar background, and a common relationship with Oxford, Cambridge, and the public schools. They also held similar views: a commitment to learning, liberalism, charity, and reform.

There were, of course, some exceptions. The churches at East Stratton (1885–90) and Northington (1887–90) were built for the Barings, Lord Northbrook, and Lord Ashburton respectively. Apart from a mutual interest in avant-garde architecture, Jackson had little in common with this exalted family of bankers.[46] Nor does evidence exist to explain Jackson's role as architect of the tiny Dorking Cottage Hospital (1870–1) or the small and insubstantial Hyde Institute (1903–4). The first was an interesting essay in the 'Old English' style; more cottage than hospital in appearance.[47] The second, a red-brick reading-room in Chipping Barnet, was also progressive—it provided a library

[45] *Architecture* 2 (1897), 96.
[46] Philip Zeigler, *The Sixth Great Power: Barings 1762–1929* (London, 1988), 204, and John Booker, *Temples of Mammon* (Edinburgh, 1990), 181.
[47] Horace Swete, *Handy Book of Cottage Hospitals* (London, 1870); SHC 2473/2.

for the lower orders—but no more prepossessing. Moreover, in neither case did Graham Jackson know his clients personally.[48] Most patrons, though, were less enigmatic or unknown. Even apparent exceptions like Walter Morrison, Jackson's promoter at Giggleswick and in the Balliol College Chapel debacle, fit the more general pattern. Morrison's money may have come from trade, but he was educated at Eton and Balliol, his father having chosen the college because of Jowett's liberalism. He was a man of 'extensive and peculiar learning'; a friend of Thomas Hughes, Edmond Warre, Darwin, Ruskin, and Mill; and the model for the Squire in Kingsley's *Water Babies*.[49] He was thus at the heart of the educated class.

Jackson's clients were frequently still more intellectual—as his work at the Acland Memorial Hospital in Oxford (1896–7) shows. This was a self-consciously progressive project, providing free nurses for the poor, and care (at a cost) for the middle classes. It was a deeply donnish endeavour, named in honour of Sir Henry Acland's late wife, and supported by the leading figures of Oxford academic life. Financial aid came from the heads of half a dozen colleges, from Ruskin, the Vernon Harcourts, the Max Müllers, and Mrs T. H. Green. The executive committee was made up of Jackson's clients, colleagues, and acquaintances.[50] Moreover, the project was utterly modern: the building was believed to be 'the first such Nursing Home erected for the purpose'.[51] There was no competition to choose an architect; nor, it seems, any doubt who he would be. Jackson, donating his services for free, was less hired hand than trusted ally.[52] Certainly, he was an architect amongst friends: selected by his peers, and preferred by his acquaintances.

This pattern of patronage is found throughout Jackson's life. Just as the Examination Schools in Oxford led on to work in the rest of the university, so the Sedgwick Museum generated further commissions in Cambridge. The party of progress, the Adullamites, and reformers in the public schools, all nurtured Jackson's vocation. Old friends often gave him new work. In Cambridge, for example, his career was materially aided by J. H. Middleton, who nominated Jackson as architect of the Geological Museum.[53] Middleton, like Jackson, was trained by G. G. Scott; he was, like Jackson, fellow of an Oxford college—in his case, Exeter. Unlike Jackson, however, he was a

---

[48] *RIBA Journal* 32 (1924–5), 49. It is possible that his clients at Chipping Barnet, the 'Misses Paget' were related to his acquaintance, Sir James Paget. *Barnet Press* 6 Jan. 1940. See also, Pamela Taylor and Joanna Cordon, *Barnet, Edgware, Hadley and Totteridge* (Chichester, 1994), 114; *Victoria County History: Hertfordshire*, vol. ii, pp. 336–7

[49] Geoffrey Dawson, 'Walter Morrison', *The National Review* 78 (1922), 854–66; Palestine Exploration Fund, *Quarterly Statement* 1921–2, 55–7; W. R. Mitchell, *Walter Morrison: a millionaire at Malham Tarn* (Settle, 1990), 7–46.

[50] Bod., GA Oxon 4° 538, 'Proposed Testimonial to Sir Henry Acland' (1895), 3–4.

[51] Bod., GA Oxon c.317 (24), 'The Story of the Acland Home' [n.d.], 5.

[52] Bod., GA Oxon 4° 538, 'Statement of Accounts' (20 April 1898).

[53] CUA, Geol. 8/6, Minutes 1891–5, 2 March 1892.

significant figure in Cambridge too, and it was this access to the university that Middleton gave him. As this suggests, Jackson was commissioned by his clients because he was their friend and their colleague. He was seen both as a safe pair of hands and a member of their world.

This was, though, more than the architecture of acquaintanceship. Friends could nominate, but they could not unilaterally commission. In Cambridge Middleton had first to persuade the Syndicate, then the Council, and then the whole university to accept the plans. Jackson's friends were only able to use his designs if they appealed to a wider audience. At Trinity College, Oxford, T. G. Jackson's buildings were, in part, paid for by appeal. Donors were attracted and funds were raised by sending lithographs of Jackson's proposals to potential benefactors. Those who gave money were sent photographs of the buildings for which they had paid.[54] The same was true at Cranbrook, where an appeal was launched, and illustrations of the new schoolhouse dispatched.[55] The success of this correspondence, and of Graham Jackson's projects, is quite clear. And it reflects his popularity amongst a much wider range of people than his close friends and relatives: he satisfied the needs of a whole social group. Jackson's patrons were in the vanguard of this new status group which had a reforming ethos and a fresh aesthetic. They were the intellectual aristocracy and he was the instrument of their ambition.[56]

The wish to create an exclusive class of thinkers with a monopoly on thought was an accusation often levelled at the Oxford party of progress, and particularly at Benjamin Jowett. Indeed, as early as 1852 he himself acknowledged the sense in this slur. 'As university reformers', wrote Jowett to Stanley, 'we must appear to the world rather as seeking to make an intellectual aristocracy or, to express it more coarsely, to form good places for ourselves out of the revenues of the Colleges . . . This appears to me to be true of all of us—myself included of course.'[57] The reforms in the university—which included the abolition of compulsory celibacy, and the creation of an academic profession—had produced a new phenomenon.[58] For the first time it became possible for an individual to live entirely by thinking, and to be paid for research and teaching alone. There were, it is true, some important precursors.[59] But, as T. W. Heyck has suggested, the idea of the intellectual, indeed, the very term itself, was a creation of the late

[54] TCA, Records, photographs (1880); letters (1887).

[55] CSA, Uncat. Corresp. 1883–6, letter (1884) with photograph.

[56] See William Whyte, 'The Intellectual Aristocracy Revisited', *Journal of Victorian Culture* 10 (2005), 15–45.

[57] Abbott and Campbell, *Benjamin Jowett*, vol. ii., pp. 212–13.

[58] A. J. Engel, *From Clergyman to Don* (Oxford, 1983); Christopher Harvie, *The Lights of Liberalism* (London, 1976); J. P. C Roach, 'Victorian Universities and the National Intelligentsia', *Victorian Studies* 3 (1959), 131–50.

[59] See especially, Jacques Le Goff, *Intellectuals in the Middle Ages* (trans. T. L. Fagan; Oxford, 1993).

nineteenth century.[60] It was for these academics that Jackson built the King's Mound, and designed tutors' apartments at Brasenose and Trinity. Married and committed to a career in college, the occupants of this accommodation were avatars of the reformed university and exemplars of a new class. Jowett's insight was acute. The reform of the universities had indeed created an intellectual aristocracy, paid for out of the revenues of the colleges.

As Noel Annan has so successfully shown, this aristocracy was one of blood as well as of brains.[61] Often with a shared evangelical background, it was a group of interrelated individuals, whose relationships grew more complex with every marriage. Annan has affectionately traced the links between this great mass of the intermarried and interbred: the Arnolds and Forsters, and Arnold-Forsters; the Darwins and Huxleys; the Butlers and Galtons and Stephens and Venns. The rise of the dons had created a new profession, and the abolition of compulsory celibacy had created a new and self-perpetuating status group. Nor was this confined to the universities. The distinction between a fellowship at Oxford and a mastership in the great public schools had yet to be made, so the intellectual aristocrats entered secondary as well as higher education. Edmond Warre, Jackson's friend and client, left his fellowship at All Souls to become a master, then Headmaster, then Provost at Eton. Oscar Browning, sacked by Warre, left Eton for King's College, Cambridge. Others gained still more glittering prizes. Montague Butler was successively Headmaster of Harrow, and Master of Trinity College, Cambridge. He was also the son of a previous Headmaster of Harrow; father of a Cambridge Professor of History; uncle of a Master of Pembroke College, Cambridge; and brother-in-law of Jackson's client, the Harrow Housemaster J. A. Cruickshank.

Of course, this change was slow and piecemeal. This was not a revolution. The move from clergyman to don was never so absolute as Engel's title implies. Butler and Warre, for example, were both ordained. Indeed, Montague Butler became Dean of Gloucester, and Examining Chaplain for two Archbishops of Canterbury. Moreover, each of Butler's primates were themselves academics. A. C. Tait succeeded Arnold at Rugby, whilst E. W. Benson was the first Headmaster of Wellington. Archbishop Benson was, in fact, as much an intellectual aristocrat as his chaplain. As a young man he was concurrently a Fellow of Trinity College, Cambridge, and an assistant master at Rugby. His relatives included W. W. Jackson, later Rector of Exeter College, Oxford, and the Cambridge philosopher Henry Sidgwick. His sister was a headmistress in Norwich, then Oxford, and finally in Bedford, whilst his son became Master of

---

[60] T. W. Heyck, *The Transformation of Intellectual Life in Victorian England* (London and Sydney, 1982), 13–21; Peter Allen, 'The Meanings of "An Intellectual": nineteenth- and twentieth-century English usage', *University of Toronto Quarterly* 55 (1986), 342–58.

[61] N. G. Annan, 'The Intellectual Aristocracy', in J. H. Plumb, ed., *Studies in Social History* (London, 1955); reprinted in Annan, *The Dons* (London, 1999), 304–41. See also Francis Galton, *English Men of Science: their nature and nurture* (1874; London, 1970), 41–73.

Magdalene. When, in 1899, Jackson built Benson's monument in Canterbury Cathedral, he was commemorating a man who was both clergyman and don.[62] Benson's life in this way exemplifies Annan's intellectual aristocracy, and quietly corrects the programmatic assertion of secularization so often found in the secondary literature. More specifically, however, it also highlights Jackson's own importance to this group. In Athelstan Riley and Edmond Warre, he shared friends with E. W. Benson.[63] With his tomb for the Archbishop, Jackson immortalized both the man and his class; both Benson and the intellectual aristocracy of which he was such a conspicuous part.

Now, as Stefan Collini has shown, the intellectual aristocracy was by no means an exclusive, or exclusively familial, outfit.[64] Although a shared social background was an advantage, this was an exceedingly open elite. John Percival provides the perfect example. Jackson's patron was variously Headmaster of Clifton; President of Trinity College, Oxford; Headmaster of Rugby; and Bishop of Hereford. But his career was not aided by connection to great academic names: he was born out of wedlock into a family of yeoman stock. It was the scholarship to The Queen's College, Oxford, from his grammar school at Appleby which propelled him towards his success. Nor was his first wife a part of the educated circles in which Percival was later to move. Only in 1899, at the age of sixty-four, did he finally connect with an academic family. He married Mary, a cousin of John Addington Symonds and a relative (by marriage) of T. H. Green.[65] In no sense, then, did his rise depend upon his relations. In fact, for him, the reverse was actually the case. And generally, a shared ethos was more important than shared genes. Although the intellectual aristocracy was indeed sustained by Annan's relationships, it was as much a freemasonry as a family—as Collini makes clear.[66] Thus it was that the outsider Percival, the insider Butler, and even the Hon. Edward Lyttelton, high-born Headmaster of Haileybury and Eton, could find themselves within its bounds.[67]

What, though, was their shared ethos? How was this a peculiarly intellectual elite? Essentially, they held a common approach to the world and its problems. They devoted their lives to teaching and to writing; to creating an academic profession. They were, more often than not, Liberals—although many became Liberal Unionists from the mid 1880s.[68] They accepted a public role, and a collective responsibility to advocate progress, reform, and the amelioration of poor social conditions.[69] Above all else, they shared an identity. Works like

---

[62] RA Library, Uncat. MSS, elevation of tomb [n.d.].

[63] A. C. Benson, *Life of Edward White Benson* (2 vols.; London, 1899), vol. ii, pp. 155, 576.

[64] Stefan Collini, *Public Moralists* (Oxford, 1991), 14.

[65] John Potter, *Headmaster: the life of John Percival, radical autocrat* (London, 1998), 6–12, 50, 217. See also William Temple, *Life of Bishop Percival* (London, 1921).

[66] Collini, *Public Moralists*, 14.   [67] Tim Card, *Eton Renewed* (London, 1994), 122–38.

[68] John Roach, 'Liberalism and the Victorian Intelligentsia', *Cambridge Historical Journal* 13 (1957), 58–81; Tom Donne, '*La trahaison des clercs*: British intellectuals and the first home rule crisis', *Irish Historical Studies* 23 (1982), 134–73.   [69] Collini, *Public Moralists*, 14–58, 114, 237.

94. 'Intellectual Culture *v.*
Aristocratic Barbarism', from
George Du Maurier, *Society
Pictures* (1891).

(*Mrs de Montmorency Jones calls
upon Lady Clara Robinson (née Vere
de Vere) about the character of a
Nursery Governess.*)

Mrs De Montmorency Jones: 'And
may I inquire if you consider Miss
Wilkinson thoroughly competent to
impart instruction to the younger
female members of my family, aged
respectively five and three?' *Lady
Clara:* 'What, teach your two little
girls? Oh, yes!'

P. G. Hamerton's 1873 *The Intellectual Life* popularized the notion of a peculiarly cerebral way of living.[70] It was this lifestyle that the intellectual aristocracy adopted. They had a problematic identity and peculiar location within society. Although, as observers indignantly noted, they appeared to claim a monopoly over all aspects of thought, they were nonetheless relatively poorly paid.[71] True, a Head of House might earn £1,500 a year, and some teaching fellows made more than £800 per annum. But these salaries declined as the century came to a close, and in comparison to the incomes of those whom they taught, the figures were trifling.[72] Jackson's clients, then, possessed what Pierre Bourdieu would call large quantities of intellectual capital, but held much lower levels of economic capital.[73] They were rich in academic prestige, but often poor in purely monetary terms.

It was a paradox acknowledged at the time, and often in the same language.[74] Unable to challenge others economically, the educated elite claimed the right to

---

[70] P. G. Hamerton, *The Intellectual Life* (London, 1873).

[71] [J. H. Millar], 'Mr. Jowett and Oxford Liberalism', *Blackwood's Magazine* 1897, 721–32 and [Julia Wedgwood], 'The Moral Influence of George Eliot', *Contemporary Review* 39 (1881), 173–85, 177–9. Sheldon Rothblatt, *Revolution of the Dons* (London, 1968), 242; Engel, *Clergyman to Don*, ch. 3.

[72] Although see, J. P. D. Dunbabin, 'Oxford and Cambridge College Finances 1871–1913', *Economic History Review* 2nd Ser., 28 (1975), 631–47.

[73] Pierre Bourdieu, *Distinction* (trans. Richard Nice; London, 1996), 176, 254, 261, 287, 292–3; *Homo Academicus* (trans. Peter Collier; Cambridge, 1990), 178; *Rules of Art* (trans. Susan Emmanuel; Oxford, 1996), 11, 48–55, 129; Bourdieu and J-C. Passeron, *Reproduction* (trans. Richard Nice; London, 1990), 201.

[74] George Eliot, for one, was blessed with 'Intellectual wealth'. Wedgwood, 'Moral Influence', 179.

dominate intellectually. Academic achievement, they argued, was far superior to commercial success. In 1876 William Loftie eulogized a typical aristocrat of the intellect, who had made 'Judgement and taste, not money . . . [his] capital'.[75] From this position mere wealth could come to seem tawdry and unworthy of the truly cultured and thoughtful individual. Indeed, as Hamerton observed, this was an occupational hazard. Addressing himself to 'a Genius Careless in Money Matters', he wrote of the ways in which

> We come to hate money-matters when we find that they exclude all thoughtful and disinterested conversation . . . Our happiest hours have been spent with poor scholars, and artists, and men of science, whose words make us rich indeed. Then we dislike money because it rules and restrains us, and because it is unintelligent and seems horrible.[76]

Indeed, just as Hamerton had feared, the intellectual aristocrats came to define themselves against the rich. In their lifestyle, their conversation, and their opinions, the educated elite reinforced the distinction between an aristocracy of wealth and one of brains. It was a situation repeatedly satirized in a series of cartoons by George Du Maurier. In his drawings 'Intellectual Culture' was sharply contrasted with 'Aristocratic Barbarism'; Sir Georgius Midas set against pale creatures living beautifully in South Kensington, where peacock feathers were only a penny apiece.[77]

In particular, the intellectuals drew a contrast between their culture and that of the super-rich. The late nineteenth century saw a drawing together of the great landlords and millionaire capitalists into a new group.[78] Social distinctions between commercial and landed wealth began to be broken down, and new money entered old families. 'English society', wrote T. H. S. Escott in 1886, 'once ruled by an aristocracy is now dominated mainly by a plutocracy . . . peer and *parvenu* frequently invert their *rôles* now-a-days.'[79] It was a phenomenon much remarked upon at the time, and with little enthusiasm. Trollope's *The Way We Live Now* (1875), Mallock's *The Old Order Changes* (1886), and Henry James' *Awkward Age* (1899) all condemned the incursions of the *nouveaux riches* and the pollution of blue blood by the merely wealthy. Moreover, this new class was seen to have constructed a new identity. Both aristocrat and millionaire, as Escott observed, 'possess much the same aspirations, the same tastes, have been similarly educated, display the same weaknesses, follow the same way of life'.[80]

[75] W. J. Loftie, *A Plea for Art in the House* (London, 1876), 46.
[76] Hamerton, *Intellectual Life*, 186.
[77] George Du Maurier, *Society Pictures* (2 vols.; London, 1891), vol. i, p. 220; vol. ii, p. 239.
[78] David Cannadine, *The Decline and Fall of the British Aristocracy* (London, 1992), 298, 342; Harold Perkin, *The Rise of Professional Society* (London and New York, 1989), 27, 62–9; W. D. Rubinstein, *Elites and the Wealthy in Modern British History* (Brighton and New York, 1987), 62–70; F. M. L. Thompson, *English Landed Society in the Nineteenth Century* (London and Toronto, 1963), 292–9.   [79] [T. H. S. Escott], *Society in London* (London, 1886), 43, 161.
[80] Ibid., 163.

The plutocrats were believed to value mere money over the knowledge and discrimination of the educated elite. As William Morris put it in 1879, 'I fear that at present the decoration of rich men's houses is mostly wrought out at the bidding of grandeur and luxury'. The overall effect, he maintained, was 'simply meant to say, "This house is built for a rich man"'.[81]

The place of the intellectuals in this society remains a vexed question. It is, as Rubinstein observes, the most difficult problem—the 'gammy leg'—of class theory.[82] But the response of the Victorian intellectual aristocracy to the new nineteenth-century plutocracy is surely without question: it was almost wholly negative. The classic statement of this position came in Matthew Arnold's *Culture and Anarchy*. Contrasting the 'men of culture and poetry'—the *'aliens'*—with the ignorant 'populace', bourgeois 'philistines', and aristocratic 'barbarians', he called for 'sweetness and light'; for 'Hellenism', 'humanity', and a search for human perfection.[83] It was particularly pointless to look to the rich for these values. In another essay he argued that the wealthy, relying on all things 'solid, material, and visible . . . are slow to attach great importance to influences impalpable, spiritual and viewless'.[84] The narrow materialism of the plutocrats was rejected in favour of cultured good taste, knowledge, and discernment.[85]

It was a call taken up by the educated elite—and not least by Arnold's niece, Mrs Humphry Ward. Granddaughter of Thomas Arnold, sister-in-law of Leonard Huxley, mother-in-law of George Trevelyan, and wife of a fellow of Brasenose, she was the intellectual aristocracy incarnate. Her early life reflected her origins. With her commitment to social reform, her agnosticism, and her liberalism, her disposition was solely cerebral. With her delicately decorated home, her reformed dress, and her love of blue china, she reflected her class's aesthetic too.[86] Mary Ward's initial ideals were entirely opposed to those of the plutocrats. Recalling her time in the Oxford of the 1870s, surrounded by the scions of the educated elite, she described their attempts to lead a life of sweetness and light. 'Most of us', she wrote, 'were very anxious to be up-to-date, and in the fashion, whether in aesthetics, or housekeeping, or education. But our fashion was not that of Belgravia or Mayfair, which indeed was scorned! It was the fashion of the movement which sprang from Morris and Burne Jones.'[87] She was not alone. The intellectual aristocracy—progressive in politics, and modern in style—eschewed all the show of the rich. By the late nineteenth century they were confidently articulating their own identity, and displaying it in their homes.

---

[81] William Morris, *Collected Works* (ed. May Morris, 24 vols.; London, 1910–15), vol. 22, pp. 113, 94. See also F. M. L. Thompson, *The Rise of Respectable Society* (London, 1988), 267.

[82] Rubinstein, *Elites and the Wealthy*, 80.

[83] Matthew Arnold, *Culture and Anarchy* (1869; Cambridge, 1993), 64–181.

[84] Arnold, 'Democracy' (1861), in *Culture and Anarchy*, 9.

[85] See, in addition, [E. M. Haweis], *Beautiful Houses* (London, 1882), 22.

[86] John Sutherland, *Mrs Humphry Ward* (Oxford, 1990), chs. 1–7; William S. Peterson, *Victorian Heretic, Mrs Humphry Ward's* Robert Elsmere (Leicester, 1976), 83.

[87] Mrs Humphry Ward, *A Writer's Recollections* (London, 1918), 190–220.

It was, of course, this Aestheticism and this class which drove T. G. Jackson's career. Mrs Humphry Ward is again a case in point. She was on the committee at Somerville which chose him as architect.[88] Her husband was a tutor at Brasenose and director of studies at Jackson's Oxford Military College.[89] Her friends, Professor and Mrs Max Müller, T. H. Green, G. G. Bradley, and H. J. S. Smith, employed Graham Jackson at the Oxford High Schools for Boys and for Girls.[90] He was able to satisfy their requirements, reflect their tastes, and respond to their rejection of vulgar wealth and untutored show. In architectural terms, his way was clearly defined. Given their progressive tastes, conservative Gothic was out. Nor was a revived classicism any more acceptable. Italianate architecture was utilitarian, and associated with both industry and commerce. French was far worse. As J. Mordaunt Crook has revealed, this was the style of choice for the super-rich. French classicism was ostentatious and expensive—and it looked it. Unlimited by cost, and unrestrained by educated taste, Crook's courtiers and cosmopolitans tended to 'gild every possible lily'.[91] This was not the way of the mind, much less of the intellectuals. They wanted to display a more discerning taste. Bernard Shaw's aesthetes are archetypal. Visiting the mansion of a rich collector, they attack his house and his ostentation. The golden dome of the hall, the crimson velvet of the saloons, the flowered damask, and decorated dadoes all stand condemned. 'It stinks', shouts one, 'of money.'[92] In contrast to the 'gold and grandeur, pomatum, powder and pride'[93] of the plutocrats, the intellectual aristocracy sought what Rhoda and Agnes Garrett called 'an atmosphere of refinement and cultivation'.[94] It was not expensive, showy, or classical. But it was original, modern, and totally distinct.

The problem, as the Garrets recognized, was to reconcile 'refined and cultivated tastes' with 'moderate incomes'.[95] Few were the intellectuals who could afford to build their own houses, much less adorn them with domes and gilded dadoes.[96] For most, dress and decoration were the only affordable means of self-expression. The adoption of pre-Raphaelite clothes and Aesthetic attitudes was a cliché of the period.[97] The most modern chose shapeless garments in sage and olive green: Newnham College seemed full of them in the early 1880s.[98] Others, in their 'curious aristocratic way', simply wore the last fashion but one.[99] Bit by

[88] SCA, Minutes of Council 1879–1908, 9.   [89] Bod., G.A. Oxon. 4° 272, Prospectus (n.d.).
[90] Bod., G.A. fol. A 139, Scheme and Deed of Trust (1878), 10; OHSA, Uncat. Material, Council (1877).
[91] J. Mordaunt Crook, *The Rise of the Nouveaux Riches: style and status in Victorian and Edwardian architecture* (London, 1999), 58–67, 167–74, 70.
[92] G. B. Shaw, *Immaturity* (written 1879; London, 1930), 105–11, 164.
[93] Anthony Trollope, *The Way We Live Now* (2 vols. in 1, 1875; Oxford, 1999), vol. i, p. 296.
[94] Rhoda and Agnes Garrett, *Suggestions for Home Decoration* (London, 1876), 7.
[95] Ibid., 8.   [96] Tanis Hinchcliffe, *North Oxford* (New Haven and London, 1992), 158–85.
[97] W. S. Gilbert, *Patience* (London, 1881), 10–12, 30.
[98] Gwen Raverat, *Period Piece* (London, 1952), 26, 201; Mary Agnes Hamilton, *Newnham: an informal biography* (London, 1936), 139.
[99] Carola Oman, *An Oxford Childhood* (London, 1976), 43.

bit, though, a distinctively academic dress developed, which—like the professor's clothes in *The Old Order Changes*—mixed 'deference for convention and contempt for it'.[100] In 1907, the Master of Caius College travelled to America, and his wife was worried about what she should wear. A friend advised her that 'University ladies dressed much the same the world over' and so she found her 'simple garments did well enough'.[101] In their homes the same taste prevailed. Ideally, William Morris wallpaper, peacock feathers, blue china, and fans were added to pre-Raphaelite prints.[102] It was a distinct aesthetic and reflected 'the union of persons of cultivated tastes to define, and to decide upon what is to be admired . . . Vulgarity, however wealthy it may be, can never be admitted into this exclusive brotherhood.'[103] In these ways, the intellectuals were able to stress their independence, and to do so inexpensively.

There were, though, occasional opportunities to make grand gestures. Some academics found themselves able to build their own homes.[104] In Oxford, T. H. Green commissioned J. J. Stevenson to design a red-brick, terracotta, white-painted, sash-windowed 'Queen Anne' home in 1882. Also in the latest style, Stevenson built Balliol Croft (1885) for the liberal economist Alfred Marshall in Cambridge.[105] Both houses were designed for couples with educated interests and high-brow tastes. In this sense they were typical of the intellectual aristocracy. But both houses, for most, also represented an unattainable dream. As a result, large corporate and collegiate projects offered isolated opportunities for architectural self-expression. It was in this field that Jackson's work became a crucial part of the intellectuals' identity.

It became a crucial part because Jackson himself was an intellectual: if not a member of the intellectual aristocracy itself, then, at the very least, part of the intellectual gentry. He spoke their language, he understood their needs and he was accepted as part of their world. Throughout his life, indeed, Jackson remained closer to academics than architects. He knew few artists as a young man, and as he aged he became still further distanced from his fellow professionals. For many more workaday designers, indeed, he seemed aloof, arrogant, and 'too much of a Don'.[106] His idea of the architect's profession reflected this distance and his lack of empathy with the less well-connected. Arguably, the campaign against compulsory registration was made up of similarly situated individuals.[107] The memorialists, as good intellectuals, thought it more

---

[100] W. H. Mallock, *The Old Order Changes* (3 vols.; London, 1886), vol. iii, p. 260.
[101] Mrs E. S. Roberts, *Sherborne, Oxford and Cambridge* (London, 1934), 97.
[102] Mary Paley Marshall, *What I Remember* (Cambridge, 1947), 20; Raverat, *Period Piece*, 125–7; M. J. Loftie, *The Dining Room* (London, 1878), 13.
[103] Walter Hamilton, *The Aesthetic Movement* (London, 1882), vii.
[104] As did artists and writers: Maurice B. Adams, *Artists' Homes* (London, 1883).
[105] Hinchcliffe, *North Oxford*, 114–15; Girouard, *Sweetness and Light*, 114–18, and 'The Architecture of John James Stevenson' in *The Connoisseur* 185 (1974), 106–12, at 108–9.
[106] Reginald Blomfield, *Memoirs of an Architect* (London, 1932), 67.
[107] Peter Stansky, *Redesigning the World: William Morris, the 1880s and the arts and crafts* (Princeton, 1985), 128.

important to be gentlemen than professionals. Jackson shared this view. He was indeed 'fundamentally an English gentleman'.[108] More than this, as his university acknowledged, Jackson was 'typically Oxford', part of an academic 'culture . . . [which] was wide and unprofessional'.[109] In that respect he was as much archetype as architect.

Jackson's academic aspirations ran throughout his life. His books identified him as a Fellow of Wadham, and later as an Honorary Doctor of both Oxford and Cambridge. He was not, of course, unique in this. Others rose higher still, with J. H. Middleton becoming Slade Professor at Cambridge in 1886, and Edward Prior achieving the same lofty eminence somewhat later. Nor was Jackson alone in writing. As has already been noted, the corollary of historicism in architecture was that architects would write history. Graham Jackson was, though, better placed and more successful: his work was widely read and much respected. His writing was clear and compelling. Thus it was that Jackson, rather than Norman Shaw, edited *Architecture: a profession or an art*.[110] Shaw was more famous, but less assured academically. Reginald Blomfield felt, in fact, that most architects were envious of Jackson's ability with words.[111] Certainly, his position and his publications marked him out amongst his fellow artists—and emphasized his membership of a much wider, more learned and more literate culture.

Through books, letters, lectures, and articles, Jackson claimed the right to call himself an intellectual. His writing, indeed, grew from his teaching—whether of his architectural pupils, students at the Royal Academy, or members of the University of Cambridge.[112] He also became an educational theorist of note— and put his theories into practice.[113] As a young Fellow of Wadham, he had of course been a part of the reform of the college rules.[114] His continued involvement—at the Royal Academy and Royal College, the Council for Art, and the Art Workers' Guild—grew from his role as an acknowledged expert on education.[115] It was, so to speak, a recognition of his dual nature: both as architect and academic. So was his membership of the Athenaeum, the quintessentially academic club.[116] Elected in 1900, under a rule designed to admit the great and the good, he joined an institution which was well-known as the common focus for 'persons of intellect and of intellectual tastes, lovers and cultured adherents of art and letters'.[117] Here he dined with writers and Royal Academicians. His circle of friends was similarly mixed, though tending to the donnish. He lunched regularly with Rutherford, the Headmaster of Westminster.[118] His relationship

[108] *Builder* 127 (1924), 753.

[109] [John Wells], 'Sir Thomas Jackson' *Oxford Magazine* 43 (1924–5), 126–7.

[110] Reginald Blomfield, *Richard Norman Shaw* (London, 1940), 81.

[111] Blomfield, *Memoirs*, 67.

[112] Jackson, *Life and Travels*, 148–9 and *Reason in Architecture* (London, 1906); *Cambridge Review* 34 (1912–13), 558.   [113] *Cambridge Review* 28 (1906–7), 192.

[114] WCA, 2/4 Convention Book 1829–1944, 162, 173.   [115] See Ch. 2.

[116] Collini, *Public Moralists*, 15–21; Humphry Ward, *History of the Athenaeum* (London, 1926), 87–92.   [117] Francis Gledstanes Waugh, *The Athenaeum* (privately printed, 1900), 117.

[118] Jackson MSS, 'Recollections', vol. ii, p. 474.

with Edmund Warre, Headmaster and Provost of Eton, was 'one of the great pleasures of [his] later years'.[119] He became close friends with T. McKenny Hughes when building the Sedgwick Museum. On Jackson's visits to Cambridge, he stayed with Hughes, and when Hughes lectured in London, he lodged with Jackson.[120] The geology professor anonymously promoted his architect friend through the pages of the *Cambridge Review*.[121] Amongst his Oxford clients, Jackson dined with Jowett[122] and sketched in Switzerland with Henry Boyd, Principal of Hertford.[123] Throughout his career, Jackson remained 'a gentleman, [and] a scholar', as well as 'a very able architect'.[124]

In his family life, too, Graham Jackson was an intellectual. An evangelical upbringing was a common experience for the leaders of the educated elite. Their philanthropy was similarly typical.[125] Moreover, as he was keen to emphasize, his relatives were also writers, teachers, and researchers. His father's family included Fellows of St John's College, Cambridge; his mother's were Fellows of Trinity. On both sides of his family there were lawyers, doctors, and minor thinkers of every sort. Even at school Jackson could not escape the clutches of the educated classes. He was a contemporary of the distinguished lawyer, Sir Erskine Holland, and just junior to Sir E. J. Poynter, later President of the Royal Academy.[126] And, sharing a background with the intellectual aristocracy, so too he held with them a common aesthetic. His home was the acme of the academic eye.[127] All was quiet good taste. The arts and crafts predominated, and his restoration and refurbishment were evidently sympathetic. He took a clear pride in the vernacular walled garden, and the house's historical associations.[128] In this, he was again entirely typical of his class.

Even Jackson's pupils tended to share his own social and intellectual position. When asked where they would get work, Jackson always replied that, like him, 'in all probability they will get it from their friends'.[129] It was an answer which reflected all the confidence of connection and the assurance of place. His pupils were usually public school and Oxbridge educated: men like Charles Bone of Radley and Exeter College, Oxford; Henry Goddard of Haileybury and Wadham; William Marshall of Cheltenham, Rugby, and King's College, Cambridge. They included the sons of Frederic Harrison, a fellow of Wadham,

---

[119] Jackson, *Life and Travels*, 233.

[120] CUA, Geol. 8/6, Site Syndicate Minutes 1891–5, 28 Sept. 1895; Geol. 8/9 Museum Syndicate Minutes 1890–1, 30 May 1892; Geol. 11/2 Jackson Corresp., (19) 8 Nov. 1892.

[121] *Cambridge Review* 21 (1899–1900), 190; CUA, Geol. 9/36, Misc. Corresp. 1892–1901 (2).

[122] OUA, UC/FF/353/1/2, Jackson (30 Nov. 1890).

[123] I must thank Mr Richard Norton for lending me transcripts of letters relating to this excursion of 1902. See also, Richard Norton, 'Henry Boyd and Thomas Graham Jackson: their rowing exploits', *Hertford College Magazine* 82 (1995–7), 106–11.   [124] Blomfield, *Memoirs*, 66.

[125] Annan, 'Intellectual Aristocracy', 244–7.

[126] *Oxford Magazine* 43 (1924–5), 126.

[127] T. G. Jackson, 'Eagle House, Wimbledon', *Surrey Archaeological Society Collections* 10 (1891), 151–64.

[128] CUA, Geol. 8/9, Geological Syndicate Notes, Jackson (30 May 1892); T. G. Jackson, *Six Ghost Stories* (London, 1919), 212, 242.   [129] Jackson, *Recollections*, 257.

and Edmond Warre, Headmaster of Eton. Frequently, his pupils were antiquarians as well as architects. William Nicholls, of Rugby and Hertford College, became an archaeological surveyor in India. Sir Charles Peers, of Charterhouse and King's College, Cambridge, became architectural editor of the *Victoria County History* and head of the Ancient Monuments Department of the Office of Works. Evelyn Hellicar epitomized Jackson's pupils. He belonged, said the *Builder*, 'to the order of architects to whom scholarship meant much'.[130]

Jackson's intellectual attitudes were echoed in his architecture. And his buildings satisfactorily resolved the inherent tensions of the academic aesthetic. They were tasteful, yet distinctive; striking, but subtle. They eschewed the banality of the bourgeoisie and the vulgarity of the plutocrats. Amongst the educated elite, as we have noted, 'conventionalism [was] giving place to intellectual decoration'.[131] Jackson's work reflected this change. Thus, at Trinity, he was able to erect buildings both 'picturesque and unlike anything else in Oxford'.[132] Similarly, in his New Examination Schools, Jackson offered a design which 'would harmonize with the traditions of Oxford' but was, nonetheless, in his 'own peculiar style'.[133] At its most extreme was Giggleswick School Chapel, which Jackson hoped, 'in spite of its swelling dome, will not be out of keeping with its surrounding in the Yorkshire dale[s]'.[134] His eclecticism allowed him to respect the *genius loci*, whilst at the same time reflecting the particular needs of his clients. His work was always sympathetic, and never overly showy. In particular, he drew on, and reinforced, the widely held association between the Jacobethan style and a scholastic ethos. Like his sixteenth-century predecessors, he was building colleges and schools 'rich in a sort of learned ease'; not classic, but looking 'to classic architecture for motives'.[135] Jackson was not alone in playing on this theme. Nor was he even the first. But his success in Oxford and beyond made him a leading exponent of this approach. More than anything, as the *Cambridge Review* recognized, Jackson's style was the apotheosis of 'scholarly refinement'.[136]

In their details, too, Jackson's buildings were designed to delight the educated. With their puns, allusions, and quotations, they shared the sense of play which he showed in his literary work.[137] In both, he revealed the 'knowledge of a scholar, [and] the appreciation of an artist'.[138] To some extent, what was really shown was simple hard work and determined research.[139] But, more than this, Jackson was producing architecture for the cognoscenti. For those in the know, a building could be read like a book. At Brasenose, for example, Jackson ornamented a chimney-piece with 'heraldic decoration in the old way i.e. to mark either the

[130] *Builder* 137 (1929), 337.   [131] *Oxford Magazine* 1 (1883), 24.
[132] *Oxford Magazine* 3 (1885), 362.
[133] Bod., G.A. Oxon. c. 33 (184), Jackson, 'Proposed New Examination Schools' (1876); *Oxford Magazine* 6 (1887–8), 296.
[134] *Giggleswick School Chronicle* 6 (1897), 168.   [135] *Builder* 37 (1879), 929–30.
[136] *Cambridge Review* 35 (1913–14), 450.   [137] Crook, 'Cult of Eclecticism', 106.
[138] *Cambridge Review* 34 (1912–13), 558.   [139] Ward, *Athenaeum*, 330.

ownership or something given, or the date'. He proposed the college crest, together with those of the Principals who had commissioned the work. 'The arms of the two Principals of old time', he added, 'would seem to falsify the date.'[140] The glass at Giggleswick was similarly suggestive.[141] In particular, the window in the south transept paid tribute to the school's benefactors: its Headmaster, and Walter Morrison, the donor of the chapel. This iconography was important to all,[142] and especially to Jackson, who was concerned that the founder, James Carr, would be shown in the vestments of a sixteenth-century priest, despite some doubts cast upon this vocation by his will.[143]

This often pedantic—though also frequently playful—scholarship was found throughout his work. At Radley, a small extension to the cloisters was built in a later style, and with lighter-coloured tiles. The motto above the door in the Eton Music Schools caused concern and amusement in equal measure.[144] There was often humour in Jackson's work, but it was invariably of a most improving sort. The Sedgwick Museum saw the triumph of his academic ebullience. 'I have', he proudly recorded, 'an ichthyosaurus for a weather-cock, and on the other capital to that with the pterodactyls, heads of the musk-sheep which make capital volutes.'[145] Dotted about the building was a menagerie of other animals.[146] Nor was the symbolism simply ephemeral. Jackson hoped Hughes would 'direct the attention of your pupils' to the beasts carved around the building,[147] whilst Hughes was pleased to find that the variety of materials used made it 'a veritable museum of geology' in itself.[148] Jackson's architecture was a puzzle to be solved by the educated: whence did that feature come? what does that motif mean?[149] These questions clearly engaged Graham Jackson's clients. This was, it should be stressed, a period in which architectural ornamentation was a source of real interest amongst what Michael Stratton terms 'the educated public'. After all, as late as 1901 the police were required to control crowds which had gathered to view the decorated façade of a factory in Bristol. They were forced to remain on duty for two whole days.[150] The impact of Jackson's erudition on the intellectuals was more subtle, though no less profound. Through his good taste, and great learning, he perfectly satisfied his clients. He understood them and they trusted him. As the Master of Emmanuel put it, 'having regard to Mr. Jackson's eminence . . . he regarded his judgement . . . as final'.[151]

[140] BNCA, B502/I Misc. Corresp., Jackson (28 Jan. 1887).
[141] [George Style and T. G. Jackson], *Giggleswick School* (Oxford, 1901), 34–40.
[142] e.g. Morrison to Brayshaw: GSA, Brayshaw Collection, Notes—extra illustrated (89), 22 July 1899.   [143] GSA, Uncat. MSS, Jackson to Morrison (17 Aug. 1900).
[144] Jackson, *Life and Travels*, 244: 'Warre said, "How would this do?—*Cave Canem*—which a lower boy the other day translated as "look out, I'm going to sing".'
[145] CUA, Geol. 9/40 Jackson Corresp., (1) 5 March 1902.
[146] Much to the horror of some: *Cambridge Review* 25 (1903–4), 202.
[147] CUA, Geol. 14, Museum Opening, (1) 4 Oct. 1900.
[148] *Cambridge Graphic* 17 Feb. 1900, 10.   [149] *Cambridge Review* 35 (1913–14), 450.
[150] Michael Stratton, *The Terracotta Revival* (London, 1993), 14.
[151] *Cambridge Review* 33 (1902–3), 892.

95. The entrance to the Sedgwick Memorial Museum, Cambridge, from Downing Street is framed by a sloth and an iguana.

96 and 97. A bison and two bears stand guard at the Sedgwick Memorial Museum.

Despite his dominance of the public schools and ancient universities, of course, Jackson never possessed a monopoly on commissions. In the capital, for example, he was far from ascendant. Not only did the colleges of the University of London remain evidently underfunded, but also, in drawing on the Greek Revival grandeur of University College, they were overwhelmingly classical.[152]

---

[152] J. Mordaunt Crook, 'The Architectural Image', in F. M. L. Thompson, ed., *The University of London and the World of Learning, 1836–1986* (London and Ronceverte, 1990), 1–34, at 4–7.

In the metropolis, school architecture was dominated by another of Scott's pupils, E. R. Robson. He was the architect of the London School Board, and the man who made 'Queen Anne' the dominant style of popular scholastic building.[153] His work was used by the intellectual aristocracy to articulate their belief in educational reform and social progress.[154] This meant an abandonment of the previously dominant Gothic idiom.[155] As Robson himself put it, 'A continuation of the semi-ecclesiastical style . . . would appear to be inappropriate and lacking in anything to mark the great change which is coming over the education of the country'.[156] Jackson, expensive and associated with other sorts of education, could not compete. His only London school remained Westminster.

Outside London Jackson was, as we have seen, far more successful. Even in the ancient universities, though, he did not have it all his own way. The intellectual aristocracy had their pick of the most original architects of the period, and they took advantage of the opportunity. In Oxford, Jackson found his preeminence threatened by Basil Champneys: artist, author, and intellectual in his own right.[157] 'Old Chapneys [*sic*]' was the biographer and confidant of Coventry Patmore.[158] His friends and Hampstead neighbours included the academic Edward Appleton and the artist George Du Maurier.[159] As an undergraduate at Trinity College, Cambridge, he had befriended Sidney Colvin and Henry Sidgwick, both of whom later became significant figures within the university.[160] The comparisons and contrasts with Jackson are obvious—and indeed they were near neighbours at work, with Jackson at 14 and Champneys at 19 Buckingham Street. But this proximity simply underlines their rivalry. Even in Oxford Jackson found his position challenged. Champneys replaced him as architect at Oriel (1908–11), Merton (1904–10), and Somerville (1902), and took the commission for the Indian Institute (1883–96), which was originally intended for Jackson.[161] Many of these jobs were the product of other friendships. Colvin was the director of the Fitzwilliam when Champneys built the Museum of Classical Archaeology (1883). Sidgwick was on the building committee which chose him as architect at Newnham (1874–1910).[162] Basil

[153] Malcolm Seaborne, 'Introduction' in E. R. Robson, *School Architecture* (1874; Leicester, 1972), 9–22.
[154] Weiner, *Architecture and Social Reform*, 3, 5, 70–81; but cf. David Englander in *Victorian Studies* 40 (1996), 143.
[155] Malcolm Seaborne and Roy Lowe, *The English School* II (London, 1977), 7–10.
[156] Robson, *School Architecture*, 321.
[157] Alain Jerôme Coignard, 'Basil Champneys, architecte, 1842–1935' (Mémoire de Maitrise, Paris IV, 1984); Stephen Robinson, 'Basil Champneys' (unpublished MS: Oxford, Lady Margaret Hall Archives); David Watkin, *The Architecture of Basil Champneys* (Cambridge, 1989).
[158] Basil Champneys, *Memoirs and Correspondence of Coventry Patmore* (2 vols.; London, 1900), vol. i, pp. 306, 351, 358.
[159] Basil Champneys, in J. H. Appleton and A. H. Sayce, *Dr. Appleton* (London, 1881), 86–8; Reginald Blomfield, 'Basil Champneys', *RIBA Journal* 42 (1935), 737–8.
[160] E. V. Lucas, *The Colvins and Their Friends* (London, 1928), 8–9, 32, 348.
[161] Coignard, 'Champneys', 21.   [162] NCA, N3, Minutes 1874–80 (25 Feb. 1874).

Champneys acknowledged the importance of these friendships in getting him the job.[163] And these commissions drove new work. Lady Margaret Hall was modelled on Newnham. What, then, could be more natural than to use the same architect? Champneys designed their first new building.[164] Later still he built for Bedford College, which provided women's education in London (1910–13).[165] Thus, in his writing and his building, Champneys joined Jackson in serving the intellectual aristocracy.

Nor was he unique. Several other architects were sustained by this new status group. One of the most interesting of these was George Gilbert Scott, junior. He was another profoundly academic architect—a man indeed who 'liked to think of himself more as a scholar than an architect'.[166] Educated at Eton and in his father's office, he read Moral Sciences at Jesus College, Cambridge, becoming Fellow in 1869.[167] Like Jackson, Scott was a writer, the author of an *Essay on the History of English Church Architecture* (1881), and he has been described by David Watkin as amongst the most important architectural historians of the nineteenth century. His career was cut short by his Catholicism, lunacy, and early death, but at its height Scott was a well-respected architect in the two ancient universities.[168] His building at Pembroke College, Cambridge (1879–83) is, according to Pevsner, 'one of the best of its date at the universities'.[169] At St John's, Oxford (1880–1) he offered two alternative plans for the college's northward expansion: one 'Queen Anne', the other Gothic.[170] This adaptability reflected Scott's understanding of his clients. He too was a truly intellectual architect.

There was plenty of competition for this description, of course, and other architects were just as well connected. A younger man, Edward Prior, later gained work from his brother-in-law, the Bursar of Pembroke College, Cambridge.[171] Still more were simply intellectual themselves: many wrote books, and even G. F. Bodley wrote poetry, albeit bad poetry.[172] Reginald Blomfield, architect at Haileybury School, Sherborne School, and Lady Margaret Hall, read Greats at Exeter College, Oxford.[173] He also produced books on all aspects of architectural history. 'Nothing', wrote Escott in 1886, 'is

---

[163] Mark Girouard, 'Victorian Sweetness and Light, Newnham College, Cambridge', *Country Life* 150 (1971), 1704–6.

[164] Margaret Birney, 'Lady Margaret Hall and Somerville College', *Victorian Society Annual* 1992, 9–24, at 10–12. [165] Margaret J. Tuke, *A History of Bedford College* (London, 1939), 212.

[166] Gavin Stamp, *An Architect of Promise: George Gilbert Scott junior (1839–1897) and the late Gothic Revival* (Donington, 2002), 3. [167] Stamp, *Architect of Promise.*

[168] Nor was he a pleasant man to work with. See his violent outbursts in Cambridge, PCA, Scott Corresp. 1–64 (1878–84), 46, 48, 51, 53 (1881). The contrast with Jackson's emollience is striking.

[169] Nikolaus Pevsner, *Buildings of England: Cambridgeshire* (London, 1970), 128.

[170] Howard Colvin, *Unbuilt Oxford* (New Haven and London, 1983), 180–2.

[171] Lynne Brown Walker, 'E. S. Prior, 1852–1932', (Ph.D., London, 1978), ch. 7.

[172] G. F. Bodley, *Poems* (London, 1899).

[173] Richard A. Fellows, *Reginald Blomfield* (London, 1985).

more noticeable than the intense respectability of the artistic society of London.'[174] What was true of painters was doubly so of architects. University and public school architects were usually college men, they were certainly gentlemen, and they were always allies of the educated elite.

Yet even amidst all this talent, Jackson remained uniquely successful. Like Blomfield, he was Oxford educated. Like Scott, he was a college fellow. Like Champneys, he had a network of influential friends. But his success transcended theirs, and his importance can be seen even in their projects. Although Giles Walkley goes somewhat too far in calling Basil Champneys a 'follower' of T. G. Jackson, there is much evidence of influence.[175] Champneys' School of Divinity at Cambridge, and Mansfield College in Oxford—as befitted theological institutions—were Gothic in style.[176] But at Merton, his Warden's Lodgings were pure Anglo-Jackson, whilst the Rhodes Building for Oriel was in many respects an almost wholly Jacksonian edifice.[177] The fellows of Oriel insisted that the elevations must be 'in accordance with the style which has become traditional in Oxford'.[178] In other words, they wanted to use the idiom which Jackson had made his own. This, they argued, was necessary if the building were to have a good 'academical character'.[179] G. G. Scott, junior, was, on occasion, equally beholden to Jackson. At Pembroke he erected lodgings based on the Fellows' Building at Christ's College, Cambridge. It was, for 1879, a strikingly modern approach. But this was more than a Christ's-like building, it was also, to some extent, an imitation of T. G. Jackson's Oxford work.[180] And in Oxford, too, in an unbuilt design for St John's, Scott adopted the 'Early Renaissance Jackson was making his own'.[181] Nor was it just the younger generation that followed Jackson's lead. Even J. L. Pearson was influenced by him—as can be seen in his work for Sidney Sussex, Cambridge, begun as late as 1894.[182] It was an impressive achievement, and one that was repeated again and again.

Curiously, the most perfect example of Jackson's relationship with the intellectual aristocracy comes not in Oxford, but in London, and not in a school, but a glassworks. This, though, was no ordinary glassworks. Powell's Whitefriars' workshop was amongst the most prestigious glassworks of the period.[183] It was at the heart of the arts and crafts movement, and of the

---

[174] [T. H. S. Escott], *Society in London* (London, 1886), 156. See also Caroline Dakers, *The Holland Park Circle* (New Haven and London, 1999), 4–5.

[175] Giles Walkley, *Artists' Houses in London* (Aldershot, 1994), 75.

[176] ManCA, *Eastern Daily News* (18 Oct. 1889), 'The profane Oxford undergraduate has nicknamed Mansfield College the "Dissenteries" '.

[177] Although in his St Alban Quad the college noted it did not 'approve of cupolas, cone-like ornaments, and spiral string courses'. MCA, 1.5 A Register (1877–1914), 374.

[178] OCA, ETCA8/4, Champneys Corresp., Notice (2 March 1907).

[179] *Oriel Record* 1 (1909–11), 77.   [180] Although cf. Stamp, *Architect of Promise*, 206.

[181] Stamp, 'G. G. Scott', 189. The building erected was in a much more sober Gothic—as befitted such a conservative college. Stamp, *Architect of Promise*, 197–201.

[182] Anthony Quiney, *John Loughborough Pearson* (New Haven and London, 1979), 184.

[183] Wendy Evans, Catherine Ross, and Alex Werner, *Whitefriars Glass* (London, 1993), 36, 45, 57–78, 158, 222; Hugh Wakefield, *Nineteenth-Century British Glass* (London, 1961), 133, 139.

98. Whitefriars' Workshop, London (1885–6 and 1891–2).

Aesthetic revolt.[184] The Powells themselves were educated at Oxford. They were related to a whole host of intellectuals—including, of course, the Oxford mathematician Baden Powell.[185] The head of the firm, Harry Powell, was an author and educationalist: a fellow of the Chemical Society and a member of the Technical Education Board.[186] The company was a commercial offshoot of the intellectual aristocracy, much like Morris Co. Its greatest artists were Philip Webb and T. G. Jackson.[187] Harry Powell regarded Graham Jackson as one of the 'two most important designers of table-glass' in the late nineteenth century.[188] Nor was Jackson's contribution confined to tableware. He designed stained glass, commissioned mosaics, and, in the late 1880s and 1890s, rebuilt the Whitefriars Glassworks, equipping it with a suitably tasteful new salesroom.[189] In part, he owed these jobs to a friendship with his employers. Jackson holidayed with James Crofts Powell, manager of the window department, and organized life classes in the workshop.[190] But his success came from more than friendship. It was, once more, proof of his ability to satisfy a wider elite. The production of glass was socially stratified. Plutocrats chose costly, gaudy cut glass— condemned by Ruskin and Morris alike. The majority of the public bought pressed glass and cheaper copies of higher status items.[191] Powell's, by contrast, was part of what Hugh Wakefield calls 'the intellectual revolt' in glass making.[192] Uncut, hand-blown, historically-based tableware was demanded by the educated elite. Jackson's scholarly methods, his knowledge and purity of design, produced drinking glasses for the thinking classes.[193]

Throughout his career, then, Graham Jackson was responding to the needs and wants of a specific group. In his monuments and his tableware, his decorations, his books and his buildings, his campaigns and his arguments, he was articulating the identity of an intellectual aristocracy. Not all were academics: Jackson built for the publisher John Murray in Albemarle Street and Dover Street and generations of authors have sat beneath the dome of an Anglo-Jackson waiting-room as Mr Murray mulled over their manuscripts.[194] Jackson's

---

[184] W. B. Honey, *Glass* (London, 1946), 124–5.

[185] MOL, 3237/2.28: programme for luncheon.

[186] MOL, Box 16: uncat. MSS, Notebook 'L.C.C., 1893–5'.

[187] Judy Rudoe and Howard Coutts, 'The Table-Glass designs of Philip Webb and T. G. Jackson', *Journal of the Decorative Arts Society* 16 (1992), 24–41.

[188] The other was William Morris, see: Harry J. Powell, 'Table Glass', *Architectural Review* 6 (1899), 51–5; Harry Powell, *Glass-Making in England* (Cambridge, 1923), 132–8.

[189] MOL, 3238/1 H. Powell, Notebook, 1884–92; 3235/1 Scrapbook, p. 22; 3220 a, Jackson to Powell, 4 Aug. 1891; 3220 b., illustration (1885); 3254/1–3, plans (1882).

[190] Jackson, *Life and Travels*, 94–100.

[191] Barbara Morris, *Victorian Table Glass and Ornaments* (London, 1978), 14.

[192] Wakefield, *British Glass*, 37, 133–9.

[193] MOL, 3195 A and 2232, Glass Designs, (1870); RA, Uncat. MSS, tableware (6 March 1883).

[194] ITA, BUI/17 Hare Court, Jackson (3 April, 4 Aug. 1894).

glasses were bought by the cultivated few outside the universities too.[195] More than anything, though, his clients were, like his friends, academics; the group that recast elite education. They brought teaching to Oxford, science to Cambridge, and standardized the public schools. They were the Adullamites, the party of progress, the reformers in Eton and Harrow and beyond. The historian A. L. Smith was typical of this group. As a married don at Balliol, he lived in a Jackson house, with Powell's glass upon his table.[196] A protégé of Jowett's, he was a convinced reformer, a teacher, and by marriage related to half of the university.[197] He and his allies remade elite education and remodelled it in their own image. They expressed their rejection of conservatism and of vulgar plutocracy. They articulated a belief in scholarship, knowledge, and cultivated taste. Their instrument in this was a friend and a colleague—T. G. Jackson. He shared these attitudes and their aesthetic. Jackson was valued above all for 'the consistency of his architecture',[198] but also for his 'scholarship and highmindedness'.[199] These were the cardinal virtues of an intellectual, and the combination of these three attributes appealed to his academic clients. Jackson failed in his ambition to win great public prizes, and build grand national monuments. He was, nonetheless, memorializing something just as important: the growth of a new group; the making of an intellectual aristocracy.

[195] Loftie, *Dining Room*, 96.
[196] [Mary Florence Smith], *Arthur Lionel Smith* (London, 1928), 110, 118.
[197] Annan, 'Intellectual Aristocracy', 266–7.
[198] *Builder* 127 (1924), 753.
[199] *Architects' Journal* 60 (1924), 761.

Conclusion

It is conventional to conclude a biography with the death of its subject. That, though, is how this study started. So it is with another, if related, death that it must end. Frederic Harrison died on 14 January 1923, aged ninety-one. As a Fellow his ashes were interred in Wadham College chapel amidst some ceremony. As was usual at such events, T. G. Jackson travelled up from London to attend. Too old now to address the mourners himself, his position as the college's most distinguished old member was taken by F. E. Smith, first Earl of Birkenhead. The results were quietly comic—and also strangely symbolic. Maurice Bowra takes up the story,

> Birkenhead began, 'We are met together today on a solemn and memorable occasion to welcome to their last resting place the ashes of a very distinguished Englishman, of a very distinguished Oxford man, of a very distinguished Wadham man, the ashes of no less a person than Mr. Jackson.' At this point Jackson perked up and wondered what could be happening to him, but [the Warden] in a loud voice prompted 'Harrison', and Birkenhead, quite unruffled, continued, 'The ashes of Mr. Harrison.'[1]

Reports of Jackson's death, though, were only slightly exaggerated. The loss of Frederic Harrison was closely connected to the end of Jackson's career. Harrison had been one of the reforming dons who had remade Oxford in the late-nineteenth century. He had been Jackson's colleague when Wadham itself was reformed. He had served on Royal Commissions and written works of history, literature, and philosophy. Harrison was, in short, the very model of an intellectual aristocrat. He had even sent his son to be trained by T. G. Jackson. His death marked the end of an era. A little under two years later, Jackson himself would also be dead.

The last twenty years of Jackson's life were scarred by the loss of old friends and relations. His wife died in 1900, leaving him utterly bereft. 'I cannot yet imagine living without her', he wrote to one correspondent. 'We were everything to one another.'[2] She was just the first. Always in demand to design memorial tablets, Jackson found himself increasingly called upon to commemorate his own friends and acquaintances.[3] In 1901 he erected a tablet to John Griffiths, the

[1] C. M. Bowra, *Memories, 1898–1939* (London, 1966), 147.

[2] NAL, Armstrong Letters, MSL/1976/541/54, Jackson to Armstrong (24 April 1900).

[3] Martin D. W. Jones, 'Gothic Enriched: Thomas Jackson's mural tablets in Brighton College Chapel', *Church Monuments* 6 (1991), 54–66. A large selection of designs can be found in the uncatalogued Jackson papers in the Royal Academy Library.

late Warden of Wadham, who had officiated at his marriage twenty years earlier.[4] In 1923 he fulfilled a similar duty for his old friend Henry Boyd, Principal of Hertford.[5] The intervening years had been filled with similarly miserable jobs. Jackson was, however, losing more than companionship. These were his clients and colleagues as well as his friends. These were memorials to a class as well as to individuals. Bit by bit, the late-Victorian intellectual aristocracy was dying away, leaving Jackson and a few relics as living monuments to its passing.

At the same time, architecture was changing too. New styles and new men were transforming British building. Jackson, however, stood aloof. Unwilling to countenance a revival of 'classic dogma' or 'Vitruvian hypocrisy', he rejected the renewed interest in classical styles that was sweeping across the architectural world.[6] The result was clear. By 1904 he had ceased to be in 'the vanguard of style'. 'The architects who were following Norman Shaw were still assuming Queen Anne was alive', recalled C. H. Reilly, 'while many, like Sir T. G. Jackson, had not got as far as that and were still in the Jacobean age. The most advanced were looking towards Wren.'[7] This was, perhaps, a little unfair. After all, Jackson was occasionally a true Wrenaissance man—as his Electrical Laboratory in Oxford shows. But, on the whole, he remained true to the style of his youth. Little wonder that by the 1920s he was regarded as a curiosity. Birkenhead was not the only one to bury Jackson prematurely. For his younger rivals, Jackson had become a figure 'from the remote past'; a 'product of the by-gone school of devoted enthusiasm to a phase of historic art'.[8] 'Poor Jackson' wrote E. S. Prior in 1914, 'is much better than his work.'[9] Ten years later, his obituarists could not deny his importance, but he had become yesterday's man.

The same was true of his work in other fields. Jackson had been a highly influential writer. His books were still in demand, but they were no longer mould-breaking. The work of men like Geoffrey Scott had made his views seem dated. Similarly, his role as an educationalist was under threat. Once the driving force of radical change, by the 1920s he had become a symbol of conservatism and even of reaction. The arts and crafts movement, which Jackson had shaped and sustained, was also in decline. The cutting edge of architecture was in Germany now—and in France, the Netherlands, and the United States. Younger men, like Lethaby, had accepted the principles of industrial design. Even mass production, even iron and steel girders, were becoming widely used. Jackson's talk of craftsmanship was apparently no longer relevant. Certainly, it was no longer avant garde. The campaign against professionalization was similarly dying. Jackson's son joined the RIBA, and within a few years of Jackson's death

[4] RA Library, Uncat. MSS, Drawing (29 May 1901).
[5] *Hertford College Magazine* 12 (1923), 4–5.
[6] T. G. Jackson, *Architecture* (London, 1925), 295; *A Holiday in Umbria* (London, 1923), 33.
[7] C. H. Reilly, *Scaffolding in the Sky* (London, 1938), 118.
[8] *Architects' Journal* 60 (1924), 756; *Builder* 127 (1924), 753.
[9] Quoted in Lynne Brown Walker, 'E. S. Prior, 1852–1932', (Ph.D., London, 1978), 230.

99. Jackson's proposed Holywell Street
building for Hertford College (1916).

100. T. H. Hughes's Holywell Street
Frontage for Hertford College (1929).

compulsory registration was established by law. Jackson had become a man out of his times. To some extent, he had simply lived too long.

The loss of his clients and the decline in his influence were closely linked. And this is best exemplified at Hertford College.[10] Boyd died in 1922; Jackson in 1924. His work there was completed in 1925. Yet, just five years later, when the college erected a new block, it utterly rejected Jackson's pre-existing plans, choosing stucco instead of stone, and eschewing any Gothic inspiration. 'It is felt that there is much to be said for a style of architecture which will to some degree harmonize with the most pleasing features of the Street, and is also well adapted to provide convenient and comfortable rooms', the College resolved.[11] Gothic was out and with it went Jackson. The changed aesthetic was quite clear, and the result quite striking: a building by T. H. Hughes which 'anybody at first sight might mistake for a Late Georgian House'.[12] It was a pattern repeated throughout Oxford, and elsewhere. The world had changed, and so had its buildings. These were changes mirrored in the lives of a new generation of intellectual aristocrats: people like Virginia Woolf. A writer and the daughter of a writer, married to a writer and with friends who were artists, poets, and academics, she was an intellectual aristocrat to her core. But this was a new aristocracy: self-consciously bohemian and defiantly unconventional. More than anything, they rejected the Victorian past. Moving to Bloomsbury in 1904, she wrote that 'Everything was going to be new; everything was going to be different; everything was on trial'. For Woolf and her friends, this meant a rather ostentatious rejection of what had come before, whether it be morality, manners, or even meals. 'We are going to do without napkins . . . to have coffee after dinner, instead of tea at nine o'clock', wrote Woolf.[13] It was a small change, but it represented a great revolt. It was symptomatic of a greater shift in ideas and identities. For Jackson, it meant a slow decline in his practice.

But this decline meant descent from a great height. Jackson had become an influential and important architect, a public moralist, and a well-known writer. In anyone's terms, this was a successful life. He was richly rewarded with honorary degrees, success in international competitions, and the only baronetcy ever given to an architect. Although the irony of it might have escaped him, this was indeed a life filled with what Birkenhead described as glittering prizes. But such success would always prove transitory. Jackson's decline was perhaps inevitable, and it is certainly explicable. Paradoxically perhaps, he had been simply too successful. For the new generation, he was guilty by association. His ability to embody the ideals of the late-Victorian intellectual aristocracy condemned him in the eyes of their heirs. A pre-eminent

[10] See also William Whyte, 'Unbuilt Hertford: T. G. Jackson's contextual dilemmas', *Architectural History* 45 (2002), 347–62.
[11] *Hertford College Magazine* 19 (1930), 1–2.   [12] Sherwood and Pevsner, *Oxfordshire*, 141.
[13] Virginia Woolf, quoted in David Newsome, *The Victorian World Picture* (London, 1998), 246.

Victorian, the turn against Victorianism undermined his achievements. Yet those achievements were many and various. As an artist, designer, writer, historian, and public figure, T. G. Jackson was an influential force in late-Victorian and Edwardian England. As an architect at Oxford, Cambridge, and in the public schools, he was unsurpassed in importance. His books were read across the world. His buildings were known throughout the country. His views on art, architecture, and education were sought out by governments, academics, and members of the educated elite.

This did not come about by accident. Jackson's position as an intellectual allowed him to work with other members of the intellectual aristocracy. He gave architectural expression to their ideals and advertised their identity. And above all else, Jackson owed his position to those who reformed his Alma Mater after 1870. Their loyalty was reciprocated: Jackson wrote that 'nothing pleases me more than to hear that I am sometimes spoken of as "Oxford Jackson" '.[14] This was more than mere sentiment. It was the acknowledgement of an important truth. In a symbiotic relationship, Oxford made his career, as he remade Oxford. The intellectual aristocracy in Oxford and elsewhere needed an artist to express their success, and Jackson filled the role perfectly.

[14] T. G. Jackson, *Recollections: the life and travels of a Victorian architect*, ed. Sir Nicholas Jackson (London, 2003), 31.

Select Bibliography

Publication is in London unless otherwise stated

PRIMARY MATERIAL

1. Manuscripts

Brighton, Sussex.

Brighton College
Minute Book D (1877–84).
Minute Book E (1885–95).
Minute Book H (1918–32).
Uncatalogued Drawings.
Papers of T. Griffiths and H. Griffith.
BCA 131—Papers of F. W. Madden.
BCA 153—Papers of T. G. Jackson.
BCA 154—Drawings, plans, and elevations.

Cambridge, Cambridgeshire

King's College
KCD/39—Materials relating to the extension of the hall (1900–3).

Museum of Archaeology and Anthropology
MM 1/1/2—A. C. Haddon, 'A brief history of the study of anthropology at Cambridge'.
MM 1/2/12—Bound collection of Reports of Antiquarian Committee (1875–99).
MM 2/1/1—Minute Book (1899–1913).
MM 2/1/2—appeal.
MM 2/1/3—correspondence (1907–13).
MM 2/1/4—correspondence (1907–14).
MM 2/1/5—plans.
MM 2/1/6—plans (1914).
MM 2/1/7—proposed frontage.
MM 2/1/8—prints of drawings (1909–15).
MM 2/1/9—correspondence (1909–17).
MM 2/1/10—subscriptions.
MM 2/1/12—typescript of electrical work.
MM 2/1/13—plans, elevations, sections (1910–11).
MM 2/1/14—appeal.
MM 2/1/16—appeal.
MM 2/1/17—memorandum.
MM 2/1/18—subscription.
MM 2/1/22—T. G. Jackson, 'Notes on Doorway'.
MM 2/1/33—photographs.

MM 2/2/8—misc. papers.
MM 2/3/22—prints.
MM 2/3/23—architect's drawings (1909–15).

Newnham College
L.4 Building (1874–1910).
N.3 Minutes of Building Committee (1874–80).
Plans and elevations by Basil Champneys.
Uncatalogued MSS (Clough Hall).

Pembroke College
Scott Acc/1–7, Scott accounts.
Scott Corr/1–64, Scott correspondence.
Uncatalogued MSS relating to Scott.

University Archives
C.U.R. 46—Senate House (1873–1903).
C.U.R. 46.1—Senate House (1900–23).
C.U.R. 110—University Registry, Sedgwick Museum.
Min. IV.16—Senate House Syndicate Minute Book (1874–1944).
Min. VI.43—Law School and Library Syndicate Minutes (1899–1905).
Min. VI.72—Minutes of the Museums and Lecture Rooms Syndicate (1906–12).
Prem. VII.4—Psychological Laboratory.
Prem. VIII.31—'Order of Proceedings and Description of Buildings Opened by their Majesties the King and Queen at Cambridge. 1 March 1904'.
U.A. Uncatalogued Drawings and Plans (Sedgwick Museum).
U.A. Geol 8/1–4—Prof. Hughes' Notes (1874–89).
U.A. Geol 8/5–8—Minutes of the Geological Syndicate (1879–86) and the Sedgwick Museum Syndicate (1891–1902).
U.A. Geol 8/9–11—Prof. Hughes' Notes (1890–1, 1896, 1898–9).
U.A. Geol 9/1–26—Department of Geology, misc. papers (1886–1903).

U.A. Geol 9/27–41—Hughes' Papers.
U.A. Geol 10/21—Letters (1886–87).
U.A. Geol 11—Correspondence with architects.
U.A. Geol 12—Museum plans and site.
U.A. Geol 14—Museum opening.
C.U.A. P II—Plans of Sedgwick Museum.
C.U.A. P IV—Archaeological museum.

Chichester, West Sussex
West Sussex County Record Office
Par 22/1/2/1—Binsted Church, Register of Baptisms (1813–1998).
Par 31/4/1—Burpham Church, Restoration (1870).
Par 175/4/1—Slindon Church, Building Accounts (1866–7).
Par 175/4/2—Slindon Church, Plans and elevations (1866–7).
Par 175/9/3—Slindon Church, Church Wardens' Accounts (1864–93).
Par 741/1/2/1—Eartham Church, Register of Baptisms (1813–1999).

Cranbrook, Kent
Cranbrook School
Uncatalogued material relating to Charles Crowden.
Uncatalogued correspondence (1883–6).

Eton, Berkshire
Eton College
60/35—Governing Body Minute Book (1888–1904).
60/26—Governing Body Minute Book (1904–8).
60/115—Standing Finance and Building Committee Minutes (1905–11).
Coll/B5/64—Lower Chapel.
Coll/B5/224—Playing Fields.
Coll/B5/299/1—Science Schools.
Coll/B5/299/2—Science Schools.
Coll/B5/301—Queen's School.
Coll/B5/303—Racquet Courts.
Coll/B5/304—Music Schools.
Coll/B5/305—Music Schools.
Coll/B5/306—Museum.

Giggleswick, Yorkshire
Giggleswick School
Minute Book (1892–1907).
Uncatalogued plans, elevations and drawings.
Uncatalogued papers relating to the chapel.
Brayshaw Collection.

Harrow, Middlesex
Harrow School
Minutes of Governing Body (1871–85).
H. Montague Butler, 'School Account' (1877–82).
Headmaster's Correspondence (1860–85).
Hills and Saunders Glass Plate Negative Collection.
Uncatalogued collection of pictures and post-cards.

London
British Architectural Library
R.I.B.A. Special Committee Minutes IV (1899–1908).
JaT/1/1/1, Emilio Shatzmayer, *La Dalmazia* (1877), extra-illustrated by T. G. Jackson.
JaT/1/1/2, T. G. Jackson, report on Hagia Sophia, Istanbul (1910).
JTS/1/9, Specifications for repairs to Duddington Church (1912–13).

Church of England Record Centre
51630—Ashbourne Church (1913).

Drapers' Hall
MB 50—Assistants' Minutes (1893–98).
MB 60—Assistants' Minutes (1898–1904).
MB 61—Assistants' Minutes (1904–8).
MB 62—Assistants' Minutes (1908–14).
MB 63—Assistants' Minutes (1914–20).
MB/E.11—Estate Committee Minutes (1895–8).
MB/E.12—Estate Committee Minutes (1898–1901).
MB/E.15—Estate Committee Minutes (1906–11).
MB/F.9—Estate Committee Minutes (1909–16).
PL. 48—Plans for Throgmorton Street.
a. 1019—Radcliffe Library, Oxford.
a. 1020—Correspondence relating to alterations at Drapers' Hall.
a. 1094—Letters concerning Drapers' Hall.

Guildhall Library
MS 11,588/29—Grocers' Company, Orders of the Court of Assistants, 1896–9.
MS 11,588/30—Grocers' Company, Orders of the Court of Assistants, 1899–1902.
MS 18,411/2—Aldenham School Minute Book (1893–1913).

MS 18,412—Aldenham School Agenda Book (1875–1905).
MS 18,416—Brewer's Company: Richard Platt Trust (1889–1919).

Inner Temple
BEN/1.30—Bench Table Orders (1892–6).
BEN/4.2—Committee Minutes (1892–8).
BUI/17—Hare Court: west side (1893–5).
PLA/16—Hare Court: plans and elevations.

Papers in the possession of Sir Nicholas Jackson
Architectural notes (1859–70).
Diaries (1869, 1876, 1877–8, 1882, 1883, 1884, 1885, 1888, 1896, 1910, 1913).
Drawings (1858–9).
Family letters (1855–64).
'Pilgrim's Progress' (1897–1902).
'Recollections'.

Lambeth Palace Library
Riley Papers:
MS 2343—correspondence (1879–95).
MS 2344—correspondence (1896–1902).
MS 2353—misc. papers (1882–1941).
MS2355—notes on travels.
MS 2362–9—engagement books (1886–9).

Incorporated Church Building Society:
ICBS 1024—Farnborough.
ICBS 6119—Madehurst.
ICBS 6707—Ripley.
ICBS 7444—St John's, Wimbledon.
ICBS 7885—Cranbrook.
ICBS 7527—Barton.
ICBS 7580—Bourton on the Water.
ICBS 7939—Flore.
ICBS 8011—Lottisham.
ICBS 8396—Narberth.
ICBS 8641—Caterham.
ICBS 8827—Bromley.
ICBS 8982—Little Bromley.
ICBS 9351—Earl Soham.
ICBS 9921—Bishop's Waltham.
ICBS 10237—Compton Martin.
ICBS 10251—Corhampton.
ICBS 10613—Bottisham.
ICBS 10683—St Augustine's, Aldershot.
ICBS 10812—St Luke's, Wimbledon.
ICBS 10956—St Michael's, Aldershot.
ICBS 11118—Eastrop.
ICBS 11378—Stapleford.

Museum of London
3254/1–3, plans and drawings by T. G. Jackson.
B13 3220a, letter from T. G. Jackson (1891).
B13 3220b, illustration (1885).
B15 3235/1, scrapbook.
B15 3378, Harry Powell, 'Notebook'.
B15 3235/i, Harry Powell, 'Notebook' (1873–1900).
B16, Harry Powell, letters.
B24 2232, design for glassware.
B211 3195A, design for glassware.

National Archives
ADM 169/362—Greenwich Hospital (1906–9).
CRES 35/1516—Eltham Palace (1896–1903).
ED 9/11—Royal Council on Art.
ED 23/4—Royal Council on Art.
ED 24/56/A—Royal College of Art.

National Art Library
86.DD.10,11—C. R. Ashbee, 'Memoirs' (typescript).
86.HH.53—Sir Thomas Armstrong Correspondence.
86.PP.2—Artists' letters to A. L. Baldry (1876–1934).
86.PP.15—Sir Isidore Spielmann Corres-pondence (1875–1923)
86.SS.69—T. G. Jackson and Alice Jackson, 'Diary of a Journey from London to Bosnia'.

Royal Academy
C XX, Council Minutes (1894–9).
C XXI, Council Minutes (1900–6).
Uncatalogued collection of drawings by T. G. Jackson.

Society for the Protection of Ancient Buildings
128—Winchester Cathedral (1884–1911).
Uncatalogued file on St Mary's, Oxford.

Oxford, Oxfordshire
Balliol College Archive
English Register, 1875–1908.
English Register, 1908–1924.
Architects' Plans and Designs VI, Chapel (1911–32).
Architects' Plans and Designs IX, Miscellaneous (1890–1965).
D.10.16, Chapel Correspondence (1911).
MBP.317, Chapel Papers (1910–25).

Bodleian Library

MS. Dep. C. 590 (649), Jackson to Percy Manning (1896).

MS. Eng. c. 2236 fol. 33, Jackson to Rosamund Horsley (1903).

MS. Eng. Misc. e. 720, T. G. and B. H. Jackson, 'The cruise of the Sprite' (1908).

MS. Eng. Misc. f. 796, T. G. Jackson, undergraduate notebook (?1856).

MS. Top. Oxon. A. 19—T. G. Jackson, 'The Schools, Oxford'.

MS. Top. Oxon. b. 164, W. Tuckwell, 'Reminiscences of Oxford' (1900).

MS. Top. Oxon. d.650, J. L. Marks, 'History of the City of Oxford High School'.

G. A. Camb 4° 30 (8)—An Account of the Opening of the Museum of Archaeology (1884).

G. A. Oxon. b 138—Misc. Pamphlets.

G. A. Oxon. b. 160—Misc. Schools.

G. A. Oxon. c. 33—Papers of C. L. Shadwell.

G. A. Oxon. c.111—'The proposed foundation of a High School for the City of Oxford' (1877).

G. A. Oxon. c. 204—Carfax Church and Tower, 1895-8.

G. A. Oxon. c. 270—Brasenose College Scrapbook.

G. A. Oxon. c. 275—Papers Relating to Hertford College.

G. A. Oxon. c. 287—Misc. Papers Relating to Trinity College.

G. A. Oxon. c. 317—The Story of the Acland Home.

G. A. Oxon. 4° 272—Misc. Papers Relating to Cowley.

G. A. Oxon. 4° 538—Papers relating to the Acland Hospital.

G. A. Oxon. 4° 606—Papers relating to city schools.

G. A. Oxon. 8° 161—Misc. Pamphlets.

G. A. Oxon. 8° 164—Misc. Pamphlets.

G. A. Oxon. 8° 540—Misc. Pamphlets.

G. A. Oxon. 8° 659—Misc. Pamphlets.

G. A. Oxon. 16° 136 (2)—Rhodes memorial tablet.

G. A. Oxon. fol. A. 139, 'City of Oxford High School for Boys, scheme and deed of trust under the seal of the Corporation of the City of Oxford' (1878).

Bodleian Library, Oxford University Archives

HC 1/2/1—Minutes of Hebdomadal Council 1854-66.

HC 1/2/2—Minutes of Hebdomadal Council 1866-79.

HC 1/2/3—Minutes of Hebdomadal Council 1879-96.

HC 1/1/46-51—Hebdomadal Council Papers 1897-8.

HC 1/1/52-57—Hebdomadal Council Papers 1899-1900.

HC 1/1/58-63—Hebdomadal Council Papers 1901-3.

HC 1/1/64-69—Hebdomadal Council Papers 1903-4.

HC 1/1/70-75—Hebdomadal Council Papers 1904-6.

HC 1/1/76-78—Hebdomadal Council Papers 1907-8.

HC 1/1/79-81—Hebdomadal Council Papers 1908.

HC 1/1/82-83—Hebdomadal Council Papers 1909.

HC 1/1/84—Hebdomadal Council Papers 1909.

HC 1/1/85—Hebdomadal Council Papers 1910.

HC 1/1/86—Hebdomadal Council Papers 1910.

HC 3/1/1—Committees of Council 1857-73.

HC 3/1/2—Committees of Council 1873-86.

NW 20/8—St Mary the Virgin 1891-.

ST 26—Sheldonian Theatre 1890-1914.

ST 28/2—Sheldonian Theatre 1882-1907.

UC 3/1—New Schools Delegacy Minute Book 1875-89.

UC/FF/48—Radcliffe Camera.

UC/FF/77/1—Electrical Laboratory 1905-23.

UC/FF/181A/1—Radcliffe Library 1897-1927.

UC/FF/197/1/1—St Mary's Church 1867-1927.

UC/FF/197/2—St Mary's Church 1878-88.

UC/FF/197/3/1-2—St Mary's Church 1889-1902.

UC/FF/197/4/1—St Mary's Church 1903-15.

UC/FF/210/1-2—Clarendon Press 1883-1927.

UC/FF/304/1/1—Bodleian Library 1876-89.

UC/FF/304/1/2—Bodleian 1890-6.

UC/FF/304/1/3—Bodleian 1897-1901.

UC/FF/304/2/1—Bodleian 1902-7.

UC/FF/304/2/3—Bodleian 1908-10.

UC/FF/304/3/1—Bodleian 1911.

UC/FF/304/3/2—Bodleian 1912.

UC/FF/304/4/1—Bodleian 1912-21.

UC/FF/304/5/2—Bodleian 1904-27.

UC/FF/304.6.1—Bodleian 1913.

UC/FF/304/6/2—Bodleian 1914.

UC/FF/304/6/3—Bodleian 1915-17.

UC/FF/305/1/1—Botanic Gardens 1875–85.
UC/FF/305/1/3—Botanic Gardens 1880–8.
UC/FF/305/2/1—Botanic Gardens 1885–91.
UC/FF/353/1/1—New Schools Delegacy: Letters, 1875–86.
UC/FF/353/1/2—New Schools Delegacy: Letters, 1887–93.

Brasenose College Archive
A.1.13—Vice Principal's Register 1874–90.
B.5—Uncat. Drawings by Jackson.
B.9.54–76—Architectural Drawings.
B.13.2—Working Drawings of New Buildings.
B.15.1—Architectural Drawings.
B.500—College New Buildings: Correspondence 1909.
B.502—College New Buildings: Correspondence 1883– .
B.1076—College Buildings, 1883–1928.
D.819—Buildings: Accounts 1881–1911.
SB (un-cat.) New Buildings 1881–1911.

Corpus Christi College Archive
B/4/1/8—College Minutes 1872–81.
B/4/1/9—College Minutes 1881–97.
B/14/1/1—Misc. papers from the President's Lodgings.
B/14/7/1—President's Letter Book 1862–1904.

Hertford College Archive
4/1/1—Minutes of the Governing Body 1874–1929.
Uncatalogued volume of plans and elevations 1887–1923.

High School
Uncatalogued collection of material relating to the foundation.

Lincoln College Archive
Order Book 1872–89.
Order Book 1889–1912.

Mansfield College Archive
Cup 1—Waterhouse papers.
Cup 24—Building Fund minute book (1885–9).
Cup 24, Book 2—News Cuttings 2.

Merton College Archive
1.5 College Register (1822–76).
1.5a College Register (1877–1924).
6.38 Bursar's Reports (1891–1900).
6.39 Bursar's Reports (1900–13).

Letter Book (1883–6).
Letter Book (1886–90).
Letter Book (1896–8).
Letter Book (1898–1902).
Plans and elevations of St Alban Quadrangle (1904).
Plans and elevations of Warden's House (1904).
Uncatalogued plans (1878).

Oriel College
GOV 4.A6, Minute Book (1906–13).
DL.2.3, Waterhouse papers (1879).
ETC.A4/4, Rhodes building.
ETC.A8/4, Champneys correspondence.
Locked Case C, BI (i), Correspondence relating to St Mary's church.

Oxfordshire County Archives
Oxford Diocesan papers: c.1938 (Oxford, St Martin).
Oxford Diocesan papers: c.1947 (Oxford, St Peter's in the East).
Oxford Diocesan papers: c.1900 (Milton under Wychwood).
PAR 189/11/F4/6 (Oxford, All Saints' Church).
PAR 213/C2/1 (Oxford, St Peter's in the East).

The Queen's College
Uncatalogued MSS relating to the chapel (1899).

Somerville College Archive
Minutes of Council 1879–1908.
Log-Book 1879–1907.
Reports and Calendars 1879–99.

Trinity College Archive
Coll. Govt. A.4 Order Book D 1852–84.
Coll. Govt. A.5 Order Book E 1885–1940.
I/C/3 Jackson Building.
I/C/4 President's Lodgings.
I/D/2 Proposed Alterations.
Uncatalogued records of new buildings.

Wadham College Archive
2/4 Convention Book 1829–1944.

Radley, Berkshire
Radley College
Register of St Peter's College, 1847–1899.
Uncatalogued MSS 1889–1913.
Uncatalogued plans and elevations 1889–21.

Sandwich, Kent
Sir Roger Manwood's School
Uncatalogued box of material (1895–1914).

Swindon, Wiltshire
National Monuments Record Archive
15555, St Mary's Church, Stamford.
101536, Emily Jackson Hospital, Sevenoaks.

Uppingham, Leicestershire
Uppingham School
Minute Book, 1875–94.
Minute Book, 1895–1906.
D.27—Correspondence on new buildings.
Uncatalogued plans, drawings, and elevations.

Winchester, Hampshire
Hampshire Record Office
21M65/37F/3—Botley Church (1891).
21M65/37F/4—Botley Church (1896).
21M65/57/7—St Michael, Aldershot (1910).
21M65/58F/7—St Michael's, Bournemouth (1919).
21M65/60F/6—St Peter's, Bournemouth (1905).
21M70/24—Botley Church (1891).
21M65/88F/12—Christchurch Priory (1908–12).
21M65/107F/1—Curdridge Church (1887–8).
21M65/115F/7—Holy Cross Church (1913).
21M65/123F/2—East Stratton Church (1887).
21M65/123F/1—Ellingham Church (1884).
21M65/132F/3—Ellingham Church (1920).
21M65/223F/4—Laverstoke Church (1919).
21M65/269F/2—Northington Church (1888).
21M65/424F/5—Whitchurch Church (1919).
21M65/448F/2—Wonston Church (1871).
21M65/448F/3—Wonston Church (1908).
21M69/PW15/1–13—Northington Church (1888).

30M77/PW29—Bishop's Waltham Church (1894).
30M77/PW34—Bishop's Waltham Church (1896).
30M77/PW35—Bishop's Waltham Church (1896).
30M77/PW36—Bishop's Waltham Church (1896).
30M77/PW36a—Bishop's Waltham Church (1896).
30M77/PW38—Bishop's Waltham Church, letters from Jackson (1894–9).
30M77/PW43—Bishop's Waltham Church (1897).
44M86/PW32–4—St Michael, Aldershot (1919).
55M81W/PWZ1—Hyde Church (1900).
98M82/PZ5—Curdridge Church (1887–8).

Woking, Surrey
Surrey History Centre
2136/8/4—St Mary's, Wimbledon.
2473/2—Malden Church.
2473/2/12—Chessington Church.
2508/2—Malden Church.
2853/3/1—St John's, Wimbledon.
3830/2/13—Chessington Church.
PSH/CL.E/9/2—East Clandon Church.
PSH/CL.E/9/3—East Clandon Church.
PSH/CL.E/9.8—East Clandon Church.
PSH/CL.E/10/1—East Clandon Church.
PSH/Cl.W/9/11/2—West Clandon Church.
PSH/PEP/5—Peper Harrow Church.

2. Periodicals

Academy Architecture (1889–1932).
American Architect (1876–1936).
Architect (1869–1926).
Architecture (1896–98).
Architectural Review (1896–).
Arts and Crafts (1904–6).
Arts and Crafts Exhibition Society, Catalogues (1888–1912).
Brazen Nose (1909–).
British Almanac and Companion (1827–1913).
British Architect (1874–1919).
Builder (1843–1966), continued since as *Building*.
Building News (1855–1926).
Cambridge Review (1879–).
Cambridge University Reporter (1870–).

Church Builder (1862–1904).
Coffee Public House News (1880–3).
Country Life (1897–).
English Historical Review (1885–).
Hertford College Magazine (1910–).
National Association for the Advancement of Art, Transactions (1888–91).
Nineteenth Century (1887–1900).
Oxford Journal (1867–).
Oxford Magazine (1883–).
Oxford University Gazette (1870–).
Public School Magazine (1898–1902).
RIBA Transactions/Papers/Journal/Proceedings (1842–).
St Paul's Ecclesiological Society, Transactions (1881–1938).
The Times (1785–)

3. Printed

Abbott, Evelyn, and Campbell, Lewis, *The Life and Letters of Benjamin Jowett* (2 vols., 1897).

Acland, H. W., *The Oxford Museum* (1859).

Adams, Maurice B., *Artists' Homes* (1883).

Aitchison, George, 'What principles should govern the restoration of ancient buildings or their preservation as memorials?', *Transactions of the National Association for the Promotion of Social Science* 1877, 712–20.

Allan, G. A. T., and Morpurgo, J. E., *Christ's Hospital* (1984).

Appleton, J. H., and Sayce, A. H., eds., *Dr. Appleton, His Life and Literary Relics* (1881).

Arnold, Matthew, *Essays in Criticism* (1865).

—— *Culture and Anarchy* (1869; Cambridge, 1993).

Arnold, T. K., *Remarks on the Rev. F. Close's 'Church Architecture Scripturally Considered, from the Earliest Ages to the Present Time'* (1844).

—— *An Examination of the Rev. F. Close's reply to 'Remarks' upon his 'Church Architecture Scripturally Considered'* (1844).

—— *A Few Words in Answer to the Attack on My 'Classical School Books' Published in Fraser's Magazine* (1853).

Arts and Crafts Essays (1893).

Ashbee, C. R., *Should We Stop Teaching Art?* (1911).

Atlay, J. B., *Sir Henry Wentworth Acland: a memoir* (1903).

Austen-Leigh, R. A., *An Illustrated Guide to the Buildings of Eton College* (3rd ed.; Eton, 1921).

Austen Leigh, William, *Augustus Austen Leigh* (1906).

Balfour, Henry, 'The Relationship of Museums to the Study of Anthropology', *Journal of Anthropological Institute* 24 (1904), 1619.

Barker, Ernest, *Age and Youth* (1953).

Bartlett, F. C., 'Cambridge, England: 1887–1937', *American Journal of Psychology* 50 (1937), 97–110.

Belcher, John, and Macartney, Mervyn, *Later Renaissance Architecture in England* (2 vols.; 1901).

Bell, Edward Allen, *A History of Giggleswick School* (Leeds, 1912).

Benson, A. C., *Life of Edward White Benson* (2 vols.; 1899).

Blakiston, H. E. D., *Trinity College, Oxford* (Oxford, 1898).

Blomfield, Reginald, *A History of Renaissance Architecture in England* (1897).

—— *Studies in Architecture* (1905).

—— *The Mistress Art* (1908).

—— *A History of French Architecture* (2 vols.; 1911–21).

—— *Memoirs of an Architect* (1932).

—— 'Basil Champneys', *RIBA Journal* 42 (1935), 737–8.

—— *Richard Norman Shaw* (1940).

Blunt, John Henry, *Dursley and its Neighbourhood* (Dursley, 1877).

Bodley, G. F., *Poems* (1899).

Botton, A. T., 'Sir Thomas Graham Jackson RA: an appreciation', *Architects' Journal* 60 (1924), 758–63.

Bowra, C. M., *Memories, 1898–1939* (1966).

Brasenose Quartercentenary Monographs (Oxford, 1909).

Brodrick, George Charles, *Memories and Impressions, 1831–1900* (1900).

Brown, Frank P., *South Kensington and its Art Training* (1912).

Buchan, John, *Brasenose College* (1898).

Buckmaster, Martin A., 'Further Remarks on Art Teaching in Secondary and Other Schools', *Art Workers' Quarterly* 4 (1905), 70–3.

Burges, William, *Architectural Drawings* (1870).

Burgoyne, F. J., *Library Construction: architecture, fittings and furniture* (1897).

Butler, H. Montague, *Public School Sermons* (1899).

Cambridge Camden Society, *Church Enlargement and Church Arrangement* (Cambridge, 1843).

—— *A Few Words to Church Builders* (3rd ed.; Cambridge, 1844).

Carlyle, Thomas, *Signs of the Times* (1829).

—— *Past and Present* (1843).

Fletcher, Carteret J., *A History of the Church and Parish of St. Martin, Carfax, Oxford* (Oxford, 1896).

Case, Thomas, *St. Mary's Clusters* (Oxford, 1893).

—— *Letters to the 'Times' 1884–1922 Written by Thomas Case*, ed. E. B. Mowat (Oxford, 1927).

Champneys, Basil, 'On the Present Relations between Art and Architecture', *Portfolio* 1874, 170–2.

—— *A Quiet Corner of England* (1875).

—— The Architecture of Queen Victoria's Reign', *Art Journal* 7 (1887), 203–9.

—— 'Style', *British Architect* 31 (1889), 41–3, 61–2, 81.

—— *Memories and Correspondence of Coventry Patmore* (2 vols.; 1900).

Childs, W. M., *Making a University: an account of the university movement at Reading* (1933).

Choisy, Auguste, *Histoire de l'Architecture* (2 vols.; Paris, 1899).

Clark, John Willis, *Old Friends at Cambridge and Elsewhere* (1900).

—— *Endowments of the University of Cambridge* (Cambridge, 1904).

—— *A Concise Guide to the Town and University of Cambridge* (6th ed.; Cambridge, 1919).

Cobden-Sanderson, T. J., *The Arts and Crafts Movement* (Hammersmith, 1905).

Colvin, Sidney, 'Restoration and Anti-Restoration' *Nineteenth Century* 11 (1877), 446–70.

Crane, Walter, *An Artist's Reminiscences* (1907).

Cundall, H. M., 'Queen Victoria Memorial', *Art Journal* 24 (1904), 198–201.

Dawson, Geoffrey, 'Walter Morrison', *The National Review* 78 (1922), 854–66.

Davenant, Francis, *What Shall My Son Be?* (1870).

Dukes, Clement, *Health at School Considered in its Mental, Moral and Physical Aspects* (1887).

Du Maurier, George, *Society Pictures* (2 vols.; 1891).

Elliot-Smith, G., 'Dr Rivers and the New Vision in Ethnology', in W. H. R. Rivers, *Psychology and Ethnology* (1926), xiv–xviii.

Emmett, J. T., *Six Essays* (1891; 1972).

—— 'Architecture, a Business, a Profession, or an Art?', *Quarterly Review* 176 (1893), 40–72.

Escott, T. H. S., *Society in London* (1886).

Farrar, F. W., ed., *Essays on a Liberal Education* (1867).

Fergusson, James, *A History of Architecture* (2nd ed.; 4 vols: London, 1873–5).

Fletcher, Banister, and Fletcher, Banister F., *A History of Architecture for the Student, Craftsman and Amateur* (1896).

Fletcher, Hanslip, ed., *Oxford and Cambridge* (1909).

Foster, Joseph, *Man at the Bar* (1885).

Fowler, Thomas, *History of Corpus Christi College* (Oxford Historical Society xxv; Oxford, 1893).

Fox, Francis, *Sixty-three Years of Engineering* (1924).

Freeman, Edward A., *Principles of Church Restoration* (1846).

—— *Sketches from the Subject and Neighbour Lands of Venice* (1881).

—— 'Oxford After Forty Years: I', *Contemporary Review* 51 (1887), 609–23.

—— 'Oxford After Forty Years: II', *Contemporary Review* 51 (1887), 814–30.

—— 'Architecture in Oxford', *The Architect* 38 (1887), 363.

Fyffe, Charles Alan, 'Study and Opinion in Oxford', *Macmillan's Magazine* 21 (1869), 184–92.

Galton, Francis, *English Men of Science: their nature and nurture* (1874; London, 1970).

Garbett, J., *University Reform* (1853).

Garrett, Rhoda and Agnes, *Suggestions for Home Decoration* (1876).

Gautrey, Thomas, '*Lux Mihi Laus*', *School Board Memories* (1937).

Geikie, Archibald, *The Founders of Geology* (2nd ed., 1905; New York, 1962).

Gilbert, W. S., *Patience* (1881).

Gill, Eric, *Autobiography* (1942).

de Gobineau, M. A., *Essai sur l'inégalité des races humaines* (4 vols.; Paris, 1853–5).

Gotch, Alfred, *Architecture of the Renaissance in England* (2 vols.; 1891).

—— *Historic Notes on Kirby Hall* (Northampton, 1899).

—— *Early Renaissance Architecture in England* (2nd ed.; 1914).

—— ed., *The Growth and Work of the Royal Institute of British Architects 1834–1924* (1934).

Gourlay, A. B., *A History of Sherborne School* (Sherborne, 1871).

Graham, Edward, *The Harrow Life of Montague Butler* (1920).

Green, T. H., 'The Work to be Done by the New Oxford High School' (1882).

Haddon, A. C., 'Baron Anatole von Hügel' *Man* 28 (1928), 169–71.

Hamerton, P. G., *The Intellectual Life* (1873).

Hamilton, Walter, *The Aesthetic Movement* (1882).

Hardy, R. H., *Public School Life: Rugby* (1911).

Haweis, E. M., *Beautiful Houses* (1882).

Headlam, Cecil, and Home, Gordon, *The Inns of Court* (1909).

Henderson, Bernard W., *Merton College* (1899).

Holdsworth, William, *A History of English Law* (17 vols.; 1905–72).

Hooper, J. J., *The Establishment of a School of Jurisprudence in the University of Oxford* (1854).

Howson, Edmund W., and Warner, George Townsend, eds., *Harrow School* (1898).

Hope, A. J. B. Beresford, *The Common Sense of Art* (1858).

Horsley, J. C., *Recollections of a Royal Academician* (1903).

Irish Loyal and Patriotic Union Publications, 'Mad Tipperary' (Dublin and London, 1890), 25–8.

Jackson, T. G., 'Some Account of Slindon Church', *Sussex Archaeological Collections* 29 (1867), 126–33.

—— *Modern Gothic Architecture* (1873).

—— 'Pyrford Church', *Surrey Archaeological Society Collections* 7 (1880), 67–70.

—— 'The Commonplace of Architecture', *Building News* 48 (1885), 425–6, 441–3.

—— *Ragusa. Il Palazzo Rettorale, il duomo, il reliquario del teschia di s.Biago.* (offprint from *Annuario Dalmatico* 2; Zadar, 1885).

—— 'The Architecture of Dalmatia', *RIBA Transactions* NS 3 (1887), 161–78.

—— *Dalmatia, the Quarnero and Istria* (3 vols.; Oxford, 1887).

—— 'The Obstacles Opposed to the Advancement of Architecture by Architects Themselves', National Association for the Advancement of Art and its Application to Industry, *Transactions* (1888), 193–201.

—— 'The High Street of Oxford and Brasenose College', *Magazine of Art* 8 (1889), 332–40.

—— 'Eagle House, Wimbledon', *Surrey Archaeological Society Collections* 10 (1891), 151–64.

—— 'Presidential Address', National Association for the Advancement of Art and its Application to Industry, *Transactions* (1891), 78–93.

—— 'The Training of Architects to the Pursuit of Architecture', *Builder* 61 (1891), 460–3.

—— 'Architecture, a Profession or an Art', *Nineteenth Century* 33 (1893), 405–15.

—— *Wadham College, Oxford* (Oxford, 1893).

—— 'Intarsia and Inlaid Woodwork', *Arts and Crafts Essays* (1893), 330–44.

—— *Some Thoughts on the Training of Architects* (Liverpool, 1895).

—— *Address to the Students of the Birmingham School of Art* (Birmingham, 1897).

—— *The Church of St Mary the Virgin, Oxford* (Oxford, 1897).

—— 'Architecture in Relation to the Crafts', *Builder* 72 (1897), 334–7.

—— 'The Libraries of the Middle Ages', *RIBA Journal* 3° Series 5 (1898), 365–85.

—— *Address to the Students of the Durham School of Art* (Durham, 1898).

—— 'A Modern Cathedral', *Guardian* 1902, 155.

—— 'Eagle House, Wimbledon; its builders and inhabitants', *Wimbledon and Merton Annual* 1903, 9–25.

—— 'Street Architecture', *Journal of the Society of Arts* 53 (1904–5), 107–18.

—— 'The Education of the Public in Architecture', *Transactions of the Seventh International Congress of Architects* (1906), 1–8 (reprinted in the *Builder* 94 [1908], 479, as 'The Weakness of the Architectural Amateur').

—— *Reason in Architecture* (1906).

—— 'Winchester Cathedral: an account of the building and of the repairs now in progress', *Transactions of the St Paul's Ecclesiological Society* 6 (1910), 217–36.

—— *Byzantine and Romanesque Architecture* (2 vols.; Cambridge, 1913; 2nd edn, 1920).

—— *Gothic Architecture in France, England and Italy* (2 vols.; Cambridge, 1915).

—— 'Avallon and the French Portals', *Country Life* 39 (1916), 736–8.

—— *A Holiday in Umbria* (1917).

—— 'The Churches of Serbia', *Proceedings of the Society of Antiquaries of London* 30 (1917–18), 10–17.

—— 'Serbian Church Architecture', in M. I. Pupin, ed., *South Slav Monuments I: the Serbian Orthodox Church* (1918).

—— *Six Ghost Stories* (1919; Ashcroft, British Columbia, 1999).

—— 'Some Account of St Mary's, the parish church of Wimbledon', *Surrey Archaeological Collections* 34 (1921), 1–14.

—— *The Renaissance of Roman Architecture* (3 vols.; Cambridge, 1921–3).

—— *Memories of Travel* (Cambridge, 1923).

—— *Architecture* (1925; reissued 1932).

—— *Recollections*, ed. Basil H. Jackson (Oxford, 1950).

—— *Recollections: the life and travels of a Victorian architect*, ed., Sir Nicholas Jackson (2003).

—— and Shaw, R. Norman, eds., *Architecture: a profession or an art* (1892).

—— and Style, George, *Giggleswick School: notes on the history of the school and an account of the new chapel* (Oxford 1901).

Johnson, A. H., *History of the Worshipful Company of Drapers* (5 vols.; Oxford, 1914–22).

Jones, Owen, 'An Attempt to Define the Principles which should Regulate the Employment of Colour in the Decorative Arts', *Lectures on the Results of the Great Exhibition of 1851* (1853), 253–300.

Lamb, Charles, *Elia and the Last Letters of Elia* (1912).

Langley, J. N., 'University of Cambridge Department of Physiology', *Methods and Problems of Medical Education* (New York, 1925), 8–13.

Laurie, J. S., *Rileyism and Bigotry versus Reason and Common Sense: an episode in the London School Board* (1890).

Leach, Arthur F., *A History of Bradfield College* (1900).

Lethaby, W. R., *Architecture, Mysticism and Myth* (1892).

—— *Medieval Art* (1904).

—— *Architecture* (1911).

—— 'Richard Phené Spiers', *RIBA Journal* 3rd series 23 (1916), 334.

—— *Form in Civilisation* (1922).

—— *Philip Webb and his Work* (1935).

Lilley, Henry T., and Everitt, Alfred T., *Portsmouth Parish Church* (Portsmouth, 1921).

Loftie, M. J., *The Dining Room* (1878).

Loftie, W. J., *A Plea for Art in the House* (1876).

—— 'Thorough Restoration', *Macmillan's Magazine* 36 (1877), 136–42.

—— *Kensington, picturesque and historical* (1888).

McDonnell, Michael F. J., *A History of St. Paul's School* (1909).

Mackail, J. W., *The Life of William Morris* (1899; 2 vols. in 1: 1995).

Mackenzie, Compton, *Sinister Street* (2 vols.; 1913–14).

Macnamara, T. J., 'Three Years Progressivism at the London School Board', *Fortnightly Review* 74 (1900), 790–802.

Mallock, W. H., *The Old Order Changes* (3 vols.; 1886).

Mallows, C. E., 'The Complete Work of T. G. Jackson', *Architectural Review* 1 (1896–7), 136–62.

Marshall, Mary Paley, *What I Remember* (Cambridge, 1947).

Maxwell-Lyte, H. C., *A History of Eton College, 1440–1910* (1911).

[Millar, J. H.], 'Mr. Jowett and Oxford Liberalism', *Blackwood's Magazine* 1897, 721–32.

Minchin, J. G. Cotton, *Our Public Schools: their influence on English History* (1901).

Morris, William, *Gothic Architecture* (1893).

—— *Art and Its Producers* (1901).

—— *Collected Works*, ed., May Morris (24 vols.; 1910–15).

—— *Collected Letters*, ed., Norman Kelvin (4 vols.; Princeton, 1984–96).

Müller, Max, *My Autobiography* (1901).

Munby, Alan E., *Laboratories: their plannings and fittings* (1921).

Murray, David, *Museums: their history and their use* (3 vols.; Glasgow, 1904).

Myers, C. S., 'The Influence of the late W. H. R. Rivers', in W. H. R. Rivers, *Psychology and Politics* (1923), 154–80.

Nettleship, R. L., *Memoir of Thomas Hill Green* (1906).

Ollivant, Alfred, *Sermon Preached in the Chapel of St. David's College, Lampeter on the 24th June 1880* (Oxford and Cambridge, 1880).

Oman, Carola, *An Oxford Childhood* (1976).

Oman, Charles, *Memories of Victorian Oxford* (1942).

Order of Proceedings and Description of the Buildings Opened by Their Majesties the King and Queen (Cambridge, 1904).

Page, T. E., ed., *The Public Schools from Within* (1906).

Parkin, George R., *Edward Thring: headmaster of Uppingham School* (2 vols.; 1898).

Parry, R. St. John, *Henry Jackson O.M.* (Cambridge, 1926).

Paton, A. A., *Highlands and Islands of the Adriatic* (2 vols.; 1844).

Pattison, Mark, *Suggestions on Academical Organisation* (Edinburgh, 1868).

Philpott, Hugh B., *London at School: the story of the School Board* (1904).

Pitt-Lewis, G., *The History of the Temple* (1898).

Plass, Victor G., *Men and Women of the Time* (15th edn; 1899).

Powell, Harry J., 'Table Glass', *Architectural Review* 6 (1899), 51–5.

—— *Glass-Making in England* (Cambridge, 1923).

Prior, Edward, *A History of Gothic Art in England* (1900).

Pugin, A. N. W., *The True Principals of 'Pointed' or 'Christian' Architecture* (1841).

—— *Contrasts* (2nd edn, 1841; Leicester, 1975).

Raikes, T. D., *Sicut Columbae, fifty years of St. Peter's College, Radley* (1897).

Rashdall, Hastings, and Rait, Robert S., *New College* (1901).

Raverat, Gwen, *Period Piece* (1952).

Reilly, C. H., *Scaffolding in the Sky* (1938).

Report of the Schools Inquiry Commission (21 vols.; 1868–70).

Rhoades, H. T., *A Handbook to Rugby School Chapel* (Rugby, 1913).

'R.H.R', *Rambles in Istria, Dalmatia, and Montenegro* (1875).

Riley, Athelstan, *The Anglican Theory of the Catholic Church* (1916).

—— *Eastern Christendom* (1930).

Rivers, W. H. R., 'The Unity of Anthropology', *Journal of the Anthropological Institute* 52 (1922), 12–25.

Roberts, Mrs E. S., *Sherborne, Oxford and Cambridge* (1934).

Robson, E. R., *School Architecture* (1874; Leicester, 1972).

Rowbotham, John Frederick, *The History of Rossall School* (Manchester, 1894).

Ruskin, John, *Complete Works*, ed., E. J. Cook and A. Wedderburn (39 vols.; London, 1903–9).

Sayce, A. H., 'Results of the Examination System at Oxford', in C. E. Appleton, ed., *Essays on the Endowment of Research* (1876), 124–48.

—— *Reminiscences* (1923).

Scott, G. G., *Plea for the Faithful Restoration of Our Ancient Churches* (1850).

—— *Remarks on Secular and Domestic Architecture* (1857).

—— *Gleanings from Westminster Abbey* (Oxford and London, 1861).

—— 'Thorough Anti-Restoration', *Macmillan's Magazine* 36 (1877), 228–37.

—— *Lectures on the Rise and Development of Medieval Architecture* (2 vols.; 1878–9).

—— *Personal and Professional Recollections* (1879; Stamford, 1995).

Scott, G. G. (junior), *An Essay on the History of English Church Architecture* (1881).

Scott, Geoffrey, *The Architecture of Humanism* (1914).

Shaw, G. B., *Immaturity* (written 1879; 1930).

Shaw, R. Norman, *Architectural Sketches from the Continent* (1858).

Shipley, A. E., *'J', a Memoir of John Willis Clark* (1913).

Smith, Goldwin, 'Oxford University Reform', in *Oxford Essays* (1858), 265–87.

[Smith, Mary Florence], *Arthur Lionel Smith* (1928).

[Social Purity Alliance], *Schoolboy Morality: an address to mothers* (1888).

Spring Gardens Sketch Book (8 vols.; 1870–90).

Stanley, A. P., *The Life and Correspondence of Thomas Arnold* (10th ed.; 1877).

Stedman, Algernon M. M., *Oxford: its social and intellectual life* (1878).

Stephen, Leslie, *Sketches from Cambridge by a Don* (1865).

Stephens, W. R. W., *The Life and Letters of Edward A. Freeman* (2 vols.; 1895).

Stevenson, J. J., 'On the Recent Reaction of Taste in English Architecture', *Architect* 11 (1874), suppl. 9–10.

—— 'Queen Anne and Other Forms of Free Classicism', *Architect* 13 (1875), 125–6.

—— 'Architectural Restoration: its principles and practice', *RIBA Transactions* 1876–7, 219–35.

—— *House Architecture* (2 vols.; 1880).

Strangford, Viscountess, *The Eastern Shores of the Adriatic* (1864).

Street, G. E., *Gothic Architecture in Spain* (1865).

Tanner, Lawrence E., *Westminster School: its buildings and their associations* (1923).

—— *Westminster School* (1951).

Taylor, J. R., Brentnall, H. C., and Turner, G. C., eds., *A History of Marlborough College* (1923).

Temple, William, *Life of Bishop Percival* (1921).

Thompson, Henry L., *Henry George Liddell: A memoir* (1899).

—— *Four Biographical Sermons* (1905).

Thornton, Percy M., *Harrow School and its Surroundings* (1885).

Thring, Edward, *Addresses* (1887).

Trollope, Anthony, *The Way We Live Now* (2 vols. in 1, 1875; Oxford, 1999).

Tyrwhitt, R. St John, *Greek and Gothic: progress and decay in the three arts of architecture, sculpture, and painting* (1881).

Underdown, E. M., 'The Inner Temple', in E. Blake Odgers, ed., *Six Lectures on the Inns of Court and of Chancery* (1912).

Vernon, H. M and K. Dorothea, *A History of the Oxford Museum* (Oxford, 1909).

Viollet-le-Duc, E., *Entretiens sur l'Architecture* (2 vols.; Paris, 1863–72).

—— *The Habitations of Man in All Ages* (trans. Benjamin Bucknall; 1876).

Ward, Humphry, *History of the Athenaeum, 1824–1925* (1926).

Ward, Mary (Mrs Humphry), *A Writer's Recollections* (1918).

Waugh, Francis Gledstanes, *The Athenaeum* (1900).

[Wedgwood, Julia], 'The Moral Influence of George Eliot', *Contemporary Review* 39 (1881), 173–85.

[Wells, John], 'Sir Thomas Jackson' *Oxford Magazine* 43 (1924–5), 126–7.

Wilkinson, J. Gardner, *Dalmatia and Montenegro* (2 vols.; 1848).

Willis, Robert, *Remarks on the Architecture of the Middle Ages, Especially of Italy* (Cambridge, 1835).

—— and Clark, John Willis, *The Architectural History of the University of Cambridge* (1886; 3 vols., 1988).

Woodward, Horace B., *History of Geology* (1911).

Wren, Christopher, *Parentalia* (1750).

Wren Society (19 vols.; 1928–42).

SECONDARY MATERIAL

1. Published

Adams, Pauline, *Somerville for Women: an Oxford college, 1897–1993* (Oxford, 1996).

Allen, G. A. T., and Allen, J. E., *Christ's Hospital* (1984).

Allen, Peter, 'The Meanings of "An Intellectual": nineteenth- and twentieth-century English usage', *University of Toronto Quarterly* 55 (1986), 342–58.

Allibone, Jill, *Anthony Salvin: pioneer of Gothic Revival Architecture* (Cambridge, 1987).

Allom, V. M., *Ex Oriente Salus: a centenary history of Eastbourne College* (Eastbourne, 1967).

Allsobrook, David Ian, *Schools for the Shires* (Manchester and New York, 1986).

Allsopp, Bruce, *The Study of Architectural History* (1970).

Annan, Noel, 'The Intellectual Aristocracy', in J. H. Plumb, ed., *Studies in Social History* (1955); reprinted in Annan, *The Dons* (1999).

Anscombe, Isabelle, *A Woman's Touch: women in design from 1860* (1986).

Arkell, W. J., *Oxford Stone* (Oxford, 1947).

Atherstone, Andrew, 'The Martyrs' Memorial at Oxford', *Journal of Ecclesiastical History* 54 (2003), 278–301.

Attwater, Aubrey, *Pembroke College Cambridge: a short history* (Cambridge, 1936).

Baker, J. H., *The Third University of England* (1990).

—— *An Introduction to English Legal History* (3rd edn.; 1990).

—— *The Inner Temple* (1991).

Bamford, T. W., *The Rise of the Public Schools* (1967).

Banham, Reyner, *Theory and Design in the First Machine Age* (1960; Oxford, 1992).

Barnard, E. K., *Parish Church to Portsmouth Cathedral, 1900–1939* (Portsmouth Papers 52, 1988).

Bassin, Joan, *Architectural Competitions in Nineteenth-Century England* (Ann Arbor, 1984).

Bell, Quentin, *The Schools of Design* (1963).

Bendall, Sarah, Brooke, Christopher, and Collinson, Patrick, *A History of Emmanuel College, Cambridge* (1999).

Bettley, James, *T. G. Jackson: an exhibition of his Oxford buildings* (Oxford, 1983).

—— 'T. G. Jackson and the Examination Schools', *Oxford Art Journal* 6/1 (1983), 57–66.

Betts, Robin, *Dr. Macnamara, 1861–1931* (1999).

Bićanić, Sonia, 'T. G. Jackson's *Recollections* and his campanile at Zadar', *Slavonica* 22/1 (1994–5), 29–38.

Blumenau, Ralph, *A History of Malvern College* (1965).

Boase, T. S. R., *English Art, 1800–1870* (Oxford, 1959).

Bonta, Juan Pablo, *Architecture and Its Interpretation* (1979).

Bonython, Elizabeth and Burton, Anthony, *The Great Exhibitor: the life and work of Henry Cole* (2003).

Booker, John, *Temples of Mammon* (Edinburgh, 1990).

Bourdieu, Pierre, *Homo Academicus* (trans. Peter Collier; Cambridge, 1990).

—— *Distinction* (trans. Richard Nice; 1996).

—— *Rules of Art* (trans. Susan Emmanuel; Oxford, 1996).

—— and Passeron, J.-C., *Reproduction* (trans. Richard Nice; 1990).

Boyd, A. K., *The History of Radley College, 1847–1947* (Oxford, 1948).

Brandon-Jones, John, 'Letters of Philip Webb and his Contemporaries', *Architectural History* 8 (1964), 52–72.

—— 'Architects and The Art-Workers' Guild', *Journal of the Royal Society of Arts* 121 (1972–3), 192–206.

—— 'W. R. Lethaby and the Art-Workers' Guild', in Sylvia Backemeyer and Theresa Gronberg, eds., *W. R. Lethaby 1857–1931* (1984), 32–41.

Bremner, G. Alex, ' "Some Imperial Institute": architecture, symbolism, and the ideal of empire in late Victorian Britain, 1887–93', *Journal of the Society of Architectural Historians* 62 (2003), 50–73.

Bridgwater, Patrick, *Schopenhauer's English Schooling* (1988).

Briggs, Asa, *Victorian Cities* (1968).

—— and Snowman, Daniel, eds., *Fins de Siècle* (1996).

Briggs, Martin S., *Goths and Vandals* (1952).

Brock, M. G., and Curthoys, M. C., eds., *The History of the University of Oxford, vol. vi: nineteenth-century Oxford, part 1* (Oxford, 1997).

—— *The History of the University of Oxford, vol. vii: nineteenth-century Oxford, part 2* (Oxford, 2000).

Brock, W. R., and Cooper, P. H. M., *Selwyn College: a history* (Durham, 1994).

Brooke, Christopher N. L., *A History of the University of Cambridge: vol. iv, 1870–1990* (Cambridge, 1993).

Brooks, Chris, *The Gothic Revival* (1999).

—— (ed.) *The Albert Memorial* (2001).

Brooks, Michael W., *John Ruskin and Victorian Architecture* (1989).

Brown, Ford K., *Fathers of the Victorians* (Cambridge, 1966).

Brown, W. J., *So Far . . .* (1943).

Brownlee, David, ' "A Regular Mongrel Affair": G. G. Scott's Design for the Government Offices', *Architectural History* 28 (1985), 159–78.

Bryans, E., *Sicut Columbae: a history of S.Peter's College, Radley, 1847–1922* (Oxford, 1925).

Budden, Lionel B., ed., *The Book of the Liverpool School of Architecture* (1932).

Burrow, J. W., *Evolution and Society* (Cambridge, 1966).

Bussby, Frederick, *Winchester Cathedral 1079–1979* (Southampton, 1979).

Butler, C. MacArthur, *The Society of Architects* (1926).

Cannadine, David, *Aspects of Aristocracy* (1994).

Carleton, John D., *Westminster School: a history* (1965).

Catleugh, Jon, et al., eds., *William De Morgan Tiles* (1983).

Cavell, John, and Kennett, Brian, *A History of Sir Roger Manwood's School, Sandwich* (1963).

Chapmen, Arthur W., *The Story of a Modern University: a history of the University of Sheffield* (1955).

Cherniavsky, M. T., and Money, A. E., *Looking at Radley: an architectural and historical survey of the earlier buildings* (Radley, 1981).

Clapp, B. W., *The University of Exeter* (Exeter, 1982).

Clark, Kenneth, *The Gothic Revival* (1928; 1995).

—— *Another Part of the Wood* (1974).

Clarke, Basil F. L., *Church Builders of the Nineteenth Century* (2nd edn; 1969).

Clarke, Dennis, and Stoyel, Anthony, *Otford in Kent: a history* (Otford, 1975).

Clegg, Jeanne, *Ruskin and Venice* (1981).

Cole, David, *The Work of Sir Gilbert Scott* (1980).

Collini, Stefan, *Public Moralists* (Oxford, 1991).

Colvin, Howard, *Unbuilt Oxford* (1983).

—— 'Architecture', in L. S. Sutherland and L. G. Mitchell, eds., *History of the University of Oxford, vol. v: the eighteenth century* (Oxford, 1986) 831–56.

Cooper, Jeremy, *Victorian and Edwardian Furniture and Interiors* (1987).

Cottrill, D. J., *Victoria College, Jersey* (1977).

Craster, Edmund, *The History of the Bodleian Library 1845–1945* (Oxford, 1952).

Crawford, Alan, *By Hammer and By Hand: the arts and crafts movement in Birmingham* (Birmingham, 1984).

—— *C. R. Ashbee: architect, designer and romantic socialist* (1985).

—— 'Sources of Inspiration in the Arts and Crafts Movement', in Sarah Macready and F. H. Thompson, eds., *Influences in Victorian Art and Architecture* (1985), 155–60.

Crinson, Mark, *Empire Building* (1996).

—— and Lubbock, Jules, *Architecture Art or Profession?* (Manchester and New York, 1994).

Crook, J. Mordaunt, 'The Pre-Victorian Architect: professionalism and patronage', *Architectural History* 12 (1969), 62–78.

—— *The Greek Revival* (1972).

—— 'Introduction', J. T. Emmett, *Six Essays* (1891; New York and London, 1972), v–xvi.

—— 'Sidney Smirke: the architecture of compromise' in Jane Fawcett, ed., *Seven Victorian Architects* (1976), 50–65.

—— *William Burges and the High Victorian Dream* (1981).

—— 'T. G. Jackson and the Cult of Eclecticism' in H. Searing, ed., *In Search of Modern Architecture* (New York, 1982), 102–20.

—— 'Ruskinian Gothic', in John Dixon Hunt and Faith M. Holland, eds., *The Ruskin Polygon* (Manchester, 1982), 68–71.

—— *The Dilemma of Style: architectural ideas from the picturesque to the post-modern* (1987).

—— 'The Architectural Image', in F. M. L. Thompson, ed., *The University of London and the World of Learning* (1990), 1–34.

—— *John Carter and the Mind of the Gothic Revival* (1995).

—— *The Rise of the Nouveaux Riches: style and status in Victorian and Edwardian architecture* (1999).

—— *The Architect's Secret: Victorian critics and the image of gravity* (2003).

Cumming, Elizabeth, and Kaplan, Wendy, *The Arts and Crafts Movement* (1991).

Cunningham, Colin, *Victorian and Edwardian Town Halls* (1981).

—— and Waterhouse, Prudence, *Alfred Waterhouse, 1830–1905: biography of a practice* (Oxford, 1992).

Dakers, Caroline, *The Holland Park Circle* (1999).

Dale, Antony, *James Wyatt* (Oxford, 1956).

Daniel, Glyn, *Cambridge and the Back-Looking Curiosity* (Cambridge, 1976).

Darby, E. and M., 'The Nation's Memorial to Victoria', *Country Life* 164 (1978), 1647–50.

Davey, Peter, *Arts and Crafts Architecture* (1995).

Davies, C. S. L. and Garnett, Jane, eds., *Wadham College* (Oxford, 1994).

Deane, Anthony Charles, *Great Malvern Priory Church* (1926).

Dixon, Roger, ed., *Sir George Gilbert Scott and the Scott Dynasty* (South Bank Architectural Papers I, 1980).

—— and Muthesius, Stefan, *Victorian Architecture* (1985).

Donne, Tom, '*La trahaison des clercs*: British intellectuals and the first home rule crisis', *Irish Historical Studies* 23 (1982), 134–73.

Donnelly, James S., *The Land and the People of Nineteenth Century Cork* (1975).

Donovan, Marcus, *After the Tractarians: from the recollections of Athelstan Riley* (Glasgow, 1933).

Draper, F. W. M., *Four Centuries of Merchant Taylors' School, 1561–1961* (1962).

Draper, Peter, ed., *Reassessing Nikolaus Pevsner* (Aldershot, 2004).

Dunbabin, J. P. D., 'Oxford and Cambridge College Finances 1871–1913', *Economic History Review* 2nd Ser., 28 (1975), 631–47.

Dunlop, John, *The Pleasant Town of Sevenoaks* (Sevenoaks, 1964).

Engel, A. J., *From Clergyman to Don: the rise of the academic profession in nineteenth-century Oxford* (Oxford, 1983).

English Heritage, *London's Town Halls* (1999).

Evans, Wendy, Ross, Catherine, and Werner, Alex, *Whitefriars Glass* (1993).

Faber, Geoffrey, *Jowett: A portrait with background* (London, 1957).

Fawcett, Jane, ed., *The Future of the Past* (London, 1976).

Fellows, Richard A., *Sir Reginald Blomfield: an Edwardian architect* (1985).

Fox, Adam, *English Hymns and Hymn Writers* (1947).

Frankl, Paul, *The Gothic* (Princeton, 1960).

Franklin, Jill, *The Gentleman's Country House and Its Plan* (1981).

Frayling, Christopher, *The Royal College of Art* (1987).

French, Stanley, *The History of Downing College, Cambridge* (Cambridge, 1978).

Friedman, Terry, *James Gibbs* (1984).

Furness, W., ed., *The Centenary History of Rossall School* (1945).

Gambler, Jacques, 'In Search of the Primitive', *Architectural Design Profile* 27 (1980), 80–3.

Geison, Gerald L., *Michael Foster and the Cambridge School of Physiology* (Princeton, 1978).

Geraghty, Anthony, 'Wren's Preliminary Design for the Sheldonian Theatre', *Architectural History* 45 (2002), 275–88.

Germann, Georg, *Gothic Revival in Europe and Britain* (1972).

Girouard, Mark, 'Attitudes to Elizabethan Architecture', in John Summerson, ed., *Concerning Architecture* (London, 1968), 13–27.

—— 'Victorian Sweetness and Light, Newnham College, Cambridge', *Country Life* 150 (1971), 1704–6.

—— 'The Architecture of John James Stevenson', *The Connoisseur* 184 (1973), 166–74; 185 (1974), 106–12.

—— *Sweetness and Light: the 'Queen Anne' movement, 1860–1900* (Oxford, 1977).

Girtin, Tom, *The Triple Crowns: a narrative history of the Drapers' Company, 1364–1964* (1964).

Golant, William, *Image of Empire: the early history of the Imperial Institute* (Exeter, 1984).

Goldman, Lawrence, *Dons and Workers: Oxford and adult education since 1850* (Oxford, 1995).

—— 'Intellectuals and the English Working Class 1870–1945: the case of Adult Education', *History of Education* 29/4 (2000), 281–300.

—— *Science, Reform, and Politics in Victorian Britain: the Social Science Association 1857–1886* (Cambridge, 2002).

Goodhart-Rendel, H. S., 'The Works of Sir T. G. Jackson', *RIBA Journal* 33 (1926), 467–77.

—— *Vitruvian Nights: papers upon architectural subjects* (1932).

—— *Architecture since the Regency* (1953).

Gosden, P. H. J. H., and Taylor, A. J., eds., *Studies in the History of a University 1874–1974* (Leeds, 1975).

Goudie, Andrew, ed., *Seven Hundred Years of an Oxford College* (Oxford, 1984).

Gray, A. Stewart, *Edwardian Architecture* (1985).

Gray, Arthur, and Brittain, Frederick, *A History of Jesus College, Cambridge* (1979).

Green, V. H. H., *Oxford Common Room: a study of Lincoln College and Mark Pattison* (1957).

—— *The Commonwealth of Lincoln College, 1427–1977* (Oxford, 1979).

Greensted, Mary, *Gimson and the Barnsleys* (Stroud, 1980).

Haig, A. G. L., 'The Church, the Universities and Learning in Later Victorian England', *Historical Journal* 29 (1986), 187–201.

Hall, Michael, 'The Rise of Refinement: G. F. Bodley's All Saints', Cambridge, and the return to English models in the Gothic architecture of the 1860s', *Architectural History* 36 (1993), 103–26.

Hamilton, Mary Agnes, *Newnham: an informal biography* (1936).

Hardy, Emma, 'Farmer and Brindley: craftsmen sculptors 1850–1930', *Victorian Society Annual* 1993, 4–17.

Hearn, M. F., *The Architectural Theory of Viollet-le-Duc* (Cambridge, Mass., 1990).

Harper, Roger H., *Victorian Architectural Competitions* (1983).

Harris, José, *Private Lives, Public Spirit: Britain, 1870–1914* (1994).

Harvey, Charles, and Press, Jon, *William Morris: design and enterprise in Victorian Britain* (Manchester and New York, 1993).

Harvie, Christopher, *The Lights of Liberalism* (1976).

Hearl, Trevor, 'Military Academies and English Education: a review of some published material', *History of Education Society Bulletin* (1968), 11–21.

Hearnshaw, L. S., *A Short History of British Psychology* (1964).

Heeney, Brian, *Mission to the Middle Classes: the Woodard Schools* (1969).

Henderson, Ian T., and Crook, John, *The Winchester Diver: the saving of a great cathedral* (Crawley, 1984).

Herle, Anita, and Rowse, Sandra, eds., *Cambridge and the Torres Strait* (Cambridge, 1998).

Herrmann, Luke, 'William Turner of Oxford', *Oxoniensia* 26/27 (1961/2), 312–18.

Hersey, George L., *High Victorian Gothic: a study in associationism* (1972).

Heseltine, Joanna, ed., *The Scott Family: a catalogue of the drawings collection of the RIBA* (1981).

Heyck, T. W., *The Transformation of Intellectual Life in Victorian England* (1982).

Hibbert, Christopher, *No Ordinary Place: Radley College and the public school system* (1997).

Hickson, Alisdaire, *The Poisoned Bowl: sex and the public school system* (1995).

Hinchcliffe, Tanis, *North Oxford* (1992).

Hinde, Thomas, *A Great Day School in London: a history of King's College School* (1995).

History of All Saints' School, Bloxham (2nd ed.; Bloxham, 1925).

Holbrook, Diana, 'The Restoration of Winchester Cathedral by Thomas G. Jackson, 1905–12', *Transactions of the Association for Studies in the Conservation of Historic Buildings* 11 (1986), 48–71.

Hollamby, Edward, *Red House* (1991).

Honey, J. R. de S., *Tom Brown's Universe* (1977).

Honey, W. B., *Glass* (1946).

Hope-Simpson, J. B., *Rugby since Arnold* (1967).

Hopkins, Clare, *Trinity: 450 years of an Oxford college community* (Oxford, 2005).

Horowitz, Helen Lefkowitz, *Alma Mater: design and experience in the women's colleges from their nineteenth-century beginnings to the 1930s* (New York, 1984).

Howarth, Janet, 'Science Teaching in late-Victorian Oxford: a curious case of failure?' *English Historical Review* 102 (1987), 334–71.

Howell, Peter, 'Architecture and Townscape since 1800', in R. C. Whiting, ed., *Oxford: studies in the history of a university town* (Manchester, 1993), 53–84.

—— 'Oxford Architecture 1800–1914', in M. G. Brock and M. C. Curthoys, eds., *The History of the University of Oxford, vol. vii: nineteenth-century Oxford, part 2*, (Oxford, 2000), 729–80.

—— ' "The Disastrous Deformation of Butterfield": Balliol College Chapel in the twentieth century', *Architectural History* 44 (2001), 283–92.

Hughes, Quentin, 'Education and the Architectural Profession in Britain at the Turn of the Century', *Art and Design Education* 1 (1982), 135–44.

—— 'Before the Bauhaus: the experiment at the Liverpool School of Architecture and its Applied Arts', *Architectural History* 25 (1982), 102–13.

Hunt, John, *Education in Evolution* (1971).

Hunt, John Dixon, *The Wider Sea: a life of John Ruskin* (New York, 1982).

Ives, Eric, 'A New Campus', in Eric Ives, Diane Drummond, and Leonard Schwarz, eds., *The First Civic University: Birmingham, 1880–1980* (Birmingham, 2000), 111–30.

Jackson, Neil, *Nineteenth-Century Bath Architects and Architecture* (Bath, 1991).

Jackson-Stops, Gervase, 'Castle Ashby, Northamptonshire', *Country Life* 179 (1986), 248–53, 310–15.

Jenkins, Frank, *Architect and Patron* (1962).

Jones, John, *Balliol College: a history* (2nd edn; Oxford, 1997).

Jones, Martin D. W., *A Short History of Brighton College* (Brighton, 1986).

—— 'Gothic Enriched: Thomas Jackson's mural tablets in Brighton College Chapel', *Church Monuments* 6 (1991), 54–66.

—— *Brighton College, 1845–1995* (Chichester, 1995).

Kaye, Barrington, *The Development of the Architectural Profession in England* (1960).

Kaye, Elaine, *Mansfield College: its origin, history, and significance* (Oxford, 1996).

Kelsall, Frank, 'The Board Schools: school building 1870–1914', in Ron Ringshall, Margaret Miles, and Frank Kelsall, eds., *The Urban School: buildings for education in London, 1870–1980* (1983), 13–28.

Laborde, E. D., *Harrow School, Yesterday and Today* (1948).

Lambourne, Lionel, *Utopian Craftsmen: the arts and crafts movement from the Cotswolds to Chicago* (1980).

Langham, Ian, *The Building of British Social Anthropology: W. H. R. Rivers and his Cambridge disciples* (1981).

Lawson, F. H., *The Oxford Law School, 1850–1965* (Oxford, 1968).

Le Goff, Jacques, *Intellectuals in the Middle Ages* (trans. T. L. Fagan; Oxford, 1993).

Leedham-Green, Elisabeth, *A Concise History of the University of Cambridge* (Cambridge, 1996).

Lewis, W. J., *A History of Lampeter* (Ceredigion, 1997).

Lowe, R. A., and Knight, Rex, 'Building the Ivory Tower: the social function of late nineteenth-century collegiate architecture', *Studies in Higher Education* 7/2 (1982), 81–91.

Lucas, E. V., *The Colvins and Their Friends* (1928).

Macaulay, James, *The Gothic Revival, 1745–1845* (1975).

McCorquodale, Duncan, ed., *The Inns of Court* (1996).

MacDonald, Alec, *A Short History of Repton* (1929).

Macdonald, Stuart, *The History and Philosophy of Art Education* (1970).

MacKinnon, Frank Douglas, *Inner Temple Papers* (1948).

Macleod, Roy, and Moseley, Russell, 'The "naturals" and Victorian Cambridge: reflections on the anatomy of an elite 1851–1914', *Oxford Review of Education* 6 (1980), 177–95.

Mack, Edward C., *Public Schools and British Opinion since 1860* (1941).

Mangan, J. A., *Athleticism in the Victorian and Edwardian Public School* (Cambridge, 1981).

Marnane, Denis G., *Land and Violence: a history of West Tipperary from 1660* (Tipperary, 1985).

Martin, Alistair, 'Oxford Jackson', *Oxoniensia* 43 (1978), 216–21.

Massé, H. J. L., *The Art-Workers' Guild* (Oxford, 1935).

Matthews, Bryan, *By God's Grace . . . a history of Uppingham School* (Maidstone, 1984).

Mead, G. C. F., Evans, R. J., and Savory, T. H., *The History and Register of Aldenham School* (1938).

Miele, Chris, ' "A small knot of cultivated people": William Morris and ideologies of protection', *Art Journal* 54 (1995), 73–9.

—— 'The First Conservation Militants', in Michael Hunter, *Preserving the Past: the rise of heritage in modern Britain* (Stroud, 1996), 20–7.

—— 'Real Antiquity and the Ancient Object: the science of Gothic architecture and the restoration of medieval buildings', in Vanessa Brand, ed., *The Study of the Past in the Victorian Age* (Oxford, 1998), 103–24.

—— ed., *From William Morris: building conservation and the arts and crafts cult of authenticity, 1877–1939* (New Haven and London, 2005).

Mitchell, W. R., *Walter Morrison: a millionaire at Malham Tarn* (Settle, 1990).

Money, Tony, *Manly and Muscular Diversions* (1997).

Morgan, M. C., *Cheltenham College: the first hundred years* (Chalfont St Giles, 1968).

Morris, Barbara, *Victorian Table Glass and Ornaments* (1978).

Muthesius, Stefan, *The High Victorian Movement in British Architecture* (1972).

Naylor, Gillian, *The Arts and Crafts Movement* (1990).

Newsome, David, *A History of Wellington College* (1959).

—— *Godliness and Good Learning* (1961).

—— *The Victorian World Picture* (1998).

Nicolson, Nigel, *Cranbrook School* (1974).

Nolan, William, ed., *Tipperary: history and society* (Dublin, 1985).

Norbury, Wendy, 'Oxford Town Hall: planning, building and financing the Oxford municipal buildings of 1897', *Oxoniensia* 65 (2000), 133–59.

Norton, Richard, 'Henry Boyd and Thomas Graham Jackson: their rowing exploits', *Hertford College Magazine* 82 (1995–7), 106–11.

Oswald, Arthur, 'Catton Hall, Derbyshire', *Country Life* 127 (1960), 566–9, 624–7.

Otto, Karl, ed., *School Buildings* (1966).

Park, Jo, *Athelstan Riley, Patron of St. Petroc Minor, Little Petherick* (Truro, 1982).

Parry, Linda, *Textiles of the Arts and Crafts Movement* (1988).

—— ed., *William Morris 1834–1896* (1996).

Percival, Alicia C., *The Origins of the Headmasters' Conference* (1969).

Perkin, Harold, *The Rise of Professional Society* (1989).

Peterson, William S., *Victorian Heretic: Mrs Humphry Ward's* Robert Elsmere (Leicester, 1976).

Pevsner, Nikolaus, *Outline of European Architecture* (1948).

—— *Studies in Art, Architecture and Design* (2 vols.; 1968).

—— et al., *The Buildings of England* (52 vols.; 1951–).

Philips, Ann, ed., *A Newnham Anthology* (Cambridge, 1979).

Physick, John, *The Victoria and Albert Museum: a history of its buildings* (Oxford, 1982).

Pickles, J. D., 'The Haddon Library, Cambridge', *Library History* 8 (1988), 1–9.

Plunkett, John, 'Remembering Victoria', *The Victorian* 1 (1999), 4–9.

Poole, Anthony, *A History of Wimbledon College* (Wimbledon, 1992).

Port, M. H., *Imperial London* (1998).

Porter, Roy, 'Gentlemen and Geology: the emergence of a scientific career, 1660–1920', *Historical Journal* (1978), 809–36.

—— 'The Natural Science Tripos and "the Cambridge School of Geology" ', *History of Universities* 2 (1982), 193–216.

Potter, Jeremy, *Headmaster: the life of John Percival, radical autocrat* (1998).

Powers, Alan, 'Liverpool and Architectural Education', in Joseph Sharples, Alan Powers, Michael Shippobottom, eds., *Charles Reilly and the Liverpool School of Architecture* (Liverpool, 1996), 1–24.

Price, D. T. W., *A History of St. David's University College, Lampeter* (2 vols.; Cardiff, 1977–90).

Prothero, H. A., and Owen, H. A., *Cheltenham College Chapel* (Cheltenham, 1928).

Proudlock, Noel, *Giggleswick School Chapel* (Leeds, 1997).

Quiggin, A. Hingston, *Haddon the Head Hunter* (Cambridge, 1942).

Quiney, Anthony, *John Loughborough Pearson* (1979).

Rankin, William, 'Trinity, Glenalmond', *Anglican World* 7/2 (1967), 38.

Rawle, Tim, *Cambridge Architecture* (1993).

Rayner, Christopher, *Sevenoaks Past* (Chichester, 1997).

Reader, W. J., *Professional Men: the rise of the professional classes in nineteenth-century England* (1966).

Richards, A. N. G., *St. Paul's School in West Kensington, 1884–1968* (1968).

Richter, Melvin, *The Politics of Conscience: T. H. Green and his age* (Bristol, 1996).

Roach, J. P. C, 'Liberalism and the Victorian Intelligentsia', *Cambridge Historical Journal* 13 (1957), 58–81.

—— 'Victorian Universities and the National Intelligentsia', *Victorian Studies* 3 (1959), 131–50.

—— *Secondary Education in England* (1991).

Roberts, Andrew, *Salisbury: Victorian titan* (1999).

Roberts, S. C., ed., *A History of Brighton College* (Brighton, 1957).

Robinson, Duncan H., *Cranbrook School* (Cranbrook, 1971).

Rogers, Malcolm, *Montacute House* (1991).

Roll-Hansen, Diderick, *The Academy 1869–1879, Victorian Intellectuals in Revolt* (Copenhagen, 1957).

Rothblatt, Sheldon, *The Revolution of the Dons: Cambridge and society in Victorian England* (1968).

Rubens, Godfrey, *William Richard Lethaby: his life and work, 1857–1931* (1986).

Rubinstein, W. D., *Elites and the Wealthy in Modern British History* (Brighton and New York, 1987).

Rückbrod, Konrad, *Universität und Kollegium Baugeschichte und Bautyp* (Darmstadt, 1977).

Rudoe, Judy, and Coutts, Howard, 'The Table-glass Designs of Philip Webb and T. G. Jackson', *Journal of the Decorative Arts Society* 16 (1992), 24–41.

Saint, Andrew, *Richard Norman Shaw* (1976).

—— *The Image of the Architect* (1983).

Schmiechen, J. A., 'The Victorians, the Historians and the Idea of History', *American Historical Review* 93/2 (1988), 287–316.

Seaborne, Malcolm, *The English School: its architecture and organisation 1370–1870* (1971).

—— 'Introduction' to E. R. Robson, *School Architecture* (1874; Leicester, 1972), 9–25.

—— 'E. R. Robson and the Board Schools of London' in History of Education Society, *Local Studies and the History of Education* (1972), 63–82.

—— 'The Architecture of the Victorian Public School', in Brian Simon and Ian Bradley, eds., *The Victorian Public School* (Dublin, 1975).

—— and Lowe, Roy, *The English School: its architecture and organisation 1870–1970* (1977).

Searby, Peter, *A History of the University of Cambridge: vol. iii, 1750–1870* (Cambridge, 1997).

Service, Alistair, ed., *Edwardian Architecture and Its Origins* (1975).

Sewter, A. Charles, *The Stained Glass of William Morris and His Circle* (2 vols.; 1974–5).

Sherborne, J. W., *University College, Bristol 1876–1909* (Bristol, 1977).

Shrosbree, Colin, *Public Schools and Private Education* (Manchester and New York, 1988).

Slobodin, Richard, *W. H. R. Rivers* (New York, 1978).

Smith, Alison, *The Victorian Nude* (Manchester and New York, 1996).

Smith, Janet Adam, *John Buchan: a biography* (1965).

Smith, Tori, ' "A Grand Work of Noble Conception": the Victoria Memorial and Imperial London', in Felix Driver and David Gilbert, eds., *Imperial Cities* (Manchester and New York, 1999), 21–39.

Sparrow, John, *Mark Pattison and the Idea of a University* (Cambridge, 1967).

Spencer, Isobel, *Walter Crane* (1975).

Stack, V. E., ed., *Oxford High School, Girls' Public Day School Trust 1875–1960* (Oxford, 1963).

Stagličić, Marija, 'Zvonik katedrale u Zadru', *Peristil* 25 (1982), 149–58.

—— 'Još o zvoniku zadarske katedrale', *Peristil* 30 (1987), 143–6.

Stamp, Gavin, 'Sir Gilbert Scott and the "Restoration" of Medieval Buildings', *AA Files* 1 (1981–2), 89–97.

—— 'George Gilbert Scott and the Cambridge Camden Society', in Christopher Webster and John Elliott, eds., *'A Church as it should be': the Cambridge Camden Society and its influence* (Stamford, 2000), 173–89.

—— *An Architect of Promise: George Gilbert Scott (1839–1897) and the Late Gothic Revival* (Donington, 2002).

—— and Goulancourt, André, *The English House 1860–1914: the flowering of English domestic architecture* (1986).

Stansky, Peter, *Redesigning the World: William Morris, the 1880s and the arts and crafts* (Princeton, 1985).

Stephens, W. B., 'The Victorian Art Schools and Technical Education: a case study, 1850–1889', *Journal of Educational Administration and History* 2/1 (1969), 13–19.

Stocking, George W., ed., *Objects and Others* (1985).

Stone, Lawrence, 'The Size and Composition of the Oxford Student Body, 1580–1909', in Lawrence Stone, ed., *The University in Society, vol. I* (1975), 3–110.

Strachey, Lytton, *Five Victorians* (1942).

Sturley, D. M., *The Royal Grammar School, Guildford* (Guildford, 1980).

Sturtevant, William C., 'Does Anthropology Need Museums?', *Proceedings of the Biological Society of Washington* 82 (1969), 619–49.

Summerson, John, *The Architectural Association* (1947).

—— 'A Victorian Architect', *New Statesman and Nation* 40 (1950), 329.

—— *Heavenly Mansions* (1963).

—— *Victorian Architecture: four studies in evaluation* (1970).

—— *The Turn of the Century: architecture in Britain around 1900* (Glasgow, 1976).

—— *Architecture in Britain, 1530–1830* (8th edn.; 1991).

Sutherland, John, *Mrs Humphry Ward* (Oxford 1990).

Sweet, Rosemary, *Antiquaries: the discovery of the past in eighteenth-century Britain* (2004).

Swenarton, Mark, *Artisans and Architects: the Ruskinian tradition in architectural thought* (1989).

Swift, John, *Changing Fortunes: the Birmingham School of Art building 1880–1995* (Birmingham, 1996).

Symonds, Richard, *Oxford and Empire* (1986).

Taylor, Pamela, and Cordon, Joanna, *Barnet, Edgware, Hadley and Totteridge* (1994).

Thompson, E. P., *William Morris: romantic to revolutionary* (New York, 1976).

Thompson, F. M. L., *English Landed Society in the Nineteenth Century* (1963).

—— *The Rise of Respectable Society* (1988).

Tillyard, S. K., *The Impact of Modernism* (1988).

Tittler, Robert, *Architecture and Power: the town hall and the English urban community c. 1500–1640* (Oxford, 1991).

Tozer, Malcolm, ' "The readiest hand and the most open heart": Uppingham's first mission to the poor', *History of Education* 18/4 (1989), 323–32.

Tuke, Margaret J., *A History of Bedford College* (1939).

Turner, Paul Venable, *Campus, an American Planning Tradition* (1984).

Tyack, Geoffrey, *Oxford: an architectural guide* (Oxford and New York, 1998).

Vickery, Margaret Birney, *Buildings for Bluestockings* (1999).

Wakefield, Hugh, *Nineteenth-century British Glass* (1961).

Walker, Frank, 'Jackson's Journey', *Building Design* 828 (1987), 28–9.

Walker, Keith, 'The Twentieth Century and the Future', in John Crook, ed., *Winchester Cathedral Nine Hundred Years, 1093–1993* (Chichester, 1993).

Walker, William George, *A History of the Oundle Schools* (1956).

Walkley, Giles, *Artists' Houses in London* (Aldershot, 1994).

Ward, Elizabeth, *A Short Guide to the Centre of Otford* (Otford, 1994).

Ward, W. Reginald, *Victorian Oxford* (1965).

Washington, Edward S., 'Vicar Grant and his Successors, 1868–1924', in Sarah Quail and Alan Wilkinson, eds., *Forever Building: essays to mark the completion of the cathedral church of St. Thomas of Canterbury, Portsmouth* (Portsmouth, 1995), 67–84.

Watkin, David, *The Rise of Architectural History* (1980).

—— 'Willis and Clark, 1886–1986', *Cambridge Review* 107 (1986), 68–9.

—— *The Architecture of Basil Champneys* (Cambridge, 1989).

Weiner, Deborah E. B., *Architecture and Social Reform in Late Victorian London* (Manchester and New York, 1994).

White, James F., *The Cambridge Movement: the ecclesiologists and the Gothic Revival* (Cambridge, 1962).

Whyte, William, ' "Rooms for the torture and shame of scholars": the New Examination Schools and the architecture of reform', *Oxoniensia* 66 (2001), 85–103.

——— 'Unbuilt Hertford: T. G. Jackson's contextual dilemmas', *Architectural History* 45 (2002), 347–62.

——— 'Building a Public School Community, 1860–1910', *History of Education* 32 (2003), 601–26.

——— 'Anglo-Jackson Attitudes: reform and the rebuilding of Oxford', *The Victorian* 12 (2003), 4–9.

——— 'The Intellectual Aristocracy Revisited', *Journal of Victorian Culture* 10/1 (2005), 15–45.

——— 'Reading Buildings Like a Book: the case of T. G. Jackson', in Peter Draper, ed., *Current Work in Architectural History: papers read at the Annual Symposium of the Society of Architectural Historians of Great Britain 2004* (2005), 27–34.

——— ' "Redbrick's unlovely quadrangles": reinterpreting the architecture of the civic universities', *History of Universities* 21 (2006), 151–77.

——— 'How do Buildings Mean? Some issues of interpretation in the history of architecture', *History and Theory* 45 (2006), 153–77.

——— 'The Englishness of English Architecture: modernism and the making of a national International Style, 1927–1957', in William Whyte, ed., *Britain and Europe: ideas, identities, institutions, 1750–2000* (forthcoming).

——— Hide, Liz, and Daultrey, Sally, *'A Fitting Tribute': 100 years of the Sedgwick Museum* (Cambridge, 2004).

Wilcock, Roland, *The Building of Oxford University Examination Schools* (Oxford, 1983).

Wilkinson, Rupert, *The Prefects: British leadership and the public school tradition* (1964).

Williamson, L. P., *A Century of King's, 1873–1972* (Cambridge, 1980).

Winstanley, D. A., *Later Victorian Cambridge* (Cambridge, 1947).

Wolffe, John, *Great Deaths: grieving, religion, and nationhood in Victorian and Edwardian Britain* (Oxford, 2000).

Woolf, Larry, *Venice and the Slavs: the discovery of Dalmatia in the age of the enlightenment* (Stanford, Calif., 2001).

Ziegler, Philip, *The Sixth Great Power: Barings 1762–1929* (1988).

2. Unpublished

Allen, Peter, 'Biographical Sketch: the Reverend Dr Charles Crowden, headmaster 1866–88' (unpublished article, 1992).

Buchanon, A. C., 'Robert Willis and the Rise of Architectural History' (Ph.D., London, 1994).

Christianson, Ellen, 'Government Architecture and British Imperialism' (Ph.D., Northwestern University, 1995).

Coignard, Alan Jerôme, 'Basil Champneys, architecte (1842–1935)' (Mémoire de Maitrisse, Paris IV, 1984).

Dungavell, Ian Robert, 'The Architectural Career of Sir Aston Webb (1849–1930)' (Ph.D., London, 1999).

Hamilton, N. G., 'A History of the Architecture and Ethos of the School Chapel' (Ph.D., Bristol, 1985).

Honey, J. R. de S., 'The Victorian Public School' (D.Phil., Oxford, 1969).

Knöll, Stefanie, 'St Mary the Virgin Church, Oxford' (MA, Oxford Brookes, 1997).

Low, R. A., 'The Organisation and Architecture of Schools in England, 1870–1939' (Ph.D., Birmingham, 1977).

Mack, B. J., 'W. H. Rivers: the contexts of social anthropology' (D.Phil., Oxford, 1975).

Miele, C. E., 'The Gothic Revival and Gothic Architecture: the restoration of medieval churches in Victorian Britain' (Ph.D., New York University, 1992).

Mowl, Timothy, 'The Norman Revival in British Architecture' (D.Phil., Oxford, 1981).

Powers, A. A. R., 'Architectural Education in Britain 1880–1914' (Ph.D., Cambridge, 1982).

Rigby, Cormac, 'The Life and Influence of Edward Thring' (D.Phil., Oxford, 1968).

Robinson, Stephen, 'Basil Champneys' (unpublished MS; Lady Margaret Hall Archives).

Stamp, Gavin, 'George Gilbert Scott, junior, 1839–1897' (Ph.D., Cambridge, 1978).

Tozer, Malcolm, 'Physical Education at Thring's Uppingham' (M.Ed., Leicester, 1974).

Walker, Lynne Brown, 'E. S. Prior, 1852–1932' (Ph.D., London, 1978).

Index

Italic numbers denote reference to illustrations.